GW00657439

Praise fo

'The book brings forth the rich vibrancy and complexity of the
historical event, mostly in the words of ordinary men and women'
—Tabish Khair, *Mint*

'What makes *Besieged* special is [Farooqui's] sense of delight
and curiosity, and a style that moves between the sober
and the theatrical'
—Narayani Gupta, *The Asian Age*

'Marvellously readable . . . Perhaps the best way to understand
Mahmood Farooqui's achievement in this book is to see him not
as the editor and translator of a compact colonial archive, but as a
disc jockey with (historical) attitude, sampling the past to give us a
medley that might startle us out of our settled view of 1857'
—Mukul Kesavan, *Biblio*

'If you want to know what Dilliwalas had to go through in 1857,
you cannot do better than read this book'
—Khushwant Singh

'A unique ringside view of daily life in the embattled city of Dehli
during the great ghadar of 1857 . . . A stupendous achievement:
a popular book with an assured shelf life'
—Shahid Amin, Professor of History, Delhi University

'Brilliant and revolutionary . . . *Besieged* is a marvel'
William Dalrymple

'Groundbreaking'
—*The Hindu*

BESIEGED
VOICES FROM DELHI 1857

Compiled and Translated by
MAHMOOD FAROOQUI

*With notes on the Mutiny Papers and
governance in Delhi 1857
by the translator*

PENGUIN BOOKS

PENGUIN BOOKS
Published by the Penguin Group
Penguin Books India Pvt. Ltd, 11 Community Centre, Panchsheel Park,
New Delhi 110 017, India
Penguin Group (USA) Inc., 375 Hudson Street, New York, New York 10014, USA
Penguin Group (Canada), 90 Eglinton Avenue East, Suite 700, Toronto, Ontario,
M4P 2Y3, Canada (a division of Pearson Penguin Canada Inc.)
Penguin Books Ltd, 80 Strand, London WC2R 0RL, England
Penguin Ireland, 25 St Stephen's Green, Dublin 2, Ireland
(a division of Penguin Books Ltd)
Penguin Group (Australia), 250 Camberwell Road, Camberwell, Victoria 3124, Australia
(a division of Pearson Australia Group Pty Ltd)
Penguin Group (NZ), 67 Apollo Drive, Rosedale, Auckland 0632, New Zealand
(a division of Pearson New Zealand Ltd)
Penguin Group (South Africa) (Pty) Ltd, 24 Sturdee Avenue, Rosebank, Johannesburg
2196, South Africa

Penguin Books Ltd, Registered Offices: 80 Strand, London WC2R 0RL, England

First published in Viking by Penguin Books India 2010
Published in Penguin Books 2012

Copyright © Mahmood Farooqui 2010

All rights reserved

10 9 8 7 6 5 4 3 2 1

The views and opinions expressed in this book are the author's own and the facts are as
reported by him which have been verified to the extent possible, and the publishers are
not in any way liable for the same.

ISBN 9780143418221

Typeset in Adobe Janson Pro by Eleven Arts, New Delhi
Printed at Replika Press Pvt. Ltd., Sonepat

For Abbu,

And

In Memoriam,
Shardul K. Chaturvedi (1972–2006)

ستارہ‌ٔ شام بن کے آیا

برنگ خواب سحر گیا وہ

(Sitara-e sham ban ke aaya,
Barang-e khvab-e sehar gaya voh)

CONTENTS

PREFACE

I moved to Delhi in 1990. I lived in Okhla and travelled every day to the university in the privileged confines of a University Special bus. The flyover beside the Salimgarh fort was then under construction. The bus always stopped at a place called Kashmiri Gate, which was not visible from the Ring Road, in order to drop off the students of the Delhi College of Engineering.

I studied modern Indian history as an undergraduate but I do not remember any of us opting for 1857 as a paper. You can look at Sumit Sarkar, you can look at Bipin Chandra, you can look at the Cambridge School or at the Subalterns, and all schools of Indian history know that modern Indian history begins after 1857. With 'Gandhi' and the 'National Movement' and 'Partition' beckoning us and the 'Drain of Wealth' and 'Revenue Settlements' behind us, the uprising of 1857 seemed dusty and fruitless. What I do remember was a joke, ascribed to the then principal of my college who, when teaching 1857, would declare from the class podium that '1857 was a turning point in Indian history'. He would then take a dramatic pause, walk all the way to the exit, turn and declaim with a flourish, 'but India refused to turn'.

However, India did turn and very much so after 1857. The college I went to was one of the outcomes of 1857, established with the assistance of and encouragement by the colonial government soon after it had finally closed the old Delhi College. The remnants of that old, old college were exactly where the Delhi College of Engineering then stood. We at the history classes of St Stephen's were the precise and fulsome fruits of the pointless struggles of 1857.

One read about 1857 here and there but never did it appear as a subject in its own right. At universities abroad I never met anyone who was specializing in 1857, nobody who found anything redeeming about it. 'Modern India' emerges as a subject after 1857, and before that there is Indian emasculation and the British conquests. In between those conquests there is this bloody piece of resistance. If anything, it aroused chagrin, the *Amar Chitra Katha*s dealing with it were actually accounts of our weakness, our disunity, our lack of patriotism and manliness.

Until, first William Dalrymple and then the hundred and fiftieth anniversary of 1857 roped me into it. I returned to the archives, I saw these documents. There were hundreds of small biographies, with no claimants. The people who appear in these stories have long vanished, their descendants have cleared out to Pakistan or Hyderabad or Lucknow or appear in magazine pages, consistently for the last hundred years, as the poor, lost, condemned descendants of the Mughals. The bylanes of Old Delhi . . . Ah, the galis, ah, the Mir couplet, *Dilli ki na hain galiyan, awraq-e musavvir hain* . . . But there were few takers. The Hindus who lived in Old Delhi have long moved out to Civil Lines, Mukherji Nagar and Rohini. The Punjabis who came to take their place in 1947 have also by now moved out to south Delhi, to Karol Bagh and elsewhere. The Muslims who now live there all seem to have descended from western Uttar Pradesh in the last thirty years. In sooth, there are no Dilliwallas.

But there is the anniversary, there are the celebrations. And so these documents in Shikastah (cursive) Urdu. There are few modern Indian historians who bother with Urdu, we cannot seriously expect them to decipher Shikastah. And the Urduwallas, all Muslims thanks substantially to 1857 and to Hindi nationalism, seem to have lost the energy to turn their heritage into a world language. The long century of modern Urdu, reformed Urdu, an Urdu with history and social sciences and humanities, began to run dry in the 1960s. Few Urdu critics do research now. The Urdu historians, even those who earlier worked on the histories of *ulema* and Urdu journalism and their own cities, oh I don't know where they are. Probably in some forlorn Urdu department, trying to turn their ad hoc posts into permanent ones by working as glorified peons in their supervisors' houses.

Yet more of third world lack really. And so there they sit, these thousands of documents and the only Urdu students who seem capable of deciphering them are unfortunately all from madrasas. So there you have it, the connection between 1857 and fundamentalism.

So I set to work, imperfectly, unenthusiastically, sometimes poring over words with an ancient magnifying glass generously provided by the staff at the National Archives, sometimes surreptitiously tracing the outlines on butter paper so that I could consult someone later. Occasionally, I was startled by the fact that Hindu officers often addressed the British as *kafir*s or that they unselfconsciously used the word jihad. Or by the number of fantasy and fiction books that topped the advert lists in the recently-emerged newspapers. Or the variety of wine makers that seemed to exist in pre-modern India.

I have been to many of these places, of course. To Turkman Gate and Ajmeri Gate and Bhojla Pahari and Sadar Bazaar and Tiraha Bairam Khan and Gali Qasimjan. I have even seen Kashmiri Gate while travelling to the Old Delhi railway station. I have searched out Carlton's, that old nineteenth-century café opposite St James Church where there is still a signboard with that name. But I am a *purabiya* and as you would learn from these pages they have ever been given short shrift in Delhi. But we keep coming here, not so much as rebels now but as migrant workers, and less frequently, as students and white-collar workers. The story of our immiserization, our cultural impoverishment and our broken connections with Delhi is the story of 1857 too. The story of my Muslimness and my Urdu are its offshoots. But there is no glory in it now.

So now with some excitement and some trepidation and a lot of uncertainty I present these unread pages, these lost sighs and these roads not taken. Here are some historical voices in search of the Dilliwallas, anyone out there?

This book contains voices from Delhi when the city was besieged by the British during the uprising of 1857. It presents aspects of the uprising that have rarely been studied before but it is *not* a history of the uprising in Delhi. Further, more than the uprising, these papers are a unique record of the city of Delhi at a time of intense turmoil. While we know an extraordinary amount about the emotions, movements and activities in the British camp when their forces had besieged Delhi between June and September 1857, we have had little insight into the city itself. Here, for the first time, is the full range of voices from an ancient city in turmoil.

These include petitions and applications from ordinary people as well as directives and commands of officials. You will encounter soldiers beyond the battlefield, when they demanded rations, wages, promotions and supplies. You will meet policemen who arranged these provisions and the constraints they faced when they sought to confiscate resources or people. There are complaints by ordinary residents when they find a huge and largely unwanted army billeted in the city. There are bankers who are bullied to make monetary contributions. There are spies who keep a tab on plans and report the slightest fall in morale. There are doctors, potters, coolies, widows, cuckolded men and runaway women, distillers, opium sellers, loitering faqirs, lunatics and, not least, firebrand editors, who are trapped in the crossfire. Such a dense record of the everyday goings-on of a city under siege, of the travails of ordinary life and the valiant attempts of an administration to simultaneously act as welfare as well as a war state is not available for any other period of Indian history.

This selection draws upon more than ten thousand documents that are stored in the National Archives of India, New Delhi, under the title Mutiny Papers. Most of them were processed for and by the administration that took charge of Delhi when the city fell to the rebels in May 1857. These papers were not produced as a conscious record of the sentiments of the rebel actors, nor were they supposed to be studied as a tool to understanding the nature of that uprising. The picture they present therefore is relatively unfiltered, and allows for as close and unmediated an access, inter alia, to the process of the uprising as can be possible.

There are three aspects of the uprising represented here that find lesser mention otherwise: first, the way it affected the common people, the labourers, artisans, shopkeepers and ordinary residents of Delhi.

The second relates to the manner in which the uprising was organized on the ground in a big city—the nature of the management and the processes through which goods and resources were provided for it. Third, how these were perceived by a self-conscious ideologue, the firebrand editor of the *Dehli Urdu Akhbar* whose sympathies lay neither with the residents, nor with the soldiers, but who was still a passionate supporter of the cause of the liberation of Hindustan from the hated firangis.

The uprising that appears in these documents, sometimes directly, at others through the crevices and interstices, is an urban phenomenon. Thanks to the works of Eric Stokes, Ranajit Guha and Rudrangshu Mukherjee, we have become more familiar with the modes of peasant participation in the uprising, but we are still not fully cognizant of the experience of the cities in 1857. However, it took me some time to realize that the narratives contained in these papers cannot be exhausted by the uprising of 1857. Many of the transactions recorded here are of a kind that any administration anywhere deals with as a matter of routine. These include, to make a random list, elopements, evictions, burglaries, bail proceedings, gambling, counterfeit currency, homeless deaths and other kinds of transgressions. These transactions, common across different times and spaces, were certainly inflected by the dynamics of the uprising in Delhi in this period, notably the presence of a very large number of somewhat unruly soldiers and the sharpened urgency with which ordinary matters were treated. But in their incidence they are exterior to it. These papers are then as much about ways of governance in the pre-modern era as they are about 1857 in particular. However, for that very reason they assume greater importance as a resource for Indian history.

The organization of trades, the clan-based artisanal realm and the conduct of the police, as reflected in these documents, show features that can reasonably be assumed to be of long antiquity. When these classes and practices appear here they provide us with an important glimpse into an era which seems out of place after a century of colonial rule. Important as these documents are for refashioning 1857, they are even more important as a source for studying pre-modern social organization.

Among other details of society and government these papers also tell us how the police conducted its investigation, how it interrogated suspects, the manner in which the deposition of witnesses was recorded and the official tags through which people identified themselves to the authorities. The details required while recording depositions provide clues to understanding the relationship between the state and its subjects. Apart from the usual tags, such as name, address, profession, caste, the deponent also had to clarify whether he was educated or not. This emphasis on education/literacy slightly complicates our expectations from a predominantly illiterate society. Did it matter in altering the status of the person, or was it merely a question of verifying whether the person can sign her name or not? The matrices of social group identity, the *qaum* a person belonged to, as explained elsewhere in the book, reveal the segmentations by which society was organized and governed. The legal status of women, to take another instance, appears in police documents not as it was being fashioned by colonial laws but as it was articulated in official terms in the pre-colonial times. Similarly, a number of times people assert that they have never been to a thana in their entire lives and therefore will not appear even if summoned. The current notoriety of the police, it appears from these documents, has a long history.

To the extent that it reflects a relatively new picture of 1857, I hope the book will interest the handful of specialists who work on the period. I also hope to attract other students of Indian history who may be interested in the ways in which a pre-colonial city was organized and governed. The general reader will find narratives and voices here which may appeal to him. More than anything else this is a record of ordinary people caught in extraordinary times. Harried by rulers and harassed by soldiers, the stories of people who suffered the loss of status, well-being, home, wealth and were condemned to shortages of all kinds, makes for a poignant narrative at any time. It is the sacrifice of the ordinary, the quotidian, the everyday that creates the joys, pains and sorrows from which grand historical themes are fashioned. This book retrieves the unsung, the ordinary, and the unheroic from the uprising of 1857. Anyone interested in Indian realities should find something of interest here.

For purposes of simplification as well as for invoking, by a sleight of hand as it were, some truth claims of my own, I have divided the documents into fifteen loose sections. These try to disaggregate the *ghadar* into several components. There are sections on soldiers, police, residents, volunteers, spies, the Court of Mutineers and others. The classification of the sections is necessarily arbitrary. When soldiers clash with the police, as they often do, the document could go either in the section on soldiers or the police. Volunteers are also soldiers and it is difficult to distinguish one from the other when it comes to a face-off with the citizens or with the police. But I have kept them apart in order to throw light on the claims and expectations of those who came from afar to fight this unpaid war. A lot of times ordinary citizens wrote to complain about the distress they had suffered because of the soldiers. The documents could belong equally to the soldiers' chapter as to the citizens'. When grocers complain about soldiers it could be listed under 'supplies' or under 'soldiers'. The police are ubiquitous, a separate section for them only highlights the difficulties under which they were labouring—the poor pay, the inability to hire and fire, the living conditions, and so on. Many 'regulations' concern the police or are implemented through them. The separate section marked for them only underscores the fact that the regulations had a wider impact on the city. If citizens complain about the soldiers or face other problems I have included it under the section on 'Dilliwallas'; if the complaint about soldiers comes from a government official, then I have put it under 'soldiers'. Sections dealing with Sikhs, doctors and spies have been organized only in order to earmark the importance of these somewhat missing facts from the annals of 1857. The introductory comments before each section are meant to guide the general reader through the contents of the particular section. They are not at all exhaustive memoranda on the themes that I have somewhat arbitrarily imposed on a protean and decentralized event.

However, I do feel that the material will benefit its processors better had it been made available to them in the original. That might yet be. I look forward to future historians to make better use of the content I have provided them and humbly accept my lot as a translator or transmitter of historic(al) legacies.

The same caveat applies to the notes which attempt to place these documents against the wider historiography of 1857. The hypotheses and claims I put forward in these should be seen not as the assertions of a historian, backed up by quotes and sources, as much as tentative forays by a non-professional. If the insights prove useful I shall be delighted and if not, well, they have been placed at the end of the book precisely so that you can wholly skip them if you wish. My attempt has been to speak to specialists and laypersons alike in the hope, vain though it may be, that *dil se jo baat nikalti hai asar rakhti hai* . . .

NOTE ON TRANSLATION

Translations, says the poet Vivek Narayanan, are like poems, never finished, merely abandoned. This applies particularly to this selection, translated entirely from Shikastah (broken, cursive) Urdu barring an occasional Persian document, because no attempt has been made here to conform to scholarly accuracy. I have interpreted the texts before me and interposed between them and the reader in English, giving to the latter a fluency which necessarily carried a different flavour in the original. As is common to writings of the period, punctuation marks occur rarely in the original and where sentences overflow, their translation is faithful only to the velocity of the original, not to the boulders, pebbles or foliage through which the stream meandered. In other words I have stuck to the outward form and ignored the internal rhythms. Where words or phrases were illegible, I have not hesitated from extrapolating the meaning of the sentence.

A large number of Urdu words recur in the translated texts. Indian readers are perforce familiar with words like gora, kafir and angrez, all of which, separately or together, stand for the British alongside the word *nassar* derived from Nazarenes or the followers of Jesus of Nazareth, which represents the British as Christians. I have let most of them stand to provide a flavour of the variety of ways in which the British were remembered or cursed in 1857. English words in italics have been reproduced from the Urdu original.

There are names of Indian officials or functionaries, zamindar, *tehsildar*, *thanadar*, *barqandaz*, which I have explained in the glossary but have often left untranslated in the text and these too should not pose a problem for any reader familiar with India. There are titles or names referring to caste and occupation which were once very common but have now become less familiar like the word *bhishti*, meaning water carrier, which is both a caste as well as an occupation, or *kahar*, both caste and occupation, or similar words such as *barhai, lohar, chamar* and so on. Most have been explained in the glossary but are found in the original, sometimes, in the main text.

The word qaum is given here in the original in order to convey the widespread usage of this flexible word and the variety of ways in which social identities could be conceived and explained. This pertains to community as well as to apprehension of caste as far as government documents are concerned. For the lower castes, unexceptionally, qaum—or as it later came to mean, nation, community, ethnicity, any social identity—refers to their occupation and for the upper castes it refers to their caste, thus qaum Kahar or Mughal or Brahman. Caste in this period, it appears, was central to social identity, across communities, at least in this city.

The numbers given at the end of the entries refer, serially, to the Collection and Item Numers under which they are stored in the Mutiny Papers. The dates can help in locating them among the bundles of the Collections.

DATELINE

May

11 May: Soldiers from Meerut arrive in Delhi. The Delhi regiments join them. The British are massacred or flee the city, looting and plunder in the bazaars. Before midnight a 21-gun salute from the royal cannon announces the restoration of Bahadur Shah Zafar's majesty.

12 May: Frances Taylor, principal of Delhi College, beaten to death in the streets. Bahadur Shah Zafar tours the city on an elephant urging shops to open.

15 May: Plundering of the magazine. Delhi aristocrats raise private police force, but this fails to stop the plunder. Princes given ranks and made in charge of the military.

16 May: Massacre of the European prisoners at Red Fort.

17 May: *Dehli Urdu Akhbar* reports that the sepoys are occupying the Diwan-e-Khas, have placed their own guards and the Red Fort looks like a cantonment.

20 May: King instructs thanadars to send in their daily diary as before. Mutiny at Agra; Mirza Abu Bakr, a prince, sent to Meerut to get cannons. Fortifications of the city under way.

21 May: Proclamation that anyone found plundering will be shot. Shops begin to reopen. City bankers raise one lakh rupees to pay the sepoys.

23 May: Turkman Gate thanadar reports that all diggers of the area have run away, and so will the shoemakers if they are not paid their wages.

25 May: A mint is opened by Munshi Ayodhya Prasad producing coins with Bahadur Shah's face imprinted on them.

28 May: Qazi Faizullah appointed kotwal to replace Muinuddin Husain Khan. Money arrives from Rohtak.

30 May: British under Brigadier Archdale Wilson attacked at Ghaziuddinnagar on the Hindon river by Delhi rebels. Rebels defeated. Mutiny at Lucknow.

31 May: Rebels defeated again by Wilson at the Hindon river. A canal worker is arrested for spying.

June

1 June: Fear in the city. Shops closed. Frantic building of entrenchments by Mirza Mughal, the C-in-C.

2 June: Shops remain shut. Rebels build a battery on the ridge.

3 June: Mutiny at Nimach. Irregular cavalry arrive from Hansi and join the rebels.

4 June: A rebel force arrives with money from Mathura.

5 June: Identity badges demanded for barqandazes.

8 June: Battle of Badli-ki-Serai. Rebels defeated. British occupy the ridge. Beginning of the siege of Delhi.

9 June: First attacks on the British at the ridge.

10 June: First British shells from the ridge hit the city. Soldiers disallow even corpses to be carried out of the city.

11 June: King orders that dues owed by soldiers should be deducted from their salaries.

16 June: Sweepers directed to remove garbage and carcasses from the city gates.

17 June: Telegraph set up at the British camp. Reopening of communications with Punjab and Calcutta.

19 June: Residents of Hauz Qazi clash with soldiers. A resident of Kucha Brijnath, Shankar Nath's daughter, arrested by a nawab who wishes to marry her.

22 June: Volunteers from Bareilly want names enrolled on the register.

23 June: Biggest rebel attack on the ridge to mark the anniversary of Plassey.

24 June: Soldiers pillage the royal ice factory. Chandni Chowk residents complain about their corrupt thanadar.

26 June: Three companies sent on assault return for want of provisions.

30 June: Prostitute Sundar uses soldiers to evict her tenant.

July

1 July: C-in-C bans forced searches by soldiers.

2 July: Bakht Khan arrives in Delhi from Bareilly with a large contingent and great fanfare. Given authority over civil and revenue administration.

3 July: A Punjabi tailor confronts barqandazes at Chandni Chowk and releases conscripted labourers.

4 July: Prisoners demand a raise in allowance.

5 July: Bakht Khan designated governor-general. Prince Abu Bakr creates a ruckus at Tiraha Bairam Khan in a drunken state.

6 July: Spy reports that mullas and pandits are preaching a holy war. Mosques active centres of uprising.

10 July: The Court of Mutineers (hereafter CoM) established in the week before makes suggestions about raising money and supplies.

13 July: Proclamation that any soldier found plundering will be shot.

14 July: The house of Khurshid Alam, a Mughal prince, plundered by soldiers.

15 July: Bibighar massacre at Kanpur.

16 July: Rebel soldier asleep on duty court-martialled by his unit.

17 July: Wilson writes to Lawrence that unless quickly reinforced, the British will soon have to retreat.

18 July: Three-pronged attack on the ridge and Sabzi Mandi. Wilson writes to John Lawrence warning that a premature assault on Delhi will end in disaster.

19 July: Proclamation in the city that anyone found killing a cow will be blown off a cannon. Gauri Shankar reports that Meerut and Delhi armies are at loggerheads.

20 July: Khuda Bakhsh's wife of twelve years elopes with her pretend-brother. Surajbali abducts his former wife Bilasia from Nigambodh Ghat.

21 July: 130 horsemen from the British camp desert to the city.

22 July: Further desertions from the British camp. King offers money and land if the ridge is taken. Gujars plunder Munshi Jiwan Lal's garden.

23 July: Sepoys arrive from Benares. Failed attack on the ridge from Kashmiri Gate. Ludlow Castle occupied by the rebels. Moti Khan, *risaldar* from Jodhpur, seeks permission to raise his own troops.

24 July: *Ghazis* from Tonk arrive in Delhi. Kotwal seeks direction for dealing with gamblers.

25 July: Sepoys plunder a haveli in Ballimaran. Azurda puts a guard on his house. Risaldar Ghulam Mohiuddin's mistress runs away with his retainer.

26 July: Arrival of the Nimach battalion under generals Sidhara Singh and Hira Singh.

27 July: Imam Bakhsh arrested for possessing lead. Imam Khan deserts from the British in order to serve the Islamic side.

28 July: Ban on cow-killing on Id ul Zuha. Two lunatics arrested on charges of spying.

30 July: Rebel force sets off in the direction of Alipore. Strict measures are put in place to stop cow slaughter. People who have been illegally collecting money are arrested by the police.

31 July: Vaziran, the courtesan, freed from jail by her Tilanga admirers. Kotwal professes helplessness.

August

1 August: Id ul Zuha (Baqrid). No cow slaughter takes place. The King summons all the thanadars to pay *nazars* to him on Baqrid.

2 August: Gambling banned in the city.

3 August: Failure to break the British despite reinforcements now alarms the court.

4 August: CoM forbids anybody from crossing the Jamuna bridge without a pass. Munshi Jiwan Lal arrested and taken to Red Fort.

5 August: Sikhs complain they are not being supported by the purabiyas. Disputes between Bakht Khan and other generals come into the open after the failure of attacks on the ridge and Alipore.

7 August: Explosion of the magazine at Gali Churiwallan. Hakim Ahsanullah Khan's house attacked by irate soldiers.

8 August: Fire still rages in the gunpowder factory and water carriers are sent there to try and put out the blaze. Ahsanullah Khan's house plundered. Bahadur Shah refuses to come out in protest. The groom of Prince Colonel Khizr Sultan conscripted as a coolie.

9 August: The King threatens the army with abdication if soldiers are not restrained. The government promises to compensate all those who have perished in the magazine fire.

10 August: Soldiers avoiding battle and hiding in the city to be arrested. Bakht Khan proposes vigorous measures to stop plundering.

11 August: Deputy kotwal urges C-in-C to stop the conscription of grain-parchers as coolies.

12 August: The poor exempted from making money contributions by the C-in-C.

13 August: C-in-C restrains his brother Colonel Khizr Sultan from making arbitrary collections of money. Gauri Shankar reports low rebel spirits and dissension following the loss of the guns at Qudsia Bagh, and the fact that many sepoys are deserting.

14 August: The Nimach force threatens to retire unless paid wages. Dilliwallas and Tilangas clash at a brothel in Faiz Bazaar. Thanadar inquires about the correct protocol of addressing newly-crowned officers.

16 August: Sidhara Singh of Nimach sends twenty lakh rupees to the C-in-C. A delegation of chaudhris and zamindars from Pataudi arrive with the complaint that their *qasba* has been completely destroyed by Gujars.

17 August: Leading bankers of the city summoned to the palace. Recalcitrant bankers of Katra Neel warned that they will be blown off a cannon if they resist.

18 August: The CoM asserts that it is the only authority to levy taxes.

21 August: C-in-C forwards Sikhs' petition complaining of discrimination and asking to be formed into a separate regiment. The potters threaten to defect if they continue to be made to work as coolies.

22 August: Bahadur Shah tries to conciliate Sikhs in the Bareilly regiment.

23 August: Deputy kotwal requests relaxation of ban on opium, says otherwise the soldiers will create a ruckus.

24 August: Beating of customary drums during Muharram banned. Bakht Khan and the Nimach brigade—9000 men in all—march out separately for Najafgarh.

25 August: Battle of Najafgarh begins at sunset. The Nimach brigade is defeated by Nicholson; Bakht Khan chooses not to engage.

26 August: Spy reports that Mirza Mughal has been dismissed from the post of commanding general. The CoM forbids soldiers from changing their regiments. Two Bengali mendicants arrested. All the Bengalis in the city already rounded up.

28 August: Further attempts at taxing rich bankers.

29 August: Soldiers hold court at Daryaganj and arraign their officers for corruption. Kotwal urges the C-in-C to pay coolies' wages so that they don't run away.

30 August: The remains of the Nimach brigade return—700 men out of 2100 are missing. Starving sepoys come before Bahadur Shah saying either they should be provided for or allowed to leave.

31 August: Kite and pigeon flying banned in the city.

September

2 September: Small amount of money distributed to sepoys.

3 September: Large number of desertions. Sepoys 'do court' to depose Bahadur Shah and crown Mirza Jawan Bakht king.

4 September: One-mile-long British siege train finally arrives from Ferozepur. Bakht Khan writes to the King that he had been warning about it, but no one listened to him.

6 September: C-in-C promises rewards to all who perish in battle.

7 September: British begin digging forward trenches and constructing batteries. Call in the city for every adult, Hindu or Muslim, to go out and fight. King orders shopkeepers to hand over three months' rent.

8 September: British capture Ludlow Castle and move their batteries forward. City wall beginning to crumble. A Hindustani woman dressed as a man attempts to cross Lahori Gate with a naked sword at midnight.

9 September: Battering of the city wall continues, as do desertions. Zinat Mahal tries to contact the British camp through Maulvi Rajab Ali.

10 September: C-in-C rallies the troops and tells them to prepare for the final battle 'for the sake of the cow and the pig and abiding by religion and faith'.

11 September: All soldiers who are martyred are promised a jagir. Ghazis gather at the Jama Masjid, preparing to attack the British batteries. Khair released from prison and cleared of the charge of theft levelled at her by her brother-in-law, Pir Bakhsh, the tinman.

13 September: All armed residents asked to assemble at Red Fort. Last edition of the *Dehli Urdu Akhbar*.

14 September: British columns begin to move at 3 a.m. and the assault begins. Kashmiri Gate blown off. One column reaches as far as the Jama Masjid before retreating in the face of 'desperate assaults' by the ghazis. By nightfall, the British have lost 1200 men (including 60 officers), but capture the wall from the Water Gate to the Kabuli Gate.

15 September: Counter-attack by sepoys on British positions in the evening. Flight from the city begins.

18 September: British advance as far as Chandni Chowk, but again fail to take Lahori Gate and Burn Bastion.

19 September: British close in on Red Fort. Bakht Khan falls back to the Purana Qila with his regiment, family and many jihadis. The King retires to Humayun's Tomb with wives and other princes. British move slowly through the streets. By night Delhi is emptied.

20 September: Resistance ends as sepoys run out of grain and supplies and flee the city. Jama Masjid, Red Fort and Salimgarh all fall to the British.

21 September: Royal salute at sunrise proclaims the British as masters of Delhi. Bahadur Shah surrenders at Humayun's Tomb. House of Munshi Jiwan Lal plundered by Sikhs.

22 September: Arrest and murder of the princes.

Through September, October, November, the sack of Delhi carried out. Prize agents plunder houses, daily hangings of dozens of people. City emptied, the population camps outside the city, set to spend the winter in the open.

27 November: The King and the nawabs of Jhajjhar, Dadri, Farrukhnagar and the raja of Ballabgarh tried by a military court martial.

End of the month: First Hindu Dilliwallas allowed to return.

1858

2 January: Raja of Ballabgarh found guilty of rebellion. Sir Colin Campbell defeats the nawab of Farrukhabad and Bakht Khan at Khudaganj.

27 January: The trial of Bahadur Shah begins. King presents his defence.

9 March: Bahadur Shah declared guilty.

17 June: Death of rani of Jhansi.

7 October: Bahadur Shah leaves Delhi for the last time to travel to Rangoon via Allahabad; general pardon issued at Delhi but many Muslims under house arrest.

10 December: Arrival of Bahadur Shah in Rangoon.

January 1859: Muslims begin to be readmitted to city, but only with passes.

November 1859: Ghalib writes of houses still lying vacant.

7 November 1862, 5 a.m.: Death of Bahadur Shah. Buried the same day at 4 p.m.

DELHI IN 1857

The houses of the umara and the rajas in Delhi were grander than that
of their counterparts in Europe.

J. Forbes, *Oriental Memoirs* (1845)

It is still fashionable to refer to Old Delhi as a walled city, although
medieval cities everywhere had perimeter walls. Delhi's walls, as
they existed in 1857, have of course long since been demolished or
have crumbled, while the outlying areas, Sabzi Mandi, Shahdara,
Mughalpura, Kilokri, Jahanuma and Shalimar Gardens, the ridge,
Okhla and Mehrauli now form a central and, going by the importance
of land and votes, even determining influence on the life of the city. But
until 1857, there were the walls, surrounded by the twelve gates, some
of which still survive—Mori, Kashmiri, Turkman, Ajmeri, Delhi. Do
not confuse them with the gates to the palace, the Qila-e Mualla, in
those days, the exalted fort, which in some cases have the same names
as city gates.

There were some hundred and fifty thousand people living in the
city, with Hindus forming a slight majority. Outside the city walls lay the
notorious badlands inhabited by the Gujars, Jats and Mewatis.

The *mohalla*s mentioned in these pages acquired their names from
their founders, or from the occupation or ethnicity of the people who
lived there. Thus one encounters references to the Kashmiri Katra,
Punjabi Katra, Mohalla Imli and Kucha Nawab Wazir. Names also
accreted from their historical associations. Notice the predominance
of *wara*s, a Marathi term for neighbourhood in the north of the
city—Teliwara, Chhippiwara and Maliwara. The names of many of

these places, which are vastly transformed of course, have survived. In Old Delhi, one can still find the sites of petitions and action mentioned in these documents such as the Khirki Farrashkhana, Tiraha Bairam Khan, Pahari Imli, Bazaar Sitaram, the sweetshop at Ghantewala and Chowk Saadullah Khan.

The British conquered Delhi in 1803, not from the Mughals, but from their then protectors, the Marathas, in the battle of Patparganj that the Marathas lost . . . so the story goes because all their British and European mercenary officers refused to fight on the day of battle. The much vaunted peace the British established in the intervening fifty years led to some restoration of Delhi's importance as a trading entrepôt between Punjab, north India and elsewhere. It also served as a diplomatic outpost for British offensives against the Punjab and Rajputana. For the denizens of Delhi though it remained the cultural capital and, as the violent events of 1857 were to remind the British, very much the political capital of India.

The cultural life of the city was dominated by the court, with Bahadur Shah acting as the presiding poet-scholar-archer-calligrapher-kite flyer-fount of all wisdom and grace. Yet his days were numbered. His many successors had constantly pledged to surrender their titles, the fort and even the privileges of being emperor (emphatically, merely, the King of Delhi in British correspondence), in return for nominal succession and pensions. There were poets, scholars and traditional artists who carried on as if there were no British, a lie which acquired credence from British participation in the literary and cultural life of the city. And also from the fact that unlike at most other Indian cities, the British chose to live inside the city walls, at Kashmiri Gate and at Daryaganj. The informal, easy hand of British governance, the famous dual system where the resident and the commissioner checked each other's powers, also contributed to this sense of continuity. Individual officers rather than an impersonal bureaucratic machine characterized British rule in the city.

'The works of the Europeans at Delhi are confined to a magnificent canal, an arsenal, a church, a college and a printing press,' commented a traveller to Delhi in 1845. The college referred to was Delhi College, formerly the Ghaziuddin Madrasa where from 1828 onwards, with largely Indian munificence, students began to study English, mathematics and the sciences. The sciences could be learnt in the Urdu stream as well. Famous scholars of the city, Maulana Mamluk Ali, Mufti Sadruddin Azurda and Momin taught there. There was certainly a buzz about it and its students went on to make a mark in the latter part of the century. The British and Indian nobles met as social equals sometimes in the College, sometimes in the newly established Archaeological Society where Syed Ahmed Khan (later, Sir Syed) read out excerpts from his soon to be published, masterly history of Delhi's peoples, places, institutions and mores. They also met at the soirées and *mushaeras* held at Fraser's mansion (now known as the Hindu Rao Hospital), Metcalfe House, and the salons of Raja Hindu Rao, Lala Chunna Mal, Lala Ramji Das, and the nawabs of Jhajjhar and Ballabgarh. The courtly Urdu culture was shared by Hindus and Muslims alike, as were the famous festivals of the city such as Basant, Phoolwalon ki Sair, the Urs at Nizamuddin and Qutub Saheb, the latter, until then regarded as the patron saint of the city. There was more tension between the Hindus and Jains, who dominated trade, banking and finance, than between Muslims and Hindus. The best exposition of that period can be found in Narayani Gupta's *Delhi Between Two Empires* and in Shamsur Rahman Faruqi's magnificent novel, *Kai Chand the Sar-e Aasman*.

There were magnificent palaces and shabby shopfronts; hundreds of descendants of former Mughal princes, the *salatin*, who lived on meagre pensions and in crowded tenements inside the palace. There were gated mohallas—rows upon rows of dilapidated hutments—and the famous Delhi swagger or *baankpan*. There were three regular newspapers, hundreds of bookbinders, portrait artists, face readers, storytellers called *dastango*s, stand-up comics called *bhand*s, mimics and face artists called *naqqal*s, and poets and artisans. And there were the bankers and merchants.

Many of the bankers mentioned in these papers went on to become the financial and industrial barons who rebuilt Delhi after 1857. Lala Girdhar Lal and Saligram (both Jains), Lala Chunna Mal, Mahesh Das, Lala Narain Das Gurwala and Narain Das Naharwala were some of the magnates who refused to aid Bahadur Shah, but built their fortunes in the aftermath of the capture of Delhi. They bought property, invested in factories, controlled trade monopolies and dominated the Delhi municipality in the following years, giving rise to a new term for making and increasing wealth—'Lalaocracy'.

The Delhi of today, rightfully, belongs to them and to the millions of Punjabi refugees who poured into the city after the holocaust of 1947. Here is to them and to all the outsiders who have forever made it home . . .

Kaun jaaye Zauq, par dilli ki galiyan chhor ke . . .

CAST OF CHARACTERS

Bahadur Shah

(1775–1862)

Abu Zafar Sirajuddin Mohammed Bahadur Shah Zafar, the last Mughal emperor, who ruled between 1837 and 1857, was demoted from emperor to the designation 'King of Delhi' in British writings of the period. Born to Akbar Shah (reign: 1806–37) and Lal Bai in 1774, he was a renowned poet of his times and celebrated for his expertise in archery, calligraphy and horse-riding. He was arrested at Humayun's Tomb on 20 September after the fall of Delhi and put on a court martial trial in January 1858. The court pronounced him guilty and sent him on exile to Rangoon later that year. He died on 7 November 1862 and was buried in Rangoon that very day.

Mirza Mughal (born Mirza Zaheeruddin), the Commander-in-Chief

(1817–1857)

The fifth son of Bahadur Shah. Following the death in 1856 of his elder brother, Mirza Fakhru, Mirza Mughal became the eldest surviving legitimately born son of Bahadur Shah Zafar and the heir apparent. Designated commander-in-chief after the arrival of rebel soldiers, he energetically sought to organize the troops, make arrangements for their billeting and provisioning, and bring a semblance of order to the city. He was superseded after the arrival of Bakht Khan, although he continued to remain an important functionary in the rebel-occupied city. He was captured by Hodson on 22 September following Bahadur Shah's arrest, and was shot dead at point-blank range at Khooni Darwaza. His body was then hanged outside the kotwali. His reported last words were, '*Hindu Musalman mere shareek ho meri yaad rahen.*'

Khizr Sultan

(1831–1857)

Among the youngest of Bahadur Shah's forty-nine children. A poetic disciple of Mirza Ghalib, he was appointed colonel of the platoons after the rebel takeover. He took a leading part in the uprising and was at the forefront of collecting money, though he was admonished by Mirza Mughal for making unauthorized collections. He was shot and hanged by Hodson along with Mirza Mughal. Ghalib wrote this couplet using his name:

> *Khizr sultan ko rakhe khaliq-e akbar sar-sabz*
> *shah ke bagh mein yih tazah nihaal achcha hai*
> (May the Great Creator keep Khizr Sultan green/flourishing
> In the shah's garden, this fresh new/young plant is good.)

Bakht Khan

(1797–1859)

Born at Bijnore in Rohilkhand, Bakht Khan was related to the ruling family there and to the Awadh lineage on his mother's side. He served in the Bengal Horse Artillery of the British Indian army for nearly fifty years as a subedar in many British campaigns including the Afghan wars. In 1857, he organized the rebel sepoys and the Rohilla warriors into a large contingent of 5000 men and reached Delhi on 1 July. He was given the supreme command of the civilian and military administration by Bahadur Shah and was designated governor-general of the city. His rivalry with Mirza Mughal and with other generals such as Sidhara Singh and Ghouse Khan constricted his room for manoeuvre. Bakht Khan earned much censure for refusing to bail out Sidhara Singh's forces when the latter was besieged by the British at Najafgarh. However, he also earned great praise for his diligence and competence in organizing the city's supplies and money collections. He continued to fight alongside Maulvi Ahmedullah Shah after the fall of Delhi and reportedly died unattended in the Terai jungles of northern India sometime in 1859.

Hakim Ahsanullah Khan alias Ihtiramuddaulah and Hikmat Panah

(1797–1873)

Hakim Ahsanullah Khan was Bahadur Shah's prime minister and head physician. An Arabic, Persian and Urdu expert, he was close friends with the poets Zauq, Ghalib and Momin, and had even published Momin's collection of poems at his own expense. The sepoys strongly suspected him of being in league with the British, and surrounded and plundered his house on more than one occasion. Imprisoned by the soldiers after the explosion of the magazine on 7 August, he was released only after Bahadur Shah threatened to kill himself. He is supposed to have played an instrumental role in Bahadur Shah's surrender to the British. His *haveli* in Lal Kuan in old Delhi survived until a few years ago.

Sidhara Singh

He was the subedar of the Nimach army, and arrived in Delhi on 26 July, commanding a contingent of 15,000 men, along with General Hira Singh. He was appointed to the post of general. Bakht Khan and he were arch rivals and when his forces were routed at the battle of Najafgarh, Bakht Khan did not come to his aid.

Maulvi Mohammed Baqar

(d.1857)

Baqar was the father of Urdu's first modern historian, Mohammed Husain 'Azad', and editor of *Dehli Urdu Akhbar*, which started publication in 1837. A leading Shia scholar of the city, he was a close friend of the poet Zauq and a prominent presence at Bahadur Shah's court. A firebrand ideologue for the uprising, he passionately expounded its cause in his paper and kept up the morale of the rebels. He was arrested and hanged soon after the British occupation of the city in September 1857.

Syed Mubarak Shah

Shah, who was a customs official under the British, was appointed kotwal of the city after the deposition of Sharful Haq and Qazi Faizullah. He survived the uprising and wrote a memoir, which can be found in English translation in the British Library's Oriental Collection.

Zinat Mahal

Zinat Mahal was Bahadur Shah's favourite wife and the mother of Prince Jawan Bakht. She corresponded with the British during the uprising to have her son crowned the successor, but was exiled to Rangoon along with Bahadur Shah.

Nawab Amed Ali Khan alias Samsaduddaulah

Nawab Amed Ali Khan was Zinat Mahal's father and a top noble of Bahadur Shah's court. He was briefly appointed the chief civilian administrator of the city, but the soldiers resented and suspected him.

Ihsanullah Khan: Thanadar, Turkman Gate
Mirza Mohammed Khan Beg: Thanadar, Guzar Qasimjan
Mohammed Saadat Ali Khan: Thanadar, Faiz Bazaar
Mohammed Mirza Amani: Thanadar, Bhojla Pahari
Kunwar Lal and Bishambher Nath: Thanadars, Dariba
Hafiz Aminuddin Khan: Thanadar, Chandni Chowk
Badal Khan: Thanadar, Rajghat
Mirza Mohammed Jaan Beg: Thanadar, Guzar Itiqad Khan
Mohammed Amir Ali: Thanadar, Nigambodh Ghat
General Taleyaar Khan: Secretary of the Court of Mutineers, liasioned with Mirza Mughal
Court of Mutineers (CoM)

INTRODUCTION
1857 and the Mutiny Papers

The *ghadar* of 1857 continues to invite different kinds of recall, many of them anniversarial. Reified as a founding moment of the Indian nation, it acts as a sanctifying event for the contemporary Indian state which yokes the liberating zeal of the rebels to the discipline of current obedience.[1] At the same time, it acts as a beacon to counter-establishment politics, a reminder of a glorious moment of resistance and protest. Marginal groups seek in it a validation for their identity politics in the contemporary, and revolutionaries search it for inspiration.[2] Scholarly interest in 1857, however, follows the high points of its calendrical existence closely, peaking every fifty years with long ebbs in between. The number of monographs or dissertations it attracts dwindles with each passing year. The historians who specialize on 1857 can be found in larger numbers outside the academy. Altogether, there is a settled air about 1857, an air of 'knowability' which leaves little room for revisionism.

It may seem churlish to lament the neglect of 1857 at a time that has witnessed, thanks to its hundred and fiftieth anniversary in 2007, such a tremendous outpouring of articles, seminars, special issues of journals and books. 1857 has been both over- and under-written. Kunwar Singh, the leader of the uprising in Bihar and eastern Uttar Pradesh, to take just one example, has been celebrated in folk songs,[3] in books and articles in Hindi, and in accounts of the uprising in Bihar, but we still do not have a full-length political, or historical biography of him in English. It is the same with other places and figures of 1857. There are popular stories galore about Begum Hazrat Mahal and Tatya Tope,

1

but no full-length studies of their careers, not in English at any rate. The only English biography of Bahadur Shah dates back fifty years and there are still no monographs about the uprising in Lucknow or Bareilly or Allahabad. Three monographs in the last thirty years—Rudrangshu Mukherjee's study of Awadh, Tapti Roy's account of Bundelkhand and William Dalrymple's narrative of the uprising in Delhi[4]—underscore the need for similar studies for other regions but they are few and far between. The narrative production of 1857 in independent India in cumulative terms, one hundred and fifty years after the event, probably still lags behind the tremendous outpouring of writings by the British, laypersons and historians alike—in the context of 1857, the difference remains blurred to this day—in its immediate aftermath.[5]

The sparseness of knowledge about some of the better-known principals creates peculiarities when 1857 is invoked for liberationist or revolutionary politics. We don't *know* the rebels of 1857, we can't see them as humane, humanitarian leaders or visionaries. They are not bearers of emancipation in the way of medieval saint-poets, or of twentieth-century nationalists. Their attributes of greatness lie neither in their characters or personalities nor in the way we idealize other national revolutionaries or patriots, say Bhagat Singh or Rana Pratap. They do not provide any role models which we could emulate. Even when the rebels are hailed as heroes, their heroics lie not in their personalities or actions, but in the ideal that they are supposed to represent, one of abstract freedom from foreigners. Their achievements lie, therefore, in the realm of the counterfactual, in what they could have done. It is difficult to tell a Bakht Khan from a Tatya Tope, their interchangeability is a given; their differences are that of their fate, or their locations or movements. This cardboard image is a result of paucity of sources too, but it is also due to a certain attitude which we have towards them. As I have argued elsewhere, invoking 1857 for patriotic purposes alone compels one to think of it purely counterfactually, which leads to a long list of 'what ifs'.[6] What if the rebels had been better organized, better led, better fed, better armed and so on and so forth? Moreover, it is not the only armed uprising against colonial rule in the nineteenth century. There were several that preceded it and some followed after. In order to achieve true singularity, 1857 would need to display traits that differentiate it from other rebellions, not only in quantitative terms—admittedly, the numbers involved were larger than ever before—but also qualitatively.

On the one hand, therefore, we have the preponderance of overviews presented by general histories of the uprising of 1857 as a whole, most of them more than thirty years old.[7] At the same time, there is a plethora of publications that have inundated us because of the hundred and fiftieth anniversary three years ago. Most books that resulted from the jamborees and celebrations have been compilations of articles, a large majority of them dealing with the historiography of the event.[8] 1857 nowadays only invites 'revisits', as if the primary level of research on it is long since done and over, and we can now go back and reflect on settled truths.

What are those settled truths about 1857? Mutiny versus war of independence, localized or general, war of religion versus secular conflict—the binaries through which 1857 has been apprehended has, by and large, left participants out in the cold.[9] Leadership, military strategy, tactics, lack of unity, absence of command—the leitmotifs of discussions on rebels—all suffer from a surfeit of lack. They are the proverbial blind men, struggling valiantly in the dark, but uncomprehending, fighters all right, but not revolutionaries proper. While historical writing is sometimes laden with popular sentiments,[10] popular writing on 1857 still sets up a contest with academic writing, taking historians to task for not being sufficiently sympathetic to the aims and achievements of the revolutionaries of 1857.[11] Such contests can range from the popular to the rhetorical and polemical.[12]

In part, this overdetermination is caused by the kind of memory, or the lack of it, that surrounds 1857 in India. We are intimately familiar with the extreme emotional responses of the British in 1857 through the fecund genre of the memoir history. Details of each execution, death, escape, triumph, including childbirths and illnesses, have allowed us to 'know' the event as it struck the British. The record of that pain and the shock which it engendered has been transcribed on to the cities and sites of the uprising. In the context of 1857, when one thinks of

Kanpur, one thinks invariably of the massacres of the Satichaura Ghat and of Bibighar. Similarly, the metaphoric expression of the uprising in Lucknow is the Residency, or in Delhi, the ridge, producing associations that inscribe the uprising as an event in British history.[13] No such emotional record, or mourning, is available by and about the rebels. The massacres committed by the British leave no written traces, their memory is ground to a certain amnesia, buttressed by the colonial censor on sedition and on invoking 1857.[14] It is instructive that some of the most illustrious men of Urdu letters in the second half of the nineteenth century, who were associated, one way or another with Delhi and with the uprising there, hardly ever commented on it in their public writings or speeches. Stalwart figures such as Mohammed Husain Azad, Altaf Husain Hali and Deputy Nazir Ahmed almost completely obliterated the memory of the uprising from their public writings and speeches. Even Sir Syed gradually ceased to comment on it after the two pamphlets he wrote in the immediate wake of the uprising.[15]

The first significant acts of recording oral memory in Urdu appear in the second and third decades of the *twentieth* century. This was mainly the result of the efforts of a pioneering pamphleteer—and a practising Sufi—Hasan Nizami (1878–1957). Nizami published almost a dozen books and pamphlets which culled narratives of grief, loss and displacement, as suffered by the Delhi elite. With titles such as *Begmat ke Ansu, Ghadar ke Subh-o Sham* and *Dehli ki Jaankuni*,[16] the books provide one of the earliest instances of creating oral and popular history in modern India. They attempted to chronicle the event through interviews, memories and popular beliefs. Apart from creating an affective record of grief, thereby compensating for the absence of rebel emotions, the narratives also reflected popular versions of the uprising. Nizami wrote in the preface to *Dehli ki Jaankuni* or 'The Agony of Delhi', in 1922, that based on written records as well as survivors' memory, he had already written eight books—he went on to write more—about the uprising in Delhi.

Apart from books I have also had the opportunity to meet and accumulate the accounts of most of the Hindus and Muslims who were in Delhi at the time of the Mutiny. From my childhood I have had a great interest in meeting people who were present during those times. However, in this book I have only included those verbal accounts from people which I could authenticate from books. This is because I have written a separate book under this series where I have included all the accounts. In the present book only authenticated accounts have been included.[17]

However, the oral accounts presented by Nizami, even when inaccurate or inauthentic in their particulars, nevertheless present a general truth about Delhi through their overall impact. The 'sack of Delhi' in 1857 created such a rupture in its aftermath that its brutality was laid over by amnesia.[18] Nizami's writings highlight the 'native' silence around Delhi. The absence of direct and recorded memory creates a gap, and a lag, in retelling the narrative.[19] As a result, the personal easily gives way to the political and the actual to the normative. The experience of the rebels, and the uprising itself, can therefore easily be subsumed in the metanarrative of patriotism or nationalism or its direct other, clan-based localism.

Saheb, Iqbal, Qaum and Jihad[20]

The uprising was widely described as a war of religion. On the surface, the rebels were indubitably fighting to preserve and protect their religious values from assaults by the British.[21] However, the definition of religion could stretch very wide. In proclamations by the Mughal prince Firoze Shah and by Hazrat Mahal, the deposed queen of Wajid Ali Shah, both of whom were fighting in Awadh, a large number of 'secular' issues were clubbed under religious angst. These included the administering of British law in the lawcourts, prohibition of prescriptions by Indian physicians, the teaching of English in government schools and the payment of stipends to attend them, and several others.[22] As Rudrangshu Mukherjee has pointed out, the proclamations often *deliberately* picked out the issues that were most likely to sting people into action.[23] It was not something contemporary British observers were entirely unaware of; the soldiers deliberately perpetrated violence and murder upon the British in order to implicate the whole regiment and so that there could be no possibility of turning back.[24] Where they could not mention specific instances, the proclamations often claimed to divine the 'real' intentions of the British, which invariably led to the conclusion that they were attempting a widespread destruction of the Hindu and Muslim religions.[25]

This divination of the real intentions of the British went hand in hand with ritualistic repetition of British perfidies; for instance, the accusation that bones of cows and pigs had been mixed in sugar and flour. This particular charge had been made even at the time of the Vellore mutiny.[26] It was repeated in several proclamations of 1857.[27] It can be argued therefore that the lurid descriptions of British tyrannies, which was a standard tactic of arousing anger and hatred, rested on incantatory repetition of the baseness to which the British could descend. The charges, therefore, were often far less descriptive of an existing state of alienation than provocative propaganda. *Religious* distress is 'at the same time the expression of *real* distress and also the *protest* against real distress', says Marx.[28] *Dehli Urdu Akhbar* was one of the most passionate proponents of the religious nature of the war, but it could elaborate its appeal as easily in the name of Hindustan or in the name of the sacred and secular histories of Hindus and Muslims.[29] If the country could not be separated from religion, religion itself could not be divorced from its specific *Hindustani* location. Miracles and unforeseen interventions by the divine played as significant a role in the invocation of religion as doctrines.[30]

The references to religion and to the two communities of Hindus and Muslims also vary in emphases depending on who is making the exhortation. In newspapers, public proclamations and utterances of the ideologues, religion comes to occupy a much more central role in the everyday descriptions of battles or preparations for war, which are the staple of these documents. In many ways, the uprising of 1857, it may be argued, provided the template for invoking communal amity in India. After that year, India would automatically be assumed to consist of two hegemonic communities, Hindus and Muslims. In doing so, 1857 emulated the medieval Bhakti and Sufi poets who had already picked out these two, from among a host of many different ways of mapping ethnicities and social group identities in India.[31] The ghadar of 1857 did not create the political identities of Hindus or Muslims—but it left a very strong imprint on the ways in which India would come to be seen—as a conglomerate of two communities, with other minor claimants, a claim which is an assertion as much as a description of an existing reality. Not surprisingly, there is very little of that propagandaic element in many of the documents in the Mutiny Papers, which are concerned far more with the day-to-day running of administration than with an ideological war.

In trying to move away from conventional matrices of approaching 1857, I have been wondering if one can build an alternative vocabulary for looking at the telos of mayhem and anarchy. It would be interesting, if not evidently useful, to track how and when the firangis came to be included in the respectful mode of addressing superiors, namely, saheb.[32] By 1857, however, the word saheb had become a self-sufficient reference for denoting the British. When the spy Gauri Shankar writes about the arrest of an Englishman, it suffices to call him a saheb—'a horseman has brought a saheb here'. Another letter mentions, simply, that 'Hindus are all well wishers of the sahebs'.[33] *Jis waqt baly gard mein sab saheban the* ('The time when all the sahebs were at the Residency') goes a folk song about the British at Lucknow in 1857.[34] Hereafter, the word saheb is so inflected that it not only comes to stand for anybody closely associated with rulers, or belonging to the ruling class, but also connotes a certain way of being. It comes to stand, in other words, for a cultural specificity which heavily partakes of the English—*Sala main to saheb ban gaya, saheb ban ke kaise tan gaya, ye suit mera dekho, ye boot mera dekho, jaise koi gora London ka*, sings Sagina Mahato, as late as the 1970s. Does this tell us something important about the changing perceptions about the British and their position in the Indian order of honour? This Indianization, as it were, rested very strongly on something else, on the *iqbal* of the firangi. The firangi was blessed, fortunate, lucky, had prestige and aura. Conquest and good fortune poured into each other in order to create a hegemonic air about the British presence in India.[35] The *buland* iqbal of the princes and emperors of yore has constantly been hailed in our dramas and films. Saheb-e alam's waning and waxing iqbal makes Mughal-e Azam, famously, expand and elongate with forceful inward breathing in that eponymous film.[36] The firangi had come to enjoy the iqbal of the Mughal dynasty—*Iqbal se firangi mulk awadh le liya*—goes another folk song about the British conquest of Awadh.[37] Not military might alone, but wisdom and sagacity, and an ascendant fortune, characterized the British victories. The word appears several times in these documents and in the *Dehli Urdu Akhbar*, denoting the connotation which I have just described.[38] When its ascendant star fell, however, in 1857, the saheb lost both his s*ahebi* and his iqbal as both his body, his august person, as well as his hegemony, his rule, came to be disrupted. In disrupting that iqbal, the rebels fell upon violence, which showed how the power enjoyed by the British was widely seen to be, in spite of the iqbal, as illegitimate. Even as sympathetic a writer as Moinuddin Hasan Khan, the former kotwal of Delhi, whose memoir written at Theo Metcalfe's behest formed the second part of the latter's *Two Native Narratives*, starts his remembrances—written for a British audience and available only in an English translation—by saying, 'I will commence my narrative with the statement that, however the English may regard themselves, they are regarded by the natives as trespassers, and this feeling was intensified on the annexation of the province of Oude.'[39] This widespread resentment, and the humiliation of the everyday experience of racism, also needs to be remembered when we try to understand the torrential outflow of violence that is the hallmark of 1857.

The counterpoint to the sahebs could have been the *qaum*, the Hindu and Muslim qaums or the qaum of Hindustan.[40] However, the word qaum appears rarely in documents and proclamations related to 1857, although the Mutiny Papers are replete with it. In the standard format of petitions here, a person identifies herself by name, patronymic, age, education and qaum. Unlike later usage which defined qaum as nationality, here it refers almost exclusively to one's caste, if upper class, or occupation-caste, if one is lower caste. Moreover, as discussed above, the *qaumiyat* or identity of those seeking to displace the British could shift and change and depended on the context. Instead of relying on qaum, invocations to *deen* and *dharam* posited a way of countering the British iqbal. If the British had been destined to rule India for some time, that same destiny now determined their downfall. Its clearest exposition can be found in the pages of the *Dehli Urdu Akhbar*.

Although now recognized to be a multiple event with varying trajectories in different spaces, altogether, the ghadar of 1857 has been overwhelmed by 'truth-claims' of many varieties.[41] Whether read as a peasant revolt, a religious war, an uprising against an alien power, or as 'a multitude of detached and almost contemporaneous incidents,'[42] its immediate ramifications for the participants are not entirely clear. The history of the process is substituted for the history of the events where 'what happened' is a narrative account modulated by a truth claim. Because of the dense focus on the motivation informing the rebels, the discussion on the ways in which the rebels acted implies, only, the political significance of their actions. There are very few accounts dealing with the 'how' of the rebels' acts. A heavy concentration on the battles, and tactics and strategy, leaves open the question of how the battles were organized. It took more than soldiers and arms to fight a battle, it took hundreds of workers to build a large wall around Lucknow, for example, or to repair the battlements every day at Delhi. So how was this organization managed? What did it mean for the residents of Delhi, especially the unenthusiastic ones, to be overwhelmed by soldiers on the streets and lanes they had long been masters of?

The search for meaning in 1857 can take many forms. In the most immediate sense, what did it mean for peoples and places which saw the longest and the most sustained action? What did the uprising mean to the residents of Delhi, whether as participants, witnesses, victims or all of these? What did the uprising mean in terms of organizing battles, raising finances and supplies, commandeering labour? What impact did the dislocation of peoples and the intense mobility of soldiers have on the process? Is a glimpse into the everyday running of a city an important component of the signification of 1857? Or is this slice of life a mere prolegomena to something else? Is the turbulence, the ghadar, to use its Urdu equivalent, which is the greatest hallmark of the times, a sideshow or the main act itself? Is there a way of narrating the ghadar without describing the actual mode by which the rebels ordered themselves—the structures through which they governed, the practices whereby they raised money and materials for war? 'I am writing about people, not about movements; about attitudes, prejudices and mentalities, not about thought,' wrote a historian of the French revolutionary movements and I find that I have unwittingly echoed him throughout.[43]

This book makes no truth claims about 1857, which is one of the reasons why it has been difficult to embed it in the existing historiography of the ghadar. Instead, it seeks to present the events of 1857 through the accounts of people in Delhi who lived through it or were intimately involved in it as officials, administrators, commanders and executives. By presenting the documents of the government established by the rebels in partnership with Delhi's royal establishment, as well as the petitions, applications and complaints of the ordinary people who interacted with or were affected by this government, it tries to present the process—the how—of the 1857 uprising. This is in that sense our first full-blooded glimpse into 1857 as an urban phenomenon. In not making a wider claim, a truth-claim about the ghadar, it does not mean to deny that broader conclusions about the motivation or the aspirations of the rebels cannot be made, or should not be made. But in so far as it studies a specific city, and that too through administrative eyes as it were, it fails to report a larger narrative. By studying the governmentality of the rebels, it tries to move beyond the idealized and grandiose claims of the proclamations and advertisements put out by the main players in order to tease out the actions of the people. It tries to describe what was going on in the city when the uprising was afoot, what it meant for the city and its dwellers, and it leaves open the question of what the uprising meant for India or Indians or Hindustanis or for the broader current of Indian history.

Notes

1. I refer to the state-sponsored commemoration of the 150th anniversary of 1857, which culminated at the Red Fort lawns on 11 May 2007.

2. For a succinct discussion on the role of 'memory, memorialisation and remembering' in recalling 1857, see Dipesh Chakrabarty, 'Remembering 1857: An Introductory Note', *Economic and Political Weekly*, Vol. 42 (19), 2007, pp.1692–95. For the invocation of 1857 by dalits, see articles in the same issue by Badri Narayan and Charu Gupta. For the way Muslims choose to remember it, see issues of *Qaumi Awaz* and *Rashtriya Sahara* in Urdu from 2007, particularly during May and June.

3. For folk songs about Kunwar Singh, see Pankaj Rag, '1857: Need for Alternative Sources', *Social Scientist*, Vol. 26 (296–99), January–April 1998, pp. 113–151.

4. See Rudrangshu Mukherjee, Mukherjee, *Awadh in Revolt, 1857–58: A Study of Popular Resistance* (Delhi, New York: Oxford University Press, 1984), Tapti Roy, *The Politics of a Popular Uprising: Bundelkhand in 1857* (New Delhi: Oxford University Press, 1994), and William Dalrymple, *The Last Mughal: The Fall of a Dynasty, Delhi, 1857* (London: Bloomsbury, 2006).

5. An indicator of this is the fact that while there is a published bibliography of British writings on 1857, there isn't one about writings by Indians. See S.B. Chaudhuri, *English Historical Writings on the Indian Mutiny, 1857–1859* (Calcutta: The World Press Ltd., 1979).

6. Mahmood Farooqui, 'A Riot of Turbulence, Wherever you Look: The Dehlvi Ghadar', *Sarai Reader 06* (Delhi: Centre for the Study of Developing Societies, 2006), pp 254–71.

7. I refer to histories of 1857 by V.D. Savarkar, S.N. Sen, R.C. Majumdar, S.B. Chaudhuri, Pandit Sunderlal (in Hindi) and Eric Stokes. For details of their publications, see Biswamoy Pati, 'Historians and Historiography: Situating 1857', *Economic and Political Weekly*, Vol. 42 (19), 2007, p. 1691.

8. I refer to collections published by the *Economic and Political Weekly*, *Biblio* and *ICHR*, and to innumerable conferences, some which I attended, at the universities of Delhi, Jamia and Edinburgh, as well as compilations such as the Sharmishtha Gooptu and Boria Majumdar (eds.), *Revisiting 1857: Myth, Memory, History* (New Delhi: Lotus-Roli, 2007).

9. With the exception, enormous of course, of Ranajit Guha. See his *Elementary Aspects of Peasant Insurgency* (New Delhi: Oxford University Press, 1983), passim. Even Guha, however, does claim to know what the rebels are up to, as different from the rebels telling us what they were doing. Gautam Bhadra's 'Four Rebels of Eighteen-Fifty-Seven', in Ranajit Guha (ed.), *Subaltern Studies IV* (New Delhi: Oxford University Press, 1985), is also successful at breaking these binaries and remains, twenty-five years later, an unusual study of different kinds of rebels.

10. See, for instance, the contributions of K.C. Yadav to *Proceedings of the National Conference on Historiography of 1857: Debates in the Past and the Present State of Knowledge, 9–10 December 2006*, published by the Indian Council of Historical Research.

11. It seeks to emphasize the planned and organized nature of the revolt, imparts it a countrywide spread, hails it as the founding moment of the Indian nation and reads in its failure a tragic story of betrayal and collaboration. Among others, this genre includes Amaresh Mishra's *War of Civilisations: The Road to Delhi* (Delhi: Rupa & Co., 2008), and also his *India AD 1857* (Delhi: Rupa & Co., 2008).

12. See issues of a recently-launched pamphlet *Ghadar Jari Hai* and *Liberation*, May 2007.

13. For a succinct elucidation of this through a close reading of John Kaye, see Shahid Amin, 'History of the Sepoy War: A View from Delhi Ridge and Cavalry Lines', in Rosie Llewellyn-Jones (ed.), *The Uprising of 1857* (New Delhi: The Alkazi Foundation for the Arts and Ahmedabad: Mapin Publishing, forthcoming). I have contributed a chapter to the book comparing the contrasting attitudes of two Delhi intellectuals, Mirza Ghalib and Maulvi Baqar.

14. The first 'Indian' history of 1857, of course, is V.D. Savarkar's *The First War of Indian Independence*, published in 1907, but banned immediately in India. Sporadic writings in Urdu began to appear in the second decade of the twentieth century. But even as late as 1929, after the event had become part of the revolutionary pantheon, shaped mainly by the Ghadar party, Pandit Sunderlal's history in Hindi, *Bharat Mein Angrezi Raj*, was banned by the colonial authorities.

15. See S.R. Faruqi, 'From Antiquary to Social Revolutionary: Syed Ahmad Khan and the Colonial Experience', Sir Syed Memorial Lecture, Aligarh, 2006. See also footnote 19 below.

16. *The Ladies' Lament, The Days and Nights of the Ghadar* and *The Agony of Delhi*, respectively. For a brief biography, see http://www.twocircles. net/2007may01/chronicler-1857-par-excellence.html. Even Nizami, however, claimed that he had written the book to wean the youth away from the path of violent confrontation with the British. His exact words were, 'The main reason for writing this book is to make the nation aware of the effects of revolt on the capital of Hindustan. It is also to show what misery and horrors are caused by war and disturbances. This book will awaken the present-day youth to the possible consequences of their war-like intentions. It will also make the youth aware that it is quite dangerous to carry out sedition against the present-day British Government as the last time the efforts of the whole of Hindustan could not manage to get rid of the British rulers' (*Agony of Delhi*, p. 3). Other than Nizami, Allama Rashid ul Khairi (1868–1936) was the other pioneering Delhi writer who obliquely wrote about the ghadar. Although he became famous for his historical fiction, he remained a social reformer and one of the first to publish a journal in Urdu called *Ismat*, which was dedicated to women's uplift and reform. I am thankful to Professor C.M. Naim for reminding me of him.

17. For Hasan Nizami and an English translation of *Dehli ki Jaankuni*, see the wonderful resource site for 1857, http://www.kapadia.com/ TheMutinyinDelhi.html

18. For a detailed account of the sack, see Dalrymple, *The Last Mughal*, chapter 10. While sporadic letters from Ghalib show his intense poignancy about the aftermath, the brutality of the massacres and other atrocities suffered by Dilliwallas has not found adequate space in written records. See Ralph Russell (ed.), *The Oxford India Ghalib: Life, Letters and Ghazals* (New Delhi: Oxford University Press, 2003).

19. Other than the colonial censor, one reason for this silence was the recasting of the relationship between the Urdu elite and the colonial regime. See S.R. Faruqi, *Early Urdu Literary Culture and History* (New Delhi: Oxford University Press, 2001), and Frances Pritchett and S.R. Faruqi (trans., and eds.), *Ab-e Hayat: Shaping the Canon of Urdu Poetry* (New Delhi: Oxford University Press, 2001).

20. This section contains very tentative hypotheses at best and should be seen as that.

21. For its most articulate exposition, see Dalrymple, *The Last Mughal*, passim. For a more sophisticated analysis of the role of religiosity in 1857 and other peasant insurgencies, see Ranajit Guha, 'The Prose of Counter-Insurgency', *Subaltern Studies II*, edited by Ranajit Guha (New Delhi: Oxford University Press, 1993), pp 1–43. See also Guha's *Elementary Aspects*, passim.

22. Mukherjee, *Awadh in Revolt*, pp. 148–52.

23. Ibid., p. 150. Emphasis mine.

24. Shahid Amin, 'Eric Stokes and the Ghadar of 1857', *Economic and Political Weekly*, 7 November 1987.

25. See the proclamation of Maulvi Liaqat Ali in Iqbal Hussain (ed.), *Proclamations of the Rebels of 1857*, draft (New Delhi: ICHR, 2007).

26. Sunderlal, *Bharat Mein Angrezi Raj*, reprint (New Delhi: Publications Division, 1961), p. 529.

27. See the first document in the section titled 'Beginnings' in Iqbal Hussain (ed.), *Proclamations of the Rebels of 1857*. See also section titled 'Rebel Proclamations'.

28. Karl Marx, 'Contribution to the Critique of Hegel's Philosophy of Law', quoted in Bhadra, 'Four Rebels'.

29. See the section 'The Ideologue' in this volume.

30. For instance, the persistence of the story about the sudden appearance of thousands of green turbaned and masked riders outside the gates of the city of Delhi when the British first made to attack it. 'Some people even swear that the day the horsemen came here, there were she-camels ahead of them on which rode green-robed riders and then they instantly vanished from sight and only the troopers remained and they killed whichever Englishman they found and cut them like carrots and radish and would pull their legs off and throw them' (*Dehli Urdu Akhbar*, 24 May 1857, National Archives of India [NAI]). For another example, see *Dehli Urdu Akhbar*, 2 August 1857, 'Such are the ways of the omnipotent Almighty that when they made towards the city, suddenly thousands of masked soldiers appeared on the ramparts of the city and its gates, holding aloft naked swords in their hands and their mere sight was so terrifying that the English were petrified.' For similar miraculous deeds committed by Maulvi Ahmedullah Shah in Awadh, see Bhadra, 'Four Rebels', p. 264. Some of these miraculous deeds and appearances share features with the highly popular fantastic oral narrative tradition of the Dastan-e Amir Hamza, in particular, with the long epic *Tilism-e Hoshruba*. See the

three-volume study by S.R. Faruqi, *Dastan-e Amir Hamza* (New Delhi: NCPUL, 2006–8).

31. See David Gilmartin and Bruce Lawrence, *Beyond Turk and Hindu: Rethinking Religious Identities in Islamicate South Asia* (Delhi: India Research Press, 2002). While this book purports to move beyond the binary, its very title confirms the existence of such a binary. The common lampooning of Hindu and Muslim orthodoxies is the stock in trade of many medieval devotional poets, most notably, Kabir.

32. This paragraph requires a more extensive and nuanced reading of the honorifics attached to the British, in titles as well as common speak, over a hundred-year period beginning 1757. I persist with them more to present directions for research than as conclusive findings. Hobson Jobson gives this description for 'sahebs': 'Europeans generally, are addressed, and spoken of, when no disrespect is intended, by natives. It is also the general title (at least where Hindustani or Persian is used) which is affixed to the name or office of a European, corresponding thus rather to Monsieur than to Mr. For Colonel Saheb, Collector Saheb, Lord Saheb, and even Sergeant Saheb are thus used, as well as the general vocative Saheb! "Sir!" In other Hindi use the word is equivalent to "Master" and it is occasionally used as a specific title both among Hindus and Musalmans . . .' (Yule, Henry, Sir, *Hobson-Jobson: A Glossary of Colloquial Anglo-Indian Words and Phrases, and of Kindred Terms, Etymological, Historical, Geographical and Discursive*, new edition, edited by William Crooke, BA (London: J. Murray, 1903).

33. Collection 19, No. 10, 19 July, and Collection 20, No. 11, Undated, in the Mutiny Papers, NAI. See the section 'Faqirs, Loiterers and Brigade Majors: The Dangerous Liaisons of Spies' in this volume for the letters. See also *Dehli Urdu Akhbar*, 12 July 1857, NAI.

34. Folk songs about the Indian mutiny were collected by W. Crooke. See his 'Songs of the Mutiny' and 'Songs about the King of Oudh', *Indian Antiquary*, 1911. For other connections of the word 'saheb' with the English or European gentlemen, see S.W. Fallon, New *Hindustani-English Dictionary* (Banaras, printed at the Medical Hall Press; Mondon: Trubner and Co., 1879).

35. See also Rajit K. Mazumder, *The Indian Army and the Making of Punjab* (Delhi: Permanent Black, 2003), pp. 44–5, especially ff 162–66.

36. The reference is to the 1960 Urdu film *Mughal-e Azam*, where Emperor Akbar (Mughal-e Azam) and the Prince Salim/Jehangir (Saheb-e Alam)

are constantly greeted by the phrase, '*Huzur ka iqbal buland ho*' or, may your fortune be on the ascendant.

37. Crooke in *Indian Antiquary*. Shahid Amin, rightly, cautions about the reliability of the 'folk songs' presented to the British a good fifty years after the event, especially by as complaisant a collector as Ram Gharib Chaube. See his forthcoming book on Ghazi Mian.

38. See *Dehli Urdu Akhbar*, 17 May, 14 June and 5 July, NAI.

39. Moinuddin Hasan Khan's narrative, *Two Native Narratives* on http://www.kapadia.com/TheMutinyinDelhi.html, p. 4.

40. The word qaum is discussed elsewhere in the book, but it means, broadly, community, group, caste, occupation, region, any social grouping. In later years, it came to stand in for the community and/or nationality, particularly in discussions of Muslim political identity. The word Hindustan traditionally referred to North India and excluded the Deccan and the south of India. It is the word that most commonly occurs for India in these documents and seems, sometimes, to suggest the entire country too.

41. For a brief, but very lucid discussion on truth-claims and its relationship with historical writing, see Qadri Ismail, '(Not) at Home in (Hindu) India: Shahid Amin, Dipesh Chakrabarty, and the Critique of History', *Cultural Critique*, Winter 2008.

42. The phrase is John Kaye's. See *History of the Sepoy War in India*, p vi.

43. Richard Cobb, *The Police and the People: French Popular Protests, 1789–1820* (London: Oxford University Press, 1970), introduction. I acquired a copy of this remarkable study of the French police far too late for it to make a substantial difference to my findings. But I was delighted to find that I had been unknowingly groping towards similar conclusions. Especially, Cobb's findings about the French police and its gradual passage from the *ancien regime* mode to a more modern way of functioning during the period of his study closely parallels the processes and practices of the police in the period in Delhi referred to in this volume. I have to acknowledge my tremendous obligation to Professor Shahid Amin who constantly importuned me to read the book and eventually procured a copy for me.

The Proceedings

IN THE NAME OF THE COW AND THE PIG
Soldiers arrive and the King fails to take charge

The uprising at Meerut began in the name of religion and was ostensibly continued for the same reason. This appeal to religion—in proclamations, speeches, pamphlets, newspapers—as argued elsewhere in the book, was a strategic move on the part of the rebel leaders, with the intention of arousing and inciting the population. They are not as descriptive of an already hurt religious sentiment as a deliberate mechanism to enthuse support for the rebel cause. There is therefore a formulaic air about the lurid details and repeated descriptions of British machinations. Reports of mixing animal bones with flour, mentioned in the first document, circulated in Vellore too during the mutiny there in 1807. A similar incantatory effect can be seen in the repeated use of the terms 'pig and the cow' to refer to all those Hindus and Muslims who did not heed the call to fight the British.

The decision of the rebellious Meerut soldiers to march to Delhi turned a local event into a much wider rebellion. There may have been uprisings at many places even without this event, but the fall of Delhi had a galvanizing effect on the rest of the country as garrisons across north India revolted one by one. Troops from as far away as Nimach, Tonk and Bareilly made their way to Delhi and, as time went on, thousands of other volunteers poured into the city.

However, unlike at other places like Kanpur or Bareilly, the arrival of soldiers in Delhi was not accompanied by a civil rebellion. The residents of the city shared a mostly uncomfortable relationship with the soldiers throughout the period of the ghadar—while some welcomed them into the city, most citizens remained indifferent or even hostile.

The long diary of a clerk at the slain commissioner's office describes the atmosphere of fear and anarchy in the city during the first week of the soldiers' arrival. Most of the British, women and children included, were killed, many after being hunted down, while a few escaped. The soldiers plundered the houses and shops of the well-to-do on the charge or suspicion of sheltering the British. Even the high and the mighty were not exempt from this—the houses of Nawab Mahboob Ali Khan, Ahsanullah Khan, Shah Nizamuddin, Agha Jaan and Chunna Mal, leading notables of the city, were plundered and attacked. The murder of fifty-two Englishmen, women and children, who were dragged out of jail and shot in cold blood, seems to have been instigated by the soldiers' distrust of the Delhi elite. The event happened on the same day as when they had surrounded the King's physician and confidant, Hakim Ahsanullah Khan's house, swords drawn, accusing him of corresponding with the English and with sheltering them. It is noteworthy too that the event encountered some resistance on religious grounds from one of the princes and that the citizens disapproved of it.

Initially, the administration was faced with a double imperative, of preventing plunder by soldiers and keeping shops open. The King and the heir apparent, Mirza Mughal, made repeated rounds of the city, urging shopkeepers and officers to reopen the shops and to prevent looting by the sepoys. Announcements were made to the effect that anyone found looting would be arrested or blown off a cannon. Many people were actually arrested for looting, including leading criminals like Kami Khan and Sarfaraz Khan. The soldiers were not alone in plundering. Some of the residents of the city were leading them from place to place, pointing out places where the British could be hiding. In one instance, two civilians dressed like soldiers were found plundering shops.

The popular nationalist account of 1857 often credits Bahadur Shah Zafar as being one of the main planners of the event. Paradoxically, modern scholarship sees him as a largely reluctant participant in the uprising. Neither view seems to be completely correct. We have absolutely no evidence to suggest any prior planning or conspiracy before the uprising. However, Bahadur Shah's conduct in taking swift charge of the government of Delhi complicates this picture of reluctance. The day after the soldiers arrived, apparently taking him by surprise, he held a royal durbar with the greatest splendour. He dressed up in ancient fineries, ordered that an old throne be taken out, and rewarded army officers and nobles with titles and special robes of honour called *khilat*s. Within a few days of the arrival of the troops at Delhi, without waiting to see which way the tide would turn, without waiting to see whether the British would regroup and return, he wrote letters to all the leading former vassals in Rajputana and at other places, asking them to appear before him with arms and money. Within a week of the arrival of the soldiers, he had even begun to recruit soldiers directly. Within a fortnight, the royal mint had been reactivated and coins bearing the King's name were being issued. None of these actions fit Bahadur Shah's image of reluctance and vacillation.

The soldiers sometimes treated the King with disdain and wholly disregarded court protocol. The King had some difficulty in getting them to vacate the palace and to observe simple court decorum like taking off shoes and not wearing arms when in his presence. As Bahadur Shah reminded soldiers later on, they had come to fight on their own, but had begun to desert and renege on the undertaking. While the situation settled down after the first month, the soldiers were never entirely amenable to control by the King. Repeated orders to them to maintain discipline, to stick to their previous platoons and to stop depredations on residents reflect the difficult relationship between the King and the soldiers. In fact, to make them amenable, Bahadur Shah used many different kinds of stratagems, sometimes successfully—boycotting durbars and public appearances, threatening to retire to Mecca or the shrine of Khwaja Saheb at Mehrauli.

The Meerut soldiers arrived in Delhi on 11 May and were joined by the regiments posted there. On the 8th of June, the British forces led by Brigadier Wilson defeated the rebel forces in an open battle at Badli ki Sarai and occupied the ridge. While the British had ostensibly laid siege to the city, in reality, as more and more rebel troops poured into Delhi and relentlessly attacked the ridge for the next four months, the British often seemed to be the besieged party. On the 14th of September, the British army, with reinforcements from Punjab, stormed the city. While the outward rebel positions fell quickly, the rebel commanders succeeded in their plan of ensnaring the British army in the lanes and streets of the city. It took an entire week for the British forces to move from Kashmiri Gate into the heart of Shahjehabad. In the final battle of Delhi, the soldiers and volunteers were joined by the majority of the city's adult population after a general levy was enforced. Many ordinary residents of the city fought with swords, sticks and household equipment, compelling the British to retake the city lane by lane and street by street. The documents in the last part of this section describe the final days, and as the exchange of one missive after another proves, the bureaucratic and administrative order created by the rebels, shaky as it may have been, held its own till the very end.

The Shastras and the obligation to fight the treacherous firangis

Copy of a printed circular letter in Urdu published at Bareilly and sent to all the 'Kings of Hindustan', Undated

The seal of God's orders over God's country
Translation of the news of the victory of faith.

All you kings who are very steadfast in faith and men of great qualities and generous and bountiful and brave and upholders of your faith and of others, wishing you well we submit that the Almighty has given you this body in order to maintain your faith, the faith of each is evident from their religion and you are steadfast on it. The Creator has produced you kings to destroy those who seek to corrupt your faith and has given you a kingdom. It is desired that whoever has the power should kill those who corrupt your faith and those who do not have the power should think in their hearts of ways to do so and save your faith because the Shastras state that it is better to die on your faith but one should not take up another faith. This is what God has said and everyone knows this. And these English are the destroyers of faith, everyone should know this because for a long time in order to corrupt the religion of the people of Hindustan they have prepared books and have distributed them through their priests all over Hindustan and used their power to propagate books which proved their religion and this has been heard from the people who are their confidants. Witness how they have come up with schemes to spoil the religion that firstly, when a woman becomes a widow they forcibly command her to remarry and secondly, there was an ancient practice of sati so they forcibly forbade it and proclaimed a law that nobody should become sati, and thirdly, they say that if you adopt our religion this will make us happy and you will be rewarded by the government. And they say you should come to the church and listen to our religious speeches and they have told the rajas that those born of the true mother will be allowed succession and those who have been adopted will not be given *rajdhan* although according to our Shastras ten kinds of adoptions are allowed. Through these stratagems they will take over your kingdoms and you can see how Nagpur and Lucknow have been taken.

And look at their designs that they were bent upon feeding prisoners from a common kitchen, many of whom preferred to starve than to eat that food and many said that our faith has been corrupted. When they realized that this plan has not worked, they wanted to grind bones and mix it in flour and sugar and feed it to the people. They made a powder of meat and bones and mixed it in rice and supplied it to shops and they devised all sorts of schemes for us to give up our faith. Then some Bengali thought of this suggestion that if your army accepts these things then the rest too will follow suit. The English really liked this suggestion and said this is a wonderful scheme, they will themselves come round. Then they told the Brahmans, etc., in their army that these bullets are laced with fat, bite them with your mouths. Seeing the loss of faith of the Pandits, the Muslim soldiers also refused to bite the bullet. The English then became bent on corrupting both their faiths and they blew from a cannon the men of any platoon who refused to bite the bullets. When the soldiers observed this tyranny, in order to save their own lives, they began to kill them and wherever they were found they were killed. There are only a few left now and they are making to dispose of them too. We all know now that if these English stay in Hindustan they will kill everyone and spoil the faith but some of our fellow believers side with them and fight for them and give them support and we say to them that know that they will not leave you or your faith either. In this scenario we ask you what you are doing to defend your faith and your lives. If your mind is the same as ours then with a little effort we can slay them all and preserve our faith and our country.

And this has been published in order to save the religion and faith and the lives of all you Hindus and Muslims. Hindus must take oath on *Ganga Tulsi Saligram* and Muslims must swear on God and the Quran and we say that the English are enemies of both, that it would be wise for the Hindus and Muslims to kill them because that way they would be able to protect their faith and religion. Hindus regard cow slaughter as a great evil and in order to prevent that all the leaders of the Muslims in the country of Hind have made a compact that the day the Hindus show eagerness to kill the English the practice of cow slaughter will be ended and if it doesn't then it will be tantamount to reneging on the Quran and eating it will be akin to eating a pig. And if the Hindus do not get ready to kill the firangis and protect them then it will be equal to killing a cow and eating its flesh. And it may be that in order to protect their interest the firangis may explain to the Hindus that if the Muslims are promising to abstain from cow slaughter for the sake of your faith then we too accept this condition and now you join us and kill them, but the wise ones will never accept this fraud because the promises made by the English are self-serving and meant to deceive; once they get what they want they will renege from the contract and it is evident to the high and the low. Therefore do not pay heed to what they say, you will never get another chance like this and a letter, as everyone knows, is half a meeting. We expect that you will agree to everything here and make a reply. Finis.

This letter has been written unanimously by Hindus and Muslims and has been published at the Bahaduri Press, Bareilly thanks to the efforts of Maulvi Syed Qutub Shah Saheb.

(194, 30)

Murder, loot and mayhem: Eyewitness account of the first week of the rebels' arrival in Delhi

Newsletter of the Saheb Bahadur Agent Commissioner of Shahjehanabad including statements of atrocities committed by the mutineers at Delhi, the King's connection with them and Delhi Commissioner's treatment of those who were friendly or hostile to the English during the mutiny, 11 May–7 December 1857

11 May, Monday. Saheb Kalan Bahadur, the commissioner of the city, was resting at his residence. In the night a letter came about the rebellion of the Tilangas and horsemen at the Meerut cantonment. Saheb Kalan Bahadur did not make any arrangements in the night. In the wee hours of the morning word came that the horsemen of the fourth cavalry and two platoons of Tilanga have rebelled at Meerut because of the cartridges issue and are making their way towards Delhi. Therefore Saheb Kalan Bahadur immediately asked the horsemen to call the agent of Nawab of Jhajjhar, and John Metcalfe Saheb came to the city and ordered the *kotwal* to close the gates of the city and told him to send guards to the *kotwali* platform and on top of the gates to secure them. The kotwal carried out the orders.

Saheb Kalan Bahadur along with the horsemen of his entourage came to the city in a carriage. It was learnt that some horsemen had reached the Jamuna bridge and had burnt it and had killed the sergeant there. The above-mentioned horsemen then came to the northern *jharoka* before his majesty and said that they had been here sometime, and that he was to kindly get the gates of the jharoka opened. His majesty immediately sent word to the keeper of the fort that some rebellious soldiers from Meerut have come here and want to create disturbances. The keeper of the fort went forth to the Emperor and told the horsemen that you are all bastards and should immediately leave. The horsemen replied by telling him that they would deal with him. Saheb Kalan Bahadur went to the Kashmiri Gate and told the Tilangas there that since you are loyal servants of the Company Bahadur, please accompany me to meet some soldiers from Meerut who have turned seditious and come to Delhi. The Tilangas said we will not go anywhere, and if some enemy should attack you then we are here to deal with them.

Saheb Kalan Bahadur went on top of the Calcutta Gate along with some other Englishmen and secured it. At that time Jwala Singh Jamadar said to Saheb Kalan Bahadur that as all the Muslims of the city are intent on rebelling we should immediately leave. Saheb Kalan Bahadur declined to consider it. The markets in the city were shut down. Priest Jenning Saheb Bahadur along with another Englishmen was on top of the tower of the keeper of the fort's house watching over the horsemen with binoculars. The commander rode on a carriage and came to Saheb Kalan Bahadur who was on top of the Calcutta Gate and gave him a letter to peruse. Saheb Kalan Bahadur immediately told the soldiers to be on alert.

The Muslims of Bazaar Khanam went on top of the Rajghat gate and after making a pact with the rebel horsemen opened the said gate. They entered the city and began to plunder and burn and kill the Englishmen present. Eventually, the horsemen killed all the Englishmen who used to live in the camp near the river and burned their houses and also killed Dr Chaman Lal who was standing outside the hospital. The Muslims of the city told the horsemen that Saheb Kalan Bahadur is on top of the Calcutta Gate so the horsemen made their way there and fired shots and volleys at Saheb Kalan Bahadur. There were two other Englishmen there along with twelve soldiers of Saheb Kalan Bahadur's guard who were non-Muslims, but they offered no resistance to the horsemen. Saheb Kalan Bahadur then himself snatched the musket off a soldier and shot and injured a rider. Saheb Kalan Bahadur then escaped in a coach with the keeper of the fort and reached the gate of the fort. There they alighted and were making their way into the keeper of the fort's house. The commander went on top of the house and even as Saheb Kalan Bahadur was climbing the stairs, some horsemen attacked him and killed him. Then they went on top and killed the keeper of the fort as well as the priest and two other Englishmen who were present there.

The Muslims of the fort and city then went on a rampage and plundered the houses of the keeper of the fort and other Englishmen. John Metcalfe Saheb Bahadur rode on a horse with a naked sword in his hands and went out of the city via the Ajmeri Gate. Some horsemen pursued him till Tar Bazaar Chawri but the Saheb escaped. Thereafter three platoons of Tilangas who were posted at the Rajpura cantonement joined hands with the rebels and killed its officers and entered the city.

Wherever the rebels found any Englishmen or women, whether in their bungalows or houses or camps, at Kashmiri Darwaza (gate) or Kothi Sikandar Saheb or elsewhere, they killed them. The city's Muslims along with some Hindus accompanied the rebels and attacked all the twelve thanas of the city and the Kotwali Chabutra and destroyed them and broke all the locks. Sharful Haq, the city kotwal, disappeared while the deputy kotwal Baldeo Singh ran away after being injured.

Afterwards, the miscreants assaulted the bank house. Two Englishmen, three ladies and two children were hidden away on top of that place. The ruffians made to kill them but were deterred by the gun in one of the Saheb's hands. One Muslim person climbed a tree but was killed by the praiseworthy Saheb. The miscreants set fire to the bank house after which the Sahebs were left with no choice. The ingrate horsemen went away and then the Muslims killed the Sahebs and the children with a sword. The Muslims and the rebels then went marauding around the city. Raja Nahar Singh of Ballabgarh who had gone to pay a visit to the Saheb in the morning returned in the late afternoon. Whatever goods were there in the Delhi treasury were looted by the Tilangas of the Rajpura platoon and the loot was distributed among them. They also set fire to the civil and military courts and to the Rajpura camp.

Later the cavalry division and two platoons of Tilangas of the Meerut camp and three platoons from Delhi appeared before his majesty and asked him to lead them saying we will ensure your sway over the whole country. The King assured them of his benediction and asked them to set up camp at Salimgarh. The shops, streets and markets of the city were shut down and plunder and looting raged everywhere. Later after hearing that some Englishmen with their ladies were assembled at the magazine and had shut its doors, a group of Tilangas and horsemen reached there after taking a cannon from the Rajpura camp. They fired a volley of shots at the magazine and then the magazine was blown up. Its impact led to the cracking and felling of hundreds of houses around the magazine. The Sahebs ran from there and reached the tower on top of the river Jamuna. The horsemen killed them and arrested two ladies and three sergeants and brought them before the King. The Sahebs pleaded with the King, saying spare our lives and we will remain at your feet, otherwise these fellows would kill us. The King ordered them to be taken to the prayer house. Raja Nahar Singh of Ballabgarh along with the queen and Ranjit Singh, the brother, and Mohan Singh, the father-in-law, left for Ballabgarh towards the early evening after hiding away some Sahebs.

The Tilangas assaulted the house of the treasurer Saligram with the intention of looting it but could not loosen the screws. At midnight the Tilangas along with Muslims of the city finally broke through the gate and looted all the goods of the *kothi*. At midnight two sergeants were going to Meerut with two cannons from the Rajpura camp when the Tilangas reached there and took the guns. The sergeants ran away. The Tilangas and the horsemen gathered together and fired a round of 21 guns outside the fort. All night looting, chaos and disorder ruled the city.

12 May, Tuesday. The King was in the palace and emerged from there and went to the Diwan-e-Khas and accepted the salutations of the officers and leaders. The *subedar*s of the five Tilanga platoons appeared and made a request that the Emperor should appoint somebody to look after supplies and provisions. After hearing this, the King ordered Narsinha Mal and Diwan Mal Modi to supply five hundred rupees worth of flour, grams and pulses to the five Tilanga platoons and the cavalry company every day.

In the house of Mohammed Ibrahim, the son of Wali Mohammed trader, four Englishmen had taken refuge. The Tilangas reached there and looted his kothi and killed the Sahebs. One lady was going to the pond wearing Indian clothes when the horsemen intercepted her and put her to the sword.

The Tilangas looted the shops of grocers, sweetmeat makers and cloth sellers. When it was reported the King appointed Mirza Aminuddin Khan as the subedar of the city and asked him to proceed to the Kotwali Chabutra and prevent the looting. A company of troops was also sent with him. Thereupon the said Mirza, seeing that Tilangas and horsemen continued to loot the bazaars of Chawri, etc., reported it and the King called the subedars of the Tilanga platoons and asked them to deploy a company of Tilanga each at the jharoka, and the Delhi Gate of the Shaharpanah, and on top of the Ajmeri Gate and Lahori Gate and Khirki Farrashkhana, etc., at all the twelve gates of the city to secure them. He said the looting of ordinary subjects is not acceptable to me and send a company of Tilangas to the Dariba.

Later the Tilangas and the horsemen tried to attack the gate of a city merchant in order to loot it. The residents of that place shut the gates from inside and began to shower the Tilangas with stones whereupon they ran away.

Some Englishmen along with their wives and children went and hid at the house of Kalyan Singh, the raja of Kishangarh. The horsemen reached there and fired a volley at the Sahebs who in turn also fired at the Tilangas. At the end the horsemen brought two cannons to the kothi, the Sahebs went and hid in the basement. The horsemen made their way back.

The King asked Mirza Mughal to take a platoon of Tilangas to control the looters. So Mirza Mughal rode inside the city at the Kotwali Chabutra on an elephant. A proclamation was issued throughout the city that whosoever was caught pillaging would lose his nose and ears and that whoever refused to open their shops to supply provisions to the soldiers would be fined and imprisoned. His majesty released Taj Mahal Begum from prison while two English Sahebs who were trying to escape wearing Hindustani clothes were beheaded by the horsemen opposite the Kotwali Chabutra.

Afterwards, the Emperor sat on an elephant and seated Mirza Jawan Bakht close to him, and with his entourage and two platoons of Tilangas, made his way to Chandni Chowk to get the shops opened. He said to the shopkeepers that you should open your shops and give provisions to the soldiers. Later, after resolving the matter, he returned to the fort. Hasan Ali Khan then appeared through Hakim Ahsanullah Khan's reference and paid an *asharfi* as a tribute. The King asked him to stay saying he wished to confer with him. Later, a shawl was presented to Mirza Aminuddin Khan for appointing him to the *subedari* of the city, who, out of gratitude, paid a tribute of four rupees.

13 May, Wednesday. The King emerged and came to the *tasbihkhana*. Nawab Mahboob Ali Khan and other officers presented themselves and paid their obeisance. A command was given to Husain Mirza Nazir to call Mirza Aminuddin Khan. The said Nazir returned and told the King that because of sickness the said Mirza could not present himself. An order was issued to Mirza Moinuddin Khan, the city kotwal, that the supplies had not yet reached the army and that he should procure them immediately.

Hasan Ali Khan appeared; the King said to him that a lot of troops have collected inside the fort and what is your suggestion. The said Khan replied that since this army is composed of murderers and has killed its rulers, one should not place any faith in such an army. A command was sent to Shah Nizamuddin Pirzada and Budhan Saheb, the son of the late Nawab Mohammed Mir Khan, that they should present themselves for consultation. Mirza Mughal, Khizr Sultan and Abdullah, etc., were appointed as colonels to the Tilanga platoons and were told to leave with two guns and to secure the Kashmiri, Lahori and Delhi Gates.

Shah Nizamuddin stated that Nawab Mir Hamid Ali Khan had been captured and brought on foot to Hakim Ahsanullah Khan at the Jawaharkhana. His captors were saying he has hidden Englishmen in his house, while the said Mir says that should you find any Englishmen in my house, ransack it and loot all my belongings, and kill me along with my wives and children. The King asked Shah Nizamuddin to take seven horsemen and Tilangas with him and search Mir's house. So Shah Nizamuddin reached there and searched the house—no Englishmen were found. Whatever property and belongings of the Mir Saheb had been looted by the horsemen and Tilangas were returned to him and he was set free.

His Lordship appointed Mirza Abu Bakr as colonel of the cavalry unit. News arrived that twenty-nine Englishmen, women and children who were hidden at the house of Kalyan Singh of Kishangarh were discovered by the Tilangas who had arrested them all and had then shot them. The horsemen went to the kothi of the late Colonel Sikandar Saheb and arrested the son of the late Yusuf Saheb and executed him opposite the Kotwali Chabutra. Acting on someone's report, the horsemen and Tilangas reached the residence of Sarai Das and the house of Ramsarandas and said we have heard that Englishmen are hidden in your house. With this excuse, they pillaged their houses and looted all their belongings. The Tilangas also killed Qazi Pannu and his successor. Two Sahebs were trying to escape in Indian clothes when they were killed by horsemen.

The King granted four hundred rupees each to all the Tilanga platoons towards food. Mirza Aminuddin Khan issued a proclamation throughout the city that whoever wants to be employed should come armed and that if an Englishman was found in anyone's house, he would be held guilty. Nawab Ahmed Ali Khan and Nawab Walidad Khan of

Malagarh appeared when commanded and the King asked them to be present at court every day. All the landowners and traders of the city were called and told that after fixing the rates of grain, they were to open the granaries and begin selling it. Aminuddin Khan deployed some two hundred soldiers at Dariba, Chandni Chowk, etc., to provide protection. Two persons were arrested for stealing oil from a trader's shop in Chandni Chah Lal. Known criminals Kami Khan and Sarfaraz Khan were arrested as well. Some people have been arrested for looting at Teliwara and Sarai Mandvi.

14 May, Thursday. The King was in the palace. He emerged from there and came to the tasbihkhana. Husain Mirza Nazir and Captains Dildar Ali Khan and Husain Ali Khan presented themselves. As commanded, Mirza Aminuddin Khan, Ziauddin Khan and Maulvi Sadruddin Khan also came and paid obeisance. Maulvi Saheb paid an asharfi as tribute and was told to preside over the civil and criminal courts. The Maulvi Saheb begged to be excused. Later Saligram, the treasurer, appeared as desired and paid an asharfi as tribute. The King asked if there was one lakh rupees in the treasury. Saligram said this slave does not know about it. The King asked him to send one of his representatives to secure the treasure.

Rehmat Ali Khan presented an asharfi as tribute through Hasan Ali Khan's reference. The King asked who he was. The latter said this is the brother of Khan Saheb Bahadur Jang Khan of Dadri. Later on, the confidant of Sohan Singh Rawal of Samut appeared and said that Rawal Saheb is very unwell and therefore could not be present before your majesty. But Rawal Saheb wishes to go to Jaipur. After hearing this, a note was sent to Maharaja Sawai Singh of Jaipur asking him to present himself with his army at the earliest. The confidant stated that he would soon leave for Jaipur. Later on, several notes were sent to Abdur Rahman Khan of Jhajjhar, Bahadur Jang Khan of Dadri, Akbar Ali Khan of Pataudi, Raja Nahar Singh of Ballabgarh, Hasan Ali Khan of Dujana and Nawab Ahmed Ali Khan of Fursatnagar to the effect that they should soon appear before his majesty.

An order was given to Mirza Aminuddin Khan and Ziauddin Khan that they should take care of Pargana Jharka Firozepur and Gurgaon district, which are lying vacant. A report came in that some Gujars had looted shops in Sabzi Mandi and Teliwara and had ransacked the tomb of Nawab Safdarjang Khan. Therefore a command was issued to Mirza Abu Bakr that he should take care of the Gujars. Mirza Abu Bakr then reached the said district with a company of horsemen and placed guns around it; the Gujars left the area and ran away, whereupon the said Mirza plundered the region and set fire to it.

Bahadur Singh, the *darogha* of the Lucknow property, appeared and paid a tribute of an asharfi. A gora was coming to spy from Ambala cantonment but was arrested and sent to jail. One Englishwoman who had been arrested was also sent to jail.

The Tilangas and the subedars stood in the palace with their shoes on. His majesty expressed his displeasure about that.

A command was given to Mirza Aminuddin Khan, the city kotwal, to take a platoon of guards to the Rajpura camp and stop the pillaging at Rajpura camp, Sabzi Mandi and Pahari. Four persons came from the Meerut cantonment and told the Tilangas that gora soldiers are making their way here from Meerut to kill you. The Tilangas were very put out and got those four people arrested.

An order was given to the thanadar of Nigambodh to bury the corpses of Saheb Kalan Bahadur and the keeper of the fort in the graveyard, and to immerse the bodies of the other Englishmen, women and children in the Jamuna river. The order was carried out. The Gujars looted all the property and goods from the kothi of Saheb Kalan Bahadur and desecrated his grave.

15 May, Friday. The King was in the palace. Maulvi Abdul Qadir prepared the salary roll of the soldiers and presented it to the King. His majesty conferred a shawl to the maulvi of Nawab Mahboob Ali Khan. The named person rode back to his house on an elephant. The darogha of Rawal Son Singh of Samut made an appearance and presented a jar of rose water and a bottle of *itr* as tribute from the said Rawal. A note asking the Raja of Jaipur to present himself was given to the darogha. Afterwards, Ghulam Nabi Khan, the darogha of Kale Mahal, along with Akbar Ali *sawar*, who was an orderly of Saheb Kalan Bahadur, presented himself and said that fifty horsemen sent by Nawab Abdur Rahman Khan of Jhajjhar are here at his lordship's service and that his client could not appear himself because of the disorder and lawlessness prevailing in the area.

Maulvi Ahmed Ali Khan appeared on behalf of Raja Nahar Singh of Ballabgarh, paid a tribute of one rupee and presented the application of Raja Nahar Singh saying that the servant could not appear himself because of the destruction wreaked by the Gujars. He would take care of the Gujars and present himself very soon. An order was given asking him to quickly present himself.

A report came in that the Saheb collector of Rohtak has run away and the treasury of that place is about to be looted, while the treasury of Gurgaon has already been pillaged. Hearing this, his majesty decreed that a platoon of Tilangas along with a company of horsemen should go and bring the treasure of Rohtak in kind. An order was given to Abdul Hakim to recruit four hundred macebearers and a company of horsemen at a salary of twenty-five and twenty rupees a month respectively. Some two hundred men were thus recruited. Maulvi Baqar prepared a note and showed it to the King and said that the servant would take care of the arrangements.

A decree was sent to all the risaldars of the cavalry that Mirza Abu Bakr has been suspended as your officer and that you should all present yourselves before his majesty as desired. Qazi Faizullah presented himself and placed a request for being granted the post of kotwal after paying a tribute of five rupees. His request was granted. One person was arrested for murdering another out of rivalry.

The Mewatis of Jaisinghpura had looted four thousand rupees and other goods off the administrator of roads of that region. The Tilangas and horsemen resolved to go to Jaisinghpura to punish those Gujars and to blow up Jaisinghpura. Upon which Lala Yudh Singh, the representative of the raja of Jaipur, moved a petition saying he was responsible for the protection of the people of Jaisinghpura.

A proclamation was made that no soldier or rider should go to Jaisinghpura without his majesty's permission.

It was mentioned that the Tilangas and horsemen march in the streets and roads of the city with bare swords in their hands, and out of fear, the shopkeepers do not open their shops. Hearing this, a decree was sent to the gates of the fort forbidding any person or soldier or rider from walking inside the city with a bare sword.

The risaldar of the Nawab of Jhajjhar was told to go and camp at Mahtab Bagh. A report came in that four boats laden with grains are on their way for Ramji Mal Korwala. An order was given to Diwan Mal Modi to disembark the grain. Two Tilangas had looted two thousand rupees from the *bankghar* and deposited it with Ramji Mal Korwala, saying we will take it in Lucknow. When the Tilangas complained about injustice, a company of Tilangas went to Ramji Mal, who then immediately returned the money.

His majesty sent a note to all the traders and moneylenders of the city asking them to present themselves before him. Later, the horsemen and the Tilangas appeared before his majesty after conferring in the Diwan-e-Khas, and pleaded that it is not possible for us to survive on the salaries given to us. It has been learnt that Hakim Ahsanullah Khan and Mahboob Ali Khan are colluding with the English.

The horsemen and the Tilangas went to the haveli of Chuna Lal and said to Shah Nizamuddin Pirzada that we have heard that two Englishwomen are hiding in your house. Shah Nizamuddin asked them to bring the spy who had reported before him. The horsemen brought a man who was a resident of Rampur. The man said that he had heard this report. Shah Nizamuddin then said that if any Englishwomen are found in my house after a search, then you are welcome to pillage all my property and belongings, and to kill me. And if you want to loot my house using this slander, then you have the power. The horsemen did not say anything. Mahboob Ali Khan placed his hand on the Quran and said that we are not conspiring with the English. The horsemen and Tilangas looted the house and property of Agha Mohammed Jaan.

16 May, Saturday. The King was in the palace and came to the Diwan-e-Khas and held court. Hakim Ahsanullah Khan, Bakhshi Agha Khan, Captain Dildar Ali Khan, Rehmat Ali Khan, etc., paid their obeisance. Afterwards, Tilangas and horsemen came with their officers. They had apprehended a sealed note of Nawab Mahboob Ali Khan and Hakim Ahsanullah Khan at the Delhi Darwaza and presented it. They said that the Hakim and the Nawab had written to the English asking them to quickly come to this place and make Mirza Jawan Bakht, the son of Zinat Mahal, the successor. They had also said that they would get all the horsemen and Tilangas present in the city arrested. The Hakim and the Nawab looked at the paper and said that somebody had forged both the seals and stamped the paper. Hakim Ahsanullah Khan and Nawab Mahboob Ali Khan then took out their seals from their hands and showed it to the Tilangas and the horsemen. They placed their hands on the Quran and swore that they did not write the note and that someone had forged it.

Somebody reported to the Tilangas and the horsemen that two Englishmen were hiding in the middle of the canal. So Mirza Abu Bakr reached the canal with some horsemen and they jumped inside the canal and fired many shots, but no Englishman was found. Afterwards, the Tilangas and the horsemen surrounded Hakim Ahsanullah Khan's house with naked swords in their hands and said that you are certainly conspiring with the English. That is why you have arrested the English so that you can hand them over to the English when they come here and get us all killed.

Eventually, the Tilangas brought fifty-two English prisoners from the jail to the *hauz* of the Naqqarkhana with the intention of executing them. The *majhle* Sultan then intervened by saying it is not in accordance with Mohammedi practice to kill innocent women and children. The horsemen then made to kill the said Mirza who ran away. The horsemen seated them all and fired volleys killing them. Later, the macebearers killed the family members of the slain Englishmen with swords. Afterwards, his majesty ordered the corpses to be taken away in two carts and to be immersed in the Jamuna river. It was implemented.

This generated a lot of unrest and fear in the city and people said that the vile purabiyas would never be victorious if they committed such cruel deeds.

The guards at the gates changed positions. Somebody reported to the horsemen that there are Englishmen hiding in the haveli of Mathura Das, the treasurer, and at Kucha Chaudhri. So the Tilangas went there and searched the said places and came back. A note was sent to Nawab Walidad Khan of Malagarh stating that the Gujars are wreaking havoc near the Jamuna and that he should go and take care of them. Two persons who were wearing Tilanga uniforms and pillaging the city were arrested. The traders of Lahori Darwaza made an application saying that Kashi Nath, the thanadar of our area, is asking us for a bribe of one thousand rupees and saying that if we don't pay him, he will arrest us and send us to the kotwali. Hakim Ahsanullah Khan then sent a note to Qazi Faizullah ordering him to arrest the said thanadar.

18 May, Sunday. The King was in the palace. All the officers and horsemen and Tilangas appeared and said we have set up camp at Salimgarh and hope that your majesty will come and inspect it. After hearing this, his majesty sat on an open palanquin and went to Salimgarh and inspected the arsenal that the Tilangas and the horsemen had set up there. He assured the sepoys that his grace was fully behind them and they should forget their suspicions of Hakim Ahsanullah Khan and Mahboob Ali Khan. His majesty added that whenever you catch an Englishman, bring him before me and I will kill him with my own hands. So a compromise was reached between the Hakim Saheb and the Tilangas. One person who was bringing a letter from some Englishmen in Meerut cantonment was arrested on the Jamuna bridge and the Tilangas tied him to a cannon. His majesty got the floor of the Diwan-e-Khas cleaned and spruced up.

Mirza Aminuddin Khan and Mirza Ziauddin Khan appeared before his majesty as desired and paid their obeisance. His majesty asked them to appear in court every day. They said they had not been keeping well, and therefore could not come. His majesty asked them to recruit some troops to prepare for battle, and they agreed to do so. Afterwards, Naqi Khan and Mir Khan, the brothers of Nawab Mustafa Khan of Jahangirabad, and Akbar Khan, the successor of Faizullah Khan Bangash, Fakhruddin Khan, etc., appeared and paid their obeisance. Everybody presented two rupees each as tribute. After this, there were discussions with the colonels of the platoons.

A rider came from Garhi Nar Saru and reported that the revenue of the southern districts comprising several lakh rupees, and guarded by a few Tilangas and horsemen, was on its way to Shahjehanabad when it was looted at Garhi Nar Saru by some three hundred Gujars and Mewatis. Hearing this, two companies of Tilangas and a cavalry unit were sent under Maulvi Baqar to punish the Gujars and to retrieve the treasure. The Tilangas severely beat up a retainer of Mirza Mughal on the charge of spying, but let him off when the latter intervened.

Two royal messengers who had gone to Meerut to get news returned and said that one thousand goras, along with some women and children and a battery, are mounting their arsenal at Surajkund. The Gujars are looting and raiding the whole area between Seelampur and Meerut. His majesty deployed two companies of Tilangas on the Jamuna bridge to take care of the matter. Hakim Abdul Haq Khan presented himself and submitted five rupees as tribute. Five companies of Tilangas from the platoon of sappers and miners were going to Meerut via the Roorkee bridge. The English told them not to leave and to stay in service. The men of the said platoon did not agree. A fight took place and some hundred men from among them escaped while many were injured or killed. Afterwards, notes were sent with four horsemen to each of these rajas asking them to quickly appear before his majesty: Maharaja Narinder Singh of Patiala, raja of Jaipur, raja of Alwar, raja of Jodhpur, raja of Kota, raja of Boondi, raja of Malair Kotla and raja of Farid Kotla. There are reports that an army has come from Ambala. Two girls died when the terrace of Diwan Kishanlal collapsed.

(39)

Obey your officers and the King and earn merit in this world and the next

King's orders to the army, Undated

In the name of the merciful God,

The order from the shadow of God on earth, the King, which was issued from the seat of perfect equity and justice about the management of Zafar's victorious armies with a few clauses.

First of all that those armies of Zafar that due to God's grace and approval joined hands with the government and became helpers and friends of this triumphant government, it is incumbent upon them to always remain obedient and comply faithfully with the orders of the great lord, the shadow of God on earth. They should spend all their energies in executing these orders and should not spare any effort in their sincerity and devotion and should not spare any enemies. They should understand that in this lies the happiness of the shadow of God and the path for their own progress and advancement.

Second, every horseman and soldier should obey and submit to their officers and the junior officer should obey the senior one. And every officer should consider it obligatory to maintain discipline in his rank and file and should do nothing to oppose his officer.

Third, it is essential that all officers and soldiers must not spare any effort in killing, arresting or destroying the enemies of religion and the claimants of this country and its wealth and should not try to evade or be derelict in fulfilling these tasks. In this lies the advantage and prosperity of all of Allah's creation.

Fourth, that whichever officer demonstrates bravery or distinction in service or has done so will get adequate rewards and increments and promotions from the royal seat. Whosoever perishes or sacrifices his life in this conflict will be compensated so by the royal seat that his son or grandson or any other relative will be appointed in his place with an increased salary.

Fifth, whoever colludes with the enemies of faith or helps them in any way or gives them aid or does anything to harm the glorious kingdom or supplies them provisions will be a culprit in the eyes of God and the Prophet and will be punished accordingly.

Sixth, on the ridge some kafirs have taken shelter and which, despite the deployment of a large and triumphant force, has still not been conquered and the debased heathens have not been meted their rightful end, and due to this delay all financial and domestic matters of government have been endangered. Since the governance and running of the country and the protection of the populace and God's creations depends on this, therefore all valiant and enemy-storming warriors should throw themselves body and soul into this battle. They should be so dedicated and persevering that the enemies of faith are totally defeated and destroyed. And may the fame of this distinguished victory and valour and bravery spread to all four corners of the globe and in every sense the imprimatur of royalty be re-established.

Seventh, that the riders and Tilangas should join and remain in service with their respective regiments and platoons as before. They should serve in the ranks in accordance with their superior officers' orders and should not aimlessly disperse here and there because there is danger in this. After the establishment and reinstatement of governance everybody will be recruited according to ability.

Now all junior soldiers and senior officers are exhorted to accept these orders of the great and exalted Emperor with heart and soul and act in accordance. By following this one earns all kinds of advantages and by opposing this one incurs loss in this world and the next.

Any soldier or officer who deserts his platoon or regiment should be reported immediately by his officer in compliance with government regulations so that he is not recruited elsewhere and is expelled after being given his just punishment.

(94, 1)

Let not a single gora escape alive

Note sent by the King to all the officers and soldiers of the artillery, infantry and cavalry platoons, Undated

The petition you sent passed through the eyes of the exalted one and thus attained its purpose. Since the issue of depredation and cruelty practised by the heathens, and since their expulsion has been sanctioned by the royal pen from this side, therefore the implementation of the order should be carried out without delay or dilation by making arrangements for the death of the kafirs, and they should be driven away and dispelled from all the surrounding areas. In fact, make it so that not a single person of the gora community should escape without meeting death. So that we can make sure that this kind of tribulation is not repeated. Meaning therefore that you should meet the enemy's blow with greater equanimity and courage so that each of your blows is fatal. After we achieve complete victory over terror, the flying forces of Bahadur Shah should move to protect the palaces. Retain your composure at all times; the exalted one shall be concerned and attentive towards this matter.

(73, 201)

Let the officers swear on oath and pig and cow to those who disobey

Amir Khan Dafadar from Lucknow cavalry proposes certain plans for attacking the English, Undated

To all officers, senior and junior, of the infantry and the cavalry,

All the officers should be summoned and should take oath before naked swords and rolls of betels and they should be thus exhorted—you are the ones who caused this war and took upon yourself the task of achieving victory. It was not the case that the King had sent you notes and commands summoning you. You all joined hands to protect your religion and your faith and were eager to fight and appeared before his majesty and said that you had no desire for money or rewards and were only concerned for your faith. When the King's sway has been established, then we will take our rewards. Over and above this fact, when you all landed here, arrangements were made to provide you food, you were looked after according to your position and rank. The King treated you better than his own sons. Now it is incumbent upon you, if you are steadfast in your faith and religion and your word and honour, to oppose and fight the enemies and achieve victory over them and reach heaven. All officers, whether senior or junior, should assemble their platoons and their soldiers and riders and read out this order to them in accordance with the royal practices and arrange them in *sections* and divisions. Officers, whether senior or junior, of the right or the left or in the middle, should stand according to their ranks. When armies go to the front, then one platoon should go via the canal and the other through the Idgah on top of the hill via the Sabzi Mandi and the Saiyyadi garden. The soldiers should constantly be encouraged and their morale boosted so that they remain confident.

The force should stay hidden in the gardens and when the battle begins then they should attack in the formation of *sections* and come on top of the Saiyyadi hill behind the guns. Half a platoon should go to Kashmiri Gate and attack on the straight road from there and the same half platoon should then come around from the other side, the Lahori Gate side, where the attack took place today, and raid that front. The cavalry should stay behind them everywhere, and their formation should be done accordingly. When the battle is in full gear, they should attack from the left and right.

Thus this order is passed and those who want to stay are welcome to stay and fight and those who do not like it can return their weapons and leave. Cow to those Hindus and pig to those Muslims who do not agree with this.

This plan was written by Amir Khan, dafadar, Lucknow cavalry, servant of the king, and at the time of writing, all the officers and soldiers were promised money and gold and valuables and other rewards.

(60, 830)

Bahadur Shah proclaims he will eat something and die or go to a shrine and become a sweeper

King's orders to the mutineers, 9 August

Royal Command to all Officers of the Army. This is the order of the King, that first of all the fact is that I did everything that suited the sepoys' pleasure and left nothing undone from my side. I had made a compact with the troops that they are like my children, and just as children insist on something and are mollified, I too agreed to all your requirements and did everything to keep you happy. Unfortunately, you showed no consideration even for my life, nor did you heed my old age. It is incumbent upon you to care for my infirmities, how I suffer from minute to minute, because my health is and was in Hakim Ahsanullah's hands. He used to look after me minute to minute. Now except for God, nobody is left to take care of me. Every minute my situation worsens. All leaders, officers and troops should look after me just as I have looked after them. The guard from Hakimji's house should be freed so that he can come at all times, check my pulse and go back. Those who declare him an enemy should pause and consider. Whoever says that this man is like that, tell him to bring me a signed note to this effect which proves that he is my enemy and I will accordingly take action. And as for all the wealth that has been looted, the royal soldiers will investigate and recover the stuff and it will be submitted before me. Those responsible for this looting will be correspondingly punished by the royal court. If it is not agreeable to you then take me to the shrine of Khwaja Saheb. He protects everyone and I will go there and become a sweeper and stay there. If that is also not possible, I will get up and leave, let us see who can stop me. How does it matter whether I am killed by you or by them? And all the oppression against my subjects is being committed not on them, but on me; therefore it should be immediately taken care of. Otherwise give me an answer. I will do as I say and sleep. And a box of his exalted highness has also gone missing when Hakim Ahsanullah Khan's house was looted. Any paper signed with the seal in the box dating after that date is invalid.

(135, 167–170)

Come to the King and he will make you happy

Colonel Khizr Sultan to the officers of the army, 8 June

The case is that the platoons present here fought for their faith and by the grace of God achieved victory. Therefore, this is being written to you that if you are steady in your faith, then you should come here and the government will satisfy you with its bounty and you will also preserve your faith and religion and it is certain that all the Englishmen will be killed. No Englishman remains here and the King rules from his throne and he has kept your brother platoons happy here and also given them rewards.

(189, 3)

Any Tilanga who plunders will be punished

C-in-C to the officers, Undated

To all the officers of the war platoons at all the twelve gates inside and outside the city falling under the area of the Paharganj thanadar,

You are warned that often the Tilangas of your platoons go to the said thana and forcibly take grain, goods and provisions from the shopkeepers in that area. They do not even pay for anything. In case anybody resists or declines, they commit excesses on the populace and take away the wood from below the corpse and destroy it. There is no way we can tolerate the destruction of our people, therefore it is being written to you that every officer should make their soldiers swear to our name so that they do not indulge in these excesses again; otherwise, after the evidence is presented, they will be duly punished.

(67, 157)

Do not believe the rumours about our defeat

Colonel Khizr Sultan to the officers, 11 August

That someone has reported to you that the splendid royal forces have met with defeat, this statement is completely false and fabricated, and this rumour has been spread by the kafirs, that is, the English. The truth about the situation is that some eighty or ninety thousand soldiers are present here and all the platoons of the east and the Punjab have come here with money and with arms and magazines, and some ten thousand horsemen are available with his majesty and give battle to the English night and day and at all times. The English camp has been ejected from the ridge and, God willing, within two or four days, you too will achieve victory and these kafirs will be humiliated and expunged and consigned to hell. Therefore you are being instructed that upon seeing this proclamation, you should instantly remove yourself to his majesty and achieve fame and goodwill and join the partisans of faith. Act promptly.

(152, 32)

Do not give ranks to newly arrived soldiers

Officers to the King, 26 August

My lord,

Earlier an order had been passed by your excellency that those soldiers who have left their service to join us will serve at the same posts at which they were serving earlier and all the soldiers were very happy and highly satisfied at this order. Now those soldiers who have come later have submitted a petition to your excellency and have got their rolls prepared. Apropos this matter, all the soldiers got together and submitted to their officers that if these soldiers who have arrived lately are given ranks, then the injustice to those who have been serving for so long and have been going to the front and have been highly obedient to his excellency is manifest and obvious. Therefore, all the officers and men of the third regiment request that since all the soldiers and officers are satisfied with your lordship, you should issue an order reverting to the previous situation.

Devoted,
Jeevram, Ajodha and other officers of the third regiment.

(152, 38)

Hold parades and headcounts of the brigades every day

Code of Conduct for the Army, Undated

The colonels of each platoon are urged to hold a *parade* of their platoon at both times of the day and whenever the platoon goes out on an assault, or if at the front, then at the time of the departure a headcount should be done and they should be divided into *sections*. And when it returns from the action, then again a count should be done and if there is any discrepancy, it should be looked into. If a sepoy is wounded or killed, it should be entered in the registers. The *Brigade Major* should ensure that at the time of the distribution of salaries, everyone is told that they will inspect the front and when the platoon departs, you will again make an inspection and inform the officer so that no complaint comes in at the time of the attack.

(93, 62)

Soldiers are ruining royal shops

King to Mirza Mughal, 16 July

Son, learn that we are informed by a petition from Ratan Chand, the superintendent of the royal garden, which is herein enclosed, that the troopers of the cavalry from Jodhpur have picketted their horses in front of the shops and have taken possession of them and that in consequence, some of the shopkeepers have vacated the place and gone away and that most of the tenants are ready to do the same. Under these circumstances, our monthly earnings are bound to suffer. You, our son, are therefore directed to cause the cavalry to remove from their present location and to assign them some other place to stay in so that no loss to our revenue may occur. Be assured of our kindness.

(199, 81)

Tell Bakht Khan not to interfere with my orders

C-in-C to the King, 17 July

The King, shield of the world,

Respectfully showeth that your majesty is cognizant that before Mohammed Bakht arrived here, active preparation of war was carried on daily without any let up and your majesty knows likewise that since the arrival of the Bareilly general, several engagements have taken place. It so occurred today that your slave proposing to make an attack had formed the army and taken it outside the city when the said general interposed and kept the whole force standing inactive a long time wanting to know upon whose order the force had gone out and saying that it was not to proceed to the attack without his permission. Saying this, he caused the whole force to return. Even an open enemy would not attempt an act like this, namely, that the army should be proceeding to an attack and one should interfere and cause it to return. Your slave therefore supplicates that if the entire control and management of the army have been bestowed on the said general, your slave may be directed by a royal order to refrain from interfering in military matters and your slave will no longer interfere but will acquaint the officers of the army that from the future they are to remain with the said general and yield obedience to him. Having his order reversed cannot but cause vexation and chagrin to any officer, high and low.

If on the other hand, if the control of the army is supposed to be vested in your slave, the said general should not interfere. He has entire authority over his own regiments, and such demands for the services of his regiments as may be made from this place, he should immediately comply with.

Mirza Zaheeruddin

(199, 186)

All the residents should assemble for a *parade* at Lahori Gate

Kotwal to the thanadars, Undated

Know that today, two hours before sunset, all residents of the city, armed, Hindu and Muslim, should collect in a *parade* formation between the Lahori Gate and the fort. The exalted General Saheb, the C-in-C, will announce something regarding the victory of the faith.

Syed Mubarak Shah, kotwal

(120, 129)

If we don't attack now we are doomed

C-in-C to all the officers of the platoons, 9 September

The goras are attacking between the Bakhshikhana and the Kashmiri Gate and all the army is standing outside the Kashmiri Gate for making an assault; therefore you are being told that as soon as you see this order, start the assault. If we don't attack now, we will be doomed, know that this is the moment to show valour and bravery, if you don't attack now, we will be able to do nothing.

Received by
Ali Husain Risaldar,
Moti Singh, subedar, seventy-fourth regiment, Kampu Nimach
Shaikh Fidauddin Khan, etc.

(57, 440–41)

The C-in-C must personally tour the front

An officer to the C-in-C, Undated

My lord,

The petition of the slave is this that it is incumbent right now on your resplendent lordship to, whether on camel or horse or on a palanquin, make a personal appearance and his inspection would boost the morale of the sepoys and the soldiers posted on the bastions no end.

Devoted,
Asaf Khan

(60, 814)

You are very prompt in collecting salaries but very lax in fighting

C-in-C to the officers, Undated

The decree for the cavalry and risala officers is that a platoon has attacked us. It is desirable that you should command all the horsemen to attack. I am present at Kabuli Gate where his lordship's summons has arrived stating that you people are very prompt in collecting your salary but are very lax when it comes to giving battle. You must all try heart and soul for this conflict because the matter pertains to faith and religion.

(93, 16)

Let all those who are armed assemble at Kashmiri Gate

Order to the kotwal of Kashmiri Gate, 13 September

You are directed to issue a general proclamation that whoever in the city is a soldier or is armed should assemble at Kashmiri Gate at night and should stay there as long as the fighting continues.
(Seal of the Court of Privy Council, administrator of military and civil.)

(111d, 171)

Let all prepare—the enemy is at the gates

C-in-C to all the officers, 8 September

You are being told that there is severe fighting today at Kashmiri Gate and Siyah Burj where the English are relentlessly exploding cannon shots, and I went and saw with my own eyes just now that there is a great shortage of soldiers at Kashmiri Gate and Siyah Burj. Therefore, the instruction for you is that all the commanders and officers and soldiers should be told that they should prepare instantly and reach the Siyah Burj and Kashmiri Gate along with guns so that they can decimate the kafirs who are in the range of shots. It is desirable that the infantry troops should appear there and give battle. We can shoot very well from the top of the bastions. There should be no delay or dereliction in the execution of this task because the enemy is at the gates and everybody should gird up their loins courageously.

(Note on the reverse of the order:
We received the *parwana* from the exalted one, and it was instantly relayed to all the soldiers.)

(73, 158)

Concentrate on Kashmiri Gate, everything is all right at Lahori Gate

Ananti Mishr, subedar, fifth infantry, to the C-in-C, 10 September

My lord,

This platoon set out for the assault. Here at Lahori Gate there are enough soldiers. The goras are concentrating on the Kashmiri Gate front. I hope that arrangements would be made for the defence of Kashmiri Gate. Everything here is all right.

Ananti Mishr, subedar, platoon deployed at Lahori Gate

(92, 77)

Darogha of the Jama Masjid—'Tell the soldiers to obey me'

Darogha of Jama Masjid to the C-in-C, 4 September

Due to sickness I have been unable to present myself. I have been serving as the darogha of the Jama Masjid for twenty-one years as appointed by his majesty. At the moment, the military guards at the mosque do not seem aware of my status. Therefore I pray that a command should be issued to the effect that Fazlullah Khan is the darogha of the mosque and everything that happens should have his concurrence and approval and does not concern anyone else. I hope the command will be issued. May the kingdom's sun shine forever,

Fazlullah Khan

(Note on the letter:
General Taleyaar Khan should do whatever is required.)

(102, 47)

Arranging drinking water at the Jama Masjid

Request to the King for public distribution of water, Undated

The exalted lordship,

The hereditary servant, after presenting salutations, submits that there should be an arrangement for public distribution of water in front of the main gate of the Jama Masjid because the people offering namaz are in distress; therefore I hope that his excellency would order a public water supply at the Jama Masjid so that the namazis are relieved and the graces accrue to your lordship.

Devoted,
Rustam Beg, Jama Masjid

(102, 84)

COMMITTEES, DEBATES AND A CONSTITUTION
The Court of Mutineers

A court of administration, which popularly came to be called Court of Mutineers (CoM), was formed in early July by some of the leading officers of the regiments that had arrived in Delhi. This was an arbitrating and decision-making committee which combined aspects of the traditional panchayat system and the contemporary 'committees' which soldiers had been exposed to whilst serving with the East India Company. It drew up a constitution and called itself the 'Court of Administration' and had defined posts such as *president, vice-president* and *committees*. These English words occur in their original in the Urdu text. The CoM was to contain six representatives from the army, two each from the artillery, infantry and cavalry, and four from the civilians. It defined elaborate rules of procedure, debate and voting. Decisions were to be consensual, the majority vote prevailed, and the manner of presentation inside the committees was also well defined.

Similar councils were formed by soldiers at Lucknow, Kanpur and at other centres of rebellion. While the nominal leadership of the uprising lay in the hands of the erstwhile princely rulers or *jagirdars*—the Queen of Awadh, Rani of Jhansi, Nana Saheb, Bahadur Shah—the soldiers exerted their power everywhere by insisting on the formation of committees and councils of governance. These councils included representatives from the local nobility, but were dominated by soldiers. The peculiarity of the Delhi CoM lay in the fact that it functioned for the longest time. Instructions and commands from the CoM can be dated almost till the day the British stormed the city in September 1857. The soldiers had devised this as a mode of governance which would be corporate and consultative, and in so far as it checked the power of the King and the nobles, it could be called semi-constitutional or even a semi-republican mode of governance. In that sense, the uprising pointed to a new mode of governance, by formal, corporatized consultation.

The CoM in Delhi remained in existence till the very end. It suggested ways and means for raising revenues, supervised the collection of taxes, examined everyday accounts and acted also as a judicial and supervisory court. The CoM functioned under the Commander-in-Chief (C-in-C), but he himself referred many matters and cases to the court and deferred to its decisions. For instance, his personal accounts could be subjected to scrutiny by the CoM. As his accountant reminded him, the elephants he used for his person could not be accommodated under military heads because the CoM would enquire after it. The court was aware of the need for bringing the hinterland under control, for revitalizing the thanas, *daks* and *tehsils*. It devised schemes for sending royal representatives out into the villages to collect taxes. However, these schemes were only implemented sporadically.

In many cases, the CoM was the ultimate authority of appeal against misconduct by soldiers. It could summon soldiers or officers, reprimand them, restrain them and even, on occasion, imprison them. Even the jihadis, the voluntary religious fighters from places such as Tonk and Patna, who had come to wage a jihad against the British, were amenable to its supervision. As a letter from their leader testifies, they looked up to the CoM and submitted to its decisions. Merchants and bankers were not to be arrested without orders from the CoM. Many of the documents addressed to the C-in-C were in effect also being addressed to the CoM since he governed in consultation with it. The CoM also supervised decisions by the police and, on occasion, could overturn police judgements or seek explanation from the police. The last document of this section is dated 7 September 1857—a week before the city was stormed by the British where the CoM directed the darogha of the Jamuna bridge to not allow deserters to pass through. Much of the historiography on 1857 has ignored these attempts at organization, discipline and the bureaucratic norms, which characterized aspects of the rebel administration.

The practice of forming a court to decide on something was evidently widespread because, as we shall see in later sections, there were frequent mentions of soldiers holding court or doing court, namely, *kot karna*, with the court acting as a verb and as a noun. There are instances where holding court, particularly to decide on dismissals or punishments for soldiers, stood as an equivalent of the military court martial. It was therefore neither a wholly traditional practice nor a completely novel one, but a contemporary and vital amalgamation of the two.

Constitution of the Court of Mutineers and its Rules and Regulations

With the idea of dispelling the disaffection of the functionaries and for better administration of the army and the government, and to establish a constitution for the military and civilians, and in order to implement the constitution, the setting up of a court is considered necessary. The following will be the guidelines for the functioning of the said court:

1. A court should be formed and it should be called *Court Administration**, that is, a committee to look after civilian and military matters.

2. Ten people should be appointed to that committee in this way that four of them may be civilians and six military. Of the military, two people should be from the infantry platoons and two from the cavalry and two people from the department of artillery, and there should be four civilians.

3. With mutual consultations of these ten persons one should be appointed *President** and one *Vice-President**. The President's vote would be considered equal to two votes, and each office, as per requirements, should have a *Secretary**. Five members would be required for a session to be conducted.

4. At the time of the appointment of these ten people, an oath would be taken to this effect that the work of the court will be carried out with sincerity and devotion and without any prejudice or laxity and with full dedication and commitment of purpose. Nothing, major or minor, will be allowed to stand in the way of performing their duty and no administrative matter would suffer intentionally or due to oversight. The suggestions made at the sessions of the court should not arise out of prejudice or negligence and no relaxation of rules will be allowed for anyone. The members will always strive to supervise and improve the administration of the kingdom in ways which will strengthen the government and benefit the public. No decision of the court will be leaked out deliberately or otherwise until the court deems it fit to make it public.

*Italicized words on this page appeared in English in the Persian document.

5. The members of the court should be selected by a majority in such a way that two people each from the infantry platoons and the cavalry units and two from the artillery office who have had a long service and are able and intelligent should be elected. Should there be a person who is very capable and very bright and very well suited to the business of the court but has not served long enough, then this single condition would not bar his appointment to the court. Similarly, four civilians will also be elected/appointed like this.

6. After the appointment of these ten people, if any member of the administrative court acts in bad faith, or dishonestly or confers favour upon anyone, then, the majority vote can suspend that person from the court and appoint a new person according to regulations in resolution number 5.

7. All administrative matters should first be presented to the court. After it is approved by the majority, the matter will be presented to the Crown Prince, and the Commander-in-Chief for approval. The court shall function under the authority of his excellency, the Crown Prince. No act or action whether civilian or military will be considered worthy of promulgation without the approval of the court and the agreement of the Crown Prince and his exalted majesty, the King. After the approval of the Crown Prince, the decisions of the court will be intimated to his majesty. In case of a difference of opinion between the Crown Prince and the court, after the court has reconsidered the matter it would be presented before his august and exalted majesty and he will be the final arbiter.

8. Other than persons appointed by the committee, and other than the Crown Prince and his exalted majesty, no one else shall be allowed to attend meetings of the committee or be present at its deliberations. If certain members are unable to present themselves for a valid reason, then the majority opinion of the people present in the court shall be considered the collective opinion of the entire court.

9. If anybody in court wishes to bring up a matter before it then he should find somebody else to second it before putting it up.

10. When a matter is presented in court in line with the ninth rule, first the person bringing the matter up should be allowed to speak on the matter and nobody should interfere until his deposition continues. If any members of the court have any objection they should also be able to express it uninterrupted. If a third person wants to add or modify anything to what the objector has said then every member of the court can express his opinion in writing. After acceptance, the matter should be forwarded to the secretaries of all the offices.

11. From each military secretariat, the persons selected as representatives according to rule number 2 will also be considered the executives and administrators of the said secretariat and four people will be appointed to work under them according to rule number 4. And as per requirements secretaries will be appointed. Whatever is the opinion of these people will be conveyed to the *Administrative Court* [sic] through the secretary and will be implemented as per rule number 7. The same system will be adopted for all military and civilian secretariats.

12. The court retains the right to amend or change these regulations as and when it likes, depending on the circumstances.

(57, 539–41)

Court's suggestions for raising money and revenues

CoM to the C-in-C, 10 July

The ordinance of his exalted majesty addressed to us had come our way stating that whatever money had come into the treasury has been spent merely in daily allowances of the army and there is a tiny amount left, which too would be expended soon and it is incumbent on the officers of the court to make arrangements for the supply of money. We were privileged to receive that note. My lord, the submission is that in our opinion the way out is this that the army should be sent out of the city. The first suggestion is that money should be borrowed from bankers on interest and after arrangements have been made, it should be returned with interest.

Second suggestion. The army should be sent out in the following manner that one thousand five hundred infantry soldiers and five hundred cavalry and two guns should be sent out and they should go out of the city and make arrangements for administration, and thanas and dak and tehsils should be brought under control and should be revived so that it becomes known that the King has taken charge of the government, and whatever government money is owed should be collected and gathered without coercion. And the army going out should be warned that whoever engages in plunder or coercion or causes harm would be punished.

The first submission is that the suggestions that have been made for collecting money should be implemented.

The second submission is that in order to make these arrangements, an officer should be sent by you who should be capable and trustworthy.

The third submission is that the officer who is being sent out should be told on behalf of the court that the court's order is this that if you go out and harass a poor zamindar or tehsildar, or accept bribe and gifts, then you will be punished according to the court's decision.

The arrangement for appointing zamindars would be made like this that those whose names are already there on the rolls of the *patwari* and *qanungo*s, and have the receipt of submitting revenues which proves that they were responsible for such and such village, then after examining these papers and after the testimony of qanungos and patwaris when the *zamindari* of that person over that village is proven, that person will be given charge. If another person contends for the rights to a village, then his application will be received and it will be acted upon after investigations, but for the moment the *lambardari* of the village would be given to the person who held it earlier.

The fourth submission is that if the officer sent out does not act in accordance with these orders, then the zamindars may appear and complain about the case to this department and if after consultation it appears that the officer is worthy of being dismissed then he would be dismissed and the rightful person would earn his right.

Devoted officers of the court,

Shivram Subedar Major, Taleyaar Khan Subedar Major, Baseram Subedar Major, Jeevaram Subedar Major

(153, 2)

Only the court can summon bankers and raise loans

C-in-C to the kotwal, 18 August

You are being commanded that today onwards this issue of raising money has been handed over to the officers of the CoM and except for members of the court, nobody else is authorized to summon bankers and raise money. If a royal order is sent to you about it, you should immediately send it to the court. Without orders from the court do not arrest anybody. Act promptly.

(Note on the order:
Protector of the poor,

My lord, the command will be carried out. Has been reported for information. May the kingdom's sun shine forever.

Devoted,
Deputy kotwal)

(129, 61)

Anybody bringing heads of gora captains or soldiers will be rewarded

Generals Sidhara Singh and Hira Singh to the C-in-C, 12 September

My lord,

Our submission is that the brave and hardy officers of the court at Delhi have decided in council in this confrontation with the kafirs that any soldier or *mujahid* who brings the head of a colonel or general or captain of the Christians will be given an award of hundred rupees by the exalted government. And that whoever brings the head of a gora will be given fifty rupees as a prize. If a proclamation to this effect can be issued in Delhi city, it will be wonderful. Surely the spirit and vigour of our brave soldiers and holy warriors will be doubled like this.

Servants,
General Sidhara Singh and General Hira Singh, Nimach camp

(57, 483)

The CoM will not pay for C-in-C's personal use of elephants

To the C-in-C from his accountant, 19 August

Lord of the world and the universe,

In accordance with your instructions the expenses for the chains and the feed of the elephants has been paid out of the army's account. Two more elephants have now come to the government. All their expenses for feed, etc., comes to seven rupees and twelve annas for one day. The *faujdar* Mir Nisar Ali demands fifty-one rupees three annas for seven days service and your lordship has approved of the payment. The submission is whether this amount should go under the expenses of the army or of your lordship. The CoM might object to the account going under the army's head. The driver's daily food amounting to two and three quarter rupees is also accounted under the army's head. Should I suspend that? Will do whatever is ordered.

(Note by the C-in-C:
Diwanji, you should do whatever you think appropriate. I will speak to the officers of the court in the evening and please issue all of these whether from our account or from theirs. I will explain everything after the consultation. And I will not use an elephant until the matter is cleared.)

(133, 53)

Nobody but the court appreciates the jihadis' services

*Maulvi Sarfaraz Ali, leader of jihadis, to
the members of the court, 10 September*

Generous and affectionate killers of the degenerate infidels, the members of the court of the C-in-C, salutations.

You gentlemen's note about the merits of the *mujahideen* and about their participation in the digging of trenches at the front was received along with the latest from the front, and the state of the situation was learnt. The patrons of the age, the fact is that these people always display the same valour and dedication, but until now have never received any appreciation for it, nor was there anybody to enquire after them. Thank God you have now filled that lacuna. We are now certain that our services will be rewarded, God willing. As per your request all the mujahideen have arrived and will participate in battle with the same vigour.

Servant of the mujahideen,
Mohammed Sarfaraz Ali

(65, 36)

I want to be appointed risaldar

To the C-in-C, 21 July

My lord,

This devoted servant Ganga Singh, dafadar, seventeenth regiment, first troopers, came here from his risala and has been here from the first day; therefore I submit that an order conferring the rank of risaldar on this devoted one should be approved. The servant has a right too and I have shown great daring at the front, therefore his lordship should laud my efforts and make me a risaldar. Dutifully submitted, may the kingdom's sun shine forever,

Devoted,
Ganga Singh
Dafadar, seventeenth regiment, first troopers from Shamsabad

(Notes on the letter:
Order—Should be presented to the CoM, the petitioner wants the post of risaldar.
CoM—Order is that all the horsemen and office holders who appear separately should gather together as one body and prepare a list and present it before his lordship, a decision will then be taken on the application.)

(194, 212)

Do not let the army come and stay in the city

C-in-C to members of the CoM, 28 June

It has been learnt that men of the army who are at present camped outside the city wish to enter the city. Consider for yourself that if these people enter the city, there will be chaos everywhere and all the residents of the city will be wrecked and destroyed. Therefore it is being ordered that please make such arrangements for the army that no soldier is able to come into the city and stays put outside. They should stick to Sabzi Mandi and Teliwara and such areas and must not interfere with the city. The order should be executed as soon as possible.

(57, 37)

Abattoir for the Muslims of the city

Taleyaar Khan to the CoM, 10 July

Protector of the poor, the C-in-C,

The privileged note from his lordship has been issued to the effect that an abattoir should be set up for members of the Muslim community in view of the ban on cow slaughter, and that the sale of beef be fixed at two places. In pursuance of the order, abattoirs have been set up and the order will be executed in accordance with his lordship's wishes. This in truth is a wonderful arrangement which has been well liked by the officers.

Taleyaar Khan, subedar major

(87, 34)

One officer of each regiment will be included in the court

Bakht Khan to the King, 23 August

Your exalted grace, the lord of the world and the universe,

Your order about dispatching an officer of each regiment and cavalry for inclusion in the proposed court was received. In accordance with your lordship's command, all the officers were summoned and warned to appear at your court at 10 a.m. All the officers submitted to the order and swore to carry it out to their utmost. Further submission is that all our stuff has presently been loaded and we shall go to Palam and returning from there make a humble appearance before the lord of the world's court. Reported to convey the information.

Devoted,
Mohammed Bakht Khan, lord governor general, C-in-C

(199, 309)

Don't decide cases on your own, send them to the court

C-in-C to the kotwal, 19 August

You are being instructed to immediately dispatch one named Abdul Haq, bead maker, resident of Chandni Chowk, and his companion Bulaqi before us in order to dispose of a case currently before us.

(Notes on the order:
Lord of the universe,

The slave had summoned Abdul Haq, the bead maker, when Ali Bakhsh, the complainant, came here and said that we have reached a mutual agreement; there is no need now to summon him. Their agreement deed is being attached along with this correspondence. With the greatest respects,

Kotwal, Syed Mubarak Shah

From General Taleyaar Khan of the court,

Since the plaintiff had earlier made a claim and your letter shows an agreement having been reached between them, it is not clear whether the plaintiff had made an honest claim or a false one. Therefore you are being warned not to decide the merits of any case by yourself but to send it here. Now send the two parties after fining them.)

If soldiers change their regiments they will be punished

From the court and the C-in-C to the kotwal of Delhi, 26 August

By decree from the court, the valiant kotwal of Delhi city,

Since a lot of the men of the Bareilly contingent have left their camps and have come here, therefore you are being directed that you should go to the Delhi Gate and wherever else the Bareilly contingent is camping and proclaim this that whichever soldier or horseman or grenadier has come here from elsewhere should immediately return to his own camp. If they don't leave and are found to be staying here after this proclamation, then on investigation as per the suggestion of the court, he will be punished by his lordship. Go immediately and issue this proclamation.

(111d, 41)

Anybody found selling stolen goods will be punished

From the C-in-C directorate to General Taleyaar Khan of the court, 7 September

It appears that articles of the magazine, namely, bayonets, matchlocks, rifles, saws and locks, are being brought by men to Jama Masjid with the intention of selling them; therefore it is urged that in order to stop the practice a decree should be sent to the kotwal that those who bring such articles to sell at the Jama Masjid should be arrested and sent to the C-in-C along with the goods.

(60, 689)

My sheep have been impounded and my belongings confiscated

A sheep merchant to the King, 16 August

My lord,

Some six days ago the slave had taken some sheep from the English front at the ridge and was coming to appear before his majesty. On the way some four horsemen stopped me and asked me who these sheep belonged to. I said they belonged to the kafirs and I am taking them before his majesty; so then the horsemen asked me what other goods I had and they took the tumbler, etc., from the slave and Ranjit Singh Risaldar got the sheep counted and entered them in the royal cattle pound, but did not return my personal effects. Therefore this slave begs that Ranjit Singh Risaldar should be made to return my personal goods and it will be an act of mercy on the poor. Urged out of necessity.

One brass tumbler,
one iron mace,
cash.

Slaves Magru and Medhi, qaum shepherds

(Notes on the letter:
King—Mirza Mughal Bahadur should look into it.
Note—The application was presented before the court and it was ordered that in accordance with the petition, an order should be sent to the cavalry unit arrived from Bareilly.)

(60, 566)

Nobody can cross the Jamuna bridge without special passes

CoM to the darogha of the Jamuna bridge, 4 September

An order has been issued today that nobody, horsemen or sepoy, etc., except for government officials, can cross the Jamuna bridge unless he has a permit from this department because sepoys and horsemen are leaving via the bridge.

General Taleyaar Khan Bahadur, the Court of Mutineers

(60, 566)

NO KITES, OPIUM OR GAMBLING

Pillaging soldiers to be shot—the order of restraint in the city

Of the several regulations in place, some have been culled here to indicate the kind of order of restraint that had been set up in the city. Gambling was the first casualty of the new set-up. The initial confusion about whether it was permissible or not, as noted in the first document, gave way to a much stricter attitude towards it. There were also other kinds of bans, sale of opium was banned leading to much disquiet, particularly among soldiers. Lead became a contraband commodity in part because it was used in the preparation of gunpowder and people could be arrested for possessing it. There was a daily schedule fixing the price of goods which was processed and sent to all the thanadars who were supposed to ensure compliance with it. The rates of exchange for asharfis or gold coins was also fixed; new coins had been struck by the government and the rates of exchange between these coins and the old double coins of the company were also fixed and publicized to facilitate exchange. People found flouting these rates could be prosecuted as a document below establishes.

The administration was responsible, in continuation with earlier practice, for unclaimed corpses and the cost of their funeral was supposed to be borne by it. Garbage could only be taken out of certain specified gates at certain times. Removing carcasses of animals was the responsibility not of the police but of the keeper of the royal stables and the kotwal appeared keen to ensure that this demarcation of responsibilities was followed. In order to prevent the plunder of people's houses and to prevent excesses by soldiers, the government came up with various regulations. It appointed guards at shops to ensure that nobody took goods without payment, it issued proclamations that soldiers plundering people's houses or shops will be punished, and generally made sure that platoons knew about the standing orders in such matters. In order to prevent excesses by the police and soldiers during investigation, the government also devised modalities which had to be followed before houses could be searched. In other cases, thanadars followed earlier norms for their investigative practices, selecting how and when to recover stolen goods and whether to conduct a general search for it or not. Once the tide turned and soldiers began to desert, regulations were introduced forbidding soldiers from leaving and the guards in charge of gates and bridges were instructed to not allow any soldier to leave.

There was also an effort to ensure compliance with earlier protocol—a document below forbade soldiers from carrying arms into the Diwan-e Khas. In order to ensure military discipline and to control the autonomy of soldiers, a regulation was brought in to prevent soldiers from leaving their earlier platoons and joining any other at will. Among regulations restraining religious practice, apart from cow slaughter mentioned in the section designated for it, the observance of Muharram too was regulated by banning the playing of big drums during the festival on the grounds that the noise would drown out the sound of the bugle. For the same consideration, kite flying, pigeon flying and the wanton use of guns and cannons was forbidden. The fact that a person belonging to the royal family gave a deposition repenting his act and promised never again to play lightly with a gun shows some compliance with these orders. The ban on buying stolen goods on punishment of death too should be seen in the same light.

A new regime brought new promotions and newer titles, and the abrupt social mobility raised questions about the protocol of addressing these officers, reflected in the kotwal's anxiety about it. A crucial announcement pertained to the fact that the government took responsibility for all those who were killed in the fire at the magazine. The announcement of pensions and compensations for them was a form of post-facto insurance for everybody who perished in the line of government duty. The same goes for the regulation promising rewards and titles for those martyred when fighting for the government.

Warn the gamblers via a proclamation before arresting them

Kotwal to the King, 24 July

My lord,

Often it happens that clandestine gambling continues again in the areas commanded by thanadars posted in the city. Since there are no standing orders on the matter, therefore I humbly enquire whether we should act against it by arresting all the gamblers, and once arrested, whether they should be charged or should only be detained and an application should be sent to you after the arrest of the accused. Whatever is commanded shall be done.

Syed Mubarak Shah

(Notes on the letter:
Order—First, issue a proclamation banning gambling. If you find anyone gambling despite the proclamation, then arrest them without any hesitation and prosecute them in the courts.
Response—Proclamation was issued.)

(111, 11)

There is heavy gambling in the city, all gamblers should be arrested

C-in-C to the deputy kotwal, 2 August

Since these days heavy gambling happens in the city, therefore it is being commanded that all the gamblers should be arrested and sent to his excellency. Act promptly.

(130, 16)

Arrest all the gamblers of your thanas

Deputy kotwal to the thanadars, 2 August

Following the issue of the ordinance by Mirza Mughal, the C-in-C, your attention is drawn to the fact that heavy gambling takes place in the city these days, therefore it would be right if you arrest all the gamblers of your area, fine them and send them to the kotwali so that they may be presented to his lordship, the commander-in-chief. Do not delay.

Khuda Bakhsh Khan

(Marked on the order: Receipts and seals of all thanadars.)

(130, 14)

Three gamblers stand up to a soldier

Thanadar, Turkman Gate, to the kotwal, 26 July–3 September

After greetings, the application is that persons named Saidi and Owaiz Ali and Ilahi Bakhsh have been arrested on the charge of gambling and for confronting a sepoy. This said Saidi stood up to a soldier, and all three are being sent to you. I hope they will be suitably punished and fined. These are all gamblers, I would have arrested them all and sent them to you but it is important right now to get the sugar weighed and the two soldiers whom they stood up to are also being sent.

Mohammed Ihsanullah Khan

(45)

The government agrees to take care of the kin of all those who perished in the gunpowder factory fire

Colonel Khizr Sultan to the kotwal, 9 August

It should be known that the government agrees to take care of the kin of all those who perished in the gunpowder factory fire. Therefore you are being asked to issue a public proclamation to this effect across the city so that they can present themselves. Be prompt.

(Note on the order:
Response—A public proclamation was issued in accordance with the exalted one's instruction that the children and successors of those who perished in the gunpowder factory will be the responsibility of the government. With the greatest respect,

Devoted,
Deputy kotwal)

(130, 42)

Government will reward all who are martyred in this battle and if victorious they can keep the loot

C-in-C to all the officers of the infantry and artillery, 6 September

In accordance with the command of his exalted majesty, the Emperor, you are all being informed that whoever emerges victorious during the assault of the ridge will be entitled to keep all the loot from there, except for the material of the magazine and the artillery. This would be in addition to the kudos and rewards of this magnificent government. Therefore you are asked to firm up your resolve and to spare no efforts in achieving a powerful victory. Furthermore, the government will handsomely reward and compensate the dependants and successors of those who are martyred in the battle. A proclamation about this order should be issued all over Delhi city and around, and should also be relayed to all the infantry, cavalry and artillery units. From all sides

Hindus and Muslims should attack the ridge because this is a battle over religion and has nothing to do with who is employed by the government and who is not. Everybody should display courage and valour and fearlessness at this hour. The attack will be made when the preparations are complete.

You should know too that all the force should be ready so that there is no delay at all when the order has been passed. As soon as the command is given everybody should together launch the attack. The officers should arrange their forces in accordance with the schedule and junior officers and soldiers should try their utmost to obey their officers' orders and should not feel that its not their responsibility. On our own we should get into battle formations and attack with valour and should ensure that the hour of attack is not pre-empted. After all the preparations are made for a joint and unified assault and everybody must keep mum and not a word should be heard about it.

(57, 403/4)

Thanadars not to raid houses without permission from the kotwali

C-in-C to the thanadar of Kashmiri Gate, 19 May–10 August

There was a note from trader Bahauddin stating that Bahauddin's shop as well as two houses of Prince Kamran Bahadur which fall in your area were searched without any reason and you even let them be stormed. Therefore the thanadar of Kashmiri Gate is being instructed that until someone's guilt is proved, you should desist from raiding or looting anybody's house. When and if you intend to raid somebody's house, you should immediately inform the kotwali. Until permission is granted by the kotwali, no raids should be conducted. If anybody complains to you about anyone, then you should get him to swear under oath and keep him in the lock-up. You will be acting against your interest if you act against the rules. In case of any doubt, please contact the kotwali right away.

(53)

Soldiers should be prevented from conducting forced searches at respectable houses

C-in-C to the kotwal, 1 July

An edict has been proclaimed to the effect that without the order of the government and the presence of the informer, no forced searches will be conducted at any respectable person's house. Yet, people of the army have been known to flout the order and act in contravention of it. It is incumbent upon you to stop them and to find out which platoons these soldiers belong to. Let us know quickly and keep the soldiers at bay. Act firmly.

(60, 253)

Rampant complaints about soldiers—officers must ensure that rampaging soldiers who are a minority should be apprehended

C-in-C to all the cavalry, infantry and artillery officers, 9 August

You are being informed that since yesterday, the situation in the markets is such that there have been innumerable suits and complaints from many places that the soldiers forcibly loot goods. It is quite obvious that the people are being overly oppressed. If this oppression continues, how will the city function? The shops will shut down and everybody will suffer. You should know these people who are a minority bring ill repute upon those office bearers or soldiers who are upright. It is desirable that officeholders and soldiers should always keep watch over all those hoodlums who wish to loot the bazaar. Whenever anyone spots anybody looting or preparing to plunder or cause some other damage he should immediately apprehend him and hand him over to the closest guard. If there is no guard nearby, then find out his name and report to us. All the guards should make sure that they take down the name and address of whoever hands over the sinful culprit and the name of the prisoner and confine him with care and send to the august presence attended by a guard.

(57, 274/83)

Poor people being oppressed by soldiers have relatives and friends in the army—there may be a civil war soon

Lord Governor Bakht Khan to the C-in-C, 10 August

As regards the large number of soldiers who are congregating in and around the house of Hakim Ahsanullah Khan and loot not only his but also others' houses and oppress the poor and the disadvantaged. This is very far from acts of grace and likely to incite the wrath and fury of the Almighty. Therefore I hope that your lordship will make some arrangements in this regard as soon as possible. Let there be no delay or hanging about in this matter for the Almighty Allah will provide just rewards and retribution on the Day of Judgement. Dutifully submitted.

It should also be clear that the people whom they oppress have relatives and friends in our armies. Supposing they come forward to defend the honour and persons of their relatives and confront the soldiers, mutual inter-fighting will break out and people will be massacred. Therefore it is imperative that arrangements are made for this situation. May the sun of the kingdom shine forever.

Devoted,
Lord Governor Bahadur

(Note on the letter:
Response—An order has been passed stating that the situation was learnt from the petition, it will be looked into. An order is being prepared.)

(57, 297)

Any soldier found looting will be shot

To all the officers of the platoon and the cavalry units, 13 July

Regarding the fact that there are often complaints by the residents of the city that the Tilangas forcibly take goods from the market without paying its price. In order to stop this practice, a patrol guard had been put in place, but even then people do not mend their ways and do not heed the admonitions of the guards. This is certain to lead to the devastation of the populace. Because of this shopkeepers do not open their shops. Therefore, out of regard and consideration for the people, you are all ordered that the officers of all the platoons should keep a copy of this decree with them and should have it read out aloud in all the platoons and the cavalry units that any sepoy who is found taking goods from the citizens without paying its price or asking the owner for it or whoever takes anything forcibly and does not heed the warnings of the guard would be shot without hesitation by the sepoys of the guard and the government would overlook it. Any sepoy who carries wood, etc., from Qudsia Bagh will be duly punished. Comply with these orders and act promptly.

(Notes on the order:
Receipt—
Copy made. Nihal Singh, Havaldar Major, Moppet platoon
Copy made. Sappers and Miners platoon
Read out aloud in Bailey platoon.
Read out in fifty-seventh regiment.)

(60, 309)

Soldiers' funeral costs borne by the government, according to regulations

Report on the death of a soldier by a subedar, 8 July

My lord,

Last night, one sepoy named Muhibbullah Khan horseman died of cholera. I write merely to inform you. Further, in accordance with the government's secretariat regulations, the cost of his burial may be forwarded to this devoted one.

With greatest respects, may the kingdom's sun shine forever.

(70, 170)

Thanadars should send schedule of rates to the kotwali every day before 9 a.m.

Deputy kotwal to all the thanadars, 24 July

Since the schedule of rates reaches the kotwali very late, all of you are being instructed that the schedule of rates for every day should be filled up at all the thanas and should reach the kotwali at eight or nine o'clock in the morning and the thanadar of Nigambodh should chastise the barqandazes of this thana that they should take the appropriate papers to the thana Chandni Chowk, and not to leave it at the kotwali.

Khuda Bakhsh Khan, Deputy kotwal

(130, 9)

Forging or using counterfeit asharfis will be strongly punished

Proclamation by the C-in-C, Undated

Since most soldiers and Tilangas and cavalry of the army buy asharfis from the city and use asharfis for their shopping, some wicked shopkeepers have started a new practice. They forge the asharfis and then sell them at one or two rupees below the market price to the members of the army. That is why this advertisement is being issued to all in the city of Delhi that whoever is caught forging asharfis or selling counterfeit coins will, after an investigation, be exemplarily punished.

(57, 543)

Moneychangers to be chastised for not sticking to conversion rates for old and new coins

Kotwal to all the thanadars, 24 July

By order of the General Saheb of the Bareilly army, a proclamation had been issued fixing the rate of exchange for the earlier double coins and the newer ones, but it is not being complied with. This creates problems for government. Therefore you are all being troubled to summon all the *chaudhri*s of the moneychangers of your area and chastise them and send them to us.

Syed Mubarak Shah

(120, 136)

Deputy kotwal proposes abolition of all customs duties

From the deputy kotwal, Undated

A proclamation should be issued that no customs duty will be charged on anything; second, whoever has taken a gun or a bayonet from the magazine and turns it into a pistol or a dagger would be regarded as a great culprit by the government.

Bhau Singh

(131, 127)

Anyone found buying stolen goods will be convicted

Kotwal to the thanadars, 13 August

Let this be known that often people purchase goods stolen from the residents of the city in order to profit themselves; therefore it has been considered appropriate that if somebody buys stolen or plundered goods off someone and if the charge of buying stolen goods can be proved before us, then that person will be punished once due evidence is presented. Therefore a pronouncement is being issued to the kotwal of Delhi city with the order that he should get a proclamation made in the city to this effect that anyone found buying stolen goods will be tried and convicted if found guilty and the goods will be returned to the owner.

(101, 26)

Soldiers are likely to create a ruckus because of ban on opium

Deputy kotwal to Samsamuddaulah Bahadur, 23 August

As per your instructions, the sale of opium has been declared illegal and a proclamation to the effect has been issued. But the situation in the city is such that most opium users are unwell and harassed and restless, and men of the army are intent on disorder and there is fear of riots due to its unavailability. Therefore I pray that you would permit the contractors to supply it. In the absence of its availability, the soldiers are shutting down other provision shops like those of salt, etc. Aware of the intent of the men of the army to create a huge ruckus, I thought it best to inform you right away.

Khuda Bakhsh Khan, Deputy kotwal

(130, 183)

Nabbu Khan avers never to blow a cannon or fire a gun as a sport

Bond for good behaviour executed by Nabbu Khan, 18 July

I am Nabbu Khan, son of Rustam Khan, resident of the exalted fort.

When this humble one was trying to torch the small cannon, which I used to often do with young children as a kind of game, I was arrested. I aver that I will never fire a gun and if I do then the government has the right to arrest me or give me any other punishment. That is why I have written these few lines as a kind of undertaking so that a certificate remains.

Nabbu Khan

(71, 117)

No drums should be played during Muharram lest the bugle sound is muted

Kotwal to the thanadars, 24 August

Right now, General Taleyaar Khan appeared in the kotwali and expressed his wish saying that you should issue a circular note to all the thanadars that during Muharram drums should not be played. The reason for that is that it should not drown out the noise of the bugle. The enemy is close at hand, there should be no confusion because this is a fight over religion and everyone should be mindful of that and remind people of the salience of that fact. In addition, the thanadars and *jamadars* should carry on with their patrols as before. Therefore, all of you are being directed accordingly that you should occupy yourselves in carrying out this order, and at the hours of evening and night and dawn, and at all hours, be very vigilant. You should make such arrangements which do not impinge too much on the public and the city too should not want safety. Copy these instructions immediately and send to all the thanas so that this is obeyed within two hours.

(Seals of police officers in confirmation)

(130, 185)

Kite and pigeon flying to be banned in the city

Deputy kotwal to all the thanadars, 31 August

Know that today, at 2 p.m., Mohammed Bakht Khan Saheb General Bahadur came to the kotwali and bade it necessary that a proclamation be issued in the city that nobody should indulge in kite flying, pigeon flying or fire in the air, neither during the day nor at night. And nobody should create a ruckus because noise and commotion startle the soldiers of war and they get into battle gear and this causes a nuisance. Anybody found transgressing this order will be punished. Therefore all of you are being thus instructed that you should proclaim this order in your areas through the sweepers and chowkidars and let everybody be warned.

Bhau Singh

(120, 190)

The protocol of addressing newly-styled generals and colonels

Thanadar, Chandni Chowk, to the kotwal, 14 August

After paying due respects, the submission is this that as the officers style themselves as colonel sahebs and as generals, please inform the humble one about their ranks and the proper forms of address for them because at the time of writing applications to them there are a lot of problems.

One doesn't know which mode of address will please them and which will displease them. Please write as soon as possible.

Mir Nazar Ali

(61–369)

'As far as being present or absent is concerned the fact is that this slave does not absent himself even for a minute'— Turkman Gate thanadar

Thanadar, Turkman Gate, to the kotwal, 25 May

After due respects, the submission is that it was learnt through your circular that Faiz Mohammed Khan has filed a petition regarding the break in and loss of goods at his house stating that when he reached this thana, there was no thanadar or clerk there. The representation is that when this Faiz Mohammed Khan came to the thana, I had gone to offer Id prayers at the hospice of Ghulam Ali Shah and the clerk was in the toilet. He stated the news of the break-in, and the barqandazes asked him to wait saying that the thanadar has gone for Id prayers. But he said I will go home and come back in a while. Then he sent his father to the kotwali. When I came back, I went and inspected the spot of the break-in and it appeared that in fact there was no break in. The fact is that these contractors receive a lot of goods on credit for trading and this one had also received a consignment and he wanted to forfeit it and so he made up the break-in story. The situation with the break-in is that if a house is broken into, the debris of the walls from where this has happened should be found lying in the room. In these kinds of situations, the plaintiff usually does not make a claim against anyone nor does he press for searches, etc. In view of this, I have not pressed hard on anyone, but still I am investigating the matter secretly and overtly too. And as far as being present or absent is concerned the fact is that this slave does not absent himself even for a minute and the clerk of this thana is an outsider, so he never leaves the thana and the statement of the plaintiff is being attached with this note. The earlier regulations were that if a plaintiff does not lay claim against anyone and does not ask for a search, then the thanadar should do nothing, whatever the new regulations demand will be done.

Mohammed Ihsanullah Khan

(61, 64)

New contractor for the excise shops of the city

Kotwal to the C-in-C, 26 July–3 September

As per the command issued by you, Pyare Lal merchant has been given charge of the excise shops of the city of Delhi and beyond through the thanadar of Dariba, and the contract of Mansa Ram, the former contractor, has been cancelled. The advance for fifteen days and the amount that was due from the former contractor has also been taken and given to the current contractor, Pyare Lal. Places for which the price schedule has been fixed sent the lists, which were sent by the thanadar of Dariba, and are being forwarded for your exalted consideration along with this application.

Kotwal

(45)

As instructed, no Tilanga will be allowed to leave the city without a pass

An officer to the C-in-C, 13 September
(one day before the British assault on the city)

His lordship had issued a decree that any Tilanga or horseman who is found deserting should be apprehended and sent back, no one should be allowed to leave. Therefore, acting on your instructions, the sepoys and horsemen who are on duty have been instructed to not let anyone go and to arrest and return to Delhi whoever is found deserting. If a horseman or Tilanga has a pass, they will be allowed passage, otherwise the deserters will be caught for sure. With greatest respects, may his lordship rest easy on the matter, may the kingdom's sun shine forever.

Devoted,
Colonel Ahmed Khan

(60, 725)

No Tilanga should carry arms inside the fort or in the Diwan-e-Aam

To the officers of the Bailey platoon, Undated

Know that this is the command of his exalted majesty that no Tilanga should carry arms inside the fort or in the Diwan-e-Aam and whoever buys anything from the shops should pay the market price for it, and if any Tilanga commits depredation, the officers should instantly report it to the government, and they would be duly punished.

(60, 829)

Sweepers should remove carcasses and garbage from the city gates

Deputy kotwal to all the thanadars, 16 June

In accordance with royal orders, you are all being urged to issue instructions to all the sweepers of your areas that they should remove all the carcasses and garbage of the city from the five designated gates. This command is being sent to you via a circular note so that you can inform all the officers manning the gates about its contents and collect their signatures on it and send it back to the kotwali. Except for these five gates, the garbage will not be taken out from anywhere else.

Lahori Gate
Farashkhana
Kashmiri Gate
Turkman Gate

Delhi Gate
Shaikh Mohammed Amir
(Seals of officers)

(128, 64)

It is not the job of the police to remove carcasses

Kotwal to the King, 3 July

A couple of hours before dusk, a sepoy from a regiment came to the kotwali and complained that carcasses of camels are strewn around our camp, and that they had to be removed. Since the job of removing dead animals from the streets has been deputed to chosen persons and is concerned with Mir Amir Ali's department, I therefore beg that an order be issued to Mir Amir Ali that he should get those carcasses removed from Daryaganj through some menials.

With the greatest respects,
Syed Mubarak Shah

(Note on the letter:
Order—Amir Ali has been called to verify the matter and do the needful.)

(111b, 14)

Soldiers cannot leave their regiments and join another

General order to all the platoons and cavalry units, 12 July

Often soldiers and horsemen leave their platoon and take up employment with other platoons and cavalry units; to put an end to this practice, you are all being instructed that no commander of a platoon or cavalry unit should recruit a soldier or horseman of another platoon and whoever gets a transfer without permission would be liable for punishment. Wherever anyone is presently serving they have to remain there. Stay firm on this order.

(Receipt seals of various units.

Repeat—The application of Ram Prasad Pande, subedar of the fifty-ninth platoon, twenty-eighth regiment, to the effect that Shiv Dayal and Ranjit Singh, sepoys of the twenty-eighth regiment have joined this platoon without their officers' orders, was received. You are being instructed that no commander of any platoon or cavalry unit should transfer any sepoy from anywhere else. You are all being urged to stay put wherever you are. Be obedient.)

(60, 301/302)

Thanadars' daily diaries should reach the kotwali before 8 a.m.

C-in-C to all thanadars, Undated

Know that the daily diary of all the thanadars reaches this department only at two o'clock in the afternoon. It is proper that the diaries should reach this department at 8 a.m. in the morning promptly. Act with alacrity.

(120, 34)

A *dafali*, Imam Bakhsh, arrested for possessing lead

Deposition of Imam Bakhsh regarding his arrest, 27 July

Name: Imam Bakhsh alias Chunnan
Son of: Mohammed Bakhsh
Qaum: Dafali
Resident of: Damoj, Sohna
Occupation: Tambourine player

Q. Why have you been arrested?
A. I came to Delhi sixteen days ago. I spent two days in a garden near Paharganj and one day at the Mochikhana at the Naqrai Gate where people of my community used to live. One day I spent with the

*ghazi*s at Zinatulmasajid, after which when I was coming out of the *khirki* of the mosque, the soldiers searched me and found some lead, one rupee, some Delhi coins, one handkerchief, etc., on me. All that stuff, the lead, etc., were taken by the soldiers and they brought me here to this prison.

Q. Where did you bring the lead from and where were you taking it?

A. I bought it from a shop in Chawri Bazaar, but I don't know its name, although I can easily identify the shop. I had bought it for an anna and six pice, etc., where two or three youngsters had brought the lead, and I bought it for one rupee, but I do not know the names, identities, etc., of those boys. I was taking it to my village.

Q. What purpose were you taking it for?

A. The zamindars used to have a lot of fights with each other. For some profit, I would sell it to them. I was only taking it for my profit.

Q. Have you ever taken any lead before?

A. I have never taken it before. This was the first time I was taking it and was arrested. I now want to be set free for I did not know that it is now forbidden to possess lead.

(Note on the deposition:
Order—It is ordered that the lead should be impounded and he should be let off.)

(67, 77)

Mehrab Khan arrested while taking lead to protect his village

Deposition of Mehrab Khan regarding his arrest, 27 July

Name: Mehrab Khan
Son of: Aqeel Khan
Qaum: Pathan

Resident of: Mohammedpur, Sohna
Occupation: Zamindari, illiterate

Q. Why have you been imprisoned?

A. I had brought three mares with the intention of finding service at Delhi. Through a juggler named Manglu Khan who lives there, I sold two horses to the ninth regiment encamped at Daryaganj. And I was taking back the third horse which was rejected, and had on it the lead which I had bought from several people. When I reached Mehrauli, the Gujars pounced on me and robbed me and then they arrested me and left me with the horsemen at Alipur. And the horsemen and the Tilangas sent us here. We beg your majesty and hope that his justice would bring me freedom and my horses.

Q. Why had you bought the lead?

A. The situation is such that the servants of the Raja of Alwar demand taxes from us and from the shire of Karori, which is merely six or seven *kos* from our village. I was taking it out of fear because the barqandazes had warned me.

Q. How much lead is there?

A. I don't know because I did not buy it all together.

Q. Who did you buy it from?

A. From many different people on the streets and even outside the city.

Q. Where is your baggage?

A. It is all in the government's custody.

Q. Why were you carrying the lead despite the government ban?

A. I was not aware that it has been banned by the government.

(67, 76)

The soldiers should not believe rumours that the magazine has blown up

From the C-in-C to all the officers of the divisions, 7 August

You are being informed that you should remain steadfast according to your sections and reinforcements are being sent your way and do not worry and do not leave the front at any cost and should someone claim that the magazine has been blown up, it is totally false, the magazine has not blown up. Be calm and act promptly and do not leave the front.

(74, 79)

All martyred soldiers will earn *jagirs* from the government

Kotwal to deputy kotwal, content for proclamation, 11 September

Any horseman who leads from the front in the assault and attacks the cannons, etc., and becomes a martyr because no help reaches him, will earn a jagir from his excellency.

(131, 118)

TYRANNY, IMPUDENCE AND POWERLESSNESS
The King's defence

Bahadur Shah Zafar was arrested on 19 September from Humayun's Tomb along with some of his wives and some princes. While some of the princes, including Mirza Mughal, the C-in-C, were shot dead by William Hodson at the Khooni Darwaza near Delhi Gate on the way back to the city, the King himself was kept in confinement in one of the dingy back quarters of the fort. Towards the end of January 1858, he was put on trial under a special court martial at the Diwan-e-Khas of the Red Fort. The compilation of the Mutiny Papers owes its existence to this very trial and selected portions of it were translated specially for it.

Bahadur Shah was charged with treason, treachery and rebellion and also with being the head of an international 'Mohammedan conspiracy involving the Kings of Iran and Turkey, Muslims of India and Muslim religious leaders'. The trial was a preposterous affair in substance and in form and was noted as such by some British observers at the time. The document reproduced in this section was the defence presented by the King which was dictated orally and presented to the court with his signature.

The defence has to be read with some scepticism. It would have helped Bahadur Shah, facing trial and imprisoned as he was by the British, to minimize his role in the rebellion. All the same, there is sufficient evidence even in these pages to show that he was often helpless and powerless to have his say. The soldiers, it has been shown, often humiliated him and persecuted his closest companions, his favourite wife Zinat Mahal and his physician Ahsanullah Khan included. The CoM and the commissariat of Mirza Mughal were largely their own masters and the misuse of the King's seal or his signature without his permission, which he dwells upon here, is not too surprising. The princes themselves had their own favourite sections of the army and the soldiers tried, more than once, to remove Bahadur Shah and crown someone else, Mirza Jawan Bakht or Mirza Mughal, as king. Bahadur Shah often failed to achieve the one thing that he most wanted to do, to protect his subjects from deprivation and cruelty.

However, we should be wary of underplaying the contribution of the King. When things reached an impasse, his word usually prevailed. The soldiers may have plundered Ahsanullah Khan's house, but they had to lift their guard when the King pushed hard for it. Through these months, he often used his own persona, even his appearance, and access to him, as a bargaining tool to achieve his ends. He would sometimes vanish inside the palace and not appear in public unless his demands were met. He would tour the city and its markets to urge the shopkeepers to keep their shops open, he would inspect battlements or watch preparations for battle from close quarters. He would insist on summoning the leading notables to the durbar, and he remained the ultimate dispenser of authority, dismissing Mirza Mughal from the post of C-in-C for instance, and appointing Bakht Khan as lord governor. He used the threat of abdication, asceticism, retirement, travel to Arabia—every possible emotional tactic—in order to discipline the wayward soldiers.

Bahadur Shah Zafar has usually been seen as an indispensable symbol of the rebellion, even as a reluctant martyr. He provided a moral authority under which a settled administration could emerge in Delhi, a standard to which others could rally. It was his ancestors after all who had bestowed sovereignty on the East India Company, and he was still the nominal ruler, the badshah of India. Demands for *sanad*s and *firman*s, even from places far away from the city, indicate that his word carried weight outside Delhi too. But his contribution to the rebellion in Delhi was more significant than that. He needn't have surrendered so easily to the soldiers, he needn't have assumed kingship so easily, he needn't have written letters to countless people across the country—although one has to be careful when sifting letters written by him from those that were written in his name. By doing these things of his own volition, Bahadur Shah indicated his partisanship with the rebel cause as well as he could. He often wrote notes on letters in his own hand, and was fairly intensely involved with the defence of Delhi, in spite of his slightly removed location.

Bahadur Shah's vacillation and indecisiveness, especially at the end, have come in for a lot of flak. Later nationalists lamented that he did not leave Delhi with Bakht Khan after the fall of Delhi, nor did he actually take to the field of battle. The eighty-two-year-old King was well aware that rebellion or no rebellion, he was the last Mughal ruler who would live in the Red Fort. The Company had laid this as a condition for nominating his successor. They would also not have been allowed to use the title 'king'. A child who grew up at Shah Alam's feet, Bahadur Shah often averred that the end of the great Mughal lineage was near and that he was the last in the line. His leadership of the rebellion can then be seen as an attempt at staking his claim for posterity, not a valiant attempt to regain an empire that was forever lost, but a mere setting straight of the record. He gambled with the soldiers, but the enterprise was doomed from the start. Bahadur Shah in Delhi was the most potent symbol of the revolt—without Delhi, he was a mere Mughal personage, like several others. Reluctant he may have been, but he played no mean part in the uprising at Delhi.

'Whatever happened was done by that army, I was powerless' —Bahadur Shah at his trial

Fair copy of the ex-king's defence attested with autograph cipher, circa January 1858

The truth is that in the beginning on the first day I had no idea about anything. Suddenly, at around noon, rebel riders came below the jharoka and began to scream. They said we have come from Meerut after killing all the Englishmen there because they asked us to bite bullets that were coated with the fat of cows and pigs. This corrupted the faith of Hindus and Muslims alike. When I heard this I got the gate below the jharoka shut and sent word to the captain of the fort. He came and wanted to go to the gate below the jharoka and get it opened. I did not let him go and did not allow the said gates to be opened. Then the fort captain went to the window and said something to the riders at which they left. After that, the captain said, 'I will go and take care of this,' and took my leave. After a while the magistrate asked for two cannons and the captain asked for two carriages and they sent a message that two English ladies are in the former's house, please have them called and hide them in the fort. I immediately sent the carriages and ordered the cannons to be sent. A little later I heard that the carriages did not reach and all of them were killed.

After that the rebel forces entered the Diwan-e-Aam and the hall, the courtyard of the Diwan-e-Khas as well as the tasbihkhana overflowed with soldiers and troopers. They surrounded me from all sides and placed guards everywhere. I said to them, 'What do you mean by this?' They said remain still otherwise we are past caring for our lives and will not stop at anything. At this, fearing for my life, I kept quiet and went inside the palace. Later, towards the evening, those disloyal ingrates brought a number of Englishmen and ladies who had been captured from the magazine and wanted to kill them. I admonished them strongly against this and their lives were saved. The soldiers then imprisoned them and afterwards again wanted to murder them, but desisted when I pleaded and reasoned with them. At last, the third time around, I again cajoled them, but the rebels disregarded me and killed the poor men and women. I did not order them to be killed and if Mirza Mughal and Khizr Sultan and Abu Bakr and Basant chamberlain, who were in collusion with that army, used my name, then I am not aware of that. And if in collusion with the rebels or due to the incitement of Mirza Mughal any of my personal retainers participated in the killing without my orders then I am not aware of that. Even afterwards nobody apprised me of the situation.

Apropos the witnesses' statements implicating my attendants in the murder of Englishmen, my plea is the same that I did not give orders to this effect. If they participated in this massacre of their own accord, then I am not aware of that. Nobody told me about this anyway. God forbid I did not order the killing of any Englishmen. Mukund Lal and other witnesses are lying when they take my name.

I will not be surprised, however, if Mirza Mughal or Khizr Sultan had given such orders because they were colluding with the rebel army. Afterwards, that army brought Mirza Mughal and Mirza Khizr Sultan and Mirza Abu Bakr and said that we want them to be our commanders. Initially I rejected it, but they insisted strongly and became upset with me. Mirza Mughal went off to his mother's house. I then kept silent out of fear of this army and after mutual consultations Mirza Mughal was appointed the commander of this army.

As for the commands and edicts bearing my seals and signature, the fact is that since the day this army arrived here and killed the rulers and imprisoned me, I was fully under their control. They would write whatever they wished and get it stamped by my *munshi*, or very often they stamped it themselves. A copy of it was given to the secretariat, therefore many such documents with a false seal are there in the file. They also got my seal put on many empty envelopes. I don't know what kind of notes they dispatched inside those envelopes and to whom. There is one note by Mukund Lal written to I don't know who which is there in the file among the collection of edicts. It clearly describes how such and such person got so many edicts written, and these many were written at someone else's behest. My name is not mentioned against any of these orders. This clearly proves that without my permission, without even my knowledge, anyone could get edicts composed. I would not even learn about the contents of many notes, and neither my munshi nor I could protest out of fear for our lives.

The same applies to signed letters. The army or the Princes Mirza Mughal, Khizr Sultan or Abu Bakr brought whatever petition they wanted. They would be accompanied by army officers, along with a separate note containing what they wanted done. In accordance with these notes, they would get a signature stamped on the petitions. They would go so far as to say aloud in my hearing that whosoever does not obey us would strongly regret it. At that time I could not say anything to them out of fear.

As for my retainers and attendants, especially Hakim Ahsanullah Khan and Mahboob Ali Khan and Zinat Mahal, the rebels claimed that they send letters to the English and are in league with them, therefore we will kill them. So one day they looted Hakim Ahsanullah Khan's house and arrested him and even wanted to kill him, but abstained after I pleaded and reasoned with them. Later on also they imprisoned many of my officers. Samsamuddaula, Zinat Mahal Begum's father, was also arrested amid announcements that we will depose the king and crown Mirza Mughal king.

At this stage it is worth pondering for the sake of justice as to whether I had any discretion or room to agree with them. Moreover, often these officers would ask me to hand over Zinat Mahal Begum to them, adding that she is colluding with the English and so they wanted to arrest her. If I had any power, why would I have allowed the arrests of Hakim Ahsanullah Khan and Zinat Mahal's father, or tolerated the looting of Hakim's house?

That army had appointed a court and acted independently after mutual consultations and discussions. I was never party to those discussions. Therefore, without my orders or my knowledge, many bazaars were plundered, and many persons looted at will or murdered. They extorted unknown amounts of money from many *mahajan*s and other respectable people of the city without my permission, and spent it on their own. Whatever happened was done by that army. I was powerless. They had caught me unawares and had taken me prisoner. Out of duress I did whatever they asked me to otherwise they would have killed me.

All the Sahebs know the fact that I was quite fed up with them and my life was at stake and there was no hope that my men's life would be spared. So I decided to become a faqir and adorned saffron robes and wanted to go to Qutub Saheb and from there to Ajmer Sharif and from Ajmer Sharif to Mecca, but the army did not let me go.

That army plundered the government magazine and treasury and did whatever it wanted to and I had nothing to do with them and took nothing of what they brought me. One day, they assaulted Zinat Mahal's house and wanted to loot it, but could not break open the gate. One should consider that if they were under my control or if I was conspiring with them, then why would these things have happened? Furthermore, nobody asks even a poor defenceless man to give up his wife, nor does anyone say to him hand us over your wife so that we can arrest her.

Siddi Qamar took his leave from me to go for Haj. I never sent him to Iran nor did I send any missives to Iran through him. Someone must have spread these false rumours to malign me. The note submitted by Mohammed Darwaish does not contain my writing and is not trustworthy. If out of enmity against Hasan Askari or me somebody sent this note then it should not be trusted.

The state of this army was such that nobody ever saluted me or showed any respect for me. They would march into the tasbihkhana or the Diwan-e-Khas with their shoes on. How could I trust an army that had killed its governors? Just as they had killed their lords they had also imprisoned me and unleashed repression. I was kept for namesake only. When they managed to murder such strong and powerful overlords as the English, then how could I who had no army, no treasury, no magazine and no cannons act against them, or have control over them.

I gave no assistance of any kind to that army. When the riders came on the first day, I got the gate below the jharoka that was under my control shut and called the captain and informed him and did not let him go to those rebels. When he sent word for carriages for the ladies, I sent them right away and acting on the wishes of the magistrate, dispatched a few cannons for his protection. That same night, I also sent a special missive to his exalted Lord Lieutenant Governor Bahadur of Agra through a camel rider detailing the events that had taken place here.

For as long as I had any power, I did whatever I could and I did not join them of my own volition. They forcibly did whatever they wanted. The small contingent of new retainers that I employed was because of the fear of those rebels, in order to protect my life against them.

When that army made ready to flee, I managed to get away from them and went and hid in Humayun's Tomb. When the government, after agreeing to spare my life, called for me, I came under their shelter. The rebel forces had wanted to take me with them but I did not go.

I aver that everything that I have dictated to be put down in writing here contains absolutely no omissions or falsehoods. God is my witness that I have dictated only the absolute truth and all that I remembered. In the beginning itself I had sworn to you that I shall speak only what is true, no more and no less.

(Signature Seal)

As for the copy of the note addressed to Mirza Mughal which is there in the file containing complaints against the rebel forces and about my intention to go to Khwaja Saheb and from there to Mecca, I don't remember this note. But the copy of this edict is in Urdu language, contrary to the usual practice of my secretariat. My secretariat usually issued edicts only in Persian. I can't explain why it was composed, but it appears that when I was fed up with the rebels and had wished to go to Mecca and had left the world to become a faqir, at that time Mirza Mughal may have got this note written by his office and affixed my seal to it.

Anyhow, the very existence of this note proves my lack of control over the events and my disagreements with the rebel forces. This confirms the truth of my first statement too. As for the copy of the note to Raja Gulab Singh along with copies of Bakht Khan's petition including my signature, and many other copies in the file, I don't remember it very well. What I do know is what I have said before that whichever officer wanted whatever kind of order would get a note composed and get my seal stamped without informing me. I am sure these notes above were also issued like that. And as for Bakht Khan's application, they would have got the signature stamped on top of it beforehand just as they did with other petitions.

(56, 7)

The Imperatives

COOLIES, WATER CARRIERS AND *PURI-KACHAURI*
Arranging supplies for the war

In addition to soldiers, wars require material and labour. A very large section of the Mutiny Papers consists of letters about supplies, both of labour and of material. The list of goods and articles being supplied every day to different regiments makes for staggering reading. How were these supplies raised and distributed?

Most of the goods and supplies were procured through the police. Working sometimes through the chaudhris (the headmen of the clans of workers), the police arranged for labour. We learn that it was the usual practice for the thanadars to send workers to the kotwali and to the C-in-C every morning. In the process, the police sometimes conscripted skilled workers for manual labour and vice versa, and there were a number of complaints about this. The services of this unpaid labour class to the uprising have never been sufficiently acknowledged. It is clear, however, that this subaltern class was only mobilized through some coercion. But that it was not all coercion is also proven by the constant demand for payments for the workers.

In addition to labour, materials of war and food were the other important supplies required by the army. Regiments requisitioned the desired goods by sending in their demands, on paper, to the office of the C-in-C who then instructed the policemen or the officers of the magazine or the artillery to supply it. Conditions in the city may have been chaotic and provisions in short supply, but there was some order to the manner in which procurements were made. Receipts had to be signed by the person who demanded and received these services, and every thanadar insisted on receipts.

Different thanas arranged for grains and provisions in their own areas or sometimes arranged for cooked food such as puri-kachauris for the army. Soldiers could directly approach thanas and demand food. Grocers' shops were billeted to particular regiments. One document forwards a complaint from the grocers via the police that the soldiers do not pay them and abuse them and that they are unwilling any more to put their stalls at the particular regiment. Not all goods or requirements could be picked up at will—a thanadar wanted to know whether the government would pay the price of the sugar at the rate being demanded before he could supply it.

Apart from the resistance offered by the shopkeepers and workers, the supplies of goods were also hindered by interference from other quarters such as the Punjabi tailors who used to make workers run away or the soldiers who resisted the forcible rounding up of coolies. All considered, what is more remarkable is the length of time for which the city held out rather than its eventual defeat.

Routine of rounding up workers—to be sent to the kotwali before dawn

Kotwal to the thanadars, 25 July

As per the usual practice, please make sure to collect coolies, doolie-bearers, jamadars, cobblers, saddle makers, tailors, and carts and carriages from your area and send them to the kotwali before dawn tomorrow morning.

(111c, 15)

Two hundred coolies, one hundred baskets, forty planks, five construction workers, twenty poles and one thousand sacks required

General Bakht Khan to the C-in-C, 13 September
(one day before the fall of Delhi)

Two hundred coolies and one hundred baskets and forty pieces of wooden planks and five construction workers and twenty poles are required for preparations at the front. Please have them dispatched immediately upon the receipt of this note. If they do not arrive by the evening, it will be a great loss for our mission. Also, along with these goods, please also send one thousand sacks. May the sun of the kingdom shine forever.

Furthermore, along with the other things, please send forty soldiers to make reparations at the trenches.

(Note on the letter:
Parwanas have been issued to all the departments to get the desired goods dispatched.)

(73, 167)

Iron, steel, brass, pewter, ammoniac, spades, shovels, axes and glass requisitioned

Qadir Bakhsh Subedar to the C-in-C, 25 June

The following material is urgently required for preparation for battle by the platoons in the battlefield. Therefore I beseech you to grant me the articles mentioned below. Dutifully submitted, may the sun of the kingdom shine forever.

Servant,
Shaikh Qadir Hasan Subedar

Iron: 3 *maunds*
Iron steel: 1 maund
Brass
Pewter/Tin
Sal-ammoniac
Spades: 300
Shovels: 200
Axes: 200
Glass
Borax

(51, 50)

Arrest all the water carriers of the city and dispatch them to the magazine

C-in-C to the kotwal, 8 August

The order is that immediately upon the receipt of this note, please arrest as many water carriers of the city as can be arrested and dispatch them to the gunpowder factory so that the saltpetre that is still left there is saved. Please regard the matter as urgent and obey the instructions promptly.

(Note on the order: Water carriers were sent.)

(111c, 139)

Please forgive the *kahars* who had run away for they are servants and masters must forgive

Kotwal to lord governor, General Bakht Khan,
26 July

Your lordship, the kahars or doolie-bearers are arranged through the chaudhris or headmen of the clan of bearers, and these people bring some people of their acquaintance and some are procured through circulars by the thanadars. It was learnt that some doolie-bearers were sent through their elders and five of them, outsiders, ran away and his lordship's wrath is directed at Jwala kahar. Therefore it is being submitted that you are the lord and master, these people are servants and they perform the government's work with great assiduity and masters are wont to forgive their servants and the dues that were paid are being returned and those people have not yet come, God knows where they are, the rest will be paid to them when they appear because one doesn't know whether they are doing service at the front or at the platoons. Your lordship's person is the fount of mercy and generosity, please forgive their errors and always the subjects are at fault and looking after the subjects is the preserve of the family.

(45)

Chaudhris of shoemakers and tailors have been dispatched

Thanadar, Turkman Gate, to the kotwal, 12 August

After greetings and respects it is stated that as per your instructions, the chaudhris or headmen of the clan of shoemakers and of tailors are being sent to you.

Mohammed Ihsanullah Khan

(61, 352)

Resend the chaudhris of *baqqals* in whatever state they are in

Kotwal to the thanadars, 30 August

After salutations, summon and resend all those chaudhris of baqqals or corn-chandlers whom you had sent earlier. Further, execute the order yourselves, send them in whatever state they are in.

(130, 225)

Thirty-one coolies and forty water carriers dispatched, please issue a receipt

Thanadar, Turkman Gate, to the kotwal, 15 June

Salutations, the application is this that in accordance with your circular, thirty-one coolies and forty water carriers have been sent to the kotwali in the company of barqandazes, I hope you will send me a receipt. Further, in accordance with your circular, the chaudhris or headmen of corn-chandlers of this area are being sent to your exalted company.

Mohammed Ihsanullah Khan

(61, 53/54)

Chaudhri of water carriers is unwell, therefore cannot be summoned

Kotwal to darogha, thana Rajghat, 6 September

It was learnt through Munnu Khan water carrier that the chaudhri of water carriers Yadallah has been a resident of Haveli Hamid Mirza Khan of your area; therefore you are directed to summon Yadallah Chaudhri right away and dispatch him to the kotwali.

Khuda Bakhsh Khan, Deputy kotwal

(Note on the order:
As per your instructions, when he was summoned, it was learnt that Yadallah, the chaudhri of water carriers, is very unwell. Whatever is commanded will be obeyed.)

(130, 243)

Sixty carts required, people sent in search

C-in-C to the kotwal, 29 July

It is hereby ordered that you should arrange for sixty carts of carriage from wherever you can, from within the city and outside, right now. Send thirty carts to the Nimach camp and thirty to his excellency. Act promptly and immediately.

(Note on the order:
People have been sent in search.)

(111c, 53)

Grocers' shops stationed at a regiment, one barqandaz posted at each

Thanadar, Turkman Gate, to the kotwal, 22 June

After salutations, the application is that in accordance with yesterday's command, grocers' shops have been set up at the quarters of the Nasirabad platoon under the charge of the jamadar of the platoon and further, that one barqandaz has also been posted at every two shops. You are being accordingly informed.

Mohammed Isanullah Khan

(61, 86)

Water carriers and coolies and carpenters sent through their chaudhris, receipt demanded

Thanadar, Turkman Gate, to the kotwal, Undated

As per your circular, three water carriers along with their headmen, and six coolies and seven carpenters of this area are being sent to your exalted presence. Hopefully a receipt will be granted for the same.

Ihsanullah Khan

(61, 82)

Kaale, the legendary gunner, requires labourers at the front

C-in-C to the kotwal, 1 July

Please send forty labourers to help Kaale, the gunner, at the front of Mori Gate as soon as possible, along with some borax.

(60, 253)

Impound carriages in advance so that you don't make an excuse when needed

C-in-C to the kotwal, 26 July–3 September

It is being commanded that you should collect as many carriages as you can and keep them on a standby, so that when the need arises, you should not make any excuses and the work of government should not suffer. Impound as many carts as you can.

(45)

Thanas collect grain and food from their areas for the army

Kotwali records, 27 July

Provisions were sent to the Nimach brigade according to the following break-up:

Collection from Guzar Qasimjan thana for the eleventh platoon—lentils, salt, black sugar, sugar

From Nigambodh thana—lentils, grams
From Lahori Gate—lentils, oil
From Kashmiri Gate—lentils, wheat
From Allahabad Road and Arab Sarai and Chandni Chowk—lentils, wheat, salt, *urad* and *moong* lentils

(103, 214)

Puri-kachauri, *sohal, revari,* sweets collected by thanas for the army

Kotwali records, Undated

The following items of provisions were received from different thanas at the kotwali:

Thana Chandni Chowk—Puri-kachauri, sweets, oil, grains
Thana Allahabad Road—Puri-kachauri, sweets
Thana Guzar Dariba—Puri-kachauri
Thana Lahori Gate—Puri-kachauri, revari, sohal, sweets
Thana Rajghat—Sweets
Thana Turkman Gate—Black sugar

(193, 220)

Other regiments get *sheerini*, sugar syrups, but we don't

Subedars to the C-in-C, 5 July

My lord,

The sepoys complain that sugar syrup is sent to all the platoons at the front but does not reach our platoon. If the syrup is being sent anywhere, kindly ensure that it reaches here too and if that is not the case, please intimate us. An application has been sent several times, but nothing has happened yet.

(83, 20)

Please pay rent for the carriages which have been parked at the kotwali for two days

Kotwal to the C-in-C, 26 July–3 September

My lord,

After enormous difficulties carriages have been procured through the headmen of the clan of cart-pullers. They have been parked at the kotwali for the last two days because when required it is difficult to find carts. Therefore, they have been arranged from outside the city, I pray that their rent be paid by the government.

Khuda Bakhsh Khan, Deputy kotwal

(45)

Forty coolies required for building
a road outside Salimgarh

C-in-C to the kotwal, 23 July

Forty coolies are required to prepare the outer road in front of Salimgarh. Therefore the order is to arrange for and send to the Salimgarh front forty coolies tomorrow morning before dawn.

(111c, 2)

Tailors and kahars and coolies sent in
custody of barqandazes

Thanadar, Turkman Gate, to the kotwal, 18 June

After salutations, it is urged that in accordance with your circular, four tailors and three doolie-bearers and twelve coolies of this area are being sent with barqandazes. Hopefully a receipt will be issued and there is a clarification that there are no construction workers in this area, otherwise they too would have been sent.

Ihsanullah Khan

(61, 66)

Opium seller dispatched

Thanadar, Chandni Chowk, to the kotwal, 25 August

After due respects, it is hereby submitted that the person named Bihari, who is a seller of opium, is being sent to the thana to appear before you as per the exalted one's instructions.

Syed Nazar Ali

(61, 447)

All liquor and opium shopkeepers to be sent before 10 a.m.

Deputy kotwal to all the thanadars, 10 August

In accordance with the ordinance issued by Samsamuddaulah, you are instructed to send all the shopkeepers of liquor and opium of your area to the kotwali at 10 a.m. today without fail. Let there be no delay.

Bhau Singh

(131, 79)

Sending Mohan, no other opium seller in the area

Thanadar, Chandni Chowk, to the kotwal, 25 August

After necessary submissions of respect, it is urged that Mohan, the seller of opium in Chandni Chowk, is being sent to the kotwali. One shopkeeper had been sent before that. Except for these two shops there is no other opium shop in the area of Chandni Chowk.

Syed Nazar Ali

(61, 448)

Diggers in the area have run away, so will the shoemakers if not paid

Thanadar, Turkman Gate, to the kotwal, 23 May

After due respects, the submission is that as per your circular, twenty-three shoemakers are being sent to your exalted presence and the situation is that the diggers who lived in the area have left the city and have gone to the outskirts and these shoemakers have also been arranged with difficulty and if they are not paid their wages, then they too would leave the city just as the diggers have left.

Mohammed Ihsanullah Khan

(61, 1)

Let us collect supplies from outside the city because shopkeepers in the city keep their shops shut

Thanadar, Bhojla Pahari, to the King, 11 June

Often, the government armies are supplied flour, provisions, etc., from the grocers, which poses grave difficulties because of lack of money, and for the same reason, the majority of shopkeepers keep their shops shut because there are no supplies left in their shops. In this situation, the plea of the devoted one is that an order should be sent for procuring supplies from outside the city and all the chaudhris of grocers should be instructed to pick up flour from the mills. Dutifully submitted, may the kingdom's sun shine forever.

Humble,
Mirza Mohammed Amani

(121, 73)

Coolies' wages at Calcutta Gate; conscript and keep more coolies in readiness

Deputy kotwal to all the thanadars, 9 August

The coolies who had been sent to the front at Calcutta Gate should be sent here to this place because their wages are with the subedar of the Calcutta Gate. Keep the people who have earlier worked at the fronts on standby at the thanas; when the need arises, a horseman will be sent to procure them and when he arrives, immediately conscript and dispatch those coolies from your area with him. Make arrangements for procuring coolies beforehand so that you can act instantly on the note when it reaches you.

Khuda Bakhsh Khan

(130, 50)

Insubordinate shopkeepers sent to the kotwali

Thanadar, Chandni Chowk, to the kotwal, 17 June

After due respects, the submission is that persons named Jata and Misanvi Chaudhri were summoned to supply provisions, but the chaudhris said that we have not opened a shop forever; if we send one today, there will be more orders tomorrow and this way we will be completely ruined. Therefore, they have been sent to the kotwali for further action.

Hafiz Aminuddin Khan

(61, 61/2)

Nimach camp's application for provisions

Kotwali records, Undated

Imam Bakhsh, the sepoy of Nimach camp, applied for provisions at the kotwali. In accordance with his application, letters were drawn up for thanadar Guzar Itiqad Khan and for thanadar Rajghat to supply some and they have been handed over to the above mentioned. Has been entered in the daily diary to convey the facts.

(103, 215)

Baker at lunatic asylum has run away, the thanadar can't send him again and again

Kotwal to thanadar, Guzar Qasimjan, 8 August

Post salutations, the word is to send a shop of bakers to the lunatic asylum right now. If the shop does not reach promptly, there is danger of a riot.

(Note on the letter:

Respected Kotwal Saheb,
Post salutations, in accordance with your directive and with the instruction of Mir Akbar Ali Saheb, horseman of the Lucknow risala, a baker's shop had been dispatched in the morning with Kamdar Khan barqandaz at that moment itself. Yesterday too, a baker had been dispatched with an oven to the lunatic asylum. It is proper and binding to obey orders and we fulfil the obligations we undertake and after being dispatched in the morning, if they turn away from there, how can this humble one be held responsible for that and even now, the shop has been dispatched; now if they run away after some time, what can be done about that? Mir Saheb did not turn up in the evening either, otherwise repetitive searches can be a cause of friction and dishonour.

Mirza Mohammed Khan, thanadar, Guzar Qasimjan)

(111c, 140)

No carpet traders can be found but fishing rods have been sent from Chandni Chowk

Thanadar, Chandni Chowk, to the kotwal, 21 August

As per the lofty one's orders, a search has been conducted for copper ewer, but there are no shopkeepers of copper ewer in this area. As far as the carpets are concerned, it is stated that their traders cannot be found.

Syed Nazar Ali Thanadar

It is further stated that two rounded fishing rods have already been sent.

(61, 426)

A doolie-bearer and a Hindu barber required for the fourteenth regiment

Deputy kotwal to darogha, Rajghat thana, 25 August

Ramrup Tiwari, sepoy of the fourteenth regiment stationed at Khas Bazaar is reaching you. Arrange a doolie-bearer for him and if you can't find a doolie-bearer, then find him a Hindu barber on the terms that if he eats along with the regiment, will get paid two rupees a month and if he does not take the provisions, will get four rupees a month, and having hired him, send him with the man from the regiment to be employed.

The kotwal

(Note on the order:
After salutations, the news is that there is no barber available in this area. Please write to some other area.)

(130, 91)

List of cattle going out to graze needs to be prepared by the thanas

Deputy kotwal to thanadars of Kashmiri Gate, Begumpura and Guzar Itiqad Khan, Undated

After salutations, an ordinance was received from Colonel Saheb to the effect that a list of all the cattle of your areas which go out to graze in the forest should be prepared and sent to the kotwali right now. If there is any delay in carrying out this order, you will earn the wrath of his lordship.

Khuda Bakhsh Khan

(130, 42)

Fifty sacks, cobblers and three maunds of rope being sent, price demanded

Kotwal to the C-in-C, 28 July

In accordance with your orders, fifty sacks and cobblers as demanded in the note by Darogha Ghulam Ali, and three maunds of rope bought from the market have been dispatched before your exalted presence. I pray for the compensation of the price paid.

Dutifully submitted,
Syed Mubarak Shah

(111c, 34)

Lord Governor Bakht Khan demands a charpoy and wood for funeral, costs will be paid

General Bakht Khan to the kotwal, 7 August

Kindly send along a charpoy and a wooden plank with this messenger. The cost of the charpoy and the plank will be paid from here. Since morning, the corpse of the Subedar Saheb has been lying here. It would not be proper to delay the matter at all. Be prompt.

(111 c, 127)

Seven *sers* of sugar at one rupee can be supplied if the kotwal finds the price agreeable

Thanadar, Turkman Gate, to the kotwal, 5 August

After due submissions, the plea is that, according to Alam Khan Darogha, Sarmast Khan has some eighteen maunds of sugar lying with him, but he says that he will not give it to anyone unless the price is paid. Moreover, there are also no sacks left here. The rate he is fixing is seven sers per rupee. Therefore I am writing to enquire whether you are agreeable to buying raw sugar at seven sers to a rupee, and if you are, then kindly arrange for the money, otherwise whatever you suggest will be carried out.

Devoted,
Mohammed Ihsanullah Khan

(61, 309)

Deputy kotwal demands wages for forty doolie-bearers summoned by Bakht Khan

Deputy kotwal to the C-in-C, 26 July–3 September

These forty doolie-bearers had been hired for the Stopper platoon, forty-eighth regiment, by the order of the general of the Bareilly forces; when their salaries were demanded, it was suggested that the matter be raised before his exalted majesty and there it was urged that the matter be presented before you and you said to raise the matter when the money came in therefore this application seeking payment for these men as soon as possible.

Devoted,
Khuda Bakhsh Khan
(Note on the letter:

The valiant kotwal,
After a study of the application mentioned above regarding payment for forty doolie-bearers appointed by the Bareilly regiment, you are being commanded to inform us as to who demanded these men and whose requirement led to their hiring. Ask whoever hired them to pay.)

(45)

Coolies not paid their wages, they work only for money, 'If not paid they will run away like the others'

Kotwal to the C-in-C, 29 August

The submission is that the coolies who had been sent to the Teliwara front from the kotwali have not received their wages of two days. Therefore the petition is that the exalted government should pay their maintenance for two days because if the coolies are not paid their wages, how will they do the work of the government? Already countless coolies have fled the city and those that are left come for service only out of greed for money; if the ones remaining also run away, then how and from where will coolies be arranged for? If they don't get their wages, then these coolies too will not turn up the next time.

(129, 80)

The workers should not confront the barqandazes

Thanadar, Turkman Gate, to the kotwal, Undated

Post greetings, it is urged that as per your circular, three doolie-bearers and some carpenters and ten litres of milk in accordance with the demand by Jagannath, the clerk of the kotwali, are being sent to your exalted presence. Hopefully a receipt will be issued.

Devoted,
Ihsanullah Khan

Further plea is that because of non-payment of wages, coolies, labourers and water carriers are difficult to come by and those that are found argue with the barqandazes. I hope their wages will be paid and they will be warned not to confront the barqandazes.

(61, 111)

Men of another thana seize a conscripted carriage

Thanadar, Chandni Chowk, to the kotwal, 29 July

After due respects, the submission is that two carpenters of this area have been dispatched to the kotwali. A receipt regarding that is requested. And Gunjan Chaudhri had gone with Mohammed Khan barqandaz to search for carriages to different thanas; he came back and stated that one cart had been seized at the Guzar Allahabad thana, but the clerk and the jamadar of that thana handed it over by force to the Tilangas. It is difficult to come by carriages, therefore I beg that a note should be sent to the thanadar of Guzar Allahabad from the kotwali asking him why the said carriage was seized and given to the Tilangas.

Syed Nazar Ali

(61, 256)

A Punjabi tailor abuses the barqandazes and makes other tailors run away

Thanadar, Chandni Chowk, to the kotwal, 3 July

After salutations, the application is that your note requisitioning four tent makers and four tailors was received. My lord, this Punjabi tailor is a scoundrel and he challenged the horsemen of the Bareilly contingent and became abusive with Hyder Ali barqandaz and this Punjabi has made many tailors run away. Therefore it is urged that unless this rascal is punished, nobody is going to obey instructions.

Aminuddin Khan

(61, 117)

Water carriers being sent but 'soldiers violently interfere with conscription'

Thanadar, Turkman Gate, to the kotwal, 26 August

After due respects, the submission is that eight water carriers, Ilahi Bakhsh, Chhota, Bholu, Azim Bakhsh, Karim Ahmed, Mohammedi, Khuda Bakhsh and Billa, are being sent to you as per your instructions. I beg for a receipt to be sent to me. Further plea is that the Tilangas and horsemen often violently interfere with the conscription of coolies and water carriers; unless that matter is sorted out, the arrest of coolies and water carriers is impossible. Today also there was a confrontation with a few soldiers.

Ihsanullah Khan

(61, 453)

Grocers billeted at Daryaganj camp, but soldiers sent them away

Kotwal to darogha, Rajghat thana, 11 July

Greetings. You had stated that you have sent provisions to Daryaganj, but an order has come from his highness that the provisions have not reached yet. On seeing this note, please immediately send a receipt about provisions reaching the Daryaganj camp.

(Note on the letter:
Respected Kotwal Saheb,

As per your orders, several shops of grocers, etc., had been sent to the Tilangas' camp at Daryaganj, but the men of the regiment said that it is now dusk, we don't want it now, send it in the morning. In the morning, the shops will be set up there and a receipt from the regiment confirming this will be forwarded to you. Otherwise, whatever you desire will be carried out.

Thanadar, Rajghat)

(128, 37)

Distillers dispatched from Turkman Gate

Thanadar, Turkman Gate, to the kotwal, 22 June

As per your command, the distillers of the area are being forced to convey themselves to you in company of the barqandazes.

Ihsanullah Khan

(61, 84)

Thanadars can procure what is available in the city but what is not available can hardly be provided

Kotwal to the C-in-C, 26 July–3 September

The decree of his lordship regarding supply of oxen was received. My lord, all the twelve thanadars have been instructed about this matter and a circular has been sent everywhere, but no cow has yet come in. His lordship is well aware that there are few oxen in the city and whatever buffaloes, etc., were available have been procured and some fifteen or sixteen buffaloes have been sent to the general of the Bareilly forces and all the noteworthy barqandazes have been sent out in the city. By evening, any oxen that are found will be sent before your lordship, but it is apparent to your lordship that it will be difficult to come by animals of carriage so quickly and in such numbers from the city. The obedient one can procure through the thanadars what is available in the city, but what is not available can hardly be provided and one must excuse oneself for that. Dutifully submitted,

Devoted,
Syed Mubarak Shah

(45)

Halwai unwilling to supply stuff without payment

Thanadar, Chandni Chowk, to the kotwal, Undated

After due respects, it is urged that your note regarding the summoning of the bakers and the confectioners was received. As for summoning them, the situation is this that the head halwai is a *banjara* and is unwilling to send the stuff required without payment.

(61, 296)

If potters are conscripted as coolies, we shall leave and the work of preparing utensils will suffer

Potters of the city to the C-in-C, Undated

My lord,

We servants belong to the potter caste and have four to five houses and our work consists of moulding pots for the armed forces. Many of our men have run away. Now the kotwal, through the thanadar of Turkman Gate, has had us arrested and sends us away for government work and makes us work as coolies. We are thus faced with total ruin. If we continue to be conscripted as coolies, we shall leave and the work of preparing utensils will suffer. We hope that your lordship will issue an order and a note will be handed to us too so that the kotwal or the thanadar of Turkman gate desist from arresting us and sending us to the front.

Devoted,
Kalka Chaudhri, Debi Prasad, Bhola, Jodha
Qaum, Potters, Kali Masjid, under Turkman Gate thana

(67, 152)

Potters continue to be conscripted as coolies

Potters of the city to the C-in-C, 21 August

My lord,

We servants of the potter qaum are engaged in the profession of making pots, but the thanadar of Turkman Gate constantly arrests us and sends us to the front. The work of making pots thus suffers greatly. We devoted ones manufacture pots and send it to the forces. This way we are faced with total ruin and we have nothing to do at the front. We hope that his lordship will issue an order to the Turkman thanadar that he should desist from sending us to the front so that justice is meted to us.

(67, 111)

Grain parchers working for the government should not be made to work as coolies in the magazine

Deputy kotwal to the C-in-C, 11 August

My lord,

The grain parchers who parch grains for the government godown and have no knowledge of gunpowder work have now, in accordance with the government orders, been arrested and brought to the kotwali. This is likely to cause delays in the work of parching grains and if they are conscripted, then how will provisions be supplied to the soldiers and the army? Therefore, the plea is that grain parchers from Shahdara and Mehrauli regions should be deployed for the magazine so that we can focus on preparing provisions and be exempted from work at the magazine. For the rest, you are the lord and master, whatever is commanded will be executed. With the greatest respects, may the kingdom's sun shine forever.

Devoted,
Khuda Bakhsh Khan

(Note by the C-in-C on the letter:
Do not conscript the grain parchers who work for the government
for working in the magazine for this will obstruct the work of the
government and the subjects.)

(130, 68)

Requisitioned carts should be returned to the owners

Cart pullers to the King, 27 August

My lord,

The carts that had been requisitioned for the assault on Alipur have all
now been released by order of the government. But the carts owned by
us have not been returned. Therefore, we pray that our carts be released
so that we earn our liberty and we devoted slaves of your lordship have
no other source of redress and we cart pullers are starving and pray for a
dose of your lordship's mercy so that the matter is investigated and our
carts returned to us. A decree should be sent to Ali Bakhsh Darogha
to return our property to us.

Slaves,
Chetan and Jai Singh, cart pullers

(60, 596)

Lack of supplies and reinforcement forced three assaulting companies to return

Prince Colonel Khizr Sultan to the C-in-C, 26 June

Today, three companies of ours went outside the city for a raid, but lay
quiet there for want of provision and reinforcements. Helpless, they
have returned now. I write to inform you.

Yours,
Khizr Sultan

(100, 55)

Regiment on the assault has run out of magazine

Officer to C-in-C, 16 August

My lord,

A platoon of the third regiment of ours has been on the assault and we have run out of magazine; therefore this petition that two measures of magazines should be issued to us because we do not have any in our platoon.

Devoted,
Jeoram, subedar major

(Note on the letter:
The order is that the magazine should be informed.)

(90, 26)

Money sanctioned for purchase of flutes and drums

C-in-C to Jeoram, subedar major, third regiment, 24 August

Your application regarding payment of money for the procurement of drums and flutes was received. A note has been prepared and sent to the jamadar of the magazine to purchase the articles and the payment has been ordered. Should be reaching you any time.

(90, 28)

Canopy required by the C-in-C

Letter from C-in-C to the kotwal, Undated

The valiant kotwal,

Your application was received stating the measurements for the canopy if the support framework is sent; therefore you are now being instructed to get a canopy of nine feet by four and a half feet prepared in accordance with the subedar's petition. Do not delay.

(Note on the letter:
A directive in consonance with the command of his lordship, Mirza Mughal Bahadur, has been issued.)

(111c, 37)

The required musical instruments should be supplied by the magazine

C-in-C to Shaikh Rajab Ali, darogha of the magazine, 17 August

The application of Dilthaman Singh, Havaldar Major, requesting musical instruments for the band passed our eyes and a command is being sent to you to issue whatever instruments that are available at the magazine to the major.

(Note on the letter:
This order was found in the book of ordinances and it was not clear whether it had been executed or had not been sent, nothing can be made out therefore it could not be dispatched.)

(135–89)

Cavalry should be redeployed at the front

C-in-C to Brigade Major Gauri Shankar, 9 July

The front that had been set up yesterday at Qudsia Bagh, where you had personally appointed the artillery and cavalry units, after your return, the artillery and cavalry positions disintegrated completely. This relates to preparation of war. Generals are present at the trenches with infantry platoons. Therefore you are instructed to replenish the front as soon as you receive this note and deploy the artillery and infantry units at the trenches as an immediate priority.

(Seal of the commissariat)

(Note on the order:
In accordance with the order, a parwana to all the officers of Nasirabad regiment and the cavalry unit, Hindu sepoys, number four, is being sent alongwith.)

(57, 55)

MERCHANTS, BANKERS AND WAGES
Raising money for the war

As we see in other sections, everybody—soldiers, volunteers, labourers and coolies—needed money. It may have been a voluntary war, but everyone involved in it expected to be paid. Indeed, how were soldiers, many of whom had forfeited several months' salaries by deciding to rebel, going to defray their daily expenses if they didn't have money? Money was required for manufacturing gunpowder, for procuring arms and for the supplies that kept the war going—sacks, grains, planks, poles, axes, shovels. Where was that money to come from?

The King did not have any money to offer the rebels. A lot of the treasure that the soldiers had plundered at different places went into private hands. Money would therefore have to be raised from the city, which primarily meant taxing the merchants and bankers. Initially, there were hopes that once government control had become more consolidated, revenues and collections from the countryside would help cover the cost of loans. The King therefore instructed the C-in-C to assure the merchants that their contributions were merely in the form of interest- free loans.

Documents in this section comprise several orders to the police asking them to produce merchants from various localities. Muslim Punjabi merchants and Hindu bankers were the two classes most in demand for making money contributions. But other notables of the city were also not spared. Men like Ziauddin Khan, Nawab Hafiz Mammo, Ahmed Ali Khan and others who were part of the elite courtly society of the city also had to make contributions. Shopkeepers and merchants were already suffering the duress of providing supplies without payment to soldiers and when pushed to make monetary contributions, they could prove recalcitrant.

In addition, as we see in other sections, the King repeatedly pressed upon the principalities surrounding Delhi—Ballabgarh, Bahadurgarh, Pataudi and Jhajjhar—to make contributions. Emissaries were sent and their agents were bullied. Sometimes, expeditions were also mounted to these estates to ensure compliance. Rao Tularam, the Jat leader from Rewari, sent in some money on occasion as did villages of Meerut and Mathura.

There was also conflict about the correct authority for collecting taxes. As Mirza Mughal's note informs us, there were at least three different sources that had been officially earmarked for the collection of money, but there were many more unofficial ones who were doing so. Soldiers were forcibly taking loans from people, princes were collecting money on behalf of the court, self-appointed middlemen were collecting money, and the CoM too was collecting money on behalf of the soldiers. There was a fine line between raising contributions and extorting money, and it was crossed more often than not. There is a document that mentions the arrest of people for raising contributions without authority. There are complaints by shopkeepers and ordinary citizens saying they are too poor to make contributions, and there are exasperated notes from the police who were unable to bend the merchants.

Yet, the process of collecting money was not entirely unregulated and indiscriminate. There was some record of people who had made their contributions and two documents below urge the lifting of guards from the houses of people who had already paid their dues. There were also specific exemptions for people too poor to pay. While soldiers were forever clamouring for more pay, even prisoners were unhappy with their daily allowance and wanted a raise.

Various schemes were periodically considered for collecting money. The CoM came up with an elaborate scheme, the *Dehli Urdu Akhbar* suggested appointing *ziladar*s wherever there used to be an English collector, but most such schemes remained on paper and were never actually implemented.

Sappers and miners from Roorkee demand money as they left everything behind when they came

Kishan Dayal, subedar major, and others to the C-in-C, 28 July

My lord,

The application is this that whatever forces have come here before your lordship are quite content and had brought their supplies and materials with them. Except, that is, for the platoon of sappers and miners which left behind all it had in Roorkee, and the goods and supplies that it managed to bring was left behind in Meerut. Therefore, many soldiers of this platoon are very hard-pressed. Some eight to ten days have passed and we have not even received any *chana*s and many soldiers are dismayed at the expenses. There are also no bankers or moneylenders here willing to give any loans. Therefore we beg that it is up to your lordship to reflect upon and consider these difficulties. Whatever is the command will be carried out. Dutifully submitted, may the sun of the kingdom and the government shine forever.

Servants,
Kishan Dayal, subedar major
Qadir Bakhsh, subedar

(Note on the letter:
King's comment—God willing, in one or two days, the salary will be distributed. Keep your spirits up.)

(57, 185/186)

The Nimach force will not fight until they are paid their expenses

General Sidhara Singh and Brigade Major Hira Singh to the C-in-C, 14 August

My lord,

The submission is about the Nimach camp's force that arrived in the capital with the expectation of serving the high seat after traversing a great distance and overcoming many obstacles. Till now, this obedient servant has paid off the allowances of the horses, cavalry, artillery, cattle, elephants and camels from whatever was there. My lord, the cavalry and the artillery and the elephants and the camels belong to the government and until now, however possible, were paid their allowance. Now for four or five days the entire force including the soldiers and the animals have been starving, and it is no longer possible to bear their expenses. Since the horses and the riders, and the elephants and the camels belong to the government, therefore please take them back because the government will have to bear their expenses. All the soldiers are determined to fight, but they ask how can a chap who has been fasting for two or three days do so. Therefore, I hope that out of the largesse of your heart and patronage can you please provide for all the expenses incurred by the royal force and honour this humble one with a reply. Otherwise, kindly call for the animals and inform the soldiers. Until arrangements are made for payments, no soldier is ready to do battle. Please do not construe this as disobedience. Should you not want the Nimach camp force to remain, then kindly give us a clear answer, whatever is ordained will happen. Innumerable petitions have been sent earlier but we have yet not received any response. With the greatest respect,

Devoted,
General Sidhara Singh and Brigade Major Hira Singh

(57, 328)

Raise money from Punjabis and other merchants and suitably punish them if they refuse to cooperate*

King to the C-in-C, Undated

Learn that no money whatever remains in the treasury to meet the expenses of the King and that accordingly there are no means for paying the daily and monthly allowances of the troops, nor yet for defraying the urgent daily expenses of the magazine, the artillery and the manufacture of powder, without which the active operation against the kafirs must be interrupted. It is therefore necessary to devise some plan quickly for raising funds through the means of a loan. You are accordingly directed to collect whatever money you may be able to realize on loan without interest from all the Punjabi and other merchants and from the rich servants of the English, and forward it to the royal treasury. You are further directed to forward drafts of notes of hand under our special seal promising the payment on the realization of the revenue of the country and the capture of the treasures. No fraction of any portion of this loan will be left unpaid. You will give full assurance to all parties on this point that in the event of their arranging for money required besides being repaid the loan, as a mark of favour, they will be elevated to appointments and emoluments proportionate to their qualification. But if notwithstanding such hopes and assurances of advantages thus held out any of the people above mentioned do not exert themselves to arrange for the money but advance unfounded excuses, you are empowered to chastise them as may be proper so that severity may cause them to come to the path of propriety and obedience to our royal orders may be the result. The expenses of the magazine, the artillery and the manufacture of gunpowder may be no longer interrupted and all necessary operations may be prosecuted daily. You will use such well-considered steps in the matter as will result in you collecting and sending the money to the treasury within three days. You are directed to enjoin our agents to refrain from making any demand now on such

*In English in the original. This document exists in translation only.

of the merchants who have already paid loans as also such of them as have given written engagements to pay the balance of their contribution within fixed periods. You will lay no further demand or claim on the whole of these men so that nothing at variance with the terms of agreements given under our special seal may occur and no cause of distrust to others may arise. Be assured of our kindness.

(199, 216)

Either only Bakht Khan or Mirza Mughal should be appointed to collect money

C-in-C to the King, Undated

It is known to your majesty that the army has been reduced to starvation in consequence of not being paid their daily allowances. Your slave as well as they were constrained to petition your grace on the subject and your majesty having considered to view the distress represented, orders were passed that some plan should be devised for raising a loan to carry on the expenses of the army; and a royal missive was bestowed on your slave in this matter. Your slave accordingly summoned the merchants and Punjabis of the city and conferred with them in regard to raising funds through the means of a loan. Some gave written engagements to pay in a day or two and then went away. It has just come to your slave's knowledge that Mohammed Bakht Khan has obtained a written order to summon the merchants and obtain money from them. A circumstance of this kind is calculated to cause dissonance and dissension in the army. Let your majesty consider this matter and recall the written order and let your majesty issue written instructions placing him on prohibition against taking steps in this matter. Arrangements for the money have already been made by me. I present this only out of necessity. May the sun of the kingdom shine forever.

(Note on the petition:
King's comment—My life! Order after order cannot be issued because just now the army is altogether disheartened. Whether the required

funds are raised according to your orders to the merchants or through the agency of the general, the desired object will be obtained. Otherwise it will become necessary to devise some other plan.)

(199, 350)

Money to be paid for the manufacture of gunpowder, but accounts should be submitted

Jwalanath, the diwan, to the C-in-C, 9 August

Mir Hyder Husain Khan, captain, asks for six thousand rupees as expenses for the magazine and yesterday two thousand rupees had been given out to him at the behest of Mirza Khizr Sultan. If six thousand rupees are given to him then how will the platoons and the cavalry be paid and the reason he requires this money is not known to me. Please advice whatever you order may be.

Slave,
Jwalanath diwan

(Note on the letter:
Diwanji should know that four thousand rupees will be given out to him and accounts for that will be taken from him because now gunpowder too has to be quickly manufactured; therefore give him four thousand rupees and say that Mir Saheb please make do with this for the moment and start work; as the money comes in, more will be given over.)

(136, 37)

Prince angry at the accountant's refusal to release money for soldiers

Mirza Khizr Sultan to Diwan Jwalanath, Undated

For four days, the daily wages of the sappers and miners and two other platoons have not been paid. The platoons are very insistent, and if there is such delay in the payment of their daily wages, then it would be very unwise. Jwalanath, whenever my men go to your clerk to demand money, he makes excuses by saying he has no money; therefore it is being instructed that you should immediately send the money for the allowance so that salaries may be distributed.

(Note on the letter:
Jwalanath's submission—The money was not received today from his lordship; will come in either by this evening or tomorrow morning. What can I do? I cannot function under such haste. His lordship should please spare me.)

(133, 69)

Over a hundred workers have not been paid for twelve days and will run away soon

Kotwal to members of the CoM, 30 August

For twelve days now the doolie-bearers present in the kotwali who do the work of ferrying carriages for the government have not been paid their wages by the exalted government. The doolie-bearers are about to run away; however much we console them, it doesn't seem to have an effect and they say that we have been present for service for twelve days, but our children are starving. How will we survive in this situation, they ask. In truth, for twelve days, some hundred bearers are here at the kotwali who have been losing their wages and they do the work of lifting doolies, etc., for the government. I pray that out of generosity and justice the wages of the bearers may be paid by the exalted government so that the bearers remain available for government work. Otherwise it would be difficult to procure even one of them. The submission is made in order to inform you, for the rest, your lordships are masters and whatever you deem fit will be executed. May the kingdom's sun shine forever.

Khuda Bakhsh Khan, deputy kotwal

(130, 220)

Soldiers starving at the front

An officer to the C-in-C, 29 July

My lord,

The submission is that for the last two days the force is starving at the front. It is requested that some food may be sent out of the salary due to the front so that there is something to eat.

Devoted,
Bhagirath Mishr, subedar major
Commanding officer, second platoon, tenth regiment

(83, 32)

Only rich bankers should be taxed, not the poor, and money will be returned with interest

C-in-C to the kotwal, 12 August

Since his majesty cannot stand the harassment of his subjects and that the money that is taken from the traders, bankers and affluent men of the city is taken as a loan which, on the arrival of revenues, will be returned with interest, and the suggestion that had been made for extracting money from the mohallas, vis-à-vis that, his majesty does not like the fact that poor people should be made to cough up money, therefore the order being given out is that only the well-off bankers, etc., should be sent up; shopkeepers and poor people should not be sent from any mohalla.

(130, 79)

Jatamal, the banker, extorting money from the poor, needs to be punished

Kalka Das and other poor people of the city to the King, 16 August

My lord,

The other day, Lala Jatamal the banker and moneylender of Delhi Gate, through four horsemen and some infantry, threatened and extorted money from the poor and weak of Chhiasath Khana in the presence of Lala Ram Din and Ummid Singh, exchangers, even from the helpless women and widows and from the indigent, against the royal orders, and has kept it all with himself. The government orders are that loans and money contributions should be restricted to those with means and money and to bankers and merchants and should not be taken from the villages and poor people.

My lord, it would be just to consider that Lala Jatamal has used great force and coercion and flouted government orders to extract money from all the residents of Delhi Gate's Chhiasath Khana through his soldiers and horsemen. He has collected money from each and every house and does not want to pay it out of his pocket. The well-off and bankers were to pay one lakh of rupees. We poor ones are deprived of two square meals and in any case nobody trusts anyone for even a single paisa; therefore we are hopeful that following Naushervan's* ideal of justice, an order would be passed against the said Lala asking him to return our money to us. Or else the government, through its servants, can get our money returned from the said Lala. He should also be given a stringent punishment from the government because he adopted crooked ways so that in future others will fear this and will not try to oppress or cheat anyone. With the greatest respects, may the kingdom's sun shine forever.

Devoted ones,
Kalkadas, Damlamal, Chaudhri Halwai, Harnam, Arjan, Jhajhhu, Juma, Baldeo, Nathhu, and other residents of Chhiasath Khana

(63, 42)

*Legendary emperor of ancient Iran, famed for his sense of justice.

Jatamal, the banker, to be summoned for flouting government orders

Deputy kotwal to the C-in-C, 16 August

The complaint of the residents of Faiz Bazaar regarding the collection of money from the deprived and the indigent people of the city against Lala Jatamal Sahukar, despite the government's orders to the contrary, has passed your eyes. There was a government order that indigent people should not be taxed. The intention is not to hurt anyone, therefore the applicants have submitted their evidence and await your lordship's command. With the greatest respects,

Khuda Bakhsh Khan

(Note:
After examining the petition in the said case, an order was passed that Jatamal Sahukar, resident of Delhi Gate, be summoned through the Faiz Bazaar thanadar.)

(63, 41)

Nobles of the city to be taxed

C-in-C to the kotwal, Undated

Send a trusted agent of yours today to the following well-to-do people of the city and submit the collections from them to the treasury of the court. Act promptly.

Nawab Syed Hamid Ali Khan Bahadur—500
Nawab Hasan Ali Khan Bahadur—500
Nawab Ziauddaula, son of Hakim Alimuddin Khan
Mohammed Haidaruddin Khan
Wife of Nawab Shamsuddin Khan—500

(63, 98)

Unauthorized money collectors arrested

Kotwali records, 30 July

Usman Khan and Alam Khan, Chiragh Ali, Jhajjhar Khan, Wazir Ali, Musandar Khan, Munir Khan, Pranay Singh, Ramcharan, Bhikhari, Ramzan Khan, Azimullah, through a note of Mirza Mughal on the charge of collecting taxes without authority, were brought to the kotwali. Will be kept here until further orders.

(103, 218)

Exchangers summoned for loans, vanished jeweller discovered

Deputy kotwal to Colonel Khizr Sultan, 17 August

My lord,

In accordance with the ordinance issued by you, Chiranjilal Gumashta and Gobardhan Das, resident of Dariba, and Nandkishore jeweller are being sent to your exalted company along with this note and the rest will be sent forthwith. Further submission is that after hearing the order from the thana the jeweller had vanished, and has only been found now; a circular had been issued for him and he has made his appearance and he is being sent again. May the kingdom's sun shine forever.

Devoted,
Khuda Bakhsh Khan, deputy kotwal

(130, 148)

Leading bankers summoned

Deputy kotwal to thanadar of Guzar Faiz Bazaar, 17 August

In pursuance of the order of Colonel Khizr Sultan, send the following well-known bankers of your area to the kotwali so that they could be sent to his presence as soon as possible.

Chunna Mal
Ramdayal
Dula Saraf
Guna Misr
Hakim Abdul Haq Khan
Wife of Raja Jawahar Singh
Saleh Ahmed Khan, former kotwal
Jamnadas, clothseller
Jwala Nath Kashmiri
Mohammed Amir Wakeel
Descendants of Nawab Zainulabdin
Diwan Basant Rai
Ahmed Mirza Khan

Further order is that you are merely to instruct Ahmed Mirza Khan and the descendants of Nawab Zainulabdin Khan and Hakim Abdul Haq Khan to present themselves before Mirza Khizr Sultan, not to summon them to the kotwali.

Khuda Bakhsh Khan

(130, 132)

Bankers, grocers and jewellers sent to the court

Deputy kotwal to Khizr Sultan, 14 August

In accordance with the ordinance issued yesterday summoning Mahanand, Shambhunath, Amir Ali, Harprasad and Ramdayal, today,

Harprasad, the grocer, and Mahanand, the jeweller, were sent before your presence in company of some barqandazes, and Shambhunath and Amir Ali are present in the exalted fort and the rest will also be summoned and sent before you.

Devoted,
Khuda Bakhsh Khan

(130, 108)

Bankers of Katra Neel disappear inside their houses and lodge complaints to evade paying money

Thanadar, Chandni Chowk, to the C-in-C, Undated

The note carrying the charismatic seal about the requisition of the bankers of Katra Neel was issued. My lord, acting on the orders of the resplendent one, the servant, along with retainers and barqandazes and other arms went to Katra Neel and reprimanded all the bankers of Katra Neel about making donations. You make promises for morning and evening and make no arrangements for money; therefore the following bankers are being sent before his lordship. Some people disappear inside their houses and do not give any response while most of them make one excuse or another to keep this servant at bay and are forever on the lookout for creating trouble or making complaints. Due to the lack of availability of money, the work of the thana and of providing supplies cannot be done. Therefore, I hope a strong reprimand will be administered to these bankers for unless that happens, the money will not come forth. Dutifully submitted. May the kingdom's sun shine forever.

Servant,
Syed Nazar Ali, thanadar, Chandni Chowk

(61, 547)

Merchants summoned to the kotwali

Kotwal to the thanadars, 19 May–10 August

As per the government's order, you should please call the following merchants and send them with Jamadar Jawahar Singh. If anybody resists, then let us know so we can send a contingent to arrest him.

Govardan Das Kabulwallah
Nuna Mal
Gulab Rai
Harihar Ram
Chandi Mal
Suraj Bhan
Lala Zorawar Chand
Lala Kirori Mal
Nandkishore Topkhanawalla
Bulaqi Das
Uttam Chand Bulaqi Das
Bihari Lal

(53)

Chandni Chowk merchants summoned to the fort

Kotwal to jamadar, Chandni Chowk, 19 May–10 August

Acting on the royal command, the Chandni Chowk jamadar should send the following merchants with Jamadar Jawahar Singh. Should anybody resist going to the fort, then a force would be sent to the kotwali to arrest these merchants.

Kanhaiyya Lal Saligram
Thakur Das Chunnumal
Jagannath Bansi Lal
Nanak Chand

(53)

Merchants summoned from different areas

Kotwal to the thanadars, 19 May–10 August

Greetings to all. It is urged that acting on Nawab Mahboob Ali Khan's order, you should collect the following merchants from your respective areas and send them to the kotwali from where they will be sent to the exalted fort.

Dharampura
Lala Zorawar Singh, Lala Ramji Das, Lala Gulab Rai, Baldeo Das
Maliwara
Lala Girdhar Lal, Uttam Chand Bulaqi Das, Pyare Lal, Chhote Mal
Dariba Kalan
Nandkishore, Govardan Das, Lala Dwarka Das, Tarachand Kinari Das
Katra Neel
Bulaqi Das, Nawal Kiran, Mathura Das, Issar Das, Jagannath

(53)

Katra Neel bankers will be blown off a cannon if they resist summons

Thanadar, Chandni Chowk, to Colonel Khizr Sultan, 17 August

The note of the miracle-bearing one about the summoning of the bankers of Katra Neel was received. Your lordship, the state of these disobedient bankers is this that whenever this servant goes to their houses to demand dues, they shut their doors and do not give any reply. They vanish. This servant cannot enter their houses without the permission of the exalted one. Therefore I submit that whatever is the command regarding these bankers will be carried out. Submitted dutifully. May the sun of the kingdom and the realm always be resplendent.

Devoted,
Syed Nazar Ali, thanadar, Chandni Chowk

(Note on the letter:
Proclaim a command to the effect that should you remain hidden,
you will eventually be blown off a cannon. The order is passed so you
should know.)

(61, 396)

Mustafa Khan is neither a banker nor a merchant, therefore should be officially exempted—but should quietly submit two thousand rupees

Colonel Khizr Sultan to the kotwal, 13 August

The gentleman named Mustafa Khan who is a resident of Gali Sayyidani
in Chandni Chowk is an elderly person and is neither a trader nor a
banker; therefore you are being directed not to demand any money or
contribution from him, nor disturb him in any way. Consider the matter
grave and act promptly on it.

(Note on the letter:
Quietly tell him to submit two thousand rupees.)

(63, 37)

Guards should be removed from Mannu Mal's house since he has already paid

C-in-C to all the guards posted at the house of Mannu Mal, 6 August

Since Mannu Mal has fulfilled the promise he had made of making a
monetary contribution, you are being instructed to lift the guard from
his house and return. Be prompt.

(63, 8)

Merchants detained at the fort should be released because they have already paid

Colonel Khizr Sultan to the C-in-C, 22 August

The jewellers who are imprisoned before you at the court, apropos them, the situation is that their contribution has already been deposited and a certificate to the effect is being sent. The money has been sent to the Diwan Lala Jwalanath and to the lord governor of Bareilly. In fact, Jwalanath had asked for the certificates, but since the papers were not ready, I am writing to inform you that please let those jewellers go, otherwise it would be an act of tyranny.

Khizr Sultan, colonel

(63, 52)

C-in-C admonishes his brother Prince Khizr Sultan about arbitrary collections of money

C-in-C to Colonel Khizr Sultan, 13 August

Dear brother,

What you have written about my complaining to his majesty is incorrect. But as far as the collection of money is concerned, it was communicated to his majesty that since money is being collected in the city by three groups, there are delays in collection of money. And nobody knows with what authority Mirza Abdullah arrests people in the city, on top of which he has not yet sent a penny. In a note of mine my name was replaced with his name and then he stamped his seal and rubbed it off so that nobody could tell whether the seal belonged to the C-in-C or to a colonel. He sends men into the city to make arrests. I have kept two notes aside with me which I will show you when we meet. I consider you my right hand. You are the joy of my life. Come. The thought of your coming and my meeting you is delightful. The everyday kind of meeting is something else. Always consider me to be with you through pleasure and pain. As God is my witness, the things you do without my permission or information: you get whoever you want arrested, you write off dues on people arbitrarily. You should issue whatever orders you want from the CoM here. Really this was unacceptable to me so I wrote frankly. Greater life and prosperity.

Please send all the platoons and the money and the magazines to the CoM. Until now the two platoons had not been paid anything because not enough money had been collected and whatever had come was claimed by the cavalry. Should one platoon receive something, then the grenadiers will also be given some remuneration.

(63, 36)

Chowkidars deserting because residents are not paying their dues

Thanadar, Chandni Chowk, to the kotwal, 28 July

After due respects, the submission is that several chowkidars of this area attend their posts and are diligent and prompt in observing their duties and do not absent themselves. But none of the residents pay the *chowkidari* cess to them and the chowkidars complain that we are not paid our dues and some have therefore now begun to leave. Whatever is ordered will be executed.

Syed Nazar Ali, thanadar, Chandni Chowk

(61, 246)

Merchants plead with the King for their release*

Habib Bakhsh and others to the King, Undated

We the slaves of your majesty have suffered great losses in the days of disturbance and have been entirely ruined. Whatever establishment

*Original in English.

of merchandise we had, whether in Calcutta, Benares, Kanpur, Delhi, Ambala or Lahore, has been subjected to plunder and desolation. The debts we owed to others formerly have remained as yet unpaid and these days we are incapable of even defraying the expenses of our own family. The truth of our state can be ascertained from trustworthy persons and from Nanhe Khan or account books. Mirza Mughal demands from us a sum of fifty thousand rupees. How can we pay this? At this time, even five thousand rupees are hard to come by. We have for the last three days been under the guards of Captain Hyder Husain Khan. The captain did not even allow us to leave the guard in order to say our prayers on Id ul Zuha. We have thus been compelled to lay our case before your majesty at the same time as praying to God to preserve and protect us that your majesty will issue an order for our release. We have for twenty days been administering to the wants of 1200 mujahideen and shall continue to do so. More than that, it is impossible for us to do. May the sun of the kingdom shine forever.

Habeeb Bakhsh
Peer Bakhsh
Jauhar Ahmed
Haji Maula Bakhsh
Sultan Mohammed
Kutubudeen
Karim Bakhsh
Mohammed Husain
Haji Hakim Bakhsh
Jawab Bakht
Munawwar Bakhsh

(Note by the king:
Mirza Mughal will take responsibility for future good behaviour so that he may not again, in infringement of positive orders, send commissariat necessaries or other supplies to the infidels, and provided the advice of the lord governor-general is coincided with, he will then release them all.)

(199, 360)

Prisoners clamouring for an increase in daily allowance

Deputy kotwal to the C-in-C, 4 July

At the present hour, the darogha of the workshop who had gone to distribute daily allowances at the rate of half anna to each prisoner has returned because the prisoners are clamouring and agitating for one anna each. Therefore this application is being sent to you to take a decision on the matter of daily allowance for prisoners. Whatever is the command will be carried out.

Bhau Singh

(132, 20)

Sepoys getting demoralized because of the lack of wages

Subedars to the King, Undated

Justice-giver, the situation is that for the last twenty-four days, no salaries have been issued by the government and because of that, the sepoys are very hard-pressed. His lordship may reflect how a fight can be waged without food and daily provisions. Most of the sepoys are getting demoralized; therefore I am hopeful that the government will make some arrangement for salaries so that we can be freed of daily needs and concentrate on eradicating the enemies. Otherwise there will be a lot of discontentment in the camps.

Umar Khan, subedar major
Ganga Singh, subedar, thirtieth regiment from Nasirabad

(91, 78)

BUTCHERS, LISTS AND UNDERTAKINGS
Preventing cow slaughter during the uprising

There are almost obsessive mentions of the pig and the cow in a large number of proclamations and placards produced in 1857. As we have seen, Hindus were constantly asked to swear on the cow and accused, sometimes, of eating beef if they did not participate in the uprising. There are also constant appeals to Hindus and Muslims to fight together as brethren. One of the most striking ways of showing solidarity between Hindus and Muslims was the ban on cow slaughter imposed by Muslim leaders of the uprising. In some proclamations, it appears as a trade-off for ensuring Hindu support. In view of the fact that for the next hundred years at least cow slaughter would prove to be a highly emotive issue for Hindu political mobilization, its proscription during the uprising stands as a stark contrast.

Cow slaughter had been greatly restricted in the Mughal dominions, but when the British took over the governance of Delhi, they legalized its practice. The rebel government at Delhi banned it soon after taking charge. However, with the approach of Baqrid that year, which fell in the first week of August, orders against it became more frantic and passionate. The British were strongly hoping for a rift between Hindus and Muslims over this issue and there is mention elsewhere that some jihadis were keen to sacrifice cows. That there was apprehension within the city about it is proved by the rumours of bribes paid by the British to ensure incidents of cow slaughter.

The documents in this section contain strictures and proclamations against cow slaughter and also detail the procedures through which this ban was implemented. They thus provide us a window into the practices of governmentality at the time. In order to ensure that no cows were slaughtered, the kotwal prepared a list of all the cows owned by Muslims. Then he tried to collect all the cows in the kotwali and when that proved logistically impossible, he made all the owners give him undertakings that they would not slaughter their cows.

Three weeks before the proclamation, there was the case of a kebab seller who had been arrested on the charge of cow slaughter. Hafiz Abdur Rahman stated in a petition to the King that he had been arrested by some soldiers while selling kebabs, a profession he had been forced to take up 'in the present when all jobs of Shahjehanabad are at an end'. When the King wrote to the kotwal asking him why Abdur Rahman had been arrested, the kotwal replied that Abdur Rahman had been reported by Debi Prashad Hawaldar of the first company, appointed at the Lahori Gate, 'on the charges of cow slaughter with the notice that he had taken five hundred rupees from the English to commit cow slaughter in front of our barracks with the intention of creating a riot between Hindus and Muslims'. Eventually, the administration successfully prevented cow slaughter in the city.

Anybody who harbours the thought of slaughtering cows is to be punished

C-in-C to the kotwal, 30 July

According to the order issued today it is decreed that on the eighth, ninth, *juma* and on the tenth of the month of Baqrid and on Baqrid, on both days, morning and evening get this order proclaimed loudly and publicly that nobody must be found sacrificing a cow in the city. Not under any circumstances. If someone who even harbours the thought or acts in defiance of the government order is detected he will receive severe punishment from the exalted one. And keep the city under close watch and if you find anybody bearing the thought even, arrest him immediately and send him before the exalted one. Send a note to all the thanadars of the city that they should take precautions in this regard in their areas. It has been heard that some of the mujahideen are harbouring this thought of sacrificing cows, so please go to Maulvi Saheb and tell him that they should not do something like it this year otherwise there will be an unnecessary conflict which is not good because it will only strengthen the enemy. And there are some mujahideen who go into the Jama Masjid, that blessed place of God, and pollute it. Please you should explain it to them that they should not do these things because they are not in accordance with faith and religion. They should desist from such activities otherwise rioting is bound to follow.

(111c, 64)

All cow-owning Muslims to be registered at the kotwali

A copy of the order to all the thanadars of Delhi, 26 July–3 September

As per the norms, a copy of the special royal order from the exalted highness is attached. You are all urged to strictly instruct and direct all the chowkidars and sweepers of your respective areas to report all the cow-owning Muslim households in their locality to the concerned thana. Based on that information you should prepare a list of all the cows being bred by the followers of Islam and dispatch it to the kotwali. On the basis of that you would be asked to act further. Kindly keep a copy of the royal order in your thana and execute the command within two hours and there should be no delay. Please carry out the instructions with sincerity and affection and to the best of your ability and make such arrangements for [preventing] cow slaughter as would please his majesty.

Please note that having taken action within the stipulated time, you should send your replies to me on the progress made.

Syed Mubarak Shah, kotwal

(45)

Anybody found sacrificing cows around Baqrid to be blown off a cannon

Syed Nazar Ali, thanadar, Chandni Chowk, to the kotwal, 28 July

After due respects, the submission of the servant is that before sending this note, the servant and the clerks and the jamadar and the policemen will accompany a general proclamation to this effect, with the exact words, in every street and house of the area stating that, the world belongs to God, the country to the Emperor, the government to the Commander-in-Chief; without the permission of the exalted General Saheb, on the day of Baqrid, or a day before or after, if anybody wants to sacrifice cow or buffalo or calf or heifer or all of them or any of them, in the slaughterhouse or sacrifices in the homes or makes arrangements to do so, will be considered a culprit before the imperial government and will be blown off a cannon.

(61, 24)

List of all cows owned by Muslims sent to the kotwali

Mohammed Ihsanullah Khan, thanadar,
Turkman Gate, to the kotwal, 29 July

After due respects, this is the submission that as per your instruction a list of the cows of this area has been sent before your lordship and the functionaries were appropriately instructed to make sure, as per the information of the witnesses, that no Muslims owning cows or buffaloes should fail to be noted down.

(61, 254)

Cows owned by all the Muslims cannot be collected at the kotwali as there is not enough room

Kotwal to the King, 29 July

The exalted and pure one, my submission pertains to the matter of cow killing, that there was a command that cows belonging to Muslim residents should be called for and tied in the kotwali for the duration of the Id ul Zuha festival. Apropos that, there is not enough space in the kotwali to accommodate even forty or fifty cows. If the cows of all the Muslims are called in then they would amount to something like five hundred to a thousand cows. For this purpose we need a large field or enclosure where they can be penned for a few days. This loyal one does not know of any such place. Even though the proposition of calling in the cows is advantageous to owners of female cows, but since all kinds of people are suspicious and worried and it may incur the displeasure of the owners, there is a lot of room for alienation. Therefore should you so desire an order may be sent to all the thanadars to take undertakings from all the cow-owning Muslims that they will not sacrifice cows, whatever is ordered shall be executed. May the kingdom's sun shine forever.

(Note on the letter:
The city kotwal instructs all the thanadars to compile a list of male, cow-owning Muslims by Friday. An undertaking will be taken from them not to let any cow slaughter happen in their areas. All those who own cows should keep them as before and store their feed. Please do not let them roam about for feeding. And know also that after three days if the list does not match, then the owner will be held responsible for the omission.)

(111c, 44)

Bonds signed by all Muslims, nobody is to allow their cows out during Baqrid

Thanadar, Turkman Gate, to the kotwal, 30 July

After due respects, I would like to let you know that an undertaking has been taken from all the Muslims and from those who have cows and buffaloes in their houses and they have all been informed that beginning from the day of Baqrid and up to three days afterwards, in the morning or evening, nobody should let loose their cows or buffaloes. Please be vigilant on this front.

(61, 265)

Undertaking by butchers against cow slaughter

C-in-C to the kotwal, 29 July

You are directed to collect all the hides, that is, the skins of the male cows, and other animals and the grease that is there in the houses and the shops of the butchers and send it before his majesty. So that nobody commits any fraud in connection with cow killing which has been banned for future. Those who used to kill or sell them should also not commit that butchery. Make sure that nobody contravenes or refutes the order.

Signatures:
Chaudhri Yaldaram
Chaudhri Yaldaram, the younger
Chaudhri Rahim Bakhsh
Haji
Naate
Shaadi
Azimullah
Juma
Ali Bakhsh
Chaudhri Qadir Bakhsh
Haji Yaar Mohammed
Husain Bakhsh

(111, 45)

Kebab seller arrested by soldiers on the charge of being a butcher

Hafiz Abdur Rahman, kebab seller, to the C-in-C, Undated

My lord,

This servant is not a butcher by caste and is not employed as one. In fact my profession was different, but these days when all the trades in Shahjehanabad have been disrupted, this humble one is starved of food and essentials. Feeling helpless, I adopted the profession of a kebab seller thinking that nobody would interfere with it. Yesterday, a few butchers having been arrested for cow slaughter were passing before this servant's shop when I was flattening the meat for the kebabs. The soldiers of war arrested this humble one too on charges of being a butcher. Thus I was brought to the kotwali and kept in custody with the butchers. All the people in Lal Kuan mohalla are aware of my profession and my state. I am attaching an undertaking from all of them attesting to the innocence of this humble one and hope that their submission would result in my release.

With the greatest respects,
Servant,
Hafiz Abdur Rahman

(Note on the letter:
Order for the release of the petitioner given.
Order passed that the petitioner has given an undertaking attesting that he is not a butcher, a note should be sent to the kotwal that he should be sent here to provide a statement and also submit a list of all who have been arrested along with their names and addresses.)

(103, 132)

The Dramatis Personae

THE PERSONAL BECOMES PUBLIC
Dilliwallas and the uprising

The arrival of soldiers from Meerut and the rebellion by the Delhi garrison, by and large, took the residents of Delhi by surprise. Although some of them, notably the Punjabis and the *badmashes*, welcomed the soldiers and joined in the plunder of British houses, the majority shut themselves indoors. The first few days of the incursion saw the situation worsen. Apart from British houses, places where they were suspected to be hiding were raided and plundered. Goods were looted off shops, buried treasures were hunted and the well-to-do found themselves highly vulnerable. As the social order turned upside down and, as Ghalib wrote, 'Every worthless fellow puffed up with pride,' the lower classes of the city happily joined hands with the soldiers to humiliate the elites. On the pretext of looking for stolen articles, or of sheltering the British and spies, any house could be searched or raided.

As more and more soldiers poured into Delhi, they began to occupy different parts of the city. They were found on the terraces of mansions—overlooking the zenanas of many houses and thus violating the modesty of the women—inside mosques, hiding away at shrines and occupying people's dwellings by force. The affected parties were vocal about the problems caused by the soldiers. Many of the following documents are complaints by ordinary people, residents, shopkeepers and even princes about the excesses being committed by the soldiers.

If there was a tyranny of arms, at some level, it did not extend to silencing the critics.

≈⊙

The situation improved after the first month and the soldiers were gradually forced to set up camp outside the city. But the army remained billeted, by and large, on the city. This was an unpleasant enough situation, and it was made worse by the soldiers' suspicion of Dilliwallas. There were repeated complaints about the lack of support for the cause among the Dilliwallas; the editor of *Dehli Urdu Akhbar* went so far as to say that there was something about the air of Delhi that 'the moment the soldiers eat the laddus of Ghantewala and take a stroll in Chandni Chowk, they lose all their virility and urge to fight'.

≈⊙

Apart from the ubiquitous soldier, the residents were harassed also by the prevailing shortages of many kinds. Vegetables did not make it to the market, meat was scarce, flour of the finer quality had become difficult to come by and paan had become very expensive. Scarcity and the high prices of essentials were made worse by physical contamination. Toilet cleaners had stopped working in many mohallas, carcasses of animals lay around in some places and they were everywhere faced with the equivalent of the modern security checks. Sometimes, as in the case of Prince Abu Bakr, royalty itself could commit depredations. The noteworthy thing about this case is the readiness of the citizens to confront the prince and resort to the police to help sort out the matter. When the matter was reported to the King, he sent orders to the kotwal to arrest any prince who strayed, and sent out a notification stating that except for Mirza Mughal and Jawan Bakht, no other prince had anything left to do with him.

≈⊙

The well-to-do and the propertied were worse affected than the ordinary people. Even the princes were not exempted from plunder. As one document, written to ensure that a former thanadar didn't come to any harm, avers, 'These days most evil-doers and scoundrels of the city have adopted methods of causing injury and harm to the gentility and the presence of large armies allows them to commit excesses on all and sundry without any proper investigation or evidence.' It has been mentioned how some of the most prominent citizens of Delhi were raided and humiliated by the soldiers. Many of them proceeded to get their own private guards, provided by the representatives of princely estates or by the volunteer mujahideen who were present in the city. Ghalib's lane was guarded by the soldiers sent in by the Raja of Patiala. Similarly, fearing an attack by the soldiers, Mufti Sadruddin Azurda requested a posse of guards from the leader of the mujahideen. The shrine of Qadam Sharif, the royal vegetable garden, shops, police stations, all had to be protected by soldiers.

Shopkeepers, artisans and workers found themselves at the forefront of a war that they had not started and which many of them did not want to fight. As the police conscripted labour and billeted shops on particular regiments, they had to often use coercion to meet their ends. There is more about them in other sections, as also about the bankers and merchants who were forced to make monetary contributions, from which sometimes the poor too weren't exempt.

The turbulence in the city also allowed the settling of old scores with the help of soldiers. The subedarni, who occupied the houses of her neighbours, taking help from soldiers is a case in point, as is the case of the shopkeeper, who contrary to the established practice of there being 'no evictions in the monsoons', is yet thrown out of his shop, in spite of government orders to the contrary. Depending on how one could use soldiers, one could benefit or suffer at their hands. The police too could cause nuisance at times, as the complaint about the thanadar of Chandni Chowk proves; on the other hand, the people of Nizamuddin were very satisfied with the police post in their area.

This immense outpouring of complaints, requests, pleas and petitions itself says something about the relationship of the residents with the government. One can read these expressions of grievance as signifying some faith in the administrative authorities, or one can read this as an application of the last resort. People wrote to the C-in-C or the King or to the CoM because they had no one else to appeal to, nowhere else to go.

However, this open expression of dissatisfaction against soldiers assumes a sympathetic reception. Harassed as many of the citizens were, they were not exactly taking it lying down. The fact that people were looking to the government for relief proves, in some measure, its success in representing order. People saw the King and other officials as some kind of a bulwark against the power of soldiers. The mode of complaint, written applications, also reflects the existence of bureaucratic norms.

Even members of the house of Timur
are not spared by soldiers

Prince Khurshid Alam to the C-in-C, 14 July

Respected Uncle Mirza Zaheeruddin Bahadur, salutations.

A month ago the soldiers of Jalesar platoon plundered my house and so I sent those treacherous moles before you and respected brother Mirza Abu Bakr's exalted presence and had got them arrested but they were released without punishment. However, none of my goods were recovered and there were no clothes left to put on and no sword was left with me and I had sent the list of looted goods to you via my respected brother, but no response was received. I had sent word to Mirza Abdullah a few times because he was the officer of that platoon and he admitted the fact but did not do anything about it. I am very distressed because of the loss of possessions. On seeing this note, please do something immediately about the recovery of my property and there is nobody other than you whom I could turn to. This is the enormity of the situation that even members of the house of Timur are not spared. My dear uncle, please do something immediately.

Humble,
Khurshid Alam

(67, 49)

Imam Ali looted my house with soldiers on the canard that
I have stolen goods

Azimullah Khan to the C-in-C, 13 August

My lord,

One Imam Ali through subterfuge and deceit charged into my house with some horsemen in tow and spread the canard that there are guns, weapons and other government property stored in my house. On that pretext he brought the soldiers into the house and plundered all my goods and possessions. No muskets or other government weapons were recovered from my house but the rascal Imam Ali still looted my entire house. I hope that he will be summoned and punished for plundering my property without any basis.

Devoted,
Azimullah Khan
Government servant
Resident of Shahdara

(68, 18)

Badmashes are looting houses with the help of soldiers at Tiraha Bairam Khan

Thanadar, Faiz Bazaar, to C-in-C, 19 May

Alif Khan and Natha and Amba and Jagia and Tota, etc., scoundrels, not known how and through what conspiracy caused two soldiers of Alexander platoon, seventy-fourth regiment, to join hands with them and said that we have been appointed by the Nawab Saheb to search every house in order to recover the goods stolen from the magazine. So they forcibly and by coercion searched the houses of Shahbaz Khan, Rupa Ganga, Kair Malin and Khushhali Chamari, etc., and the houses of fifteen to sixteen people, and plundered what they could from each house. Hearing this, the manager of the provisions Ali Ahmed Khan stated that this case cannot be acted upon by the thana but is fit for the intervention of the council of war. So he himself heard the statements of the accused and recorded the evidence and kept them under arrest at the lock-up of the soldier guards at the Faiz Bazaar thana and investigated the matter himself and arrested people at will and let them off at will too. And it was heard that Qarar Beg the horseman of Ali Ahmed searched two or three houses of residents of Tiraha Bairam Khan and arrested them and then released them. Three of those men are still under arrest at the lock-up of the soldier guards of the said platoon. I don't know under whose order and by what authority he decided upon the case by himself and how did he determine the case to be under the purview of the platoon. The matter is presented to convey the news, dutifully submitted.

Devoted,
Thanadar, Faiz Bazaar

(185, 2)

Soldiers search our houses with the abetment of the thanadar

Residents of Nigambodh Ghat to the King, 1 June

We write for the reason that we are respectable citizens subsisting out of the bounty of your exalted self. Due to the abetment of the thanadar of Nigambodh Ghat, the people of the city and the soldiers search our houses without reason or cause on the excuse of looking for goods of the magazine and insult and humiliate us respectable folk. It is worthy of note that we are no plunderers but honest people whose job is to provide service. This occurrence causes offence to our families and if this state of affairs continues, we will be destroyed. Therefore we beseech you to take action out of your philanthropic goodness.

(King's note on the letter:
The order is that an edict should be issued to the thanadars of Faiz Bazaar and Nigambodh Ghat.)

(158, 2)

Qadir Bakhsh, tailor, arrested for forcibly searching houses

Kotwali records, Undated

The accused Qadir Bakhsh, tailor, was brought into the kotwali through the note of the thanadar of Faiz Bazaar on the charge of forcibly entering the house of Ahmed, complainant, resident of Hayat Bakhsh Gardens, with the intention of plunder, on the pretext of there being

Englishmen and goods from the magazine in the house. Has been kept in the lock-up, the matter is under investigation, will be conducted as per the regulations.

(103, 215)

Soldiers are hiding at Qadam Sharif during battles and stealing planks, beams and cots from here

Servants in charge of the shrine of Qadam Sharif to the King, 14 July

My lord,

The request is that when the excesses and heresies were first visited by the soldiers on Kotla Dargah Naqshi, patronized by his lordship, a posse of guards of the sixty-ninth platoon was deployed by his lordship there. The soldiers came for a few days and guarded it and the situation remained peaceful. Now the guard does not come therefore soldiers of the army come here and trouble us greatly and plunder the planks, beams, rings, cots, whatever is left here. These people have rendered desolate the habitations of the bird catchers, the lime makers and several others. They are now set upon looting and destroying the holy dargah of Kotla and boast that we will destroy this shrine like the rest of the *bastis*. We servants had informed the General Saheb about this but no arrangements have yet been made for it. Many soldiers come here during battle hours and instead of fighting, hide here, and if we try to prevent them they threaten us with their muskets and warn that they will kill us.

Since your majesty is the shadow of God on earth and the deputy of the Prophet and is responsible for the safety of the shrine, therefore, we devoted ones decided to inform you of the situation. We hope your majesty would issue instructions to the General Saheb Bahadur that he should deploy a guard in place of the sixty-ninth platoon and brief them properly that no soldier should create a nuisance or oppress anybody here. Also so that no soldier should malinger from battle and take shelter here. With the greatest respect,

Devoted,
All the servants of Dargah Qadam Sharif

(67, 50)

Saaru *telin* brought soldiers and looted my entire house

Faiz Khan to the King, 5 June

Yesterday, from 11 a.m. till the afternoon, a woman called Saaru telin, resident of Kauriya Pul, took seven Tilangas with her and looted all the goods and properties at my house, worth one hundred rupees. After a complaint made by the pleader, when the thanadar of Kashmiri Gate visited my house with some Tilangas to make arrangements for security, etc., the woman said to the thanadar that a lot of stolen and plundered goods are stored in this house. So he got my entire house dug up. My claim is against Saaru telin and after investigation, I want my goods to be recovered from that woman and a sword, an imported musket and some utensils which are my property and lying at the kotwali should be returned to me. The kotwal of the city has let that woman go and has asked me to present a certificate proving my ownership.

Devoted,
Faiz Khan
Resident of Gali Kunjna, Kashmiri Gate

(67, 7)

Scoundrels gamble, abuse and ogle at women of our house next to my house

Mir Akbar Ali to the C-in-C, 3 August

In the house next to this humble one's residence, who is an earnest servant of your lordship, a lot of miscreants have taken abode and they trouble me greatly. First they indulge in gambling and shout reprehensible abuses and ogle at the women of my house. Much though they have been warned, they refuse to change their ways. When I went to the landlord to request him to get his house vacated, the rascal said that I have the right to give my house to anyone I want. Protector of the weak, I am being greatly harassed therefore I submit this application.

Hoping that an order would be passed for the city kotwal to get the building vacated after due investigations so that I can escape the clutches of these rogues.

Respectfully,
Devoted Mir Akbar Ali
Special servant, resident of Faiz Bazaar

(62, 80)

Soldiers guarding the neighbouring house
stare at our women

Rangilal to the C-in-C, Undated

Sepoys of the thirty-eighth regiment have been posted at the house of the Raja of Patiala next to the kotwali. The soldiers climb on top of the house to keep a watch and this exposes the women of our house to their gaze. We are hopeful that an order will be sent to all the officers in charge of the watch at the Raja of Patiala's house so that they are prohibited from climbing on top.

Dutifully submitted,
Rangilal

(Note on the letter:
Order—The order is that a decree should be sent to all the officers of the platoon not to do anything which leads to the violation of modesty of someone's house.)

(60, 305)

Banda Husain, a self-appointed subedar, has abducted our relatives and has plundered our house

Kaniz Jaan to the C-in-C, 13 August

My lord,

The submission is that last May, Nawab Ahmed Yar Khan, my real brother and an innocent soul, was murdered at midnight by Banda Husain and Karim Bakhsh caretaker along with a woman named Pyari, the mother-in-law of Banda Husain, who came armed and assisted by some other men, and my brother was martyred. Afterwards, they went inside the house and plundered goods worth a thousand rupees by raising swords over the head of Aimana Begum and Butan, the wives of the slain man. They got the locks of the boxes and stores opened and plundered everything there and took it all to Karim Bakhsh's house. Until now this humble one had refrained from reporting the matter thinking it would add to your lordship's troubles and had resolved to wait for the outcome of the assault on the ridge so that I get my just desserts. The situation now my lord is that for the last four days Banda Husain has abducted Aimana Begum and Lotan and two minor daughters and nobody is allowed to go to them, and if anybody goes there he says that this is by orders of his majesty and the General Bahadur. And that man Banda Husain is a swindler. When the disturbances broke out he collected a group of people and petitioned before his lordship and was awarded the rank of a subedar and now he is committing excesses upon men. He also arrests everyone who interposes on their behalf out of pity. My lord, if every ruler becomes like this, then the populace of the city will be ruined and the city will be abandoned and destroyed. The truth of my submission will be proved by the evidence of everybody in the mohalla. Therefore, having presented this petition, the plea is that those scoundrels should be summoned and suitably punished and this widow should be given justice.

Dutifully submitted,
Kaniz Jaan
Real sister of Ahmed Yar Khan, martyr

(Note on the letter:

The order is that the application is presented in the court and the officers of the court should quickly dispense the case.

The order of the court is that it should be sent to the Brigade Major and the Brigade Major should reprimand those officers and soldiers and ask them to refrain from troubling her, otherwise they will be transferred.)

(70, 210)

Brothers arrested on the false charge of being spies

Shaikh Rajab Ali to the C-in-C, 11 July

My lord,

The petition of this slave is this that Shaikh Mangu and Shaikh Haidar and Karim Bakhsh, the sons of Shaikh Mangu, are brothers of this humble one. We have been living in Mohalla Kaghazian beside the windmill for a long time. Some spy complained to the exalted, out of malice, that there were Englishmen hidden in our house. Consequently, all three of them, Shaikh Mangu and his two sons, were arrested and imprisoned by your officers. The house and all the property were looted although no Englishmen were found in our house. Therefore I beseech you that the compassionate one would enquire after their situation. If their guilt is proven, the lord is free to do whatever you wish—hang them, blow them off a cannon. But if they are not proved guilty, then your grace may release them soon. May the kingdom's sun shine forever.

Slave Shaikh Rajab Ali Havaldar, sappers and miners

(51, 57)

Horsemen and Tilangas have forcibly intruded and occupied my house

Widow of Qasim Khan to the King, 14 July

This poor and helpless widow keeps a house and thirteen shops at Guzar Kashmiri Gate as support for her subsistence. Four or five days ago thirty horsemen and some Tilangas intruded into the house by force and coercion and have encamped there. The poor servant could not protest or do anything out of fear and terror. The submission is that the truth is that that kothi and those shops are my only assets and even their rent barely provides for me and my dependants. Further plea is that because of the army's stay, my house is likely to be spoilt and wrecked. Therefore I hope that out of your inestimable generosity and mercy your majesty would cast a glance and issue orders that this poor one's house should be vacated so that this servant can achieve justice and spend the rest of her life praying for the everlasting strength of your majesty.

Widow, Qasim Khan, deceased

(Note on the letter:
Order—By this order the officers of the army are directed to get the house and the shops of the widow vacated. Act promptly.)

(67, 46)

The Gwalior cavalry has threatened to plunder the entire mohalla

Gobind Rai and others to the C-in-C, Undated

The Gwalior cavalry camping on top of the haveli of Farashu Saheb has so oppressed the entire mohalla that it is impossible to describe it. Initially they used to dish out some money to the mohallawallas for expenses, etc., but in spite of that, they treated the residents in such a way that they would catch hold of each of us and forcibly demand money and seize something here and there. After our request, a guard of the thirteenth platoon was appointed by the government. So the residents give maintenance dues to the guards but the horsemen broke all limits last night when they went to the thanadar and told him that we do not get to eat, therefore we are going to plunder the mohalla. The residents therefore spent a terribly sleepless and anxious night. This can be verified by the report of the thanadar or the havaldar of the platoon. Therefore we plead that orders be given to the risaldar of the said platoon that they should leave this mohalla and go someplace else. Then it will be true mastership and justice.

Devoted,
Gobind Rai, Pratap Singh and all the residents of the mohalla

(67, 143)

The gates to the cart pullers lane at Kauria Pul have been locked

Colonel Mohammed Khizr Sultan to the kotwal, 13 June

One Lekha, a runner with the government, stated that I live in the cart pullers' lane near Kauria Pul. The gates of the mohalla have been locked up. The humble one hopes that the gates would be opened because the residents of the mohalla are faced with great hardships because of lack of food, water, etc. Since it is wrong to let the subjects suffer, therefore you are being instructed to get the gates open. Act promptly.

(Seal of Khizr Sultan's secretariat)

(Note on the letter:
As per the order the *hirkara* was given the key to open the gate.)

(111a, 32)

All the produce and arms of the Pataudi notables have been plundered

Landlords of Pataudi to the C-in-C, 16 August

We the oppressed chaudhris, zamindars and lambardars of the qasba of Pataudi have been completely destroyed. All the produce of the villages, qasba and the cantonment, watermelons from our fields, and three cannons and horses and elephants have all been plundered. The situation now is so grim that every day thousands of troublemakers from far and near come to raid and oppress us and there is no shelter for our families and children or for the notables of the qasba. The well-to-do have been wrecked and have left and only we unfortunate ones are left. Only your lordship's command can ensure order, so we are hopeful that some horsemen will be deputed to accompany us and a command be handed to us that nobody should plunder us devoted ones and it should be shown to the riders who are going from here.

With greatest respects,
Devoted slaves,
Ahmed Khan, Khurram Khan, Chaudhris Mushtaq Khan, Shahzad Khan, Bhawani Singh
Lambardars and others from Pataudi

(68, 19)

The produce of the gardens are plundered, the Tilangas disregard the guards

Kishan Sahai and Mohan Singh to the C-in-C, 24 June

My lord,

Our crop worth some one thousand rupees consisting of bananas and grapes and plums was ready, but the Tilangas came and plundered it and they are making away with whatever was left too. The guards deployed by the government at the gate of the garden are wholly ineffective because the Tilangas do not heed them at all and snatch away their guns; the government can keep them here or recall them, it doesn't matter. The darogha here troubles your devotees for taxes and levies; how can we give money to the government like this. Therefore we hope that either the government shall make some arrangement for it or the garden should look after itself.

Devotees,
Kishan Sahai, Mohan Singh
Contractors of the garden

(Note on the letter:
Order given that a couple of soldiers of the sixty-ninth platoon should be sent there.)

(67, 12)

Tilangas came in to take shelter and ended up occupying the house

Saheb Jaan, a prostitute, to the C-in-C, 5 September

My lord,

Some two months ago, two Tilangas came to my house to take shelter when it was raining, with the understanding that they would leave after some time. Since yesterday, they have imposed one more Tilanga along with a woman in my house and have thrown out this helpless widow along with my possessions and have seized the house. And when I go there, they viciously abuse me and say that if I enter the house they will shoot me. My lord, this poor and elderly widow has no other source of redress and support and if I do not get justice here also then I am convinced of their word that they will kill me. Therefore this servant beseeches you that I should reach my home and my house should be vacated so that I can pray for his lordship.

Servant,
Slave Jaan Saheb
Resident of Bazaar Khanam, expecting mercy and justice

(Note on the letter:
The application was received from the court.)

(67, 133)

How his sisters had to jump a wall to escape the depredations of a drunk prince

Deposition of Mirza Ghulam Ghaus regarding disturbances created by Mirza Abu Bakr and others at Faiz Bazaar when they were in an inebriated state, 5 July

In the court of Mirza Mohammed Zaheeruddin, C-in-C,
My name is Mirza Ghulam Ghaus
Q. What is your statement?
A. It is this that yesterday afternoon, the prince Mirza Abu Bakr Saheb, along with Mirza Mir, Mirza Majnu, son of Mirza Haji, and Mirza Nadir, son of Mirza Khizr, came to the Bairam Khan trifurcation and said that I have come from the ridge and am very drunk. After that, they began to use foul words. When I told my sisters to go away from there, they went away and then Mirza Abu Bakr raised his sword over me and pointed his pistol at me, but I consoled and pacified him and persuaded him to go away. Then he came into the fort and in the evening asked who had shut the gates of the mohalla. Is it being looted or what? The residents of the area replied that lord and master, we are your humble servants and the gates were locked to prevent any untoward incidents, and in fact, everywhere in the city the gates are kept shut.

Then when there was a delay in getting the keys, he abused the residents of the mohalla and began to attack them. First he fired three shots of the pistol and then he fired countless volleys from double-barrelled guns on the gate. When Naseer Ali and others snatched the sword from Mirza Abu Bakr, in the process of snatching it, Mirza

Nadir was slightly bruised, and when the grenadier of Faiz Bazaar said something, he struck him thrice with a sword. Then forty people from the Alexander platoon and Tilangas came there and established order in the mohalla. Then I got my sisters to jump over the wall and had them sent to the Lal Khan area for safety.

Mirza Ghulam Ghaus

(71, 96)

The prince proceeded to attack the deputy kotwal too

Deposition of Mohammed Ihsan ul Haque regarding
the disturbances created by Mirza Abu Bakr and others, 5 July

My name, Mohammed Ihsan ul Haque, son of Munshi Imranuddin
Resident, the Bairam Khan three-way
Education, educated, can read and write
Q. What is your statement?
A. That yesterday afternoon Mirza Abu Bakr along with Mirza Mehru, Mirza Abu Nasr Bahadur, Mirza Majnu, son of Maulvi Kallu, Mirza Humayun, son of Mirza Latif Bakhsh, and Mirza Nazim Sultan, son of Mirza Haji, came to the house of Farkhanda Zamani Begum Saheb at Tiraha [three-way] Bairam Khan, the tenants of this petitioner. Through the servants of Farkhanda Zamani Begum sahiba I learnt that the Prince, etc., are engaged in drinking. When two parts of the night had passed, they went away somewhere and returned after an hour or so. As usual, the gates to the lane used for passing to and fro had been closed, but we had left a window open to allow passage.

Meanwhile, a retainer of the Prince came to me and asked for the keys. As per his request I handed him the keys and he opened the locks of the gate with his own hands. The Prince became angry at that man and began asking him why he had locked the gates and told him that he would punish him right there. The person replied by saying, 'Your lordship, I am your servant.' He then asked for the watchman and said present him before me. So then the chap who had opened the locks caught hold of my servant Karim Bakhsh and dragged him before the Prince. The Prince made to alight from the horse and whip him, but he ran to me and when the soldiers ran to catch him, he disappeared. Nasruddin, the son of the petitioner, was coming from the haveli when the Prince reached there and they pounced on him and began to hit him. The Prince fired three rounds from his pistol, it is the blessings of the master that saved him.

When the petitioner came there from the house and apprehended the situation that the Prince is beating my son, my nephew Saiyyid Mir Ali seized the Prince's pistol. The Prince then took many solemn oaths promising he will not do anything and implored me to release the pistol. When the Prince said this, I immediately got the pistol freed from the said Saiyyid. The Prince immediately took two steps back and began to fire at me. I was somehow saved and thereupon shut the door to my house and went away inside the house. The Prince and his retainers fired their muskets at the devoted one's house and broke the bars of the gates and wanted to enter the house and kill the family and kin of this humble one, but in the meantime, Mirza Abdullah arrived there and rebuked and dismissed the soldiers of the platoons and the horsemen and their retainers who had surrounded the servant's house and were firing at it.

The Prince Mirza Abu Bakr Saheb Bahadur attacked the deputy kotwal of the city with a sword and injured a guard of thana Faiz Bazaar and the deputy kotwal, and galloped to the fort so that he could carry some cannons and platoons to blow up this petitioner's house. All the belongings of the servant's house were looted as well as a horse and a pair of oxen. I can provide witnesses to the incident. I hope the affair will be properly looked into.

In the court of Mirza Mughal, C-in-C

(71, 95)

Nizamuddin residents very pleased with the local police post, even the Gujars are restrained

Statement by Muslims and Hindus of
Dargah Nizamuddin Chishti, 27 May

We, the well-to-do residents of the Dargah Hazrat Nizamuddin, the saint of Muslims and Hindus, aver,

From the day that this police post has been appointed at Arab Sarai, Thana Badarpur, there has been so much calm and quiet that nobody high or low has suffered at all. Before the establishment of this thana our days and nights used to pass in great fear and in keeping watch against the Gujars and other marauders. Since the establishment of the thana everybody in Basti Hazrat Nizamuddin and Arab Sarai and Katra can sleep peacefully in their houses while looting and plundering in nearby villages has come to a stop.

The Thanadar Saheb collected all the Gujars of the area and got them to sign an undertaking establishing their accountability. Since the establishment of the thana we have not heard anybody, high or low, complaining against the personnel of the thana. That is why we have written this out like a legal statement so that if anybody makes a complaint then this will come in handy.

Signatories:
Mir Khurshid Ali, resident of Sargah
Jagan Rath, resident of the Dargah
Ram Parshad Brahman, resident of Arab Sarai
Tikaram, resident of Katra Irawat
Sukhram Lambardar, resident of Katra Irawat
Shakirji Zamindar, resident of Katra Irawat
Qamruddin Zamindar, resident of Dargah
Sadafuddin, resident of Dargah
Sayyid Zahoor Hazan, resident of Dargah
Sayyid Badiuddin, resident of Dargah

Gulab Singh, resident of Dargah
Bhagwandas, resident of Dargah
Gaurimal Zamindar, resident of Dargah

(68, 5)

Gujars are raiding and looting the villages of Kilokri

Deen Mohammed to the King, 18 May

My lord,

Taking advantage of the turbulence created by the change of government these days, the Gujars of Sarai Kale Khan and Taimurnagar have collected their kinsmen and for the last two days have been constantly attacking all the residents of Kilokri village, Nawal Shahi, and have destroyed our houses and belongings, especially mine, the lambardar's house, and have destroyed all the crops. They are intent on murdering and pillaging but we escaped with the greatest difficulties and have appeared before his majesty with the hope of receiving justice. Since his majesty is our lord and master so we have nowhere to turn to except to you. We hope that your lordship would help us out of his compassion for the needy and that we would get a reprieve from those tyrants and save our lives otherwise the villages of your lordship will be completely destroyed.

With the greatest respects, may the sun of the kingdom shine forever.

Devoted,
Deen Mohammed Lambardar,
Village Kilokri, Nawal Shahi

(68, 2)

Gujars undertake to protect certain areas

*Gujars of Aliganj declare that they will
maintain peace in their area, 16 May*

We, Chaudhris Randhir and Jhajjhu, Gujars of Aliganj, the Khalifa
lambardars of the area, undertake and promise that beginning
with Paharganj and until Arab Sarai, we are responsible for the
area of Paharganj, etc., as per the notice issued by Mirza Mughal
Bahadur General; according to the royal orders we agree to take
responsibility for any crime committed in this region and will recover
and produce the stolen goods and if we cannot produce them then
we will be held accountable for it and will compensate the victims
for their loss.

Randhir, Jhajjhu
Khalifa

(68, 1)

The subedarni got my husband killed in these turbulent days because of previous rivalry

Chhati Bi and Sultan Bi to the King, Undated

My lord,

Paimru subedarni, resident of Badru Darwaza, falling under thana
Bangla Said Firozepur, got my husband killed during the turbulent days
owing to a previous feud. She got all our wealth and property looted
and left this widow wrecked and distraught. The humble one stayed it
out and thanks God, for there was little else left to do. But for the last
three days, this servant, along with her sister has been under military
house arrest. The retainer of that subedarni greatly troubles us with
his machinations and louts. Even the exalted guide, the Prince Mirza
Mohammed Khizr Sultan, has been misled into supporting this case.
So he also enquires where the rest of the wealth and property is. This

poor one is in great difficulties therefore I exhort the exalted court that these two maidens should be released from the hands of these brutes and the latter meet their justified punishment. May the kingdom's sun shine forever.

Servants,
Chhati Bi and Sultan Bi
Residents of Badru Darwaza, thana, Bangla Said Firozepur

(67, 141)

Five hundred soldiers and hundred and fifty ruffians surround a house in Chandni Chowk

Thanadar, Chandni Chowk, to C-in-C, 5 September

Your lordship,

At some eleven o'clock, Allah Bakhsh, resident of Chandni Chowk, came and said that five to six hundred men have surrounded Munshi Abdul Waheed and are about to humiliate him and are demanding two hundred rupees. The devoted one instantly reached the house of the said Munshi with a police patrol and ammunition and took stock to discover that in truth there were some five to six hundred people and some one hundred and fifty ruffians of the city present there. They were saying that give us the money otherwise we will humiliate you and had also stopped a cow and a carriage from making its way to Saharanpur and were demanding a hundred rupees failing which they would commit plunder. When the devoted one tried to dissuade them from rioting they unsheathed their swords and made to attack the devoted one and the soldiers. My lord, had I not been accompanied by grenadiers and soldiers of war I am sure we would have lost our lives and they would have looted all the shops in Bazaar Chandni Chowk. Therefore the soldiers placed all the swords they had before the jamadar of the sappers and miners platoon, whereupon the men said that if you kill any one of us then five hundred people would be willing to lay down their lives with them.

So, with the permission of the exalted one the devoted servant took Tahawwaur Ali, Wazir Ali and Samand Khan under house arrest and I accompanied them to the kotwali and the Kotwal Saheb then sent us all to the C-in-C Saheb at the exalted fort. But the C-in-C was out and the situation was orally conveyed by Nawab Saheb Mohammed who asked me to personally accompany the gentlemen to the kotwali. A communique would later be sent from the C-in-C. With the greatest respects, may the sun of the kingdom shine forever.

Devoted,
Syed Nazar Ali, thanadar, Chandni Chowk

(62, 167)

Radha and Kanhaiyya who had been arrested have been freed and now threaten to attack again

Residents of Mohalla Maliwara to the C-in-C, Undated

Your lordship,

We residents of Maliwara had prosecuted Kanhaiyya and Radha before his majesty's court for vacating some houses. My lord, it is worth reflecting that the defendants, of whom there were three present have been freed after presenting one guarantor and they have not been asked to produce any witnesses nor have their statements been recorded. Now those people threaten us and say what harm you have caused us by filing a suit. We will now attack you because as it is there is no government and we are all afraid for our lives and therefore plead that you would ask the kotwal to investigate the matter and punish them otherwise they will get our colony looted. With the greatest respects, may the sun of the kingdom shine forever.

Devoted ones of Mohalla Maliwara

(62, 165)

Royal grass cutters are destroying the garden crops

Pehelwan Singh and Chunni Lal to the King, 24 June

Generous and exalted lord,

It is submitted before your august presence that the contract for the village of Shamsapur has been given to us by the zamindars. We have melon farms there worth some five thousand rupees. Sometimes grass cutters come there on behalf of your lordship the protector of the poor accompanied by a mounted soldier of your corps. They hardly cut any grass but instead destroy whatever we have planted. We hope that the preserver of the poor would prevent these grass cutters from coming here otherwise we shall be destroyed. We cannot fight the soldiers of your lordship. We would like the exalted one to forbid his soldiers from coming here.

Devoted,
Pehelwan Singh and Chunni Lal

(62, 54)

Soldiers have occupied a haveli of the exalted Begum Sahiba

Fazil Beg to the C-in-C, Undated

Men of a platoon who are quartered in the haveli of her highness the Begum Sahiba, it is not known whether they are staying there by your orders or have taken up residence on their own or on someone else' authority. Nothing seems to be the purpose of their staying there and in fact the constriction of space causes great hardship to Begum Sahiba and they also cause problems and make unreasonable demands. Therefore her highness has stated that an ordinance should be issued dismissing the soldiers from there. This devoted one could not present himself today as the Begum Sahiba desires to go and visit the shrine of

Shah Mardan and will appear in the afternoon. Urged out of necessity, may the kingdom's sun shine forever.

Devoted,
Fazil Beg

(177, 10)

It is an ancient practice in the city that no house owner evicts a tenant during the monsoon, but Badruddin has done this twice, against royal orders

Maula Bakhsh to the C-in-C, 24 July

After presenting my salutations as a devoted slave, I beg to submit that Badruddin Khan, seal-engraver, had bought a shop some three months ago belonging to me at a reduced price on the understanding that I will not evict you from my shop for three years for charging a reduced price and will not increase the rent. All the people of the bazaar and mohalla are witness to this agreement. And my lord it is an ancient practice in the city that no house owner evicts a tenant during the monsoon and in this condition. But the person named has become so intoxicated on his wealth that he acted against his word and disregarding the monsoon season, with the support of Tilangas of Alexander platoon who are staying right here, regarding me as being poor and helpless, without the orders of his majesty and of yourself sent some Tilangas and got the lock of my shop broken into and got the Tilangas to occupy it and got my belongings thrown out. At his instigation the Tilangas abused me and beat me up. Since my lord's justice is famous all over the world therefore I supplicate that an ordinance should be issued to the kotwal and to the commander of the platoon to the effect that the Tilangas should be admonished that they have nothing to do with the said shop and I should regain possession otherwise the shop that he had bought off me at reduced price should be returned to me and there is no vacant shop in the area. Dutifully submitted. May the kingdom's sun shine forever.

Devoted,
Maula Bakhsh

(Note on the letter:
The order is that he should be given possession.)

(185, 16)

In spite of the C-in-C's orders
Badruddin has again got me evicted

Maula Bakhsh to the C-in-C, 28 August

After presenting my greetings as a devoted servant I wish to state that the day before yesterday Husain Bakhsh Darogha and Badruddin Khan seal-engraver came to his servant's shop along with some horsemen and threw all the wares of my shop out in the middle of the bazaar and having confiscated two cots of mine from it put his own lock on my shop. When the devoted one showed your lordship's orders to them the darogha got me beaten up by the horsemen and out of the pride of wealth showed no regard for his lordship's order. Since his lordship's justice is famous all over the world and there is nobody else in this city who can redress the grievances of the poor and the helpless therefore I beg for justice that your lordship should summon the said darogha and punish him for flouting orders and get the lock on my shop broken so that it teaches a lesson to the others in future. And I should receive justice and unless they are summoned I would not get my dues nor will the subjects pay heed to his lordship's commands. Dutifully submitted, may the kingdom's sun shine forever.

Devoted,
Maula Bakhsh

(Note on the letter:
General Taleyaar Khan: Husain Bakhsh Darogha should be summoned through the thanadar.)

(185, 20)

Government to compensate the families
who died in the magazine fire

Colonel Khizr Sultan to the deputy kotwal, 9 August

Let this be clear that as regards the men who died yesterday in the gunpowder factory at the magazine, the government has agreed to look after their families, therefore you are directed to issue a proclamation in the whole city announcing pensions for them from the government so that they may present their claims.

Lord of the world and the universe,

In accordance with your command a proclamation has been issued in the whole city that for those who have died in the blast at the gunpowder factory the government will look after their families and pay them compensation and pensions. With the greatest respect,

Khuda Bakhsh Khan,
Deputy kotwal

(130, 42)

Compensation for the husband who died in the magazine

Widow of Qurban Ali to the King, 12 August

The situation of this widow is this that I was married in the thirteenth regnal year and was blessed with an unfortunate son in the fourteenth, who is one year old and I am now pregnant again. The reason for the son's misfortune is obvious. His father used to labour in your excellency's magazine for some time when owing to the upturning of fortune this ungodly accident happened and the magazine was blown up and he too lost his life. Except for your excellency there is nobody left to take care of me therefore I beg for my children and my living so that I am provided for and I spend my days praying for the progress and prosperity of the kingdom. May the kingdom's sun shine forever.

Wife of Qurban Ali, deceased

(Note on the letter:
Order that the petitioner's name should be entered in the list.)

(136, 48)

Compensation for father killed in the magazine

Jassu Beg to the C-in-C, 13 August

The father of us slaves lost his life owing to his devotion to your
lordship and due to his death we have become destitute and now we
and our mother have no source of income to keep us going. Therefore
we pray that your lordship should have mercy on our destitution
and find employment for us so that we may be fed and clothed. Our
father was an officer in the magazine and a pension should be issued
for him.

Slaves,
Jassu Beg, Mohammed Beg, three daughters, mother and seven
persons dependent on Mirza Saggi Beg and Mirza Afsar Beg, the
brother of the deceased. Your lordship can make enquiries before
issuing the pension.

(136, 49)

I have never ever set foot in a thana or a kotwali, so a solicitor will appear on my behalf

Mohammed Ali to the darogha of Faiz Bazaar, 22 June

After greetings, the request is that a note from the kotwali through
the messenger Natha was received regarding the suit filed against me.
Therefore the reply is that the only purpose of this suit is to insult and
humiliate me and this humble one has never ever set foot in a thana or
a kotwali, so a solicitor will appear on my behalf and present a response

to the suit and since the case is completely baseless a representation will also be made to his exalted lordship.

Writer,
Mohammed Ali

(61, 87)

Scoundrels of the city have adopted methods of causing harm to the gentility

C-in-C to the kotwal, 22 June

This is about our devoted servant Shaikh Qasim Ali, late thanadar. Since these days most evil-doers and scoundrels of the city have adopted methods of causing injury and harm to the gentility and the presence of large armies allows them to commit excesses on all and sundry without due investigation or evidence therefore all the thanadars and the kotwal are being instructed to ensure the safety of the family and property of the servant mentioned above so that no criminal thwarts them in any way.

(120, 17)

Munna, a sweet shop vendor, arrested by a Tilanga for demanding dues of twenty-five paise

C-in-C to the kotwal, 27 July

The application of the woman, Chandi, mother of Munna prisoner, passed before our eyes stating that the said Munna used to run a sweet shop and some Tilanga owed him twenty-five paise. When the sum was demanded some ten days ago, he got my son arrested on a criminal charge. You are hereby instructed to investigate the matter and report.

(89, 4)

Money demanded from government for the funeral of an indigent prostitute

Thanadar, Guzar Qasimjan, to the kotwal, 20 June

After salutations, the application is that a woman called Umdan, a prostitute, a destitute soul who had been lying sick and invalid at the Lal Kuan bazaar for the last three months died last night. There was not a single penny that was found on her. Therefore you are being informed so that you can advance some money for her funeral services so that she can be removed from there. Further, at the time of informing you via Mir Khan Barqandaz of this thana, Sairu sweeper was sent to search her along with the clerk and the jamadar of the thana, and nothing was found on her.

With the highest respect,
Mirza Mohammed Khan Beg, thanadar, Guzar Qasimjan

(124, 115)

Released mendicants demand their belongings

Mendicants to C-in-C, 6 July

The following of our personal effects had been submitted to the government. Now that we have been released we beg for our stuff to be returned as we are poor outsider mendicants.

Tumbler, clothes, bowl, sheets and other things.

(60, 271)

Clothes lying with the arrested washerman should be retrieved

Banda Ali to the King, 17 July

My lord,

A few days ago this slave's washerman who had run away from the front at the kothi had presented himself and had then been arrested, thankfully he has now been released. Thirty pieces of cloth of this slave are still with that washerman. I beg that my clothes be returned to me. Dutifully submitted, may the kingdom's sun shine forever.

Slave,
Mirza Banda Ali Beg, jamadar, horsemen of Punjab regiment

(Note on the letter:
Order that a note be issued to Mirza Khizr Sultan that his clothes should be returned.)

(61, 181)

Mohallas asked to maintain vigil on their own

Thanadar, Turkman Gate to the kotwal, 15 June

After salutations, let this be mentioned that your circular enquiring into the complaint lodged by the residents of Turkman Gate was received. The situation is that the residents of mohalla Hauz Qazi, Turkman Gate, located near the city wall and the grocers of the area, with a view to maintaining security, have placed a guard there and the thana has demanded nothing of them, nor does this thanadar have any personal favour to ask of them that their complaint can have any merit. Other than this a further fact is that the Tilangas posted at Turkman Gate often ask the residents of the mohallas nearby to remain vigilant and therefore many men of the said mohalla remain on standby and sit on the parapet, otherwise we have nothing to do with all this. But it is incumbent upon the residents of the city that they should take on the task of guarding their houses and mohallas because this is a period of disturbance and riot. For the rest, everybody is free to do whatever they see fit and the thana will not demand anything of anyone. Let everyone do what they will. These were the facts so I stated them.

Mohammed Ihsanullah Khan, thanadar, Turkman Gate

(61, 52)

Thanadar of Chandni Chowk is a scoundrel who keeps company with thugs

Residents of Chandni Chowk to the C-in-C, 24 June

At thana Chandni Chowk, one Hafiz Aminuddin Khan, a charlatan who earlier spent all his time with thugs has been appointed as the thanadar. He has unleashed such a reign of terror that if such people are appointed thanadars it is the surest way to bring destruction upon the subjects. The thanadar and the police staff have not been appointed with the approval of the residents. When we old retainers of old upbraid him he threatens us with our life. One thief who had been apprehended has been released by this thanadar after the payment of some bribe. We urge the government to investigate the matter so that your subjects are freed of this cruelty. Our further plea is that he has swindled us of some of our belongings and inveigles us into the thana but we are well aware of his tricks.

Residents of Chandni Chowk

(61, 95)

Government horsemen loot a shop beside the fort

Kanhaiyya Lal to the C-in-C, 13 July

This servant owns a shop of merchandise of long standing below the fort. Today some ten–twelve horsemen of the government came and forcibly looted the goods of my shop and there was a lot of raw stock which they wanted to lift too. Next to the devoted one's shop there was a government-owned store. Therefore I beg that after investigation my goods should be returned to me or its market price paid to me. Dutifully submitted, may the kingdom's sun shine forever.

Slave,
Kanhaiyya Lal Shankar Das
Trader below the exalted fort

(67, 39)

Nobody comes to my shop because the soldiers have been quartered nearby

Hafiz Aminuddin Khan, thanadar, Chandni Chowk, to the kotwal, 20 June

After due submissions, the matter is this that a certain wood seller by the name of Amirchand came and complained that for the duration of the last eleven days, my shop in Bagh Begum, where the cavalry has stationed itself, is doing no business and now I am suffering enormous losses there. Nobody buys any wood from me. Therefore I am taking the liberty to bring to your attention that if permission is granted then this said shopkeeper may remove his shop from there and take his wares elsewhere. The order will be carried out.

Hafiz Aminuddin Khan, thanadar, Chandni Chowk

(Note on the letter:
A note was written to the thanadar of Chandni Chowk allowing the
wood shop to be shifted.)

(61, 76)

Bakhta Halwai is arrested and his shop is looted by soldiers

C-in-C to Syed Mubarak Shah, kotwal, 1 July

The valiant Syed Mubarak Shah Kotwal of Delhi city.

The application of Atta, the resident of Ballimaran, has passed
through our eyes claiming that yesterday, from the centre of the street,
Bakhta Halwai and his son were apprehended by the Tilangas and then
arrested at the kotwali. And then his shop was also ransacked. This is
against the rules. You are directed to release Bakhta Halwai along with
his son. Already his shop has been looted.

(60, 253)

Unable to open shops because soldiers are living in front of them

Shopkeepers of Chhatta to the King, Undated

Salutations,

The plea is that a set of soldiers have established their residence in front
of our shops and the slaves are consequently unable to open them. We
therefore pray that in conformity with justice, orders may be issued to
officers of the state for the removal of these soldiers from their present
location or that otherwise the guards in the shops may be made over to
us slaves in the presence of the servants of your majesty's government.
May the kingdom's sun shine forever.

(Note on the letter:
King—Mirza Mughal will have their shops restored to these
shopkeepers.)

(199, 401)

PILLAGE, EXTORTION AND DERELICTION
Soldiers billeted in the city

The uprising was started by soldiers, but sometimes, they could prove to be the biggest obstacle to its prosecution. The documents in this section outline the difficulties of maintaining order and discipline amidst the presence of a large number of soldiers. Soldiers could search houses at will, extort money from people, refuse to pay for the supplies and abuse their suppliers. They hid in the city during battles, raided the ice factory, demanded bribes for allowing the movement of goods and documents, and attacked public property such as the planks and beams of the Jamuna bridge. They could also clash with residents as the altercation at the residence of Imaman the prostitute shows. They often obstructed the police by attacking its functionaries or not allowing them to perform their duty. In other instances, the police was forced to register cases, even weak ones, because they had been filed by soldiers. The police was also the interface when there was fear of disorder because of conflicts between soldiers and residents.

There was a perpetual fear of rioting and turbulence within the city, justifying the use of the term ghadar to refer to the times. Many of these situations are common enough when a large number of soldiers are billeted in a city. These were compounded by the fact that the soldiers came to Delhi to fight a war which they thought was a public one, but which did not find sufficient support from the Dilliwallas. If one looks at these documents alone, the soldiers appear to have been a grave public nuisance. But this is a fragmentary record. It only records matters from the point of view of the administration—there is no inventory of war here, no account of the action that went on every day where scores of soldiers died, often with great bravery. Moreover, they had their own difficulties, fighting often without pay and with no certainty of salaries, fearful of spies and betrayal at every turn and surrounded by a population that was sometimes downright hostile.

However, this section also contains documents that show a mechanism for dealing with many of these problems. The soldiers missing from their platoons could be traced through the police. If their response was not satisfactory their belongings could be confiscated. That this had some impact is shown by the application of the soldiers who beg pardon and promise to return to action provided their belongings are returned. There was a procedure for conducting house searches and sometimes people could be punished for extortion or forcible searches. The case of the risaldar Zorawar Singh establishes this. Soldiers could themselves act as vigilantes as in the case of a soldier who was found to be negligent on duty. This case also establishes the practice of dispensing community justice. The word court here stands for a consultative and participatory mechanism where everybody had a say in decision making. There was thus a self-regulated system of accountability in place as well.

Orders for troop movements also point to some organization because they are implemented through written commands for which receipts are issued by the adjutants of the regiments. In cases where they could not be carried out, an explanation was provided. While soldiers could use force to get their way, they were still subject to checks and punitive actions, and often preferred to use legal channels to prosecute their case. This reveals some efficacy of institutions such as the police and sometimes the police could even arrest the soldiers. On occasion, the soldiers spoke up for conscripted labour.

In a striking representation, the grocers who were attached to a regiment threatened the kotwal with a hartal in case they were forced to carry on working there. Unfortunately, we don't know if the threat was carried out or the manner in which it was effected. But in one instance, the soldiers' salary was deducted to pay for their dues against grocers. Soldiers could best be countered by other soldiers and wherever raids were feared, soldiers from other platoons were posted there. Orders and proclamations to soldiers stress the fact this was a war started by soldiers and one that was being fought in the name of religion and faith, therefore it was incumbent on everyone to give their best.

Soldiers arrest a jeweller and demand two hundred rupees

Bhuri Beg to the kotwal, 25 May

Right now, Mohammed Vazir and Khublal appeared in the thana and deposed that some eight or nine Tilangas have arrested one Mohan Lal jeweller and have taken him and have kept him in captivity and are demanding two hundred rupees from him. Therefore you are being troubled to send a posse of guards to protect the functionaries otherwise it is quite likely that a riot will break out.

Bhuri Beg

(111a, 10)

Soldiers often release conscripted coolies and this hinders government work

Deputy kotwal to the C-in-C, 26 July–3 September

My lord,

We take enormous efforts to procure coolies, etc., for the front but often the Tilangas interfere and siding with them they resist us and get them released. On the other hand the government is constantly asking us to send coolies to the front so even today the thanadar of Paharganj sent in some coolies but the Tilangas on the way got them off. This hinders the work of government therefore this petition urging that a command be issued to the officers of the Tilangas of all the platoons asking them to desist from doing so.

Devoted,
Khuda Bakhsh Khan

(45)

Soldiers clash with residents of Hauz Qazi— kotwal directed to take charge

C-in-C to the kotwal, 19 June

It has been heard that at Qazi Hauz there is an altercation between the Tilangas and the residents of the mohalla. You are directed to go there and immediately take control of the situation. Soldiers and horsemen have been dispatched from here. You go and enquire which platoon these Tilangas belong to. Be prompt.

(110, 270)

Soldiers hide in shops and gardens and do not go for battle in spite of repeated commands

C-in-C to all the officers of the platoons and the cavalry who have not gone to the front, 23 June

Despite repeated commands and in spite of the fact that this war started over faith and religion many of you do not go for battle and while your time away in gardens, shops and at other houses where your sepoys are hiding and protecting their lives. His lordship has made them swear on his salt that all the platoons should go for the attack and annihilate the kafirs but you show no consideration. How sad that this confrontation started over religion and faith and then his lordship gave you his protection and still you refrain from going for battle. You are again being exhorted to go to battle otherwise remember we well know the consequences which might follow. Remember, the platoon that does not go to battle even now will have its emoluments stopped from tomorrow and it will not lead to any good.

The platoons and cavalry units that have displayed courage and fortitude today, and earlier, will receive rewards, medals and honours from the court and his lordship will be highly gratified.

To All the Officers of the Platoon,

The parwana that had been issued to you that the second unit should go towards Teliwara and attack, it has been learnt that you did not go to the front and are lounging in the gardens. This is completely unacceptable. You should go there immediately and destroy the kafirs for standing true to your salt is a matter of religion and faith.

(Seal of the secretariat of the C-in-C)

(60, 213/214)

Soldiers hiding in the city should be arrested and sent back to their platoons

Generals Sidhara Singh and Hira Singh to the kotwal, 10 August

Learn that Prem Singh Havaldar and Mathura Singh Naik and Nathu grenadier and Shiv Singh grenadier of the Nimach artillery have gone to live in the city therefore you are being instructed to send some barqandazes and chastise these men and immediately dispatch them this side otherwise they are liable to suffer greatly. The work of the government is getting impeded.

Mohammed Faiz Bakhsh
Department of the royal army

(173, 10)

Absconding soldiers arrested by the police

C-in-C to the kotwal, 16 August

Know that Thakur Tiwari Naik, Shiv Singh grenadier, Nathu grenadier are staying in the city and do not present themselves at the time of the assault. A decree has been issued too, and in accordance with it, arrest the soldiers and send them to his highness. Act promptly.

(Response by the kotwal:
Shiv Singh and Nathu grenadiers have been sent, Thakur Tiwari Naik
has not been found. The person sent to identify them has remained
behind.)

(173, R11)

Confiscated property of some absconding soldiers should be returned because they have rejoined their platoons

Durga, the havaldar, to munshi of the platoon, 16 June

Munshi of the platoon, let this be known, the case of the Tilangas whose
property and belongings had been confiscated because they had shown
cowardice and run away from battle has been examined. Durga, the
havaldar, stands surety that all those Tilangas are now ready to fight
and lay down their lives, therefore you are being ordered to return all
the goods and confiscated belongings of the said Tilangas and include
them amidst those fighting.

Signature,
Durga

(71, 39)

Soldier found asleep on duty court-martialled by his unit

Officers of the fifty-ninth platoon to the C-in-C, 16 July

Yesterday, during the day, Mahabal Singh, soldier of the sixty-ninth
platoon, eleventh regiment, second company, was on duty at the guns
and he had deputed a sentry on patrol. At around noon yesterday, when
Kalyan Singh Naik of the guard went to the barracks after having his
meal he found the soldier who was supposed to man the guns asleep.
Finding him negligent he picked up his gun and then woke him up

and asked him where his gun was. He said I don't know who has taken my gun. That very instant the said Naik reported the matter to Samay Singh Subedar Bahadur and that soldier was arrested on the latter's order. Today all the officers and leaders of the platoon got together as a court and Mahabal Singh the prisoner was brought in front of the officers of the court and was questioned and he accepted that in truth he was sleeping on duty. Since due to his confession before the court the charge was proven against the sepoy therefore he was dispatched along with this note to your lordship. Whatever punishment is handed out to him by your excellency is acceptable to all of us.

Dutifully submitted,
All the leaders and officers of the fifty-ninth platoon, eleventh regiment posted at Ajmeri Gate

(Note of the C-in-C:
Whatever you members of the court think is deserving punishment for him will be acceptable to us.)

(152, 23)

Barqandazes thrashed by soldiers when they enquire into sacks of plunder

Darogha, Guzar Qasimjan, to the kotwal, 22 June

After due respects, the submission is that Fakhruddin Jamadar and Mirza Khan and Vazir Khan barqandazes of the thana were sent for their daily rounds as is the practice. Below the ramparts they noted some sacks of loot stacked by the wall and they challenged the owner. The owner argued back and unsheathed a sword and there was some jostling and raised voices when some Tilangas posted at Lahori Gate came and hit Mirza Khan barqandaz and he started bleeding and they then detained the jamadar and the barqandaz in their custody. Although

I sent word many times they do not listen and do not heed anybody's words. Therefore I am submitting the details because the Tilangas posted at that gate are royal servants. If this goes on then it would be impossible to maintain order and discipline because the daily rounds are conducted to keep an eye on mischief and disorder. Whatever you command shall be obeyed.

Mirza Mohammed Khan

(103, 24)

Farrashkhana guards demand bribes to allow goods and documents to pass

Thanadar, Guzar Qasimjan, to the kotwal, Undated

Salutations. The request is about the guards appointed at the Farrashkhana gate who are creating a ruckus. They extract a bribe for all the goods that pass and if they are paid they let them be but whoever does not give bribes, etc., is greatly harassed by the guards. When the barqandazes of this thana who are posted there object to this they abuse and threaten them. A number of times the barqandazes posted at this thana have sent complaints against them but all I could do was to change the set of officials and I then kept quiet. From today they have started this practice that even for records and documents if they cannot extort money they impound them and do not let them go. Despite protestations they say that you should withdraw your barqandazes from the thana, they have no business in this. Therefore I submit to you, if you grant permission then we can remove the bunch.

(Response:
And if his lordship asks what are we going to say to him?)

(110, 293)

Civil court's order for attachment of property subverted with soldiers' help

Kotwal to Colonel Khizr Sultan Bahadur, 26 July–3 September

My lord,

The situation is that Shankar Das plaintiff had won a degree of attachment against Philuram from the court of the munsif and it had been decided that his property would be attached. When the order came to the kotwali what that man did was that he instigated soldiers to intervene on his side and they became ready to shoot on his behalf and it was with the greatest difficulty that they were restrained. The case was sent to the courts and the magistrate asked him to be kept behind bars for two days and said to *challan* or certify him again after two days. Whatever is now desired by your lordship should be commanded to the magistrate, and the matter is now beyond the purview of this devoted one. The file of the case is in the court and I hope I will be intimated with whatever is the ruling.

(45)

Two horsemen injured at a prostitute's house by residents of the mohalla

Statement of Imaman regarding the assault made on some horsemen in her house, 14 August

Name: Imaman
Father's name: Husain Bakhsh
Qaum: Prostitute
Resident of: Bhojla Pahari

Q. What is your statement?
A. Yasin Khan and Shamsher Khan, two horsemen, along with their dependants live in this mohalla and I also live in one of the bastis

nearby. A woman whose name I do not know was singing in my house and following her singing both the horsemen meaning Shamsher Khan and Yasin Khan came up to my house. Mohammed Latif, resident of Suiwalla, came to my door along with some fifty other people and began to abuse me and said open the door and eject the two horsemen hidden there. Out of fear I did not open the gate. Shamsher Khan and Yasin Khan, the horsemen, opened the veranda's shutter and went up to the terrace from the veranda. When the horsemen reached the veranda Mohammed Latif and his friend shot at them with pistols from below and Yasin Khan and Shamsher Khan were injured by those shots.

Q. Did you have any conflict or intimacy with Mohammed Latif or any other relation?

A. I have no friendship or enmity with him.

Q. Do you have any friendship or enmity with the horsemen?

A. The horsemen live in the neighbourhood and being neighbours they sometimes drop in at my place. There is no friendship as such.

(67, 94)

Soldiers pillage the hooks, beams and planks of the Jamuna bridge

C-in-C to Colonel Mohammed Khizr Sultan, 29 June

The soldiers of the regiment are removing the hooks, beams and planks from the bridge on the Jamuna river and the whole bridge is being pillaged. An order has come from his majesty about the management of the bridge. Therefore you are being instructed to immediately make arrangements for securing the bridge so that no soldier can take the rings or the planks from the bridge otherwise it will be destroyed.

Mirza Zaheeruddin

(Response:
The orders have been executed as demanded.)

(100, 60)

Soldiers pillage the royal ice factory

Imam Bakhsh, ice maker, to the King, 24 June

My lord,

The submission is that the ice factory is constantly raided by the Tilangas of the army therefore I hope that the government would do something to prevent them so that they don't do it again. Otherwise all the ice would be completely destroyed and when needed will not be available to the government. May the kingdom's sun shine forever.

Devoted,
Imam Bakhsh, ice maker

(Note on the letter:
An order was passed that a decree should be sent to all the officers of all the platoons collected at Ajmeri Gate asking them to deploy one soldier each at the ice factory.)

(67, 14)

Soldiers can only search houses with the kotwali's permission

C-in-C to the kotwal, 1 July

Your application, along with the note of the thanadar of the Kashmiri Darwaza, to the effect that because of the unavailability of materials of war the soldiers are hell-bent on conducting a house search there passed our eyes. It is hereby ordered that you should go and figure out which platoons these soldiers belong to. A proclamation has been passed in all platoons that whoever suspects the presence of any magazine stuff anywhere should first inform the government, along with the informant who spotted it. A search can only be conducted in the presence of a representative of the kotwali. Tell the soldiers that they should first go to the lord governor with the informant and submit an application there. When an order is passed from there a search will be conducted.

Without the application of the informant no houses of the respectable will be searched. Also show them this sealed letter. In case they still refuse to obey, tell the soldiers of the guard that without our orders they should not allow any search. For further emphasis a proclamation about this issue addressed to all subedar majors resident in Kothi Sikandar is being sent to you along with this letter.

(60, 253)

No soldier should come armed inside the Diwan-e-Khas of the qila

Instructions from the C-in-C to the officers, 11 June

The command of his majesty is that no soldier should come armed inside the Diwan-e-Khas of the qila and no Tilanga should get into an altercation or a fight with a shopkeeper for the purpose of extending the bazaar. If any Tilanga disobeys, his officers should immediately report him and he will be punished by the government. The roll of the officers of the platoon and risalas, including dates of months and years should be prepared.

(60, 72)

Soldiers patrolling the gates do not allow the garbage of the city to pass

C-in-C to officers of the eleventh regiment serving at Ajmeri Gate, 13 August

The petition of Ghulam Hasan Khan, thanadar of Allahabad Road, passed our eyes with the content that the soldiers patrolling the said gate do not allow the garbage of the city to pass out and because of that the mohallas and the city are suffering and if the garbage is not removed the city will be infected with stink and disease. Day before yesterday, two sweepers were wounded by the gunfire of Tilangas at Ajmeri Gate and one of them succumbed to injuries. Therefore you are being instructed that the moment sweepers reach the gate with garbage you should let them pass out immediately so that the citizens do not suffer and know that if in future any soldier interferes with or harasses any sweeper he will be suitably punished by the CoM. Act promptly.

(130, 91)

Kotwal registers a case with weak evidence because of soldiers' insistence

Deputy kotwal to the C-in-C, Undated

A note of the Faiz Bazaar thanadar arrived outlining the particulars of the case and the depositions filed by Shaikh Gulzar, Sutrin Singh and Shivnarain, sepoys, against Hyder Bakhsh, Bhawani, Jangyaar Khan and Budhoo, accused, on the charge of recovery of stolen goods but without written response of the accused. From the deposition of the complainants it transpired that goods had been stolen and the accused had been arrested at Delhi Gate near the old fort and the goods had been recovered from their beddings, etc. During their replies the accused denied all charges of theft and claimed they had been falsely implicated and had been looted by the Tilangas and claimed that they had never been arrested on any charge earlier. The investigation and examination of depositions indicated that the evidence was very weak and there was no conclusive proof but since the suit has been filed by soldiers the accused have been kept in the lock-up and the particulars have been sent to you for further action.

Devoted,
Bhau Singh

(45)

Grocers beaten up by soldiers threaten a strike

Darogha, Guzar Qasimjan, to the kotwal, 23 August

After greetings, the submission is that the grocers of this area who had been deployed at the lunatic asylum for the seventh cavalry came to the thana and deposed that since the time we have set up shop there we have received nothing but abuses and beatings. All our sales happen on credit and on nothing else. Until now we have endured that too but now we are not willing to suffer any beatings. Today too one of us was so badly beaten that he is near death and eventually he ran away from there. The grocers are all lamenting that it is better to die than to suffer this treatment. We can't even go anywhere, if this continues we will all go on a strike. They are being sent to you to do whatever you think best. And they say that please have pity on our situation and let us remove our shops from there.

Mirza Mohammed Khan Beg

(124, 306)

Soldiers' outstanding bills to be deducted from their salaries

Deputy kotwal to the King, 11 June

In accordance with your order the grocers of the Dariba had been directed to ensure that provisions reach the platoons stationed outside the Delhi Darwaza but the grocers complain that the men of the platoon take goods but do not pay their price and they treat the grocers harshly and beat them up. Therefore the grocers are all awaiting orders from his majesty. Submitted dutifully. The receipts of the supply of provisions issued by the subedars are available with the grocers.

Abdul Hakim and Shaikh Mohammed Amir

(King's order:
Jwalanath is being ordered to deduct the grocers' account from the salaries.)

(125, 12)

Two companies required to protect the Jamuna bridge

C-in-C to all the officers of the police platoons, 13 September

You are being instructed that you must anyhow arrange for two companies of your platoon for the night patrol for the protection of the Jamuna bridge and send them right now. Do not delay and let them be vigilant. Act promptly,

(Response:
Protector of the poor,
The submission is that your edict demanding two companies was received. My lord the plea is that two companies left this morning for the assault therefore I have no men left to spare.

Subedar Prithi Singh)

(112, 54)

Fifty horsemen sent to the C-in-C

To the C-in-C, Undated

Your command demanding fifty horsemen was received. In accordance with your lordship's order fifty horsemen have been raised and are being sent to you.

The officers of the thirteenth regiment, Hindustani

(86, 48)

Pillaging soldier sent to the CoM

C-in-C to Zorawar Singh, risaldar, 7 September

Since people named Musahib Ali and Lal Mohammed and Azimullah, residents of Mehrauli, have charged you with plunder and the theft of their goods and property, you are being commanded to present yourself to the court immediately on seeing this note.

(60, 692)

Companies deputed to guard Mori Gate already sent for the assault

C-in-C to the officers of the thirtieth regiment, 7 August

You are being commanded to send two of your companies to the Mori Gate for doing duty tonight. Show promptness.

(Response:
My lord,

The soldiers of this regiment have gone for the assault since four o'clock, there are no soldiers present here.

Ranjit Singh, jamadar)

(60, 508)

'This platoon has no soldiers except those on guard duty'

C-in-C to the officers of an unspecified platoon, 7 August

You are being instructed to send one company from your platoon to the Rajghat gate.

(Note on the order:
Lord of the universe,

His lordship's order was received. The situation is that this platoon has no soldiers except those on guard duty and the rest are all serving at the front, there is no other soldier here otherwise the order would have been executed.

Jaimangal Singh, colonel of the platoon)

(60, 507)

No grenadiers left with the platoon to send to the front

C-in-C to Hyder Husain, 12 September

Dear Hyder Husain, special devotee,

You are being instructed that you should right away send some grenadiers to the *kuchehri* bastion and hand them to Fazal Ahmed Khan, the risaldar of Gwalior, who is present there and supply to him whatever he asks of you. Do not show any laxity. There are no grenadiers there. Show promptness.

(Note on the order:
Lord of the world and the universe,
Arrangements for the kuchehri bastion have been made, that is to say that the grenadiers who were present with the servant have been dispatched and whatever supplies were there for the guns-sacks, lead and shots, etc., have been handed over to Bailey platoon, and the havaldar of the sappers and miners along with coolies and two masons have been handed over to the said platoon. The servant has no more grenadiers.

Writing to inform you,
Syed Hyder Husain Mominuddaulah)

(59, 321)

Hindu corpses not allowed through the gate by the guards

Deputy kotwal to the King, 10 June

The biers of Hindu corpses are not allowed out of the city via the Nigambodh gate by the guards posted there. The guards do not heed the orders of the Nigambodh thanadar to open the gate and corpses are left to lie within the city. Therefore this application that whatever order is passed on this issue will be carried out. And a command should be issued to the officers of the guards about this. Dutifully submitted.

Slave,
Shaikh Mohammed Amir

(Note by the King:
Kotwal of the city should see to it that no obstructions are placed in the way of burials and cremations because most Hindus and Muslims of the city are buried outside the city. The corpses of Hindus and Muslims should immediately be allowed out.)

(128, 34)

Horsemen requisitioned cannot be supplied as they are already at the front

To the C-in-C, Undated

My lord,

Your order requisitioning forty horsemen was received. The situation is that forty horsemen and Arbaz Khan, deputy risaldar, and two *dafadars* are there at the front since morning for the assault and there are no more horsemen here. Therefore I beg that you should order the cavalry unit of Sirsa because today they haven't gone on the assault and there are some two hundred horsemen there. Dutifully submitted, may the kingdom's sun shine forever.

Mirza Abdal Beg, risaldar

(60, 824)

'You should have regard for the fact that you have fought on the grounds of religion and faith and you should remain constant on that'

*C-in-C to all the officers of the platoons,
cavalry and artillery, 10 September*

His lordship has passed an order reminding the Hindus and Muslims that for the sake of the cow and the pig and abiding by religion and faith, if you want to make progress and earn merit in this life then let us see whether as per the order you can prepare your infantry and cavalry and artillery and reach Kashmiri Gate and attack the debased opponents, the villanous kafirs. Let there be no delay or dilation in this. Act in accordance with his lordship's orders. Act promptly.

And you should have regard for the fact that you have fought on the grounds of religion and faith and you should remain constant on that. Every officer should form sections of his platoon and cavalry and after arranging them should inform them of the order and then attack. Should anybody, officer or soldier, make any excuse, please immediately send a report about them to his lordship.

(57, 461)

BAIL, BEGGARS AND BENGALIS
Conditions of policing the city

The police force of Delhi was the mainstay of the rebel administration in the city. Government proclamations, arrangement of supplies and the procurement of labour were all carried out by the police. The police summoned bankers and conducted searches too.

This section examines the organization and the functioning of the police force in Delhi. How were policemen recruited, who recruited them, did the thanadars and the kotwal have the right to hire and fire constables, pay their salaries and arrange their accommodation? We learn that the thanadars were dependent on approval from the C-in-C or the CoM for something as minor as dismissing old and incompetent barqandazes. The police officers often had to petition the administration for their own salaries as well as for arranging accommodation, identity badges and provisions for their men. Immediately after the resumption of government by the King, the number of barqandazes in each establishment increased substantially. We also learn how much each of them was earning, and how they were recruited. Since it was the barqandazes, the constables, who actually implemented the orders on the ground, were there any cases of insubordination at any level? I found two instances of resistance by the barqandazes; there may have been others which did not make it into the papers. If every barqandaz, states the thanadar, gets the courage to rebel then it will be impossible to perform the work of government.

The administration ensured compliance from the police through a variety of ways. It insisted on a daily record of all activities at each thana—the daily diaries of the thanadars were supposed to reach the C-in-C every morning before eight. The records of the thanadar were also scrutinized by the kotwal who processed them for the higher authorities. Requests and complaints from thanadars were sent up via the kotwal, as the demand for badges indicates. The administration also tried to yoke the police officers in the old order of courtly culture by insisting that they all address the King in a particular way and pay nazars to him on important festive occasions which marked the royal calendar according to tradition.

This section also shows the variety of tasks the police was called upon to perform. Indigent deaths were the responsibility of the police. Heirless property was appropriated through the police; proclamations were issued for such cases and the property was attached after the expiry of the notice. Bail pleas were entertained after verification of the worth of the bail giver by the police. Ethnic identification and rounding up of specific groups was also a part of police duties, for example, summoning Punjabi bankers or sequestering all the Bengalis of the city. In addition, the police also performed its normal duties of searching for missing persons—whose recovery depended on descriptions provided—and of solving regular crime like theft and burglary and the documents at the end indicate its mode of investigation in such matters. One company each of soldiers was billeted at every thana to assist the police in its functioning, and the letter addressed to the officers of the police platoon refers to this.

While executing orders, the police could face interference from many quarters—most notably from soldiers, which is mentioned in a different section—also from criminals, notables and private militia of the well-to-do and a few documents of this section include instances of these. On occasion, persons described as badmash or criminals could actually be standing up for hapless labourers up for conscription, as in the case of Afzal Beg below. At the same time as being asked to conduct forcible searches, the police was also warned to maintain good conduct and not to offend anyone, a contradictory demand at the best of times, showing how the administration was constrained to draw upon the very same people whose cooperation and goodwill was crucial to its survival. All the same the picture of turbulence, of ghadar, is offset by the demands for order, regularity, accountability and the pursuance of bureaucratic norms. A barqandaz may insist on a written order or a thanadar may take issue with being pulled up for executing a written order. The soldiers interfering with police work could also be aware of the importance of a written report and could show penitence in order to prevent a report being filed.

Apart from the regular staff of the thana, the chowkidars and sweepers—medieval posts that rendered useful service in gathering information—were important irregular appendages to the functioning of the police.

The King instructs thanadars to be diligent and to send their daily diaries promptly

King to all the thanadars, 20 May

It has been learnt through the kotwal that the reports and diaries of different thanas do not reach the kotwali on time and the thanadars are not present at their thanas day and night. Therefore they are being commanded to be present and prompt through the day and at night in administering the city and should present reports of each case to the kotwal every day. If they act contrary to this they will be dismissed.

(120, 1)

Sanctioned salaries for old and new employees of a thana—and the outstanding dues

Thanadar, Guzar Itiqad Khan, to the C-in-C, 27 May

My lord,

In this thana there is one clerk, one jamadar and one barqandaz who does the work of a clerk and there are five barqandazes who are old employees and nine barqandazes who are new employees. In total fourteen barqandazes are posted at this thana and they carry out the tasks of patrolling and executing commissions and implementing orders of the government. Ten days ago I had received a sum of money from the exalted fort for the staff of the thana in accordance with the list prepared by the kotwal. I distributed two rupees each to the old barqandazes and three rupees to the jamadar and Shaikh Abdullah and Asad Ali Khan, new barqandazes, fifty paise each. Some of the newer barqandazes have now been employed at the artillery and I took four rupees for myself and the salary for two months of this humble one and of the older employees still remains outstanding out of which only two rupees for the barqandazes and three for the jamadar and four rupees for myself have been allotted. I pray for the disbursal of two months' salaries for the older employees so that we are released from the clutches of the creditors and pray for the longevity of the government and some help should be given for distribution of salaries for the recent employees. The list of officers and barqandazes has been prepared and is being appended along with this note. Dutifully submitted, may the kingdom's sun shine forever.

Humble,
Mohammed Faiztalab Khan

(123, 6)

Contrary to the outgoing kotwal's statement, there is no paper at the kotwali

Kotwal to C-in-C, 20 May

My lord,

Your exalted note asking for paper via Jiwan Singh messenger was received with honour and privilege. My lord and master, there is no paper in the kotwali, what little is left is being brought to use. If you so command it can be purchased from the market. May the kingdom's sun shine forever.

(Note by the C-in-C:
Mohammed Moinuddin Khan, the former kotwal, had said he had left some sixty quires of ordinary paper in the almirah in the kotwali. Send twenty quires out of those.

Response—Moinuddin Hasan Khan's statement is completely false, there is not a shred of Indian paper left, there is only English paper and that too very little and a sample is being sent to you for inspection. And he had stated that there is paper in the almirah at the kotwali, God knows where it is, nothing of it can be found. Written in order to inform.

Qazi Mohammed Faizullah)

(132, 1)

List of old and new employees at the Dariba thana

Thanadar, Dariba, to the kotwal, 24 May

List of old and new employees in Dariba thana.

After due respects, the submission is that as per your circular the list of old and new employees of the thana has been prepared and is being sent forthwith. Further plea is that the sum that had been issued has been distributed to the barqandazes and now more is required.

Old employees
Mohammed Hasan, clerk
Roshan Khan, barqandaz
Umar Beg, barqandaz
Imam Ali, barqandaz
Roshan Beg, barqandaz
Shaikh Maseeha, barqandaz
Bannu Singh, barqandaz

New employees
Hasan Beg, barqandaz
Karim Bakhsh
Karim Bakhsh
Bannu Ali
Mohammed Mansur
Imam Khan
Sher Khan
Ahmed Ali
Ahmed Husain

(104, 1)

Thanadars must report vacant posts, missing officers and negligent barqandazes

Kotwal to all the thanadars, 22 June

After salutations, the matter is that you should state the situation in your thana as to whether any posts of barqandaz or jamadar or *mohurrir* in your thana is vacant and of posts where the appointee is missing or if there is a barqandaz who shows dereliction of duty, send information about it and send a reply to this note.

Syed Mubarak Shah

(120, 16)

Identity badges requested for barqandazes of Turkman Gate thana

Thanadar, Turkman Gate, to the kotwal, 5 June

After greetings and salutations, the plea is that for the last one month all the barqandazes of this thana have been busy executing their respective duties but no badges have yet been issued to them which will allow them to be distinguished as barqandazes of this thana. I pray that the application for granting them badges will be approved and badges will be issued to them. Further plea is that Ghulam Husain the clerk of the thana has also appeared before you for the same purpose.

(Order:
The application requesting badges has been forwarded.)

(124, 16)

New badges much smaller than the older ones

Deputy kotwal to the King, 5 June

Your lordship,

The badges that had been issued to the barqandazes of the kotwali were very small in size therefore this humble one begs that thirty badges of the kind that were formerly given out to the barqandazes should kindly be given out so that the work of the government continues unimpeded. Whoever has a badge will be known to be a government servant and the work of government will proceed smoothly. Much obliged. May the kingdom's sun shine forever.

Humble,
Shaikh Mohammed Amir

(128, 12)

Barqandazes need to rent a separate room, can't sleep outside in the rain

Thanadar, Bhojla Pahari, to the C-in-C, 30 July

My lord,

In the barrack of the thana, the section for the barqandazes is too small, and since the assumption of governance by his majesty the number of barqandazes has increased therefore there is no space left for the cots. They managed to tide over during the summer by laying their cots out in the open in the bazaars, etc., but now that the rainy season is here there are enormous difficulties. In this situation if they are permitted to rent a room near the thana at two rupees a month then it will be an act of great benevolence. Dutifully submitted, with the greatest respects, may the kingdom's sun shine forever.

Devoted,
Mohammed Mirza Amani

(122, 22)

Address the King as 'Protector of the Poor'

Deputy kotwal to all the thanadars, 27 July

Since you usually address his majesty as 'your exalted majesty' when you send petitions and submissions to him, therefore it is being directed that from this date you should, at the beginning of your submission, write 'Protector of the Poor', not his exalted majesty. Act firmly.

Khuda Bakhsh Khan

(Receipts and seals of all the thanadars)

(120, 142)

An officer from Paharganj seeks promotion

Saadullah Khan of Paharganj thana to the C-in-C, 30 June

My lord,

The submission of this servant is this that from the day Almighty God consigned those kafirs to hell and illuminated the faith, this devoted one was serving at Mahalganj under Paharganj thana and had been posted for four–five years and two barqandazes served under this humble one. The barqandazes went away the same day and although I had friendship and acquaintance with many in that town I too had intended to leave for home but one Akbar Ali, a resident of that town and a royal employee called this sinner and said you are now a royal employee and rest content and administer properly because you are familiar with everyone here. So I served in that place from that day and I was allotted a salary out of the royal munificence. Yesterday when I came to the Paharganj thana, the thanadar said you have been suspended. Therefore I am submitting this application to your lordship to enquire the charge due to which I have been suspended and I had actually hoped for advancement and your lordship had stated several times that the day we make progress we will confer advancement upon you. I pray that your lordship will dispense justice and will look after this devoted one so that I spend the rest of my days in praying for his prosperity. Dutifully submitted, may the kingdom's sun shine forever.

Humble,
Saadullah Khan

(185, 13)

Two visually impaired barqandazes need to be replaced

Kotwal to the King, 21 July

Persons named Khuda Bakhsh Khan and Lal Mohammed, barqandazes of thana Chandni Chowk who had been transferred from Rajghat and Faiz Bazaar, are impaired of sight and therefore it is difficult for them to do the work of government. The note from the jamadar of Chandni Chowk is attached. Therefore the prayer is that in their place, Madad Ali and Amjad Ali, two able-bodied and alert young men, be hired. The application has been forwarded to the royal secretariat.

With the greatest respects,
Kotwal

(111b, 65)

Thanadars must be vigilant and patrol their areas at night

Kotwal to all the thanadars, 30 August

In accordance with the orders you are being instructed to remain vigilant in your areas at night and to patrol your areas properly.

Syed Mubarak Shah

(Seals and receipts of all the thanadars)

(130, 228)

Officers of Dariba thana absent, orders sent there are not executed

Deputy kotwal to the C-in-C, 26 July–3 September

The orders that go out from the court and the kotwali to the Dariba thana are not executed and when an order reaches there no officer can be found and it comes back for the same reason. There is no thanadar or clerk or other officers to receive the orders, just a couple of completely illiterate barqandazes are to be found. A further plea is that there is no officer at night at the said thana nor during the day except for the barqandazes, can't say if anyone turns up for a couple of hours. If the senior officers don't turn up why would juniors be present there, at the time of sending circular notes nobody can be found there and in this way there is nothing but loss of government work.

Khuda Bakhsh Khan

(45)

Thanadars are lax in executing kotwali orders

Kotwal to the C-in-C, 26 July–3 September

The commands that are issued from the kotwali to the thanadars of the city are not promptly acted upon, instead of executing them the thanadars keep the orders aside and do not show the effort and application that is required of them. Therefore this petition that an edict be sent to all the thanadars of the city to show promptitude and alacrity in acting upon the orders of the kotwali. For the rest, his lordship is the master.

Kotwal

(45)

Reprimand for thanadar of Bhojla Pahari—he is penitent

C-in-C to the thanadar, Bhojla Pahari, 14 August

It has been learnt from the submission of the kotwal that you do not show alacrity in obeying the orders of the kotwal, therefore you are being instructed that if in future you do not show alacrity in acting upon the instructions and notes from the kotwal you will meet with a dire punishment.

(Response:

The devoted one was privileged to behold your exalted note. I will act in accordance with the instructions and I have never shown any delay or dereliction in obeying orders from the kotwali. Whatever orders have come at any time have been immediately complied with. I will now show greater zeal in executing orders from the kotwal. With the greatest respects, may the kingdom's sun shine forever.

Devoted,
Mohammed Mirza Amani)

(122–32)

Daily reports to be sent to Nawab Ahmed Quli Khan

C-in-C to the kotwal, 8 August

In accordance with his majesty's orders you are being directed that the reports, etc., of the kotwali department and all the thanas under you that you used to send to the court of Ihtiramuddaulah Bahadur, from this date you should send the information and report of each act to the kuchehri of Samsamuddaulah Nawab Ahmed Quli Khan Bahadur and inform every thanadar of this change too. Let everyone act promptly on this and send a copy of this edict to each thana and inform them and send a receipt back to us.

(120, 175)

King summons all thanadars to pay nazars on the festival of Baqrid

Kotwal to all the thanadars, 1 August

After greetings let this be clear that a royal edict from his majesty to the effect that at 2 p.m. all the thanadars of the city should present themselves before him in order to present nazars on the occasion of Id ul Zuha. Therefore all of you are being put to trouble to ensure that at the appointed hour you should all present yourselves at the durbar in front of his resplendent majesty. In case the order is not complied with you are likely to earn the royal wrath.

Syed Mubarak Shah

(120, 158)

Thanadar, Begumpura, executed written orders but the kotwali denies issuing them

Thanadar, Begumpura, to the kotwal, 2 September

In accordance with the circular issued yesterday, Dahimma and Chana and others listed in the circular were summoned and dispatched to the kotwali along with the jamadar of the thana. It was learnt through the jamadar that the kotwal and the deputy kotwal and the clerks of the thana stated unanimously that we had not summoned the people dispatched nor was any circular issued from the kotwali summoning them, on whose order have you brought them here. Your worship, it is worth reflection that a circular was received from the kotwali summoning six wood sellers from this area and how was it possible to not obey an order from the kotwali and it is a habit of this humble one that the moment an order arrives it is immediately executed and if it is not obeyed I may be considered worthy of censure. This is how the Kotwal Saheb appreciates my services that when an order is obeyed I am questioned, it is a problem if I act and a problem if I don't. However, it is done. I now urge the respected one to investigate on whose orders was this circular issued and who had called for the wood sellers. Outwardly the circular states the name of Khuda Bakhsh Khan, deputy kotwal, at the end. I beg for the matter to be enquired into and to be informed about it forthwith as to whether in future circulars issued by the kotwali are to be implemented or not.

Mohammed Amir Ali

(130, 238)

Four barqandazes refuse to execute orders, if they begin to rebel how will the work of government be conducted

Kotwal to the C-in-C, 26 July–3 September

My lord,

The petition of the thanadar of Turkman Gate in the matter of negligence and laxity of the barqandazes is being attached. It states that at twelve o'clock at night, a note was received from the kotwali requisitioning four water carriers. So the clerk called out all the barqandazes and asked them to get four water carriers whereupon Ghazi Khan, etc., four barqandazes who were on duty when asked to go they said we are not going just now, we will get them in the morning and such urgent orders come every day. Eventually, they did not go at night and then in the morning the clerk had to issue them written orders and only then did they go. If this goes on and the barqandazes do not obey the command of the officers then how will the work of government get done. Earlier too a complaint about the barqandazes had been sent in by the said thanadar. If the barqandazes do not obey their officers then it will be impossible for government orders to be executed. If every barqandaz makes bold to rebel [to do ghadar] and at a time of urgency begins to make excuses then that will be the end of it. Therefore the devoted one is hopeful that Ghazi Khan and the four barqandazes will be dismissed and then they will learn their lesson otherwise they will not obey anyone, therefore this petition is being sent to your lordship.

Syed Mubarak Shah

(45)

Hyder Ali, barqandaz, who rioted and created disorder being sent to the kotwali

Kotwal to the thanadar of Dariba, 3 July

Please send Hyder Ali and Mohammed Khan, barqandazes of your thana, to the kotwali right away so that their statements could be recorded. If you hear anything about one Hyder Ali and that other rascal send them also to the kotwali. Let there be no delay.

Syed Mubarak Shah

(Response:
As per the exalted one's instructions, Hyder Ali is being sent to the kotwali for his statement and it was Hyder Ali, barqandaz, who rioted and created disorder, not Mohammed Khan.)

(111b, 30)

All the weapons owned by the residents are to be impounded, but nobody should be insulted during the searches

C-in-C to the kotwal, Undated

It has been learnt that many residents of the city keep muskets, guns and other weapons in their houses. You are therefore instructed to impound all the swords, guns, etc., wherever their existence is learnt about. If they hand it over freely then it is best, otherwise forcibly search their houses and seize the goods mentioned and have it sent over. But be very careful during the search that except for swords, guns and bullets no harm should accrue to anybody's house. Nobody should misbehave with them or insult them. You are made responsible for the good conduct, if any complaints are made on this score, you will be held accountable.

The government has learnt that there is a gun at the house of a resident of Hauz Qazi, so you are asked to search his house and recover the weapon and send him here.

(110, 294)

The badmash Afzal Beg releases the conscripted workers

Thanadar, Bhojla Pahari, to the kotwal, Undated

Today, in execution of your order, four barqandazes of this thana had been sent to requisition a hundred coolies and diggers. Afzal Beg, the notorious badmash, confronted the barqandazes and stated that you take people from here without my orders, [but] we too are rulers here [and] if you use force, we will stand up to you and use force too. He is well known to all in the city for his ways and how will people work if this goes on? Therefore it is being reported to you for information so that you do whatever you see best and whatever you order shall be carried out. The coolies and barqandazes who had been conscripted were freed by him and he said if you are armed, we too are armed.

Mirza Mohammed Khan Beg

(124, 327)

Soldiers guarding a begum's house seize
the impounded carriages but later beg forgiveness

Thanadar, Guzar Qasimjan, to the kotwal, 5 August

After greetings and salutations, the submission is this that in execution of your command carts, animals and diggers had been confiscated from Ajmeri Gate and were sent to the kotwali with Kale Khan barqandaz. When they reached the outhouse of Begum Sahiba Zinat Mahal, the soldiers posted there as patrol forcibly took away the carriages from the barqandazes of the thana and in fact abused this humble one too.

They roundly abused the barqandazes and loaded their guns and fired; and when he made to retaliate, the people of the bazaar interceded and sent him back to the thana. They kept the confiscated carriages and when towards that evening the devoted one learnt of the situation, a note was sent to the C-in-C apprising him of the situation. The soldiers appeared in front of the horsemen of Samsamuddaulah Bahadur and said we will not do anything like this again, we have forbidden all our soldiers from doing any such thing, do not dispatch the note; therefore I desisted from doing so. Now a command has arrived from his lordship summoning Kale Khan, who has been sent there with an application. Kindly pay heed to the situation, I did nothing except on orders and neither did the barqandaz do anything wrong. Since it was important to inform, therefore I have reported the matter.

Mirza Mohammed Khan Beg

(124, 173)

The groom of Prince Khizr Sultan conscripted as a labourer

Deputy kotwal to the darogha, Dariba thana, 8 August

After salutations, an ordinance has been issued by the Colonel Saheb Khizr Sultan with the content that his groom has been conscripted along with the coolies by the thanadar of Dariba. He should be released, therefore you are being informed that the groom Ghasita should be released immediately on receipt of this note and if he has been sent elsewhere, then inform Colonel Saheb's servant where he has gone.

Bhau Singh

(Response:
Ghasita the groom had been sent along with the doolie-bearers who had been dispatched to the kotwali, he is not here that he could be released but is at the kotwali.
Will be careful in the future.

Kunwar Lal)

(131, 75)

Pyrotechnists summoned for putting out fire don't know how to fire rockets

Deputy kotwal to the darogha of the magazine, 7 August

This concerns the matter of the command issued by the C-in-C; in accordance with it you are directed to identify all the pyrotechnists who can fire rockets and send them to the kotwali immediately upon seeing this note.

(Response:
The pyrotechnists in this factory were asked the question you had enquired about in your note and they said we have never fired a rocket nor do they know how to do so, they are only familiar with embroidering; therefore the pyrotechnists of the magazine were not sent before your exalted presence and their response is being communicated to you.

Mir Rajab Ali)

(130, 36)

Craftsmen of rocket makers summoned for repairing rockets

Deputy kotwal to the thanadar, Guzar Allahabad, 9 August

The rockets that have gone to Hakim Ahsanullah Khan saheb's house to put out the fire are not working [and] the upper portion of the house is now cracking, therefore you are instructed to get the rocket of the fire annihilator repaired through the craftsmen of your area so that work may be resumed and the fire put out.

(Response:
The craftsmen of the rocket makers live in the Kauria Pul area and none of them live in this area, therefore the barqandazes have been urged to send the rocket makers of Kauria Pul here and the craftsmen here will be made to learn from them.

Mir Amanat Ali Khan)

(130, 40)

Fire annihilator needs to be repaired

Deputy kotwal to Samsamuddaulah Bahadur, 12 August

My lord,

The submission is that the servant had taken hundreds of water carriers to put out the fire and the fire that was put out began to rage again and the rockets that had been sent were defective and they could not spray strongly enough on the terrace, especially since the stairs were broken because of the fire. The water carriers are unable to function effectively, therefore the delay. I have done what I could. If the fire annihilators were repaired, the fire could have been contained and I have sent all the help that I could and I would/will inform you as soon as the fire is put out.

Devoted,
Khuda Bakhsh Khan

(Note on the letter:
If the annihilator can be repaired better at the kotwali, have it done and send it here. There should be no delay in the matter because the government stands to lose property worth hundreds of rupees in this fire; no negligence will be tolerated.)

(130, 88)

Four senior Hindus summoned by the C-in-C

Circular to all the thanadars, 9 August

You are being instructed to arrange for four senior men of the Hindu qaum from your areas and to send them to the kotwali. Do not be negligent for these men have to be forwarded to Mirza Mughal Bahadur.

Deputy kotwal

(130, 46)

Four able men summoned from each mohalla

C-in-C to the kotwal, 8 August

You are being instructed to ensure that four men capable and experts from each mohalla should be sent to his majesty through the thanadars, let this be clear that it is not important to call those people to the kotwali.

(130, 37)

Canal running through the fort needs to be repaired

Deputy kotwal to the manager of the canal, 19 May

The royal order is that the water of the canal does not reach inside the fort and the channel has completely dried up, therefore you are being instructed to clear the pathway so that water can flow inside the fort, otherwise write what the situation is.

Abdul Hakim Khan

(126, 4)

Heirless property of a manufacturer attached by the government

Thanadar, Guzar Itiqad Khan, to the kotwal, 2 July

My lord,

On the third of this month, Chaitram chowkidar of Kabuli Gate bazaar came and stated that the two-storeyed house left behind by Harsukh Teli, deceased, which due to lack of claimants had been confiscated and had been lying under government lock was occupied at night by Budhha Teli. The said Budhha was immediately summoned and kept under watch at the thana and was released after bail was guaranteed by Lachhman Teli. My lord, the status of the case is this that Harsukh Teli was blind and heirless and used to be employed in selling tobacco and betel nuts. It has been two years since he died and the two attached houses which belonged to him had been confiscated by the government due to lack of heirs and the above-mentioned Teli had filed a claim staking ownership in the civil court, which was yet undecided when the city was overtaken by rioting and killing. Under these circumstances, Budhha was let off and he went and put a lock on the confiscated government property. If Budhha had not taken over the house and had not put his own lock there, he would have been presented to the royal court for reasserting his claim. Whatever happened has been stated.

Humbly,
Faiztalab Khan

(Note on the letter:
Kotwal to C-in-C
The application of the thanadar of Guzar Itiqad Khan regarding the charge of the reoccupation of the locked government property against Budhha Teli and regarding summoning him to the thana and releasing him on the bail of Lachhman Teli has reached the kotwali and is being attached with this note. It is being forwarded with the report to your lordship.

Devoted,
Syed Mubarak Shah, kotwal

The papers have been entered at the secretariat.
Order—The kotwal of the city should protect the property.
Note by the kotwal—In accordance with your order a note has been sent to the thanadar of Guzar Itiqad Khan to protect the government property and the kotwali too will keep an eye on it.)

(123, 30)

Proclamation about heirless property: if no claimants come forward in fifteen days it will be entered in the royal treasury

A proclamation order by the kotwali, 5 August

The property of a woman called Harkunwar, resident of Dariba, as a case of there being no heirs, has been brought to the notice of this kotwali from Dariba thana. Therefore in accordance with the orders of his excellency, this proclamation is issued that if there are any heirs or claimants to the property they should present themselves within fifteen days of the issuance of this notice and take possession of the property after presenting evidence for their claims. Otherwise, after the passage of the deadline, the property will be entered in the royal treasury.

(120, 165)

Thanadar consigns dead blind beggar to last rites with money found on him

Thanadar, Bhojla Pahari, to the C-in-C, 28 July

My lord,

Today at about one o'clock Mendhu, the sweeper of Mir Aashiq lane, reported that one named Lachhu beggar, blind and heirless, belonging to the kahar qaum, who had been ill from fever for the last ten–fifteen days has died. Instantly, this humble one went to the said lane where the people of the area attested to his illness and two and a quarter rupees were recovered from him. After stating the particulars of the case, the corpse was handed over to the people of the mohalla when Munnan Kahar and others used the said money and added some of their own and consigned the body to flames in accordance with Hindu rituals. The case was reported in the diary and this note is being written to inform you.

With the greatest respects, may the kingdom's sun shine forever.

Faithful devotee,
Mirza Amani

(122, 17)

All the Bengalis of the city already arrested, two Bengali mendicants also being sent

Deputy kotwal to the C-in-C, 26 August

Some twenty days ago, an order had come from the General Saheb that the Bengalis staying at the *sarai* of Chhar Tanko should be sent here, therefore all the Bengalis of the city had been sent there. In pursuance of that order, today the thanadar of Badarpur has arrested and sent two Bengalis, residents of Benares, staying at Kali Bari, Begumpura, who were going to Mathura as mendicants. They are being sent as per the command. For the rest, my lord is the master.

Devoted,
Bhau Singh

(131, 107)

List of all Punjabi shopkeepers to be prepared and they are to appear in person before the C-in-C

C-in-C to the thanadar, Guzar Itiqad Khan, 9 August

It is desired that a list of all the buildings owned by Punjabi shopkeepers in the Guzar Itiqad Khan area be prepared and be sent to us with the clerk. Announce to all the Punjabis that they should present themselves before us tomorrow at 2 p.m. Whoever does not do so will be deserving of punishment.

(Response:
A list of all the Punjabi shopkeepers of this area was prepared and sent

with the clerk and all of them have been informed to present themselves as ordered.

Dutifully submitted,
Thanadar, Guzar Itiqad Khan)

(123, 172)

Karam Ali horseman's case pending for several days at the kotwali

Karam Ali, horseman, to the C-in-C, 3 August

My lord,

It has been several days since my case went to the kotwal and no decision has yet been taken on it; therefore this application that an order should be sent to the kotwal to decide quickly upon my case.

Karam Ali, horseman, third cavalry

(60, 465)

Shahjahani cannon to fire, nobody should stay inside dilapidated houses

C-in-C to the kotwal, 22 June

The big gun at Salimgarh of Shahjahani vintage is about to fire; therefore the order is that you should immediately, as far as possible, send out a proclamation that nobody should stay inside dilapidated houses.

(111a, 48)

Bail giver's worth ascertained

Deputy kotwal to the thanadar, Guzar Qasimjan, 10 August

A person named Baldeo Sahai, son of Dhonilal, is present and stands bail for Ram Prasad. Therefore you are being directed to enquire into his status and inform whether he owns property or not and if he has assets then what is the strength of those, whether it is up to seven or five hundred or less than that.

Khuda Bakhsh Khan

(Response:
Post-salutations, the submission is that in accordance with your order, the assets of Baldeo Sahai were investigated through Pakwai sweeper and people of the mohalla. It has been learnt that in truth his haveli is a pucca one and would not be less than a thousand rupees in worth. The sweeper and Ganga Sahai and Hardayal and Saligram were witnesses to the enquiry and their signatures are appended.

Mirza Umarkhan Beg
Signatures in Hindi of Pakwai, Hardayal, Ganga Sahai and Saligram, son of Nekchand)

(111c, 160)

Drain from a courtesan's house needs to be blocked as it empties into a noble's house

Prince Colonel Khizr Sultan to the kotwal, Undated

The house of Mirza Ghayasuddin is in Kucha Bulaqi Begum where a drain falls overhead from the house of Miranjan courtesan; therefore his majesty has ordered that the courtesan should block the part of the drain which falls in Mirza Ghayasuddin's house; therefore you are being directed to go there instantly and get the drain covered.

(111d, 109)

The concerned thanadar has got the drain blocked

Kotwal to Mirza Khizr Sultan, 4 September

My lord,

Acting on your directions, the drain from the house of Miranjan courtesan which used to fall in Mirza Ghayasuddin's house has been blocked through the intervention of the Nigambodh thanadar. This submission is made to inform you while the thanadar's note is attached.

With the greatest respects,
Devoted,
Syed Mubarak Shah

(103, 361)

Barqandazes required to act as guards for a criminal court

Kotwal to all the thanadars, 6 August

Send one barqandaz each from your thana with the bearer of this note to Mehtab Bagh in the exalted fort before Ghulam Ahmed Khan, the judge of the criminal court, as he wants to post them there. Send them right away, do not delay, act promptly.

Syed Mubarak Shah

(120, 168)

A ten-year-old boy separated from his family, relatives need to be identified

Kotwal to all the thanadars of the city, 22 May

The jamadar of the Nigambodh Ghat thana has sent a boy aged ten years, lost, without jewels, to this kotwali. Therefore you are all being given the trouble of identifying the relatives of the boy in the areas under your thana and in case of any identifications to ask them to come to the kotwali so that they may take their ward after presenting some evidence.

Dark complexioned, head clean shaven, a small tonsure, wearing a green kurta.

(120, 3)

Janki of Haveli Khanam reports her missing son

Kotwal to all the thanadars, Undated

After salutations, the word is that a woman named Janki, resident of Haveli Khanam, Turkman Gate, came and deposed that her son wearing an *angarkha* of coarse cloth and leather socks, three years old, of wheatish complexion, with small eyes, has gone missing since three o'clock. Therefore you are all urged to conduct a search in your areas after receiving this note.

(120, 201)

Two boys, three and seven years old, go missing

Kotwal to all the thanadars, 4 September

After greetings, the matter is that one Mir Mahboob Alam, horseman of the second cavalry, risala fourteenth regiment, arrived from Jhansi and Mir Ahmed Beg, risaldar, posted at the house of Naraindas banker came and deposed that two boys, one aged three and a half years, fair-complexioned, wearing an angarkha and cap, and the other aged seven, dark complexioned, wearing a pyjama and cap, have gone missing. Therefore you are all instructed that as far as possible have a search conducted for the two missing children.

(120, 196)

Five English books found behind Jama Masjid

Thanadar, Bhojla Pahari, to the kotwal, 21 May

After greetings and salutations, the submission is that right now in the morning Mohammed Khan, chowkidar of Jama Masjid, brought five volumes of English books and a leather saddle and stated that somebody had left this behind the Jama Masjid. Since it appears to be goods looted from a firangi which was plundered or stolen by a criminal of the city who then left it on the road for fear of being apprehended, this is being sent to you.

Mohammed Mirza Amani

(121, 4)

Modus operandi of the thief Ramzan, arrested by the thanadar of Bhojla Pahari

Kotwal to the C-in-C, 26 July–3 September

My lord,

The file of the thanadar of Bhojla Pahari about one named Abdul Ghafoor, resident of Bazaar Khanam, plaintiff, and Ramzan badmash, defendant, for the purpose of a registration challan has reached the court. It is clear from the statements of the thanadar that the thug Ramzan stole three rupees of the plaintiff from a knot in his sheet and handed it over to an accomplice because of which the stolen goods were not recovered from him. The statements of the witnesses confirm the fact of the theft of money. Although the defendant denies the charges of theft, he is a convicted offender and a known criminal. As per the thanadar's investigation, the charge of theft on the defendant has been proven; therefore he has been kept in the lock-up and the file of the case is being forwarded to you for consideration.

(45)

Three badmashes arrested for stealing a silver bracelet

Deputy kotwal to the C-in-C, 26 July–3 September

My lord,

The thanadar of Faiz Bazaar has sent persons named Jassu, Ilahi Bakhsh and Imam Bakhsh, all badmashes, along with their statements on the charge of taking a silver bracelet off the plaintiff. The plaintiff has charged the three defendants with stealing the silver bracelet off the wrist of his granddaughter aged one and a half years. Khwaja Bakhsh barqandaz stood witness that when I reached there, these three scoundrels were running away and the stolen good was recovered from the site, and Ram Prashad, witness for the plaintiff, testified how it had happened. The defendants resolutely denied the charge and each of them expressed unfamiliarity with the other. When the charge appeared to be correct, the thanadar of Faiz Bazaar sent the file and charged them and during investigation, the plaintiff deposed that they took off the bracelet and threw it into a well, and this appears to be the truth because it is a known practice among the thieves to throw away stolen goods at the time of arrest. The three defendants deny the charge of theft, but Jassu is a seasoned criminal and has been arrested in the past and he was the one who snatched the bracelet and the case seems quite clear and straightforward. The three accused are being sent to you along with the stolen and recovered bracelet.

Devoted,
Khuda Bakhsh Khan

(45)

The complainant found to be the guilty one

Thanadar, Chandni Chowk, to the kotwal, 28 July

Respected Kotwal Saheb,

After due respects, the submission is that yesterday one man named Radha Kishan came and complained that some ornaments had been stolen from his kothi and he wanted the houses of his tenants searched on the suspicion that they were the ones most likely to have stolen them. My lord, as per the complainant's request, one house was searched yesterday, but nothing was found and today, a shop of one of the defendants was searched and a pair of gold rings was found. The screws of the door of this shop have been loosened, so it would not be surprising if the complainant himself threw it inside the shop.

Thanadar, Chandni Chowk

(61, 247)

Frames and panes of a collapsing house may be given away to soldiers

C-in-C to Ram Charan Singh, subedar, police platoon posted at Kothi Ballabgarh, 25 July

Your petition containing the following passed our eyes that at your post at the compound of the Ballabgarh kothi, excessive rain had caused the collapse of the building and that you would carry out whatever order was given out regarding the frames of doors and windows that survived the collapse. You are being instructed that if the forces want to take away doors and windows, then allow them to do so because it is part of their area and possession.

C-in-C

(Response:
To the respected general, C-in-C
My lord,

In accordance with your orders, the frames, etc., have been given to the carpenter and a receipt has been taken which has been sent to your lordship.

Servant,
Ramcharan Singh, subedar, police platoon)

(115, 43)

Wazir Khan and Noor Khan, accused of plundering a mohalla, being sent to the C-in-C

Syed Mubarak Shah, kotwal, to the C-in-C, 22 June

In accordance with the exalted and beneficent one's order, Noor Khan and Wazir Khan are being sent in the custody of Adil Khan barqandaz on the charge of plundering a mohalla.

Dutifully submitted, may the kingdom's sun shine forever.

Syed Mubarak Shah, kotwal

(103, 27)

FAQIRS, LOITERERS AND BRIGADE MAJORS
The dangerous liaisons of spies

The uprising was as much a war of information and propaganda as a military one. The rebels made full use of modern forms of communication available to them by printing proclamations, pamphlets and newspapers and by attacking telegraph poles and post routes set up by the British. The telegraph, it has been said, won the war for the British but an equally critical role was played by human intelligence. In addition to newsletters, court *akhbarat*s of the old variety, there was a network of spies that conveyed information about the events in the city to British intelligence officers. As the British force arrived at the ridge to besiege the city in the first week of June, its intelligence officers led by William Hodson began to reconstruct their information network in the city, relying mainly on merchants, spies and deserters from the rebel side. Mir Rajab Ali, the head munshi of Hodson, got in touch with Jiwan Lal, formerly a munshi in the justice department. Through his own retainers and through his daily visits to Bahadur Shah's court, Jiwan Lal supplied crucial news of the state of the city to the English. Jiwan Lal's diary was later published by Thomas Metcalfe as *Two Native Narratives*. There was also Gauri Shankar, a brigade major and one of the leading officers on the rebel side who was close to Mirza Mughal, who wrote frequently to the British. This was in addition to information supplied by newswriters, one of the most important being the representative of the Jhind state whose ruler relayed it to the British in Punjab from where it spread all over India.

The rebels were often superior in terms of numbers, but not in information. They were unaware of how precarious the British position on the ridge was and failed to make the final push on more than one occasion. We have already noted the importance of timely information reaching key British officers in the Punjab where all Indian soldiers were summarily and quickly disarmed.

The spies worked in difficult conditions and conveyed information on tiny scraps of paper. Many of the texts translated below were written on strips smaller than one's palm, which were hidden away in pipes or stitched on to clothes. The city's gates were not easy to cross for the soldiers manned them diligently and were suspicious of all unexplained movement. People crossing the Jamuna bridge could be arrested for doing so. Often, soldiers didn't even allow corpses to be carried through the gates. The soldiers raided the house of the King's prime minister, Ahsanullah Khan, on more than one occasion, accusing him of corresponding with the British and even plundered it once. An atmosphere of dread and suspicion overlay the whole city.

The rebels' fear of spying was reflected in the number of people who were arrested for loitering or for being unable to explain their movements. Some of them were killed on the spot or blown off a gun when discovered to be spies. Clearly, it was not negligence which allowed information to be conveyed out of the city.

The spies' letters in the first part of this section present a livelier picture of the city than later narratives. Their sense of immediacy conveys a picture of a city in great movement, where the air is charged with tension, expectancy and fear. We already know about the role played by religious rhetoric in the mobilization of people. The first two letters included here show us another aspect—the role played by maulvis and pandits in the actual organization of battle. The mosques became centres of resistance and served as camps, and the astrological predictions of the pandits sometimes determined battle timings. The presence of doctors in each unit also informs us of the spirit of wider participation in the battle.

Rivalries between officers often impeded the work of the rebels. In Delhi, Bakht Khan was made the lord governor, but his promotion was resented by other officers and as the letter below demonstrates, they could sometimes leave each other stranded. In addition, there is constant mention of Jhajjhar, Bahadurgarh, Ballabgarh and other principalities surrounding Delhi. The King wrote repeatedly to them requesting money and resources—requests that often went unfulfilled.

The many references to the court and 'doing court' refer to the CoM that we have encountered in another section. A startling document is the letter which describes a court conducted by soldiers where all officers were dismissed on charges of corruption. Another mentions a court which deliberated on crowning Prince Jawan Bakht as king, provided his mother Zinat Mahal paid enough money.

Information about the movement and impending arrivals of troops, and of the fate of other rebel centres could trigger hope or cause setbacks to the morale of the soldiers located within the city. Gunpowder and other necessities of war were obviously at a premium and when desperate, the government sent people to Mathura and Sohna to procure it.

The last few translations in this section are of documents outlining the arrests and the statements of those who were accused of spying. Mendicants, loiterers, lunatics, deserters from the British and sick persons, in other words, anybody, could be arrested on the charge of spying. The rebels were not unaware of the importance of spies, but it was not possible for them to control all movement of information from the city, especially when some of the highest figures such as Zinat Mahal were involved in communication with the British. The fact that most of those who were suspected of spying were actually sent to the police or the C-in-C also points to the strength of the administration.

In these documents, the word *sarkar* or government refers invariably to that of the East India Company. It is almost as if, as far as the spies were concerned, the legitimate sarkar continued to be that of the erstwhile regime.

Mullahs preach a holy war against the British

Letter from Gauri Shankar, 6 July

The mujahideen are very popular in the city. The maulvis give speeches in all the mosques and exhort people to do jihad against the Christians. The mujahideen are pouring in from all directions. The fourteenth regiment and two platoons have come here from Jhansi and have brought along one lakh rupees. The generals took oath before the King that they will offer the early evening prayer at the Jama Masjid only after the battlefront of the ridge had been conquered. But when the army returned in the evening, there was great embarrassment and all the officers remained in council all through the night. They have decided that this time around the force should be deployed near the Gadariya Gate so that supplies can be maintained. There was a proclamation throughout the city that the King has decided to pay twelve rupees capital and one rupee daily for the forces and they will continue with the other perks which had been in existence at the time of the British.

(18, 1)

A *mahurat* that on the day of Badshar there will be a great battle and the Mahabharata will be repeated and then you will become rulers

Letter from an unknown spy, Undated

You might know that Pandit Harichandra, who was implicated in the case of Sardar Ranjur Singh, is here. That kafir is spoiling the Hindus here. He encourages the officers of the army by saying that through his expertise in astrology and astronomy, he can see that they will rule in these parts. And he has given a mahurat that on the day of Badshar, which is on Wednesday, there will be [such] a great battle such that the mare's hoof will be dripping with blood. And on this ground a Mahabharata, like the one that took place at the time of the rajas of yore, the Kauravas and Pandavas, will be repeated and then you will become rulers. Every person in the force believes in what he says so much so that the attacks happen on the day and the moment chosen by him.

So General Bakht Khan feels that there should be a battle every day and not a single day should go by without engagement. For this purpose he has appointed three units so that one unit fights every day.

Disaffection within the army rises day by day. And many sepoys, both infantry and horsemen, some merely with their clothes and others with their possessions and belongings keep leaving. One very bad thing is that gatekeepers do not allow the troopers to leave. The Gujar community is very wicked. They took a bugle and a flag as a reward from the Emperor saying that they will not let any sepoy leave. So when people flee, they catch them and seize all their valuables and possessions. Some escape them and many go their way.

There is a hospital in every unit. A hakim who has come with the medicines is busy treating the soldiers.

The ruler of Jhajjhar has not yet responded to the call for money but he is greatly pressed. The Ballabgarh ruler has replied. He says that Abdul Hakim, his former manager, has looted his treasury and is presently at Delhi. He says, if you can send him, I will take the money from him and send it to you. Or you can take it from him in Delhi. Let us see what happens but that person is a friend of Hakim Ahsanullah Khan, the confidant of the King.

Mirza Jawan Bakht, son of Zinat Mahal, who had gone to Malagarh across the Jamuna, returned yesterday. Zinat Mahal has come to her house in the city from the fort. Nawab Aminuddin Khan and Ziauddin, the two brothers, went to meet her. They paid some nazar and returned.

And this is a clear advice that the shot which comes from that side does not cause any damage here and does not reach the fort either. In my opinion if the cannon is placed in Qudsia Bagh and a shot fired from there, it will certainly reach the fort. And if the force can be increased near Ajmeri Gate and a cannon fired, the shot will certainly find its mark.

(15, 19)

The Meerut and Delhi armies at loggerheads with each other

Letter from Gauri Shankar, 19 July

Yesterday, that is on Saturday afternoon, the situation is this that Bakht Khan, general of the Bareilly army, and Mohammed Shafi, risaldar, and the subedars of other platoons including generals and colonels, went to the fort and presented a petition to the King that the existing Delhi army and those newly arrived from Meerut are busy fighting with each other and out of greed for money do not go to the front and do not obey orders. Upon this, three generals were appointed. Bakht Khan, the general for the armies of Bareilly, Jabawli, Nasirabad and Jhansi, and Sham Singh, the second general for the Meerut and Delhi armies, and there is another general whose name and whose army is not yet known. So today, on 19 July, one general's forces have launched an attack. The name of the general and other details will be sent after the fighting is over.

When in the evening the officers took their leave the King recited the following couplet:

The skies have felled us down, I have lost all rest and sleep
Departure is certain, whether one goes in the morning or evening.

The news given out about the two Jhansi platoons is false. The truth is that two platoons had started out from there but some of them were detained by Jiyaji Rao Scindia and six companies, three cannons and one regiment managed to come here. Whatever property and wealth and horses and carriages they found, they looted and murdered all the Englishmen and Christians who were present in Jhansi.

A horseman called Alif Khan has brought a saheb here. This writer had gone to see him there but because of the attack the army people did not allow me in. I will find out more about it and write. It is reported that the thirteenth regiment is on its way from Kanpur. The Agra force has come to Mathura in a state of great disappointment and is demanding money from Lakshmichand Seth.

(19, 10)

The army keeps strict vigil, the pickets are guarded and forty maunds of gunpowder are manufactured every day

Letter from Gauri Shankar, Undated

Yesterday, Mirza Mughal came to the kotwal of the city to discuss ways of raising money for the supplies to the army and told him that there is a shortage of supplies in the army, ask all the traders of the bazaar to supply provisions to all the soldiers of the army, money will be paid when salaries are distributed. So the kotwal is pressurizing all the traders in the city but nothing has been decided yet.

The King had sent word to General Bakht Khan through Mirza Mughal that he should go with his troops and help out the besieged forces of Nimach, but Bakht Khan refused saying that I am not anyone's servant.

Food is still available for the army for some time, but there is great shortage of money. The remaining survivors of the Nimach force are said to be in Maduhti district. One platoon and cavalry and two carts of magazines along with four cannons which had gone to Nangal and Najafgarh day before yesterday returned yesterday afternoon. Some soldiers of that camp are coming back in a bad state. It is not a fighting force. From all the three platoons some five to six hundred soldiers have come back here while the rest have disappeared. Whoever managed to get away has left.

At night Bakht Khan's contingent had gone to the Gadariya front and came back in the morning.

From the day that a surprise raid occurred the night guard has been made very strict. On the city's boundaries and the battlefronts the army keeps strict vigil and remains awake. The pickets are alertly guarded and there is a bugle master everywhere.

The news of the arrival of the Gwalior contingent gets stronger every day.

The magazine remains active where forty maunds of gunpowder are manufactured every day. Although not all of it is used.

On the tenth of Muharram, going by astrological predictions and soothsayers, a lot more force has been called for. The Muslims are hoping to attain martyrdom on that day.

The digging at Salimgarh continues apace. People say to the King that treasures of past kings are buried here, with some even mentioning exact spots, but nothing has emerged yet.

(20, 14)

The King reconciled the officers to each other and they all came to an agreement and General Sidhara Singh who was alienated has now been mollified

Letter from Gauri Shankar, 5 August

Yesterday, on Monday, General Mohammed Bakht Khan went to visit the King, as has been the accepted practice. The King took him to the prayer room and expressed his resentment. He said, 'If you want to stay then stay, otherwise you are welcome to leave. Why did you let down General Sidhara Singh's camp so? First of all his men went to fight and stayed in the water for two days and fought. You did not send him any help and on top of that your men also looted the supplies sent to his unit.'

It has been heard that with the aid of the Raja of Bikaner, the [British] government's control has been established in Hansi Hissar. There is a report here that some forces will go to Haryana district to engage them.

So there is a meeting of all the officers at the CoM. The fact is that General Sidhara Singh, the officer of the Nimach camp, is rather upset at the conduct of the officers here. There are reports that he intends to go to Rajasthan to seek help from one of the kings there. It has also been learnt that he has taken some money from the king of Chittor as well as ten thousand rupees from the king of Alwar's men after surrounding them at Kot Potli. Khembaji Rao, a sardar of the Alwar army, is also with him along with his men since the battle of Agra.

A religious leader has come to the King with several followers from

Swat Mir with the intention of launching a jihad. He has presented a sword to the King and swore that a huge contingent under the religious leader is coming to help the King, and there are rumours that it is very near. Mohammed Shafi, risaldar, claims that their strength is fourteen thousand, and their leader is near. Earlier we suspected an English hand in this but now that doubt has been cleared. There are many views about its location. Some claim it has reached Rai ki Sarai, some say it has reached Karnal in Panipat and some say it is in Shahabad. God knows better. Madho Narain is also in that force on behalf of the raja of Ballabgarh and he has brought the news of that force to the King. His note arrived here through Kale Saheb and was read before the King.

A petition was received by the King from the raja of Ballabgarh saying that it is his responsibility to take care of the supplies, and that from ancient days the fort of Tughlaqabad has been under his control and so it should be restored to him. His plea was accepted and Ramzani Zamindar was appointed to that fort and the arrangement of supplies by the said raja has begun.

You would know of that Major Badruddin of the tenth regiment who was a great friend of Major Fisher. It has now been discovered that Major Fisher suffered a great loss from the evil-doers. Major Badruddin's real brother Saduddin Khan is the tehsildar of Ambala. It does not become the government to appoint the relatives of such a traitor to positions of high rank.

Today the King reconciled the officers to each other and they all came to an agreement and General Sidhara Singh who was alienated has now been mollified.

In the evening there is a parade of all the camps. Most likely there will be an attack today or tomorrow evening and three units will be deployed for that. As far as the mujahids of Swat are concerned, a doubt has now crept in about them among the army that the English must have set them up, otherwise it is impossible for such a large contingent to come unchecked all the way from Peshawar.

(19, 2)

The King is now very upset with the army and does not come out of the palace

Letter of a spy, 10 August

Today, on Sunday, the writer went to visit the army. The news from the front is that the cannon fight continues apace. From this side the deployment has been strengthened a little and more cannons have been brought out from the magazine and have been sent to the front. The mutual alienation and enmity between the officers increases day by day. Mirza Mughal Beg dislikes the rule of the generals and the generals dislike him. In a while the fight will worsen. There is a durbar in the court today and all the officers of the commission will gather there, let us see what turns out.

Two English soldiers who came here in a bad state are imprisoned in Bakht Khan's camp. To make preparations for the gunpowder manufacture, the kothi of Nawab Abdur Rahman Khan of Jhajjhar has been earmarked. It is located in Daryaganj.

Bahadur Ali Khan of Bahadurgarh has been granted the subedari of Rohtak. The news is that some soldiers, infantry and cavalry, will go with him. Information will be sent as soon as they depart from here. Today, that is, Monday the tenth, the above-mentioned Khan left with his followers but he did not get any force to accompany him.

Yesterday, the officers of the commission held court and decided to relieve Hakim Saheb of his duties and to free him. So from that day Hakim Saheb remains free and aloof.

In the fort, Prince Mughal Beg has made up with Bakht Khan and the King has told all the officers that I don't need this kingship and that I have handed over all the princes to you, you may keep them if you want or let them go. Just have me sent to Qutub Saheb in Mehrauli. Upon this, the officers held court again and told the King that they would reply to him soon. General Sidhara Singh did not take part in these proceedings; he has been taken into confidence by Zinat Mahal and Nawab Ahmed Ali Khan. Meanwhile, Hakim Saheb has been questioned.

As a matter of fact, Mirza Mughal wishes to depose the King and crown himself. He decided to go to the front to get stationed there. Sidhara Singh also wanted to go there but Mirza Mughal did not let him go.

The King is now very upset with the army and does not come out of the palace. Another court will be held today to bring the King around.

It has been learnt that the force that had gone to Hansi had a skirmish with the government forces. A few hundred horsemen along with a few risaldars escaped and have come here. Some twelve risaldars and six sawars and their mares have come here in a wounded condition. As a result the fourteenth regiment along with two cannons and magazines has been prepared to help them out. It will leave by today evening via Najafgarh.

In yesterday's fighting, a cannon was destroyed. There are rumours that some reinforcements are on their way to Delhi from Morar near Gwalior. Some claim that the king of Gwalior did not allow this force to make its way. The majority say that the Morar troops have crossed the river Chambal from Gwalior and are about to arrive. In the city, there is a lot of activity on the collection of levies front. Mirza Khizr Sultan, the younger son of the King, is in charge of these matters.

(15, 3/4)

Twenty lakh rupees have gone to Mirza Mughal at the fort from Sidhara Singh's camp, so an order has been issued for the distribution of salaries to all soldiers

Letters of spies to English officials, 16 August

The attack that was launched on Danda sometime before dusk was carried out by Mirza Mughal's camp.

I visited the camps located inside the city. Yesterday, some hundred–two hundred Tilangas, fully armed, dressed and mounted, were on their way to leave the city when some rebel forces stopped them and reported it to the fort. The King called them to the court and asked them why they were upset. They said our wives and families would be worried about us, and there is nothing left to eat here, that is why we are going.

So the King asked them to deposit whatever arms and mounts they had and allowed them to go. He then openly declared in court that I do not care who goes or stays, I did not ask anybody to come here and I do not stop anyone, nor prevent anyone from leaving. Whoever wants to stay can do so, otherwise they can go away, I have no objections. I have detained these arms so that if the English come here I can hand it over to them. If the troops want them, they can take them, I have no stake in the matter.

The forces of Nawab Doondi along with their followers departed today. The cavalry of various other regiments are also on their way out. Now the army is employed in looking for provisions. In a few days, the suburbs of Delhi will be fully cleared.

A note from the princes demanding levies for rations has been prepared. When the King heard of it, he called for the note and studied it while expressing anger at the princes. The note demanded hundred rupees from some, and two hundred from others. The King examined the note and then tore it. He said he would not countenance raising money like that. So, on his own, he wrote down the names of eleven sardars from among Muslims and others. Nawab Aminuddin Khan and Ziauddin Khan, Hakim Abdul Haq, Raja Dambe Singh, and Saligram, Nawab Mohammed Ali Khan, and the sons of Zainuddin Khan Arif, the son of Nawab Mammo Khan, and Ahmed Mirza and others. He asked the princes to collect eleven lakh rupees from these people. Today Aminuddin Khan went to visit the King, and was told that he may rest assured, nothing would be demanded of him.

Today, that is Monday, this writer went to the army camp, and stayed for long at the camp of Sidhara Singh. I found the soldiers very demoralized. The soldiers all talk back to the officers and do not obey orders at all. The force will rebel because of the lack of supplies. The soldiers are crying out that if we are not paid, we will not stay. More than a hundred Tilangas made off today. Such departures and desertions continue every day. But Mirza Mughal Beg consoles the forces and every day, orders for the payment of salaries are issued, because of which some troops have remained; otherwise, all of them would have left by now. Today, twenty lakh rupees have gone to Mirza

Mughal at the fort from Sidhara Singh's camp, so an order has been issued for the distribution of salaries to all soldiers, which has reassured the soldiers a little.

(15, 5/6)

Mirza Mughal Beg deposed from his post of commanding general

Letter from a spy, 26 August

Today, on Tuesday, news came in the evening that the Nimach camp which had left yesterday, getting carried away with their bravado, crossed the Najafgarh bridge, and overtaking Bakht Khan's camp, gave battle thirteen miles from here. Because of the intensity of the fighting and the destruction of the bridge, the entire force was annihilated and all its treasures and artillery were captured by the benevolent government's army. And all the three platoons who are present at the front do not have any cartridges and Bakht Khan is sitting pretty with his camp and has sent no help. All the cavalry that had gone with Sidhara Singh has run away. A lot of the cavalry has come back here and the Najafgarh bridge which has been destroyed has left a big river between government and rebel forces. Some grenadiers were killed and the remaining city forces have gone to the front to do battle. Surely all the three platoons would have been decimated.

Mirza Mughal Beg was deposed from his post of commanding general yesterday so he has come to the city in anger.

Nawab Ahmed Ali Khan, the King's father-in-law, has been appointed the chief administrator. The reinforcements asked for from here have still not been sent. If General Bakht Khan who is merely four miles away cannot send forces to help, what will the army here do. Some one lakh shots which were sent with Sidhara Singh have been destroyed.

(15, 13)

Men have been sent to Sohna and Mathura to procure sulphur

Letter from Gauri Shankar, Undated

A British camp follower was arrested and along with him, a Sikh company of the government was also arrested. The condition of the government's forces was being enquired from him. He said that the news from the British camp is that there will be an attack from their side, but after a month, because this force will surrender on its own due to hunger. Then the attack will be launched. And the newly arrived Englishmen are straining for a quick attack. There is a very large force in the English camp.

The committee of levies at the court has suggested that Muslims are in general at one with us in our pleasure and pain, whereas the Hindus are the well-wishers of the Sahebs and in fact, are in unison with them. Therefore they suggested it would be appropriate to exempt the Muslims from compulsory levy and that the taxes for the maintenance of the army and for the court salaries should be collected from Hindus. So the Muslims were happy at this decision whereas there was great mourning in the Hindus' houses.

The ruler of Jhajjhar has still not sent the money that was demanded of him so the King and the leaders of the court are very angry with him. Malik Mirza Khizr Bakhsh, a prince, has been deputed to visit him, and he is getting ready to leave. Most probably, he will leave either today or tomorrow. The King showed his displeasure to General Abdus Samad Khan who is commanding the forces of Jhajjhar, and said, 'Write to that toady that the enemy forces are near, so he should not delay sending the required money'.

Yesterday, four days' worth salary was distributed to the army. Every mounted soldier was given three rupees and the infantry were paid one rupee each with a promise that they would receive more after eight days. The total forces in and out of the city amount to some seventeen thousand. Bakht Khan, the general from Bareilly, has a large number of cavalry and infantry; Sidhara Singh has one thousand five hundred cavalry and infantry soldiers, while within the city there are eleven thousand infantry and cavalry soldiers. These numbers are falling every day.

The force at Mahadpur, some hundred–two hundred mounted soldiers-strong, disappeared over the course of day before, yesterday and today due to starvation and hunger. Yesterday afternoon, five companies of foot soldiers and some two hundred newly employed cavalry were dispatched to Mehrauli to guard the front. One messenger has been sent there, he will come back and report the details.

The lack of sulphur has greatly hampered the preparation of gunpowder here. There is no sulphur available in the city. The stored amount is not sufficient to keep up the supply required by the forces. Therefore men have been sent to Sohna and Mathura to procure it. The two hundred kilos of sulphur sent by the raja of Ballabgarh is what is being used right now. There is a report that some forces will be sent to help Walidad Khan of Malagarh. It is not known yet whether the news of the approach of the government magazine will lead them to cross from Gadariya Gate or from somewhere else. Consequently, there have been rumours in the court since yesterday. The government should now make arrangements to post forces nearby, and should also deploy some units in Gurgaon.

(20, 11)

Soldiers conduct a court and arraign the officers

Letter from Gauri Shankar, 29 August

Till the evening yesterday, there was a great fight. Bakht Khan's contingent and the Nasirabad contingent and the force inside the city fought with great valour.

In the army, the Hindus and Muslims have taken mutual oaths that nobody is going to desert but some horsemen deserted today, and although they were stopped at the gate, it was to no avail. The soldiers run away every day and the market of desertion is hot. Formerly, the subedars and officers used to mutually hold court over the conduct of war and about raising revenues; now the sepoys have set that aside and have discharged them from the work of the court saying that they collect money in our name and then these officers pilfer it away and those who have the officers' ears are let off and the soldiers get nothing. The officers make merry while the soldiers starve, therefore the officers are dismissed and the soldiers would themselves conduct court for raising the money. So now, a hundred and fifty sepoys have been appointed to do court and on their suggestion, Nawab Ahmed Quli Khan, Hakim Abdul Haq and Nawab Hamid Ali Khan and some rich notables have been put under house arrest in the court pending the demand for contibutions. Three months' rent has been collected from the houses and the shops in the city as contribution to the war fund and has gone to the court. This then is the situation.

The writer had gone today to the gates to enquire into the state of the bastions at the parapet when it emerged that the Salimgarh gun continues to fire away and the cannons fired by the government do not impact Salimgarh and the Lal Gate's wicket gate has been opened for bathing at the Jamuna. The guns continue to fire at the kuchehri bastion and the movement of troops has completely stopped from Kashmiri Gate. The shots continue to fall in the city and in fact, a few passers-by and some soldiers of the Jalesar platoon at the mansion of Sikander Saheb were injured because of the shots. The church remains a steady target for government shots and in some places, the parapet has been damaged. The black bastion which is located near the Badru Gate and the Kabuli Gate has been damaged and its gun has fallen silent. In fact, this is the one bastion left and one door of the Lahori Gate is open and one is shut and now the movement of the troops happens through that door. Soldiers and guns have been sent via the Ajmeri and Delhi Gates and it moves outside along the city walls. At Kotla Firoze Shah, which is located outside the city's habitation, the sepoys suspect the presence of a treasure there and so it is being dug up.

Know also that the powder that was used in yesterday's fight has come from the earlier stock which is being distributed from inside the fort. The King has not come out since yesterday and no durbar has been held and there are reports that he is unwell.

(20, 20)

From the day that there was a riot over the arrest of Hakim Ahsanullah Khan, the King has not appeared outside

Letter from a spy, Undated

Today, that is Wednesday, a letter arrived from Lucknow stating that on the 23rd of July, the God-ordained government has taken possession of Awadh and the government forces have properly destroyed and pillaged Lucknow and now the cities of that area are being repressed. Fifty horsemen had gone to Nawab Akbar Khan of Pataudi to demand money and when they couldn't find him, they abducted his son instead. He asked, why do you take my son, the riders said we will let him off when the time is right. The nawab of Pataudi offered the soldiers food, and when they sat down to eat, he attacked them with his force, some eight or ten were killed and five were left. The nawab himself ran away. The zamindars from around Pataudi laid into it properly and this news has been about since yesterday. The mujahideen of Rampur and Shahjahanpur were going homewards by that route and there was also a caravan of doolie-bearers with them; when they reached Hapur, they ran into a gora force which killed everyone. One or two doolie-bearers who have come back narrated the whole story. It has been learnt that the horsemen who had gone yesterday to Pataudi were not actual soldiers but pretenders. The King has sent a missive to the nawab of Pataudi saying that they were not our riders.

From the day that there was a riot over the arrest of Hakim Ahsanullah Khan, the King has not appeared outside. The officers go there and present obeisance via the *khwaja sara*.

As per the instructions, the state of the front at Qudsia Bagh and at Kashmiri Gate was enquired into. There is no big gun at Kashmiri Gate, but there are six smaller ones and there are two big guns at the entrenchments that have been formed at Qudsia Bagh. Some say that these guns have been brought out from the fort and the shots of these guns strike the mansion of Thomas Metcalfe and this is the spot from where the guns fire most heavily at day and at night.

(19, 13)

The government should treat subjects with leniency and should be more indulgent

Letter from a spy, Undated

The residents of Haryana should be urged to recall the soldiers who are their brethren and should be assured that the government will not prosecute them. When the armies learn that the government has nothing against us or our families or our booty, then they will go away on their own and very few soldiers will be left here. Now at this time, the government should treat the subjects with leniency and should be more indulgent. This is a moment to be loving towards friends and to be merciful towards enemies. Know also that as far as possible, the government should try and put down the *balwa* [rebellion] by the Tilangas with affection and clemency. Wherever there is a large presence of Tilangas in the army, that spot should be overlooked during firing because the rebellion by the Tilangas and platoons and the army will not be easily put down. And a rebellion by the Tilangas is not a good thing and this uprising should not be regarded as sedition. And it is imperative to propagate this among the populace and the army that whoever acts to cause sedition will be heavily punished and the government will take away his arms and weapons, and afterwards, the government will have the right to take his life and then his family should have no objection.

(18, 13)

Soldiers hold court to depose the King and appoint Jawan Bakht instead

Letter from a spy, 3 September

One fellow was arrested on suspicion of spying. His lips and all his teeth were broken and he was so mercilessly beaten that he is now beyond description. One Khaki, that is, a British soldier, was arrested at the front and brought here. He was tied up and so severely beaten by men of the Nimach platoon that his whole body was in bits. In the evening, about a hundred soldiers of the Hindustani horsemen and soldiers of some platoon gathered at Daryaganj bazaar and were holding court that all these princes should be suspended and Jawan Bakht, son of Zinat Mahal, should be anointed the successor and, once we achieve victory, the king. And the old man, meaning the King, should be dismissed. On that promise you can collect all the salary from Zinat Mahal Begum. This devoted one himself witnessed this meeting. They continued the discussions till the evening. Let us see what is decided. It is difficult to believe that the Begum Sahiba will agree to this plan.

(16, 16)

Bakht Khan upset that nothing was done to check the arrival of the English battery

Letter from a spy, 6 September

My lord,

Today the army is very downcast after hearing the news of the arrival of the government battery. Bakht Khan, the general, sent word to his majesty that I have been saying for four or five days that the battery is coming, some force should be sent to stop them at Panipat, but nobody listened to me. Now the reinforcement will arrive and there will be heavy fighting and the city will be wrecked. News came from Malagarh that the gora forces have come to Malagarh from Ajmer. A court was held to send reinforcements to Malagarh. At four o'clock I had a meeting with Mirza Saheb. Tomorrow the appointment to the bridge will come through and then it will soon be repaired. Today some five hundred horsemen sneaked away after being sick of the army. Today the court ordered that the force besieging Ghaziabad should stay there and armies should also be sent towards the Qutub and should keep a watch there because the British now have large numbers and lest they besiege the city in a moment of abandon. I am quite sick of the army.

(26, 2)

Queen Zinat Mahal communicates with the British

Letter from a spy, 9 September

This morning Mirza Saheb summoned me and said that Begum Sahiba had called him at night and said that while as far as I am concerned, I accept whatever you suggest. But the arrangement should be official, however it is done. She said, whether Maulvi Rajab Ali is called or Mazhar Ali Saheb is summoned, whatever aid they request, I will give them; whatever they desire, will be accepted. Without their advice, nothing can be done. All precautions will be taken for their security, my confidants will guide them along the way and bring them here safely. And should you come in accordance with the sarkar's permission, then everything will be all right. And whatever is necessary today, please enquire about it and let me know the response today itself as I am waiting.

The other thing is that I went to Kashmiri Gate today and saw the front from this side; because of the field, there will be a more or less equal contest with guns, etc. But at Lahori Gate or Kabuli Gate, there will be great mayhem, and the least loss of lives of troops is desired, for the rest, whatever the blessed one sees fit.

(16, 24)

Gauri Shankar refuses the C-in-C's overtures

Gauri Shankar to the C-in-C, 25 August

The petition is this that right now, one macebearer came to me and stated that the crown prince [i.e., Mirza Mughal] has called you and there are other commanders present there also. I replied why is it that his lord has not remembered me so far, and since the eighteenth, when the order was passed, I have been suspended from my duties of being a brigade major; so now even if a prince calls me, I don't go. My advice to you is that you should not worry yourself at all on my account because this is not the time to fritter one's attention in worries and our enemies desire us to have differences and disputes amongst ourselves, so please do not fulfil the enemies' wishes. Please go over to the exalted fort and continue to look after the arrangements of the battle as before, lest you should suffer on my account. Thanks to your kindness, I am very well and contented and in any event, I would always require your benediction. As far as your command regarding taking up brigade major-ship again is concerned, my submission is that it is unfair to visit such a court where there is no justice. I thought I would inform you about the details of the situation.

May the kingdom's sun shine forever.

Devoted,
Gauri Shankar Sukul, brigade major

(70, 228)

A faqir arrested for loitering

Thanadar, Chandni Chowk, to the kotwal, Undated

Greetings.

The submission is that a sepoy of the Lahori Gate artillery came and stated that this faqir was standing near our guns; therefore I have arrested him and brought him here. Let him go when he is properly identified by someone. Therefore the said faqir was arrested and is being sent to the kotwali through Gulab Khan, barqandaz.

Aminuddin Khan

(61, 29)

Grocer arrested for spying is innocent

Subedar, sappers and miners, to the C-in-C, 4 September

My lord,

The application is about one Ramdas grocer, resident of Peshawar, who had been arrested on the charge of spying and has appeared before his lordship. The situation is that for the last four months, he has been living with us at the sappers and miners' platoon and his mother and uncle are present here with the platoon. Due to destitution and penury, he had gone towards Chandni Chowk to beg when someone had him arrested on suspicion of being a spy. Therefore I submit that that man is not a spy and he should be let off as an act of mercy and it will be a sign of great kindness.
Dutifully submitted, may the kingdom's sun shine forever.

Slave,
Akbar Khan

(51, 76)

A worker on the canal arrested for spying

Darogha, Guzar Qasimjan, to the C-in-C, 31 May

At this very instant, Baijnath Misr, havaldar of the eighty-eighth regiment, arrested one Zabardast Khan who worked in the canal area on the charge of spying and brought him to this thana. Since it was necessary to send the man to you, therefore he has been dispatched along with this note. If he is in fact a spy, then he should be meted a deserving end and if not, then his lordship is the master to do as he deems fit. Dutifully submitted,

May the kingdom's sun shine forever.

Devoted,

Mirza Mohammed Khan Beg

(194, 7)

A man suffering from jaundice arrested on the charge of spying

Deposition of an accused, 29 August

Name: Chinta
Father's name: Rakhnath
Qaum: Rajput
Resident of: Risali
Occupation: Service

My statement is that I was earlier employed at a bridge in Meerut when the ghadar happened, and when the army came to Delhi from Mathura, I came with that force to Delhi and stayed at Daryaganj for five to seven days where, by the prowess of the Almighty, I contracted jaundice and became completely unconscious. The soldiers thought I was a spy or an informer because I could not speak and had me arrested at the kotwali. I remained unconscious for many days at the kotwali and could not identify myself. Now that I have gained consciousness, I have got this statement recorded. There is no deceit or falsehood in anything I have said.

(185, 21)

C-in-C investigates the case of two lunatics arrested for spying

C-in-C to the kotwal, 28 July

Your submission passed our eyes stating that the prisoners Saheb Singh and Jadunath had been arrested on the charge of spying and are imprisoned at the kotwali; further that these people are insane and always stay at the lunatic asylum and create a nuisance and cause difficulties for other prisoners. Looking into it an order has been passed that you should send the two insane people before us, they will be released after investigation.

(Note on the letter:
Lord of the world,

In accordance with your order, Saheb Singh and Jadunath, lunatics under imprisonment, have been dispatched to your lordship.)

(132, 25)

A chowkidar working for the Delhi government arrested as a spy

C-in-C to the kotwal, Undated

Through the application of Faizullah Khan, subedar of the platoon posted at Lahori Gate, one Kale Khan has been sent on the charge of spying. He states, I am the chowkidar of Khirki Ibrahim Khan and had gone there to collect the chowkidari dues on the instructions of the thanadar, but the man was not there and these people apprehended me on suspicion of being a spy; I am a government servant, not a spy. Therefore he is being sent to you that if he in fact is a chowkidar of

Khirki Ibrahim Khan, then release him and send a report of execution otherwise send him back for imprisonment to us.

C-in-C

(Note on the letter:
Protector of the poor,

My lord, the situation is that Kale Khan is in fact the chowkidar of Khirki Ibrahim Khan, not a spy.

Bhure Beg, clerk, Guzar Itiqad Khan)

(123, 179)

An enemy officer hiding in the city

C-in-C to the King, 9 July

Sarfaraz Khan, dafadar, and Mohammed Khan, grenadier, who have joined us from the enemy camp—an application has already been sent to your lordship regarding them—have deposed on oath that one named Ahmed Khan, resident of Lal Kuan, is a risaldar of the enemy and is posted here to spy on us and he reports all the goings-on of this place to them. Yesterday, he took three thousand rupees in front of us and has brought it here and is currently staying here. Something should immediately be done about him. My lord, since it was imperative to convey the facts to you, therefore this application, and the humble urge is that should you issue instructions then arrangements for arresting that errant risaldar may be made.

Whatever you desire will be carried out.

Devoted,
Zaheeruddin

(57, 66)

A mendicant who crossed the Jamuna bridge is arrested

Arjun's deposition regarding arrest, 1 August

Name: Arjun
Son of: Aminchand
Occupation: Mendicancy, *dadupanthi sarbhangi* [a class of faqirs who did not believe in ideas of caste and pollution]

Q. Why were you arrested?

A. It has been ten or twelve days since I came to Delhi and I went wherever I found food and slept there at night. Yesterday, I had gone to bathe in the Jamuna and when I returned and got off the bridge, a Muslim person arrested me.

Q. State the name of the person who arrested you.

A. I don't know his name.

Q. If you wanted to bathe in the Jamuna, why did you cross the bridge to the other side?

A. I went there to relieve myself and was arrested when returning. Didar Bakhsh and Maula Bakhsh, grocers, whose shop I can identify, know of my being a faqir. The government can call them.

(67, 82)

A worker for the British gives details of their positions

*Statement of Zalim, a servant of
the English who has been arrested, 16 June*

Name: Zalim
Father's name: Lotan
Qaum: Ahir
Age: 18 years
Profession: Service in the English cannon factory, illiterate

Q. Explain in detail the state of the English forces that have come here to fight, explain fully its extent.

A. The total force of the English is some five thousand and its details are as follows:

Gora platoons: 2000 approx.

Black platoons: 600 approx.

Black cavalry: 400 approx.

Two companies, approximately two hundred people.

Q. You say there are five thousand people, but in this break-up there is a shortfall, what is the reason for that?

A. I only mentioned numbers from memory. I do not exactly remember how many.

Q. How many guns are there and how much magazine?

A. There are forty-two cannons and nine magazines, but I don't know where they are. At the cannon factory, there are some eighty-five magazines.

Q. Is there any news there of the arrival of forces?

A. There is no news about the impending arrival of any troops as far as the English soldiers in Peshawar are concerned.

(71, 41)

A captive spy's statement

Statement of a captive spy regarding the fighting strength of the English, 16 June

There are seven platoons in Kalika and there is a dispute among them over who should depart first

Q. Do you know which rajas and nawabs are assisting the English?

A. Only the Nawab of Rajshala has sent approximately a thousand horsemen and some provisions to the English while declaring that he is the raja of Jaipur. No other king has sent his force and no troops have arrived.

Q. What did you mean by coming here?

A. Two to three hundred men of our platoon had come here, so I came here to enquire after them.

Q. Which platoon is that?

A. The platoon that came from Meerut.

Q. Do you have any brothers or acquaintances in the said platoon?

A. Mir Nabi and Surat Singh know me.

Q. Regarding what you state about coming to meet the platoon that has come from Meerut, tell us, why didn't you come here when that platoon came here?

A. That platoon was near the jail and I am in the city, so they came from the jail while I could not go alone.

(Note on top of the page:
Should be sent to the council for perusal. The case should be brought today.)

(71, 42)

A horseman punished by the English is arrested by the Tilangas

Statement of Jaswandi Khan before the C-in-C, 4 July

Name: Jaswandi Khan
Son of: Bole Khan
Qaum: Rajput Muslim
Resident of: Ramgarh
Profession: Service
Age: 50 years, uneducated

Q. What is your statement?

A. The answer is that I was serving the firangis as a horseman. I ran away from there but was arrested by the firangis because my horse was lame. There my *court* was conducted, after which my belongings and my horse were confiscated and my name was cut from the rolls. I came here with the intention of finding employment. I went to the front and enquired about the possibility of a job, but the Tilangas there arrested me saying I was a spy. Twenty days have passed since I was arrested and now I am feverish and suffering from dysentery and am very ill. I am humbly hopeful.

Q. Do you have any acquaintances here?
A. No, none.
Q. Which Tilanga arrested you?
A. I don't know the name or identity of those who arrested me.

(67, 33)

An impostor pretending to be insane arrested for spying

Thanadar, Chandni Chowk, to the kotwal, 15 June

After due respects, it is submitted that one Shahbaz Khan who arrived with the Lucknow cavalry came and said that one named Jhunga is a conniving spy. Arrest him and send him to the kotwali tomorrow. And this man was completely in control of his senses, but now pretends to be insane and is putting on an act. Therefore this impostor has been sent to the kotwali.

With the greatest respects,
Hafiz Aminuddin

(Note on the letter:
The one named Jhunga spy should remain in the lock-up.)

(61, 50)

Chandni Chowk, Delhi, Unknown Photographer, Photochrom Zurich, 8.8 x 10 inches, 1890s.
Courtesy the Alkazi Collection of Photography.

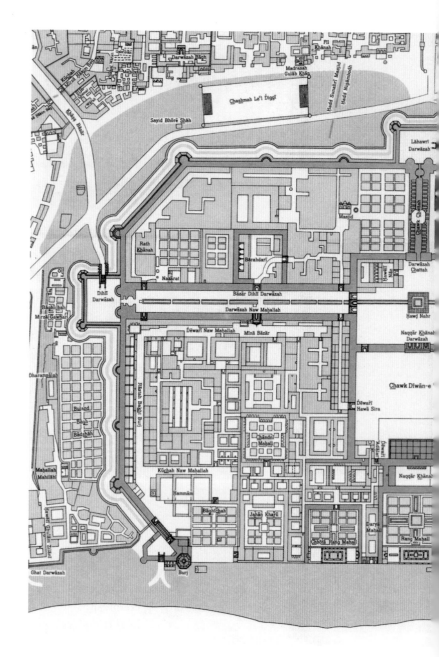

Reproduction of a map of Shahjehanabad showing the Red Fort.

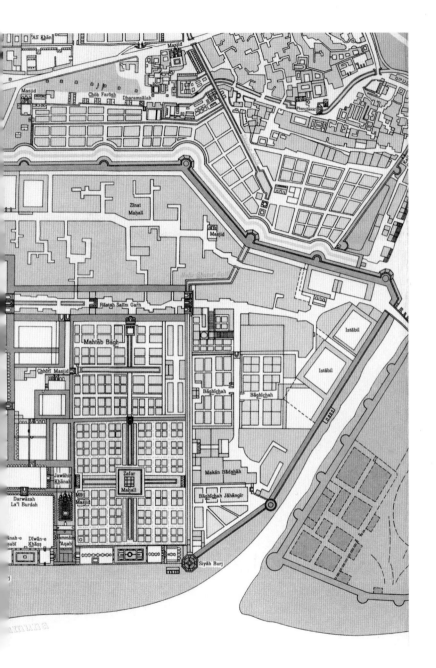

'Alī Khān

Masjid

Masjid

Chōb Farōsh   Dharamsālah

Phanshakkī

Zīnat
Maḥallī

Masjid

Rāstah Salīm Garh

Istābil

Maḥtāb Bāgh

Istābil

Chhōtī Masjid

Bāghīchah   Bāghīchah

Jawāhir
Khānah

Makān Bādshāh

Zafar
Maḥallī

Darwāzah
La'l Bardah   Mōtī
                   Masjid   Bāghīchah Jāhāngīr

ānah-e   Dīwān-e   Hammām
sabī   Khāṣṣ   'Aqab

                                    Siyāh Burj

amuna

Reproduction of a section of a scroll painting by Mazhar Ali showing a panoramic view of Shahjehanabad from the Lahore Gate of the Red Fort (1846) © The British Library Board (Add.Or.4126).

GIVE US MONEY, RANK AND COMPENSATION
Volunteers and jihadis

While the revolt of 1857 was started by soldiers, it drew its longevity and its passion from the large number of civilians who joined in the fighting. The sepoy mutiny turned into a wider rebellion, at least in Hindustan or north India, when volunteers began to participate in it. People fought in different ways—peasants of Awadh joined their landlords and poured into Lucknow to besiege the English, clansmen of Kunwar Singh conducted a guerrilla war in Bihar, and Delhi witnessed a large turnout of ordinary people from places as far away as Tonk in Rajasthan and Bareilly in Uttar Pradesh.

There are three kinds of people who have been lumped together here. There were soldiers, formerly in the employ of the East India Company, who deserted their previous positions and came to fight for the King. The second group comprised civilians who volunteered in search of employment and service. Then there were the jihadis, those who came to fight a religious war against the British. People could also assemble a body of men and seek appointment to a particular military post such as risaldar. There are instances, included in other sections, when people who had earned such honorifics misused their position to extort goods and money from ordinary people. There were others who applied for promotion, hoping to advance their rank. Soldiers expected their outstanding dues from the British to be paid to them by the King. One former jamadar of Bareilly jail mentions freeing over three thousand prisoners from the jail before he came to Delhi. Other than soldiers, there were also volunteers of other kinds; the section on spies tells us that there were volunteer doctors and hakims who had set up a hospital with each unit of the army.

The word mujahid, a derivative of the term jihad, refers to somebody who 'does' jihad. As a generic term, it also refers to any volunteer. When someone describes himself as a mujahid, it is not clear whether he is a religious warrior or simply a volunteer. At one level, however, this is a facile distinction because, as the proclamations never tire of repeating, this was a war started by religion and a war that was being fought over religion. In such a scenario, it is difficult to isolate any motivation as being completely secular. However, when the British translate the word mujahid, they completely elide its other connotation and invariably translate it as fanatics. Anybody who came of his own to fight against them, understandably from their point of view, was a fanatic but as a translation of the term mujahid, fanatic poses many problems.

If the services of the mujahids were going unappreciated, as is shown by their complaint below, they themselves were unhappy and suspicious of the attitude of the residents. As one of them wrote to the King, 'Except for you, everybody in Delhi is in league with the British.' This disgruntlement is also evident from the letter written by one of their leaders to the CoM, thanking it for appreciating their services. Mujahids were useful, however, also as a private militia, as the request from Mufti Sadruddin Azurda to the leaders of the mujahideen shows. They could face off against soldiers bent on causing mischief.

There was also an entire platoon called the 'Balam tair' platoon and it took me some time to work out that this was an indigenized pronunciation of the word volunteer, much like the *otiyar*s of Chauri Chaura.* All three categories of volunteers expected the King to provide

* From Shahid Amin, *Event, Metaphor, Memory: Chauri Chaura, 1922–92* (New Delhi: Penguin Books India, 2006).

for them, give them arms, ammunition, salaries and maintenance. They all came to fight a war on their own, but they expected to be appreciated and rewarded for doing so and looked to the established authority for this. Many of them presented accounts of their wealth, sometimes extravagant, which had been destroyed during the uprising and who therefore sought reimbursement of some kind. The fact that a soldier had missed out on plunder could be presented as a situation of hardship and one could demand compensation, in a way, from the King as the case of the Indore trooper shows. The number of men was not a problem, money was. Therefore, by the end, the King had to ask the C-in-C to send volunteers away and not to recruit anybody except those who were willing to serve without payment.

Forming a platoon or a company of volunteers by itself was not enough, it was also important to be officially enlisted. Recognition by the King or the government was useful even if it brought no money. In some instances, the reason given for joining the rebel side was the desire to serve the Islamic cause, as in the case of the soldier who deserted from his position at the ridge because he did not want to die and go to hell serving the kafirs. Similarly, a soldier from Peshawar claims that he had only joined Company service because the King's fortunes were at a low and now that the wheel had turned, he wanted to serve the right cause.

While Gujars are usually mentioned as marauders in 1857, there are some documents in other sections which show them as helping the rebel cause by not allowing deserters to escape. However, petitions about them seem to be based on the assumption that an order from the King could help release soldiers besieged by Gujars, which shows that the soldiers believed the King's writ to be stronger than it actually was. This also shows the possibility that an order from the King could have some effect, even in regions far away from the capital.

Soldiers from Bareilly want their names enrolled in the government register

Amanullah Khan, Ali Mohammed Khan and others to the C-in-C, 22 June

My lord,

The following servants of yours, employed in the regiment of Hindustani horsemen posted at Bareilly cantonment, have come here before your majesty and are praying that in this struggle, the names of us servants should also be written down in the government register so that we may execute the orders and tasks of the government as per the established regulations.

Dutifully submitted,
Amanullah Khan, sawar
Ali Khan, sawar
Amir Khan, sawar
Bakhshullah Khan, sawar

(60, 211)

God has given you this chance after a long time. Allah wants the era of Muslims to begin

Nanhe Khan, naib risaldar from Jaipur, to the C-in-C, 30 July

For the last ten days, twenty-six men of my risala from Jaipur have arrived here and are living with this humble one. They maintain that we are here with the intention of serving in his lordship's army and desire nothing more than to lose our lives at your feet. God has given you this chance after a long time. Allah wants the era of Muslims to begin. This servant is hopeful that the maintenance of the said horsemen from the servant's risala be granted.

Submitted dutifully, may the sun of the kingdom always shine brightly.

Servant,
Nanhe Khan, deputy risaldar, first rank

(61, 7)

A jamadar seeks promotion to the rank of risaldar

Faiz Mohammed Khan, jamadar, to the King, 29 July

An application consisting of the details of my officership involving me and twenty horsemen had been dispatched to your majesty earlier. I had also sought permission for raising a regiment of troops of my horsemen who are present here already with one or two who arrive here daily. The regiment is staying at Gwalior because of the beneficence of the maharaja of that place. The letter would have passed your eyes about that. Those who have come into the regiment now inform me that I have become a jamadar in my regiment. I wish to serve his majesty's government and am submitting before his lordship that my lord patronize me and give me permission to raise a corps of troops so that I may form a regiment. Right now, the servant has twenty-one horsemen and one dafadar and two deputy dafadars along with him. I hope your lordship will show generosity and issue an order appointing me as risaldar and allow the servant to raise troops so that I can show my dedication to the imperial government and serve it with diligence and purpose.

Submitted dutifully, may the sun of the kingdom and its fame always burn brightly.

Applicant,
Faiz Mohammed Khan, jamadar

(61, 253)

Jamadar from Bareilly wants promotion and the limelight

A jamadar from Bareilly to the King, Undated

My situation is this that formerly I used to be the jamadar of the guards at the Bareilly jail. When the kafirs were put down, this devoted one released some two and a half thousand prisoners and on the way, the goras and the firangis that were found were put to the sword and I did everything that would be of advantage to this government. Since the day I have appeared here, I go every day on a sortie and in fact, one gora had struck me with a bullet and I was wounded. But thanks to his majesty's iqbal, I beheaded him and snatched his gun. Now this slave has a large group of men under him and they fight under my supervision, but my efforts do not come into the limelight and the men who have come from Mathura, if they are given under the slave's charge, then I will organize them and lead them into battle. Further, your lordship had earlier issued directions for promotion but the slave has not yet been promoted, therefore this petition that the slave should be handed charge of a group and should also be promoted.

A volunteer from Bareilly

(115, 48)

An Indore cavalryman who missed out on the plunder wants to be recompensed

Noor Ali Khan, risaldar, to the C-in-C, 20 September

My lord,

The submission is that the condition of Indore is this that at the time when the army made consultations about killing the British and all the soldiers took oath, the obedient one too was present and in unison with them. And when the fight broke out and the Englishmen were killed, I too killed them and thanks to your lordship's iqbal, emerged victorious.

The obedient one received two horses from the plunder at Indore, but not a penny of cash. The soldiers all sent the obedient one to the guns along with my companions and sent off the guns, and the obedient one went ahead to make arrangements and behind him, the soldiers plundered the treasury and did not give me a penny. In fact, three days ago, the cavalry horsemen seized the two plundered horses and one that belonged to me and when we reached a place called Biawra, there was a munshi of the English there and the soldiers arrested him, and having taken a few thousand rupees from him, left him at Morar. And the situation at Dhaulpur is this, my lord, that at the time the assault took place, the obedient one too along with most of the companions reached there and thanks to his lordship's iqbal, prevailed thereupon, and the obedient one got two horses in plunder, which this humble one has presented to his excellency, and the soldiers took a few guns from them. Your grace, the submission is this that our six months' salary was forfeited at Indore and three months were spent in travel and we did not get a penny. My lord, I have stated the situation as it was and you are our lord and master and we are all obedient and subservient, we will keep his grace informed of whatever we do.

May the kingdom's sun shine forever,

The humble,
Noor Ali Khan, risaldar

(194, 28)

A trooper from Jhansi wants the King to give a name to his volunteer platoon

Tehseen Ali of Jhansi to the King, 18 August

My lord,

Regarding the application of this slave about the recruitment of men. Other than those already serving, up to five hundred soldiers are needed so that they make up a platoon, whatever is the command of your exalted self is acceptable to this slave. My lord, this slave wishes to give the platoon the name suggested and preferred by you and since the soldiers present with me are all familiar with the drill, therefore whatever name is accorded to them will remain for all time to come and the request is for the grant of an ordinance along with the seal.

Dutifully submitted, may the kingdom's sun shine forever.

Humble,
Mohammad Tehseen Ali
Officer, Jhansi

(Note by the King:
The name of the platoon will be Faiz.)

(152, 34)

From the day his majesty's fortunes were blighted, this slave too came under a black cloud—its revival brings him here

Ghulam Murtaza Khan, risaldar, to the King, Undated

This is to submit that my ancestors were long the loyal servants of his majesty's lineage and the honours and privileges they were granted are recorded in the books of the secretariat. From the day his majesty's fortunes were blighted, this slave too came under a black cloud. After a while, out of helplessness, this slave took service with the kafirs and served with them as risaldar for a number of years. Now at Peshawar, where the slave's regiment is stationed and serving to this date, I heard of the revival of his excellency's fortunes, and after making a thousand excuses to my commanding officer, I somehow took leave from there and appeared at your doorstep. I left all my belongings worth a thousand rupees at the regiment because of the displeasure of the English. Other than that, a single-storey newly built haveli worth five thousand and five hundred rupees and five old havelis worth three thousand rupees belonging to the slave were destroyed during railway construction at Gurgaon. Before leaving, I had dispatched a bill worth three thousand five hundred rupees to the said district, but in this pandemonium, that too got lost and in fact, that district itself became turmoil infested. On the way, the ruler of Patiala plundered my tent, cattle and all my other paraphernalia of travel, so much so that I was not even left with a horse to ride. Now for many days I have been present in the realm and am submitting my case with this petition that some force or district should be assigned to me so that I can distinguish myself in service to your excellency. My daily expenses including the camel and retainers amount to seven–eight rupees.

Submitted dutifully,
May the kingdom's sun shine forever,

Devoted,
Syed Ghulam Murtaza Khan, risaldar, eighteenth regiment
Resident: Gurgaon, Pargana Babool, village Sadatpur

(Note on the letter:
Mirza Mughal has sent him here saying he is an old soldier.)

(152, 52)

Except for your majesty, everybody in the city of Delhi, including the civil servants, is in cahoots with the English

Officers of a brigade to the King, 30 August

My lord,

The plea is that from the day we devoted ones have prostrated themselves at your majesty's feet till today, your majesty has not provided any maintenance to us and whatever we had left has also been expended. Either your majesty should provide for us or he should give these servants a clear answer so that we know we are in the hands of the

Almighty and after paying obeisance at your majesty's feet, we will leave Delhi. The time is ripe for your majesty's aid. If there is such starvation, then we will have to break away from your majesty and go someplace else. Except for your majesty, everybody in the city of Delhi, including the civil servants, is in cohorts with the English.

With the greatest respects,

Devoted,
All the sardars of the brigade,
Delhi

(70, 243)

When we were engaged in a bitter fight with the kafirs nobody came to our aid

Ghulam Mohiuddin, risaldar, to the King, 2 August

This humble servant, Ghulam Mohiuddin Khan, senior risaldar from Tonk, along with five hundred young men and fifteen hundred others came into this city to wage jihad. Yesterday, the servant along with retainers went to the front and took part in the assault. Some eighty kafirs were sent to death by our hands while twenty-five of our men were killed and five were injured. My lord, when we were engaged in a bitter fight with the kafirs nobody came to our aid. Even if they had just stood by our side, we would have achieved victory with divine help. There is no arguing against fate. We beg that our men should be given some arms and some expenses for their maintenance so that we are fortified in our jihad to kill kafirs and we reach our goal.

May the kingdom's sun shine forever,

Humble,
Ghulam Mohiuddin Khan, senior risaldar from Tonk

(Note by the King:
Mirza Mughal should do whatever is appropriate.)

(152, 29)

Volunteers from Rampur want money or passports to return home

Abdul Ghaffar Khan and others from Tonk to the C-in-C, 24 August

Lord and master,

This morning, we mujahideen have received two hundred rupees as expenses for the way. Apart from that, the devoted one also has fifty rupees. It cannot be distributed for the reason that the devoted one has far too many dependants. Even if I distribute all the money I have, it will amount to two or four annas per person. We are in great distress due to the lack of money. Therefore I submit that please grant us emoluments in accordance with our needs or else issue a passport so that we can return unhindered to Rampur.

With the greatest respects,

May the sun of the kingdom shine forever,

Application of servant Abdul Ghaffar Khan of Tonk

(Note by the King:
Arrangements are being made to pay towards expenses.)

(65–29)

Sadruddin Azurda requires a hundred men to protect himself from the Tilangas

Sadruddin to Maulana Ahmed, 8 August

Respected and affectionate Maulana Maulvi Mohammed Sarfaraz Ahmed, after due salutations,

Let this be known to you that Mufti Sadruddin Saheb sent some men before our preceptor and said that I fear an evil deed by some Tilangas; lest out of enmity they concoct a charge and cause harm to me, please send me a hundred mujahideen for protection. So the guide and preceptor sent sixty men from his contingent and sixty men from the contingent of Maulvi Mohammed Munir under my command. I am writing to inform you as you are my officer and whatever you command will be obeyed.

Writer,
Saifurrahman

(151, 87)

An announcer calling out to all mujahideen is attacked by Punjabis

Colonel Khizr Sultan to the C-in-C, 22 August

Rustam Beg, announcer, has filed a suit stating that yesterday a command had been issued by Mirza Mughal to all the mujahideen to go for the assault; so the slave read out the pronouncement to everyone, upon which two men of the Punjabi qaum drew out their swords on hearing the announcement and made to kill me. If soldiers of war had not been present they would have killed me. Therefore, this is being forwarded for suitable action.

(Note on the letter:
Send a note to the officers of the mujahideen that whoever identifies them should present them to me.)

(100, 123)

A deputy risaldar falls out with his officer and demands his dues

Ghulam Nabi Khan, deputy risaldar, to the C-in-C, 27 July

My lord,

From the day that this servant gave up his position as deputy risaldar in the government of Jaipur and appeared before his lordship and was registered as an officer in the secretariat of his lord, from the day of arrival whatever emolument was distributed, including the portion for the risaldar, I took from your lordship and gave the risaldar's share to him and distributed the share of the horsemen, supplies and others to each of them separately. Now Amir Ali Khan, risaldar, unjustly and falsely accuses this servant and wishes to separate the servant from the horsemen in my unit and wants to deny me justice. My lord is well aware that this slave is present in his service from the first day itself and regularly goes on attacks. Out of the expectation of justice from his lordship I am submitting this application so that my grievance may be investigated and justice meted out. The money owed to him should be given to him and what is mine should be given to me. I do not want to be involved with him, nor work with him in any way.

Hoping for mercy for my life,

Slave,
Ghulam Mir Khan

(61, 238)

A blacksmith sets soldiers against a jihadi to demand his dues

Khuda Bakhsh, jihadi, to the C-in-C, 30 July

My lord,

The situation is that the day the English rods were taken into the possession of the government, this slave too had taken some and had brought them the same day to Siva blacksmith who had processed it for a due. I had not paid the wages to him then saying I have no money today and will pay you tomorrow and he said it was all right. The next day, at the front I received a bullet wound in my leg and I could not get up because of its severity. That Siva came to me, and I said to him I have been wounded and have not been able to go anywhere so how can I pay you. I will give you the money in a day or two. Upon this he started to abuse me and beat me up, and as a matter of fact, soldiers of war stay in his house and he got them to beat me up and plundered my house and he is still bent on wreaking havoc. All my possessions have been looted, the situation is as grave right now and they say pay up ten rupees otherwise we will kill you. I now beg for the safety of my being and my life.

Dutifully submitted,

May the kingdom's sun shine forever,

Slave,

Khuda Bakhsh, jihadi and loyalist

(65, 15)

Mewati mujahideen will return home unless given their dues

Mujahideen from Mewat to the C-in-C, 13 August

My lord,

Hundreds of us mujahideen from Mewat district, leaving our families and children to the care of God, have been presenting ourselves for the past several months at your exalted doorstep to lay down our lives for the righteous cause. While other volunteers are given salaries, for us mujahideen, our blood is our victual and many of us were martyred in a state of starvation, and the intensity with which we sacrifice ourselves is obvious to everyone. But alas, let alone providing for our living, we have not even been granted a horse or the compensation for things that have been plundered off us by Gujars. Alif Khan, the leader of our caravan, has made representations many times, but your lordship did not respond to it and the charge of hoarding lead which has been brought against us is a complete fabrication. Those possessing lead have escaped and we have been unjustly arrested and his lordship is yet to look into the matter. This is far from the tenets of justice. Your lordship has to show his face on the Day of Judgement and the life here on earth is an undependable one and is borrowed time, therefore we beg for justice to be done. Otherwise, after presenting the matter once more before his majesty, we hundreds of mujahideen will return to our homes and we will be given our due on the Day of Judgement. It is useless to say anything more.

Devoted,
All the mujahideen of Mewat

(65, 24)

A deserter from the British camp wants to serve the Islamic cause

Deposition of Imam Khan regarding his arrest, 27 July

Name: Imam Khan
Son of: Mutawakkil Khan
Qaum: Pathan
Resident of: Akbarabad
Occupation: Shopkeeper, illiterate

Q. Why have you been arrested?

A. The deponent was a shopkeeper of flour and pulses, etc., with the sixty-seventh English platoon. I had come here to the ridge with the platoon at the English camp. I imagined that if I die here, I will go straight to hell. Somehow I should join the Islamic forces. When I found a way, I left at nine in the morning with only a pair of clothes and some cash. When I reached the ridge, some ten–twelve soldiers caught me and took me to a garden. They seized the money and the clothes and left me. It has been five days since I presented myself to his majesty. I had wished to take the arms from his majesty to go and fight the enemies. Now I beseech his majesty that I should be given some arms so that I can join the Islamic force and fight the enemies.

Q. Do you have any acquaintances here?

A. I have no acquaintance here. Only my faith for I am a Muslim, and that is my only proof and witness.

(67, 73)

Deserter from the British camp is arrested by soldiers

Deposition of Mihr Ali regarding his arrest, 27 July

Name: Mihir Ali
Son of: Karim Bakhsh
Qaum: Shaikh
Resident of: Khurja
Occupation: Service, illiterate

Q. Why were you arrested?

A. Yesterday, when I found the opportunity, I ran away from the English army, from the camp at the ridge, and came to Delhi. Some horsemen said to me that come to his lordship, we will get you a job there. Accompanied by these horsemen whose names I don't know, I came to the exalted fort. When I came here, I was handed over to this guard and have been imprisoned since.

Q. Did you come with the intention of spying?

A. God is my witness that I did not come here for spying but only to honour my religion.

Q. Is there anybody who knows you?

A. Nobody.

Q. What do you want now?

A. I only want to be set free and to get employment from the government. I have left all my belongings there and there is nothing with me.

(67, 72)

Recruitment of volunteers should stop because there is no money to pay them*

King to the C-in-C, Undated

Learn that the numerous applications presented by men of valiant aspirations who have already done much service in the hope of obtaining employment as foot soldiers which had been sent along with your enclosing petition has been received. Considering, however, the want of funds in the state treasury, the absence of all present prospects for the realization of land revenue from the different subdivisions of districts owing to the circumstance that no military force has as yet gone out to arrange this matter, and the prevalence of murder and pillage in the immediate vicinity of the seat of government, and further, in consideration of the collection in the city of large organized military forces from all parts of the country, and the insufficiency of the treasures brought by those troops for their own daily expenses, permission to employ these men cannot be accorded for whence can they be aided with funds as pay to meet their expenses? Such being the case, it is injudicious to give hopes to people whose homes are far distant. It is therefore ordered that you will distinctly inform the men giving the petitions referred to and all others that may hereafter present similar petitions that such of them as can remain for one or two months without requiring pecuniary assistance may stay. When order shall have been established and the revenue of the country realized, they will be rewarded with appointments commensurate with their several qualifications, but this even then can only be done when the prior claims of the regular military troops shall have been satisfied. It is inexpedient therefore retaining men that are in pecuniary destitution on the indistinct hope of employment hereafter based on the contingency of the establishment of order. Please God that when the present disturbed state of affairs shall have given

* Original in English.

place to order, when officers to receive the revenue shall have been established throughout the country and the revenue shall have begun to come in from all directions, thousands of men may be employed. At present there is no option. Be assured of our kindness.

(199, 407)

A volunteer platoon from Benares is waylaid by Gujars

Bir Singh, a soldier from Benares, to the King, Undated

My lord,

A platoon of the thirty-seventh regiment and a platoon of the second regiment left Benares to report to your lordship. They were about to reach here, bearing great hardship and discomfort, when they were waylaid. Now, fifty of my soldiers are besieged by Gujars at Mandawali, ten miles away from Delhi. They wanted to seize all the arms and ammunitions possessed by my men and to strip them naked but the sepoys of the regiment are still resisting. I firmly believe that if your majesty does not pass an order demanding the release of the sepoys of the said regiment and reprimanding the Gujars by this evening, there will be much bloodshed and tremendous loss of wealth and property. Some one hundred and fifty of this humble one's soldiers are present at the camp but many of them are caught by the Gujars at Mandawali, therefore this servant is hopeful that out of patronage and protection, a command will soon be issued urging the Gujars to lift the siege and to free the soldiers so that they may shortly be united with us.

Dutifully submitted,
Bir Singh, soldier, second regiment

(57, 511)

A risaldar wants to raise a body of men

Moti Khan, risaldar, to the King, 23 July

My lord,

The submission of this slave is that tomorrow I will present myself at the exalted doorstep along with ten to twelve horsemen formerly of the Jodhpur regiment of the Bengal army, and the slave got delayed in presenting himself because of the situation in his qasba Zalta. The situation is that the scoundrel Gujars pillage the area. The slave had come here two months ago to seek leave and my regiment along with the army had come from Bombay via Jaipur, and this slave now wants to recruit horsemen and others to service the cause of your lordship. Some of my fellow soldiers have already presented themselves and this note is being sent to you as a reminder via the dafadar, Shaikh Abdullah.

Faithful slave,
Moti Khan, risaldar

(61, 200)

UNHAPPY WIVES, TROUBLESOME PROSTITUTES AND ELOPEMENTS
Women in the city

The surest sign of the dislocation and turbulence caused by the presence of a large floating population and intense mobility was the number of cases of missing and eloped women. Women ran away with soldiers, soldiers' wives deserted them, and sometimes, servants ran away with their mistresses. The first part of this section contains reports of missing or eloped women of this kind. Khuda Bakhsh's wife did not run away with the man she had presented as her long-lost brother until the uprising began. The unsettled state of affairs at the time presented her an opportunity that she may not have got earlier. In a peculiar emphasis, in more than one instance, the officials ask the complainants whether their spouse was unhappy with them—did that consideration matter in weighing the offence? It is also apparent that marriage was not the only relationship that ensured conjugal rights over a woman. Was Zia a keep of Pir Bakhsh? Did he intend to marry her? Was she was just a tribute or booty, and did he intend to pay her meher or endowment? Relations could be organized along a matrix of different kinds of informal contracts.

Following a complaint, descriptions were sent out of the women's physical features and the marvellous fact is that in some instances they were actually spotted or recovered. In cases where soldiers were involved, recovery posed complications. Pir Bakhsh's sister-in-law was summoned through the officer in charge of the soldier with whom she was staying. But the wife of Gopal, the barqandaz of a thana, was with some soldiers and the kotwal expressed his apprehensions about recovering her by saying that the matter involved soldiers and 'his lordship is aware of their situation'. In cases where soldiers' partners went missing, they came to the police for help only with identification. Hira Singh sepoy, the thanadar was instructed, would arrest the culprits himself.

Then there were women of many different kinds—the singer-courtesan called the *tawaif*, the professional worker called the *kasbi* and other kinds of adult entertainers. Soldiers usually congregated where these women lived or at their establishments and we have already encountered the disturbances they could create. Sundar Kasbi could lean on soldiers to get her tenant to vacate while Vaziran was implicated in many cases of theft but could act with impunity because her admirers would always intercede on her behalf. Such places were a problem for the police and created what in modern parlance is called a 'law and order' situation. As the thanadar wrote about a badmash, his visits to Sundar the prostitute's house held the potential of a riot. Sometimes, such women could become prized possessions and repeated orders from the C-in-C proved incapable of securing their release. Manglu Tawaif, claimed Chhedi, had been abducted by Rustam Khan and he secured at least three different orders for her release. The officer of the platoon, Faiz Khan, claimed that she had been lawfully married and there was no question of releasing her, royal orders notwithstanding.

In cases where there was a discrepancy between the versions presented by complainants and the accused, it was very difficult to determine who was speaking the truth. Pir Bakhsh complained about his sister-in-law eloping with a soldier and with valuables, but she claimed that she had left the house because she had been beaten up. Eventually, she was released without charges.

There is a detailed description of a case involving Surajbali and his former wife Bilasia who were both from Meerut. Surajbali had sold Bilasia to a sweeper. Bilasia's father then bought her off the sweeper, after which she started living with Bhikhari, with whom she was happy. The fact that Bilasia had three different companions in a space of a few years and the fact that she was asked to identify the father of the child as also her preference for the man she wanted to stay with reveals the kind of choices and rights enjoyed by women in specific circumstances of legal proceedings. Women had to make their own statements, but whether this applied to all irrespective of class cannot be determined. All the same, without the turbulence caused by the large-scale mobility of soldiers and men, Surajbali might not have been able to launch a private settlement procedure.

Women were affected in other ways as well. As we see in the section on the residents of Delhi, the presence of guards at every nook and corner could lead to violations of the modesty of the zenana or the private quarters of houses. Stories of women fighters are substantiated by the report about the woman who dressed as a man and tried to cross the city gates at night.

A horseman's wife elopes with a young man when he is fighting at the front

Thanadar, Bhojla Pahari, to the kotwal, 16 August

After greetings and salutations, let this be known that Hyder Ali, horseman of the sixth risala, fourteenth regiment of Datiya, Jhansi, came and deposed that some four days ago when I had gone for the attack, my wife, Begum, whom I had kept at Chitli Qabar area, ran away with a young man named Hussaini, with two hundred rupees cash, which I had kept with her and a tumbler, a *paandaan* and a jug. I apply for a search to be conducted. Therefore, all of you are being instructed to search for the missing woman and in case of discovery, to send her to me.

Woman, Begum: Fair-complexioned, wide forehead, broad-faced, big eyes, well built, average nose and height, clear face, wearing a tight pyjama of *chheent* and lace with a kurti, wrapped in a chadar, sporting a silver necklace.

(121, 105)

A barber's wife elopes with a man from the mohalla along with cash and valuables

*Thanadar, Nigambodh, to the kotwal and all
the thanadars of the city, 2 August*

After greetings and salutations, let this be clear that today at three o' clock, one named Prem Singh, barber, resident of mohalla Pirkhatti, came to the thana and deposed that a woman called Gulabi, his wife, eloped last night with Meherchand Khatri, a resident of this mohalla, along with the goods listed below. Her description is appended below. Prem Singh wants a search conducted. Therefore, in accordance with the petitioner's wishes, you are all being requested to hold a search in your area through the barqandazes and sweepers for the woman as well as the valuables and if recovered, please send it to the writer.

Goods: Cash, brass tumbler, brass cup, bangles, bracelet
Gulabi: qaum—barber, young, wheatish complexion, wide forehead, woven brows, average build.

(120, 161)

A risaldar's keep runs away with his servant and he promises a reward for her recovery

Thanadar, Faiz Bazaar, to all the thanadars, 25 July

Last night, a woman named Dilpasand, a retainer of Ghulam Mohiuddin Khan, risaldar of the eighteenth risala, was forced to run away by his former servant Amani. The said risaldar was quartered at Tiraha Bairam Khan and came here after having searched in that area. Therefore, you are all requested to search in your areas through sweepers and barqandazes and if somebody matches the description of the man or the woman, to send them to this thana.

Dilpasand: Fair-complexioned, average height, black hair, brows slanted, wearing gold earrings
Amani: Dark-complexioned, *missi* in his eyes, pockmarked, black moustache

The risaldar saheb promises a reward to anyone who discovers them.

(120, 137)

A sepoy's eloped companion spotted with a soldier from Bareilly

Deputy kotwal to the darogha of Guzar Itiqad Khan, 24 July

After salutations, the matter is this that Hira Singh sepoy came to the kotwali and deposed that it has been six days since a woman called Kasbo, who used to live with me, took all my belongings and ran away, and I had reported the matter to the kotwali. Now that woman has been identified by the wife of Harbans Singh, sepoy at the residence of Baldeo sepoy from Agra, who is presently a grenadier at the Bareilly camp. She should be arrested. Therefore the case is being handed to all of you that the said woman along with the stolen goods should be arrested through soldiers as identified by the plaintiff. Do not arrest her by yourself, the plaintiff would arrest her himself with help from soldiers.

Khuda Bakhsh Khan

(Response:
A search was conducted for the sepoy Baldeo as identified by the plaintiff, but the said sepoy could not be found in this area. Right now, the plaintiff came to the thana and said that Baldeo sepoy is present at the haveli of Ballabgarh. Baldeo sepoy was summoned through a note, though that area falls under the Faiz Bazaar thana, but the sepoy said let me know where the haveli is, therefore he has been sent there.)

(123, 143)

Was your wife unhappy with you that she ran away?

Deposition of Khuda Bakhsh, 20 July

Name: Khuda Bakhsh
Son of: Shaikh Mohammed Bakhsh
Qaum: Shaikh
Occupation: Employed by the government, can't read or write

Q. What is your suit about?
A. My wife of twelve years had come to Delhi from her *watan* and four months ago, one Syed Ali came from Lucknow and said he was the real brother of my wife, and that he had left home when young and had just come back. I said fine and that man started living here as my wife's brother. When his majesty's government took over, then I gave him twenty-eight rupees to buy a horse—this was one or half a month ago. But these two have now adopted licentious ways and after leaving my house, which was in Haveli Azam Khan, they have gone to Kucha Chelan and have started living there, and they took away jewels and valuables worth two hundred and fifty rupees. I want those goods to be returned and if the woman waives her meher then I will divorce her.

Q. State the details of the stolen jewels.

A. Gold foot chain, gold bangle, gold bracelet, silver bangles, silver anklet, earrings.

Q. You have deposed above that it was worth two and hundred fifty rupees, but this does not amount to that.

A. I did not mention other articles.

Q. Was your wife unhappy with you that she ran away?

A. There was nothing wrong; Syed Ali has made her run away.

(62, 67)

Pyari goes missing after going out to buy wheat

Kotwal to all the thanadars, 2 August

Right now, Pir Bakhsh, servant in the thirteenth risala stationed at Ajmeri Gate, came and deposed that Pyari, his wife, without any jewels, had gone out of the house to buy some wheat and has not returned home yet. He wants that a search be conducted for his wife through a circular note; therefore, in accordance with his application, all of you are urged to conduct a general search and find the woman as soon as possible and send her over.

Pyari: age—Twenty-five years, wheatish complexion, average height, slender build, wearing a pyjama-choli, pierced brows.

(Seals of all the thanas on the reverse)

(111c, 189)

Shaikh Islam's wife, a tawaif, leaves him to live with a spy and a gambler

Shaikh Islam to the King, 4 August

My lord,

In the past, this servant belonged to the Hindu community and then converted to Islam. The servant has lived long in Meerut where the kafirs have struck. Having accepted the Mohammedi path, I came here to appear before your lordship and seek blessings. There was a woman named Hussaini, tawaif, with whom I got married. This servant and the woman came to Delhi. That woman then, after having appeared at Sarai Idgah, left me and befriended one named Khuda Bakhsh who is a spy and a gambler. She also took away all the valuables that this servant had brought from home. Therefore, I am filing this application before his majesty and hope that the accused will be summoned and my valuables returned to me. If this cannot happen, then at least my wife should be recovered so that I may receive justice from his lord's bounty. The humble one has no source other than your resplendent lordship to seek help.

Dutifully submitted,
Servant,
Shaikh Islam,
Resident of Meerut and Delhi

(62, 84)

Pir Bakhsh's sister-in-law elopes with a sepoy and threatens to get him beaten up

Pir Bakhsh to the C-in-C, 7 September

Some four years ago, this slave's brother Roshan died and his wife Khair stayed in the house and was the apple of everyone's eyes because she happens also to be my wife's sister, and we spared no effort to make her comfortable. Now, on the instigation of Jabar, a sepoy of the volunteer regiment, who stays near the Cooper Hospital, she has run away. In the afternoon, when I was absent from the shop, my sister-in-law eloped with the said sepoy along with goods worth one hundred rupees. Whatever I used to earn, I would hand over to her. I had made a report at the Dariba thana about this. And the woman says that I will get you beaten up by soldiers of the platoon. I beg that the woman along with the looted property be returned to me.

(60, 686)

The commander of the soldier she eloped with asked to return Pir Bakhsh's sister-in-law

Order for Kulwant Singh, commander of the fourth platoon, thirty-eighth regiment, from the C-in-C, 7 September

From the application of Pir Bakhsh, tinman, it has been learnt that the sister-in-law of the man mentioned above has eloped with the sepoy Jabar of your platoon and has also taken away some cash and jewels. Therefore you are being instructed to send Jabar along with that woman. Act promptly.

(75, 22)

The woman is freed by the court

Deposition of Pir Bakhsh's sister-in-law, 11 September

My name: Khair
Daughter of: Madar
Wife of: Shaikh Roshan
Qaum: Shaikh

Q. Pir Bakhsh, tinman, has deposed that his sister-in-law has been abducted by Jabar, sepoy of volunteer regiment.

A. Jabar sepoy did not abduct me. Pir Bakhsh, tinman, beat me up so I left him and went and stayed with Jabar's wife.

Q. Did you take any goods with you?

A. No sir, I did not take any goods.

Q. How long has it been since you ran away?

A. I was thrown out day before yesterday by Pir Bakhsh.

Q. Is there any witness for proving you did not take anything, and of Pir Bakhsh beating you up?

A. All the residents of the mohalla are witness to it.

Q. Where are you staying?

A. I stay in Bazaar Khanam, beside the haveli of Mahboob Khan.

(Note on the deposition:

The one named Jabar should remain in prison until the matter is decided.

Today, after the presentation of statements in court, it was decided that nothing could be proved against the woman, therefore she should be released.)

(60, 688)

Pir Bakhsh, the complainant, to be fined if he beats his sister-in-law

Deposition of Pir Bakhsh regarding his complaint, 7 September

Name: Pir Bakhsh
Son of: Saheb Jaan
Resident of: Katra Mahboob Khoja
Profession: Tinman, makes pots and pans

Q. What is your statement regarding the petition you submitted asking for the return of your brother's wife?

A. In the afternoon, the one named Khair, the wife of my brother, ran away with two large bangles, one necklace and fifty rupees cash—altogether it would all be worth a hundred rupees.

Q. The goods that you mention, in front of whom did she take them?

A. In front of my wife.

Q. Was there anyone else?

A. There was nobody else.

Q. Why did you beat up that woman?

A. It was a fight between women. All I did was that I slapped that woman once. I did not physically evict her from the house.

Q. Did you intend to marry her with meher?

A. I did not intend to do nikah with her.

Q. For four years since your brother died, was this woman there with you as a keep or not?

A. No, she was not my keep.

Q. Did you marry her and take the vows or was she a tribute?

A. I did not take the vows. It was all illicit.

Q. Then why did you beat and evict her?

A. I only slapped her once and did not throw her out.

(Note on the deposition:
An undertaking should be taken to the following effect—
After hearing the statements, I swear that I will not commit any oppression on that woman and if I cause any harm, then I will pay fifty rupees as fine.)

(60, 687)

A barqandaz's wife is forcibly detained by soldiers

Deputy kotwal to the C-in-C, 26 July–3 September

Your lordship's command about the arrest of the wife of Gopal, the barqandaz of thana Paharganj, was received. Today, a note arrived from the thanadar of Dariba to the effect that after a hectic search, it was learnt that that woman has been detained by Jiwan Khan and Nawab Khan, havaldar of the third company, sappers and miners platoon, and they keep her under watch. In case of arrest, a riot may break out, therefore, the note of the thanadar is being sent along with this application. What should now be done about the issue? Your lordship is well aware of the situation of the soldiers of war. The matter is now beyond this humble one's power, whatever you desire will be carried out.

Guide of the universe,

As per your instructions after a general search conducted by the thanadar of Dariba, the woman Raju, wife of Gopal barqandaz of Paharganj, has been arrested and has been sent to your lordship. Since the Paharganj thana lies outside the jurisdiction of the kotwali, it is requested that her statements should be recorded through the Paharganj thanadar. The matter now lies at your discretion.

(45)

The order for a tawaif's release has been sent twice and both times the order has not been carried out

Chhedi, traveller, to the C-in-C, 22 July

My lord,

This is the second application of this oppressed one. It is about the order for the release of a courtesan named Manglu, which had been sent to Faiz Ali, risaldar of the fourteenth regiment. The risaldar kept it in his pocket and acting against the order, has sent word through the clerk that after investigation, the said woman has admitted that she has married horseman Rustam Khan of her free will. It is worth pondering that from your lordship's court the order of her release has been sent twice and both times the order has not been carried out. In fact, this statement of the risaldar contravenes the truth because he has kept everything hidden from the courtesan and writes whatever he wants without informing her. My lord, one gruesome incident has already taken place in this regiment when Farzand Ali, court dafadar, murdered a courtesan named Imaman, the keep of Gulab, by choking her to death. That poor soul could not reach your lordship's court and had to keep silent. This slave fears horseman Rustam Khan might kill the said woman because he threatens and beats her up all day and night. If such blatant omissions of justice continue, then the populace that has run away from the depredations of the godless firangis and taken shelter here would not survive and prosper.

Whatever the good lord decides. To investigate my charges, an edict should be issued to all the clerks of the court so that they do not ignore it any further. And an order to this effect should be sent to the said risaldar that he was asked to hand over the courtesan but he disobeyed the court clerk by not sending her and shielded his own horseman and responded to this stranger's plight by concocting facts. He should now send the above-mentioned courtesan by a carriage if she is veiled or by a cart. An order should be sent out in accordance with which a court order can be drawn up so that this poor one receives justice and the courtesan, freed of captivity, can sing the praises of your kingdom and realm.

With the greatest respects,
May the sun of the kingdom shine forever,

Helpless slave,
Chhedi, a traveller from camp Gurgaon

(Note on the letter:
After consideration it has been ordered that this application should be
sent to Faiz Ali, risaldar of the fourteenth regiment, with the order that
he should study the contents and without delay send the said courtesan
by carriage or cart so that she can give her statement.)

(62, 71)

A nawab wants to marry a woman and on her refusal gets her arrested as a spy

*Statement of Shankar Nath regarding the arrest of
his daughter, 19 June*

Name: Shankar Nath
Son of: Sita Ram
Qaum: Khatri
Resident of: Kucha Brijnath
Age: 63 years
Profession: Service

Q. Complainant, what is your suit?

A. Nawab Amir Mirza got my daughter Koyal Rai falsely arrested
on the charge of being a spy for the firangis. I hope she will be released
soon.

Q. Why has he got her arrested?

A. The answer is that he is friends with Afsar Khan, so he managed
to get her arrested. Amir Mirza wants to marry that girl but that woman
does not want to marry him. Therefore he got her arrested through
some horsemen; otherwise what does my daughter have to do with
spying or firangis?

(67, 9)

A prostitute, Sundar, gets soldiers to fight her tenants

Darogha, Dariba, to the kotwal, 30 June

Karim Bakhsh of this thana came and stated that a fracas is going on at Sundar the prostitute's house in Shankar Bagh. Immediately, I took two sepoys of the platoon billeted at the thana and two barqandazes and reached there and brought the prostitute and Abdurrazzaq to the thana. Abdurrazzaq said he stays on rent at the prostitute's house and she wants to get her house vacated now, but he is unable to find any other place. Owing to this, she abused him and three Tilangas who were sitting in her house fired three times at the wall, and then they barged into his house. The prostitute deposed that she had come to ask Abdurrazzaq for rent and that he abused her and the Tilangas who were sitting at her place came and forbade Abdurrazzaq from abusing her, and they did not fire. Sundar didn't know the names of the said Tilangas and when summoned to the thana, they refused to obey. Afterwards, two sepoys, names unknown, came and said why have you imprisoned Abdurrazzaq, our brother? We will take our brother and the prostitute to Mirza Mughal. Since the case pertains to rent and getting the house vacated, and it was not learnt whether anybody fired any shots, and if they did, then who did it, therefore, the said prostitute and Abdurrazzaq having been sent to the kotwali, the report has been entered in the daily diary.

Kunwar Lal

(106–31)

A ruffian, Gopal, visits Sundar and there is danger of a disturbance

Clerk, thana Dariba, to the kotwal, Undated

After greetings, the submission is that Gopal, a vagrant ruffian, visits the house of Sundar, the prostitute, and there is a danger of a riot there.

Therefore I pray that he should be warned not to visit that house and we don't have jurisdiction over that area; so the Dariba *chobdar* should be asked to pull him up and warn him with punishment.

Mohammed Husain

(104, 67)

'She should be called forth and chastised because she is always surrounded by roguish soldiers'— Vaziran, the thieving prostitute

Thanadar, Chandni Chowk, to the C-in-C, 31 July

My lord,

A couple of days ago, one Ram Prashad, a cavalry soldier in the seventh risala of Lucknow, came and stated in the early hours of the night that my goods, valuables, jewellery, etc., worth seven hundred and four rupees have been stolen and are kept at the house of a woman called Vaziran, a prostitute. Ram Prashad said I would like her house to be searched and if a search is not conducted immediately, she will have the goods removed. Thus a search was conducted at her house and two gold earrings, one gold chain, some gems, one rifle, a bundle of cartridges, a magazine and four crackers and four lead bullets were recovered from the attic of the kothi. When I brought the said woman to the kotwali to record her written statement, Subhan, Nandan, Bahadur, Puran and Ajaipal, soldiers of the Bailey platoon, forcibly took away the said woman even before her statement had been recorded and threatened to plunder the thana. Before the soldiers came, the woman had promised to return the unfound goods and most likely, all of the stolen goods would have been recovered. Bansi, goldsmith and the claimant's witness, stated that both the rings and the locket present in the thana belong to the complainant, and Munna Singh, the second witness of the complainant, stated that he has often seen the latter wear those rings and locket and identifies them as belonging to the claimant. My lord, from the account of the case and the recovery of the stolen goods from the said Vaziran's house, the charge of theft against the defendant is amply proven. First of all, the goods have been recovered from her house and second, the woman had promised to return the rest of the goods and it was only the intervention and protection of the sepoys that caused her to change her mind and withhold the rest of the goods. These are soldiers of war and therefore no force can be used against them and an application was sent to the government on the same day that these soldiers illegally intruded to the extent that when the woman was again ordered to report to the thana, the sepoys still did not allow her to come here. In the past too this woman has been called to the thana on the charge of cheating and stealing the jewellery of Bidhan Singh and other sepoys, and a bond of fifty rupees was taken from her as a guarantee of good conduct; but still she refuses to mend her ways. She should be called forth and chastised because she is always surrounded by roguish soldiers and there is always a danger of a serious disturbance. Therefore, we hope that some arrangements would be made to take care of her so that she desists from such acts.

Devoted,
Syed Nazar Ali, thanadar, Chandni Chowk

(103, 247)

Bhikhari has eloped with the wife of this devoted one, a woman named Bilasia from Meerut

Surajbali to the C-in-C, Undated

My lord,

One named Bhikhari has eloped with the wife of this devoted one, a woman named Bilasia from Meerut, and having looted all my wealth and property, has managed to take it away with him by stealth. After many days of struggle, the case was finally presented at your lordship's court and proceedings ordered. That Bhikhari rascal does not reside here and there is no relative of his who can be caught. Therefore I am hopeful that after due consideration of this application, the defendant should be summoned to hand my wife back and he should be punished after his crime is proven, so that in the future nobody should oppress anybody else like that.

With the greatest respects, may the sun of the kingdom shine forever.

Devoted,
Surajbali, seeker of justice

(62, 173)

Bilasia sold to Chapati and then given away to Bhikhari—Surajbali and his father beat up Bilasia and abduct her from Nigambodh Ghat

Statements against Surajbali, 20 July

Name: Bhikhari
Son of: Duhar
Qaum: Kori
Resident of: Nigambodh Ghat
Occupation: Service, uneducated

Name: Jamna
Daughter of: Basti
Qaum: Kori
Resident of: Fort, uneducated

Name: Basti
Son of: Narihar
Qaum: Kori
Resident of: Nigambodh Ghat
Occupation: Service, uneducated

Name: Mahangu
Son of: Jakku
Qaum: Kori

Resident of: Nigambodh Ghat
Occupation: Service

Q. What is your claim?

A. That Ghulam Husain, etc., and a lot of horsemen from a cavalry unit whose name we do not know, on the instigation of and in support of Chhote, son of an unknown person, Mendhi, son of an unknown person, Surajbali, son of Chhote, Jorawan, son of an unknown person and Budhhu, son of an unknown person, all qaum Kori, residents of the third risala, beat us, the four deponents, the woman Bilasia and her father Basti so brutally with sticks and whips that there are bruises on our body and Surajbali slashed the woman Bilasia's neck with a knife and the woman Bilasia was so badly beaten by the horsemen that she is bleeding from her chest and nose.

Q. What was the reason for this scuffle?

A. The truth is that formerly, the woman Bilasia, the daughter of me, the deponent Basti, was married to Surajbali. It has been about one year since Surajbali left her and she became destitute. Afterwards he sold her off to Chapati sweeper. Then the *panch*es called me, Basti, from Meerut and I gave ten rupees to Chapati and got her off and then the case was conducted at Meerut in front of Cook Saheb's court, and there too my daughter was handed over to me. This happened sometime last year and since then she has been with us. Now when the turmoil took place, the accused conspired with the horsemen and beat us black and blue and seized Bilasia from us and she is injured too.

Q. Is there a witness to the scuffle?

A. Budan, Bholu and Mahangu are the witnesses.

Q. Will you present them to the court?

A. I will present them.

Q. What else do you have to say?

A. Furthermore, less than a year ago, I, Basti, had given Bilasia over to Bhikhari and Bilasia is now pregnant by seven months through Bhikhari.

Q. What do you want now?

A. We want Bilasia back and dire punishment for the accused and I have a letter from the panches of Meerut which I will present to the government. And Bakhtawar and Bhawani and Jorawan are also witnesses.

After noting the deposition the complainant's witnesses were asked whether Budan, Bholu and Mahangu wish to give witness now.

A. Not necessary right now.

(60, 349)

'Do you now prefer Surajbali, the first husband, or Bhikhari, the second'—Bilasia's choices

In the court of the C-in-C, 21 July

Name: Bilasia
Daughter of: Basti
Qaum: Kori
Resident at the moment of: Delhi
Occupation: Labour

Q. Basti, etc., have complained that Surajbali and Mendhi and Chhote of qaum Kori have beaten you up and slashed your neck with a knife and have taken you away by force. What do you have to say?

A. Yes, they have hit me and there is a knife bruise on my neck and they took me away by force.

Q. Were you first married to Surajbali?

A. Yes, at first I was married to Surajbali.

Q. Why does Bhikhari describe you as his wife?

A. I took Bhikhari as my second husband.

Q. Did Surajbali, your first husband, fight with you that you adopted a second husband?

A. He sold me to a sweeper in Meerut. Basti, my father, paid ten rupees to have me freed.

Q. Do you now prefer Surajbali, the first husband, or Bhikhari, the second?

A. I do not prefer Surajbali, I prefer Bhikhari.

Q. Which husband has made you pregnant?

A. Bhikhari has made me pregnant.

Q. Has there been a dispute earlier between Surajbali and you?

A. For a year and a half now there has been nothing between Surajbali and myself and Surajbali and I never had a fight and it has been a year since I have had Bhikhari as a husband.

Q. What do you want now?

A. I want to go with Bhikhari, the second husband.

'Why is Bilasia, your wife, upset with you?'— Surajbali's response

Name: Surajbali
Son of: Chhote
Qaum: Kori
Resident of: Meerut camp
Occupation: Service, illiterate

Q. Basti, Jamna, Bhikhari, etc., complainants, have filed a suit against you, Mendhi, etc., accusing you of having beaten Bilasia and her mother etc., and a knife wound has been inflicted on Bilasia's neck. What do you have to say?

A. Bilasia, the woman, is my married wife. During a cholera epidemic, her father Basti brought her to Delhi and sent word to me that Bilasia died of cholera; so I thought she is dead and I endured the news and remained quiet. Now, this year, my brother sent news from Delhi that my wife is alive here. Learning of this, I came here from Meerut and yesterday, my father Chhote and I went and brought the woman back and we did not hit anyone, they are all lying.

Q. You sold Bilasia to a sweeper.

A. I did not sell her, they are all lying.

Q. Why is Bilasia, your wife, upset with you?

A. I don't know why she is upset.

Q. What do you want now?

A. I want my wife Bilasia who is now with me.

'Bilasia is a married wife to my son Surajbali. What does it matter now whether she is happy or not happy?'— Surajbali's father

Name: Chhote
Son of: Amir
Qaum: Kori
Resident of: Meerut
Occupation: Service and labour, illiterate

Q. Basti, Jamna and Bhikhari, complainants, have claimed that Surajbali and his father Chhote hit us and Bilasia and her mother.

A. I and Surajbali, my son, went yesterday to the complainants and brought back Bilasia, the wife of my son, and there was no scuffle or beating.

Q. Surajbali had earlier sold Bilasia, his wife, to Chapati, the sweeper.

A. I and Surajbali, my son, did not sell her, they are lying.

Q. Now Bilasia has taken Bhikhari as another husband and she is pregnant by him and she is happy with Bhikhari and not with Surajbali.

A. Bilasia is a married wife to my son Surajbali, what does it matter now whether she is happy or not happy?

(Order:
Since the accused deny the charge of beating and scuffle, the complainants should be urged to produce witnesses and Bilasia and Chhote and Surajbali should remain in the lock-up.)

'Bhikhari has the right because Surajbali left her and did not file a claim for her'—Witness

Name: Jorawan
Son of: Vimsa
Qaum: Kori
Occupation: Service, illiterate

Q. Basti, Bhikhari and Jamna have made you a witness in the case of Surajbali, Mendhi and Chhote beating them up, what do you know?

A. In front of me, Chhote and Surajbali and Mendhi hit all the complainants with a stick and a whip, and then they forcibly took away Bilasia, the daughter of the deponent Basti, and they tied her hands and took her by force.

Q. What is the relation between Bhikhari and Bilasia?

A. He is Bilasia's second husband and Surajbali is the first husband. He had left her and then when the rule of this government began, he came from Meerut and hit her with a whip and then forcibly took her away.

Q. How many days has it been since Surajbali left her?

A. A year and a half ago. Eight months ago, she took on Bhikhari by her free will as her second husband and now she is pregnant by seven months from Bhikhari and she has been taken away by force and coercion.

Q. Who do you think has a right to Bilasia?

A. Bhikhari has the right because Surajbali left her and did not file a claim for her in these past eight or nine months; so, in my opinion, he has no right of husbandship left over Bilasia.

(60, 352, 9)

Bail for Bilasia

Name: Bakhtawar
Son of: Sukhiram
Qaum: Kori
Occupation: Service as cleaner with his majesty

That the woman, Bilasia, daughter of Basti, who has been kept in the lock up after Surajbali forcibly snatched her away, with this application, I stand bail for her and testify that whenever his lordship summons her, I will produce her instantly and if I don't produce her, then I will submit to whatever punishment or fine that the government sees fit. I write this bail guarantee so that a certificate remains.

(Order:
The bail has been accepted, she should be released.)

(60, 360)

Bilasia's child is stillborn while Surajbali and Chhote are released after an undertaking

Statement, 22 July

Lord of the world and the universe,

The servant had been under arrest and because of the beatings, the child has been stillborn, her situation is quite critical.

Dutifully submitted.

(Order:
A person should be sent to the deponent who has given birth to a dead boy and should report on her situation.)

Today, at 10 a.m., Bhikha, the servant of his lordship, went to examine Bilasia. He returned and deposed that the woman has had a dead baby and she herself was in a critical situation, unsure whether there is still life left in her.

Today, the case was put up, the papers were examined, since Bilasia has already been released on bail, and Chhote and Surajbali gave an undertaking of twenty-five rupees each that they will not engage in any scuffle again and whatever claims they have, they will file them before the government. They were then released and the case was dismissed.

(60–361)

At twelve o' clock at night, an armed woman dressed like a man attempted to go out of the city gate

To the C-in-C, 8 September

My lord,

At twelve o' clock at night, a woman dressed like a man and armed attempted to go out of the city gate. The sepoys of the guard arrested her and kept her at the post at the gate suspecting an ulterior motive behind the fact that she was wearing a man's dress and was holding a naked sword and going outside. When there was light in the morning, it transpired that she was a Hindustani person, therefore, she was released. Since this is not on and causes suspicion among the soldiers, therefore, I hope that nobody else should do anything like this and whoever does so will be punished.

Ananti Mishr, subedar of the platoon posted at the Lahori Gate

(92, 73)

BUILDINGS, NURSES AND CERTIFICATES
The hospitals and doctors of the army

This section examines the functioning of hospitals and doctors. We know from a spy's letter that there were doctors and hospitals attached to every regiment. Many of those tending to the sick were volunteers, the most famous one being a British-trained doctor called Wazir Hasan Khan who had come from Agra. There were also hakims and, presumably, vaids who were tending to the sick. The existence of doctors and hospitals points, once again, to some measure of organization and order in the rebel government. The fact that professionals, in addition to soldiers and civilians, were also trying to serve the cause also attests to the wide support base enjoyed by the uprising.

In this section, we learn how hospitals for the sick were organized, how money for them was allotted and how they raised their supplies. There were people who were permanently employed in hospitals, while the wounded were tended to by fellow soldiers who were granted special leave to do so. A sick person had to produce a medical certificate by the doctor attached to his regiment in order to legitimize his leave. The volunteers or mujahideen who did not belong to any of the regiments had their own hospital.

Even as the rebels fought the British, they retained many of their practices and names. Apart from styling themselves as colonels or generals, the medical officers identified themselves as doctors, even in Urdu. Similarly, when they issued medical certificates, they use the English term 'certify' to describe it; there are even references to a 'sick-van' for treating the wounded.

Thatchers required for preparing bamboo frames for hospital walls

Umar Khan to the kotwal, 29 July

After greetings, the requirement is for six thatchers for preparing the bamboo frame of the walls of the hospital. I hope the thatchers will be sent.

Umar Khan, subedar major, thirtieth regiment

(Note on the letter:
A circular has been sent to the thanadar of Turkman Gate.)

(111c, 49)

The wounded are exposed to rain and need a shelter

Umar Khan, subedar, to the C-in-C, 24 July

My lord,

A petition had been submitted earlier for making arrangements for housing the sick and the wounded, and in accordance with the order, a demand was placed with the darogha of supplies, whereupon the darogha replied that no curtain, screen or canvas can be found here. The wounded are in great distress for being exposed to rain, etc. Either the government, like the English, should make arrangements for a matted frame, or allow the servant to arrange for bamboo frames and let the government defray the expenses. Otherwise the wounded will be in great pain during the monsoons.

Much obliged,
Umar Khan, subedar major
Ganga Singh, thirtieth regiment from Nasirabad

(Note on the letter:
Order is that the government is making arrangements to supply
bamboo frames and sackcloth, it will be supplied.)

(91, 46)

Court should approve leave for Kale Khan who has been
certified as wounded

Medical certificate, 29 July

Certified that when I today examined the one named Kale Khan,
jamadar of the third company, thirty-sixth volunteer regiment, it was
learnt that Kale Khan had fallen ill with back pain because of riding
on a camel, and when I examined him properly, I found that there is
still pain in his legs and he still cannot walk. Therefore with this form
certified hereby, he has been given leave for ten days. The officers of the
court are urged to approve it.

Syed Mohammed Jaan, doctor volunteer

(60, 444)

Havaldar Puran Chaube given leave for four days

Doctor to Lala Durgraj Singh, havaldar major, 6 August

After salutations,

Let this be known that when I examined one named Puran Chaube,
havaldar of the third company, I found that he has a boil on the
right thigh and he finds it difficult to walk because of that; therefore,
the havaldar has been given leave for four days so that the boil
may heal.

Syed Mohammed Jaan, doctor volunteer

(70, 205)

Sepoy Shiv Ghulam Sukul given leave for gout

Medical certificate, 8 September

Certified the one named Shiv Ghulam Sukul, sepoy of the first company, thirty-sixth volunteer regiment, suffers from gout and his left knee has cramped up; in truth, this illness is terrible and painful and the sepoy is testified to be constantly present at the hospital and is not fit for service of the government.

(Seal of Mir Mohammed Jaan, doctor volunteer, thirty-sixth regiment)

(60, 700)

Sib Karan sepoy should be given leave to attend to a wounded soldier

Dr Mohammed Jaan to Lala Durga Singh, jamadar, 28 July

After due salutations, let this be known that a sepoy of the seventh company, Sib Karan Singh, had been granted leave to attend to a person called Ramrup Singh, naik, sixth company, in the hospital. But the said sepoy has fallen low due to fever, whereas the naik remains badly injured. Therefore, we beseech you that out of kindness, Ram Sahay Tiwari, a sepoy of the said company, should be relieved and sent here and we will be very grateful.

Syed Mohammed Jaan, doctor, volunteers platoon

(70, 200)

Salary of hospital employees due for a month

Doctor to the C-in-C, 19 August

My lord,

The submission is that the salary of those employed in the hospital has been due for over a month. We beg that an order is passed to the treasurer so that our salaries are given to us.

Slave,
Mohammed Naseem Khan, doctor, hospital, Lal Diggi

(74, 113)

Hospital has no money to buy supplies

Doctor to the C-in-C, 7 August

My lord,

We have not been paid any dues for a month now and until now I was marking expenses by borrowing money against myself and now nobody lends any money; therefore there is no way to procure bandages and medicines and now the wounds of the injured are getting aggravated. Meanwhile, all the mujahideen of the city have been put under my charge by an order of your lordship and the slave has no time other than to look into wounds day and night, and the debts are mounting up and nobody is extending any credit. I am suffering great hardship in keeping the supply of food going and there are so many wounded mujahideen and they are all in a poor state for lack of food; therefore I pray for some money to be granted so that I can pay off the debts and the wounded get some food to eat.
May the kingdom's sun shine forever.

Slave,
Shaikh Ghulam Bakhsh, doctor at the general's hospital

(60, 510)

Request to occupy a portion of a building as a sick-van

Kishan Dayal, subedar, to the C-in-C, Undated

My lord,

A haveli had been built by the brigadier for a Brahman near the windmill. The haveli currently houses the extra stock of the stopper platoon and the outer house is vacant. Therefore, his lordship is being informed that if permission is granted, we can convert that into a sick-van for our platoon because in the absence of a building, the injured suffer greatly due to rain, etc.

Slave,
Kishan Dayal, subedar, sappers and miners platoon

(Order:
It is decreed that an order should be drawn up for the officers of the platoon to vacate the building so that ten to twelve injured men of sappers and miners may be kept there.)

(51, 61)

Expropriation of a courtesan's house for the sick and wounded, and agreement deed to the effect

C-in-C to the kotwal, 26 July–3 September

The valiant kotwal, Syed Mubarak Shah, kotwal of the city of Delhi, the petition of Surajbali, the doctor of the platoon, states that the house of Mohammedi, courtesan, located at Chandni Chowk, is vacant; therefore you are being instructed that if that house is vacant, then make arrangements for the wounded to stay there and whatever belongings of the courtesan are lying there, stack it up in one part.

Kotwal's reply to the C-in-C. The exalted C-in-C,
As per your command, the house of Mohammedi, courtesan, in accordance with the petition of Surajbali, doctor, has been vacated for

the wounded via the thanadar of Chandni Chowk. Some rooms of the building have been left free for the use of the owner and an agreement was drawn up with the courtesan Mohammedi via her servant Karam Ali, and is being sent along with this note.

Devoted,
Ram Bhau Singh,
Deputy kotwal

Statement by Mohammedi, courtesan, and Mir Karam Ali, her servant. Me, Mohammedi, daughter of Shaikh Sheikhan, and Mir Karam Ali, son of Mir Ahmed Ali, resident of mohalla Imli, and a retainer of Mohammedi, state that a house belonging to Mohammedi has been vacated by the thanadar of Chandni Chowk on the instructions of the C-in-C for the use of the wounded of the platoon, and we have vacated the house of our own will and volition and we clarify that nobody has forced us or coerced us and nobody has threatened or abused us; therefore these few words by way of an agreement and acceptance so that a certificate remains for the use of the platoon when required.

(45)

EITHER TRUST US OR DISBAND US
Sikhs fight for the King

The role of the Sikhs in the suppression of the uprising is well known. There have been innumerable explanations for the role played by the Sikhs and the Punjabi Muslims in quelling the rebellion. What is not so well known, or not known at all, is the fact that Sikhs also fought on the side of the rebels. The documents in this section attest to a sizeable number of Sikhs fighting for the rebels. There was at least one regiment of Sikhs within the city, consisting of more than eight platoons. Their presence was not uncomplicated. It was met with suspicion and there were persistent doubts about their loyalty. The Sikhs themselves were not unaware of this. One document below asserts their loyalty and warns that if they continue to be suspected, they will go away. Apart from a separate regiment, Sikh soldiers were also interspersed within other platoons. It is not clear how many of them were part of regiments which rebelled and how many were volunteers who enlisted on the King's side. One document mentions the arrival of thirty-five Sikh soldiers from Benares. Notwithstanding the claims and counter-claims about the loyalty of the Sikhs, they seem to have fought to the end as one of the documents dating from the end of August establishes. What happened to these soldiers once Delhi was reconquered is not clear. Nobody seems to have noticed them and they are not mentioned in any of the known accounts. Their presence is a completely unacknowledged fact, hence the particular importance of this section and the reason why these documents have been included separately.

The Sikh regiment is allowed to shift camp from a church to a haveli

C-in-C to the officers of the Sikh regiment, 1 July

All the officers of the Sikh platoon,

Your application to the effect that the church where we are putting up is no place and that if permission is granted, may we shift to the haveli of Mansoor Ali Khan, was received. The instruction about that is that if there is place to live available in the said haveli and nobody is disturbed, then you may shift there.

(60, 253)

Sikh officers take the oath of obedience and loyalty

Sikh subedars to the King, Undated

The exalted Emperor,

The submission of the devoted servants is this that in accordance with the orders of the resplendent one, all the senior and junior officers of the Sikh regiment have taken an oath on their religion and faith that whatever command is issued by the Emperor will be followed by them heart and soul. All the soldiers pledge their obedience and loyalty.

Saja Singh, subedar
Bahadur Singh, subedar
Kharak Singh, subedar
Mehtab Singh, subedar
Bhagwan Singh, subedar

May the kingdom's sun shine forever.

Devoted,
Kan Singh, colonel of the Sikh regiment, Delhi Gate

(150, 11)

Sikh soldiers are in league with the firangis and it has also been heard that Gulab Singh keeps enticing all Sikh soldiers to his side

Bulhan Singh, commander of the fifteenth regiment, to the C-in-C, 29 August

My lord,

The order issued by your lordship about seven companies of the Sikh regiment to move to Bahadurgarh, vis-à-vis that, my submission is that the companies should not go towards Bahadurgarh because just now it has been learnt that the Nasirabad cavalry is to go there. There are no sepoys or cannons of our party there. It has been heard that your lordship has instructed three companies to go across the Jamuna. My lord, the submission is that you should not let the Sikh company proceed because I suspect that these Sikh soldiers are in league with the firangis and it has also been heard that Gulab Singh keeps enticing all Sikh soldiers to his side and all the Punjabi sepoys are in league with the British and it has been heard from your lordship's side that soldiers and guns of our side are posted at Bahadurgarh, then where is the need?

With the greatest respects,

Devoted,
Bulhan Singh, commanding officer, second platoon, fifteenth regiment
(70, 240)

Disband the Sikhs or form a separate unit for them and send them to the bloodiest battle front

C-in-C to the CoM, 21 August

The Sikh infantry and cavalry of the Sikh officers have requested that all the Sikhs should be separated from the army and should be sent to the toughest and most bloody front. As far as the suspicion of our colluding with the English is concerned, we have taken an oath about it and if we really wanted to leave who could have stopped us and who can stop us now? We fight for the sake of our faith and our religion. The government should disaggregate the Sikhs from all the infantry and cavalry units and let them form an independent unit. We cannot fight like this. And if my lord is not willing to separate us, then he can have all the Sikhs paraded and ejected from their regiments and get them to surrender their weapons.

Therefore, in accordance with the wishes of the Sikhs, you are instructed to discuss it and decide what is best.

(70, 224)

The King praises the Sikhs

Colonel Khizr Sultan to all the officers of the Sikh regiment,
23 August

We were called by his majesty who stated that he was confident that the Sikh platoon would give a brilliant illustration of their valour and bravery, and out of generosity, expressed great praises of you; therefore you are being directed that immediately on seeing this note, five companies should get ready and reach the Shamgarh front. There should be no delay.

(Note on the letter:
My lord, the ordinance of his lordship was received. The submission is that our platoons went to the Teliwara front at four o' clock in the day.)

(152, 35)

The Ideologue

THE *DEHLI URDU AKHBAR*
May–September 1857

The *Dehli Urdu Akhbar* was one of the three newspapers that remained in print in Delhi during the uprising. *Siraj-ul-Akhbar*, a Persian court newsletter of the old kind that mainly printed news of Bahadur Shah's court, and *Sadiq-ul-Akhbar*, an Urdu newspaper, were the other two. All three had been in existence from before the uprising, but ceased publication afterwards. The two Urdu newspapers borrowed liberally from publications in English, the newspapers and the *Delhi Gazette*, as well as from old-style court newsletters to disseminate information about the old and new to the incipient print community which was taking shape before the uprising. However, the content and roles of both newspapers changed drastically during the uprising. Whereas earlier they had provided detailed notices of the colonial government—news of campaigns, transfers, retirements and other government announcements—during the uprising, they turned into enthusiastic supporters of the King and the rebels. They adopted a tone of shrill racism against the British and espoused high religious rhetoric to justify the uprising and to raise support for it. This transformation of tone and sentiment is too abrupt and can only possibly be explained by the existence of severe subterranean resentment and anger against the British.

We do not know enough about the circulation and reception of the two newspapers to make authoritative claims about their role in the uprising. The *Dehli Urdu Akhbar*'s circulation was confined to the city. The pamphlet that its editor Maulvi Baqar had prepared to justify and exhort jihad on the population found few takers in spite of his repeated pleas. On the other hand, his hard-hitting line against the rich and the privileged elicited strong criticism from some quarters. However, Baqar was part of the old elite of the city, he was close to Bahadur Shah and had access to his court, and therefore, it is not far-fetched to view the paper as an important voice of the city.

While he was often venomous and racist in his descriptions of the British, Baqar's partisanship of the rebel cause was not indiscriminate. He came down heavily, by turns, on the army, on the residents of the city and on the administration. He criticized the army for oppressing the Dilliwallas, condemned the residents, especially the well-off for not supporting the soldiers enough, and constantly lamented the neglect of the postal system and of the collection of revenues from outlying areas. He urged soldiers to avoid congregating in Delhi and exhorted them to instead take charge of the districts they were in and pressed the city rulers to send out troops to areas beyond the capital. Along with all this, he reported extensively on the state of the city, prices of goods, scarcity, hygiene and neglect of other civic amenities.

Although Baqar saw himself as a committed journalist and stated in the first issue after the uprising began that he chose to risk his life for the edification of his readers, he should also be seen as one of the most articulate ideologues on the rebel side. He reminded his readers of the supercilious and racist attitude of the British in the past, gloated at their present discomfiture, tirelessly contested their propaganda and strongly rebutted their claims to sovereignty, governance and authority. Accounts of British perfidies and breaches of treaties were the staple of rebel proclamations everywhere. But clearly, the religious and cultural interrogation of Indians, which marked the colonial interaction with them before the uprising, had jarred greatly with Baqar for some time, as well as on his readers, and he gave ample vent to his feelings when the uprising began.

While appeals to Hindu–Muslim unity and elaborations on the theme were common features of propaganda, Baqar showed intense familiarity with Hindu religious myths and histories. Yoking mythology, history and jihad into a seamless whole, Baqar adduced a whole gamut of religious and secular arguments about why the British needed to be ousted. This included the plea of 'drain of wealth', demilitarization of Indians and the need for religious parity and tolerance. In addition, he urged his compatriots to reform their attitude to business and enterprise and acquire military training.

The emphasis on reform, self-strengthening and self-criticism notwithstanding, Baqar's most consistent priority was to boost the morale of the rebels. In doing so he resorted most frequently to divine sanction and how divine will was manifested in the fall of the British. Of the total number of times the word jihad has been mentioned in the selections presented below, more than half occur in one particular issue. This shows that while religious exhortations were necessary and easily deployed, the focus was not on jihad as much as on piety, repentance and steadfastness of faith. The emphasis on religious appeals should, however, be offset against Baqar's own lamentation at the indifference of Dilliwallas to fundamental aspects of religious duty. Religion may have been a dominant and overt sentiment during the uprising, but not everyone affected by it was as full of religious fervour as the ideologues and the proclamations desired them to be.

17 May 1857

Love of religion gushes over and the goras and
the Christians are decimated

When I reached [the site of commotion, on the day the soldiers arrived from Meerut] I saw that in front of Fakhrulmasjid, a motley group of some twenty to twenty-five Tilangas were standing around and people were directing them towards the mosque. I saw that some Tilangas went inside the mosque and there they shot a number of people and instantly sent them on a journey to the hereafter. Further ahead, I saw the church and Collins Saheb's kothi where two to three hundred Tilangas and horsemen were standing and from there different groups were spreading here and there and asking everyone the whereabouts of the English.

If anybody gave any information, four–five soldiers would immediately accompany that man and in no time two or three dead Englishmen or Christians were found lying in every lane and street. They entered each kothi and killed the Englishmen along with their women and children and whoever went into a house or hid in a drain escaped at that time and all the goods and properties of the kothis were plundered. All the property from the church and kuchehri including the chairs and tables, the floorings, etc., and the marble of the floor were taken away. After a while, when this humble one went towards the magazine and crossed the masjid of Nawab Hamid Ali Khan, I saw the corpse of Nixon Saheb, the leader of the commissionery. Some wit had even placed a biscuit in his mouth.

The mujahideen had taken control of the magazine barracks and it was heard that some Englishmen along with cleaners were holed up inside the magazine and had locked the gate from inside. When I went towards the madrasa [Delhi College] I found that all the property including the tables, chairs, portraits, pictures and instruments, chemicals and medicines and a library of English and Persian books worth thousands of rupees and maps, etc., were all being taken as loot by people and it reached such a pass that even the flooring and coverings and joints of the gates were dug out.

It was heard that Taylor, the principal of the Delhi College, was also hiding there and he was yet destined to live and had to enjoy the air of the world for some more time, but the next day, that is on Wednesday, he was killed near the same thana in the afternoon. This man was very prejudiced towards the Christian religion and often misled the undiscerning and Dr Chaman Lal's death too is on his head.

In the city and around, the Gujars and Jats have created havoc, the roads are blocked, thousands of kothis have been plundered and burnt. Upon reaching the kotwali of Delhi, the ghazis enquired after the kotwal. The prisoners came and sought release. At first the guards showed some disinclination, but afterwards, they and the kotwal could not do anything except to obey the Tilangas. From that moment, the former kotwal has been missing and there is no news of him.

It is heard that the prisoners of jail were all released. In order to console and reassure his subjects, his majesty rode on an elephant and took a tour of the city. On the 18th, Sadar Aala Mufti Sadruddin Khan Bahadur and Maulvi Abbas Ali Bahadur and Janab Karam Ali Khan Saheb Munsif were appointed to look after the civil and military courts. On the twentieth, letters inviting the rulers of Jaipur, Bikaner and Alwar were dispatched. On the 21st, the princes Mirza Khizr Sultan Bahadur, Janab Mirza Abdullah Bahadur, Mirza Mughal Bahadur and Janab Mirza Koochak Sultan Bahadur were appointed to command the platoons and drums and other materials of war were issued to them.

24 May 1857

The English will not escape because there is divine wrath upon them but Dilliwallas are sick of the plunder

Compared to last year a much smaller crowd gathered at the Jama Masjid on the last Friday of Ramzan this year. His exalted majesty did not grace the masjid because of indisposition and because of the heat of the sun. Most of the princes too did not come because they were busy looking after military preparations.

Kol

It has been heard that after blackening the face of the English, four companies of Kol have also appeared before his majesty. Whichever Englishman was found was put to death and the treasury was looted. All the people too engaged in plunder and whatever anyone found was looted. The platoon of which these soldiers are a part is called after Jalesar and the rest of the sepoys too, God willing, are also about to come.

Jhajjhar

The ruler of Jhajjhar has sent his son to his majesty and it is also said that Jhajjhar's father-in-law has also come here. People were apprehensive that the honourable ruler had intentions of disobeying his majesty and had given shelter to Englishmen. Now it has been learnt that those Englishmen who were there in Jhajjhar were cast out under protection of troopers from there towards the hills. But most holy men say that people are mistaken if they think the English will escape safely because there is divine wrath upon them. They maintain that now wherever the English go, they will not find shelter.

One venerable man had a dream that our Prophet Mohammed is saying to Jesus that your followers have risen very high and have become an enemy of my name and wish to efface my religion. To this Lord Jesus replied that they are not my followers, they do not follow my path, they have joined ranks with Satan's followers. Eventually, the Prophet said the last *kalima*, upon which Lord Jesus pulled out his sword and presented it to the Prophet saying this sword was given by you and here it is. The Prophet said to Jesus that he should give it to Ali; and when he tried to give it to Ali, he said give it to Husain, meaning that sword was given over to Imam Husain.

Some people even swear that the day the horsemen came here, there were she-camels ahead of them on which rode green-robed riders, and then they instantly vanished from sight and only the troopers remained and they killed whichever Englishman they found and cut them like carrots and radish and pulled their legs off and threw them.

Sikandra

The treasury there too was looted and the Englishmen killed and the offices were gutted.

Ghaziabad

It is said that the Gujars somehow got hold of a couple of cannons and blew up Ghaziabad and committed great plunder. These Gujars too are a strange caste. Three days ago, they had given an undertaking to the tehsildar and had taken over the responsibility of administration and now the situation is such that they have taken Ghaziabad to this pass.

The city of Delhi—the people are sick of the looting, and the police have no control

The population here is greatly harassed and sick of all the pillaging and plundering. Everyone, whether of the city or outsiders, is busy looting and plundering. The thanas do not have even an iota of control and authority compared to earlier times. Sepoys are badly needed to provide help and support. From the son of Shaikh Wali Mohammed, merchant, that is from the house of Shaikh Mohammed Ibrahim Zauq, horses were stolen and marched away. One horse was retrieved by someone after great difficulty. Great dangers beset all the respectable and well-off people of the city.

One government functionary, it is said, took over a woman's property worth thousands and even took her alone to the kothi. Eventually, the subedar of the platoon imprisoned him. Colonel James Skinner's kothi was plundered so badly that it cannot even be described. The soldiers marched into a man's house and sprayed him with bullets. God knows! The city is being ravaged and a lot of people have adopted this habit that they dress up like Tilangas and plunder the city—having pillaged the guns, arms and ammunition from the magazine and from English kothis, people dress up like Tilangas and commit plunder. Five men were arrested yesterday. It was eventually revealed that one was a kahar with Simon Saheb, one an ahir, one a chamar who used to work in the cantonment, and there were two more chamars. They were taken to the platoon, where they said where they were from and when their lie and deceit was discovered, the subedar and the sepoys gave them a heavy lashing and they are now in captivity.

A petition was presented to his majesty that sepoy lookalikes are plundering the people of the city. His majesty ordered the kotwal to make arrests and the officers too were reprimanded. This should actually be taken as divine chastisement and revenge for the kind of sinful lies, deceits and evil deeds that had begun to prosper in the city and this plundering and pillaging is a fallout of those misdeeds from the true avenger. Of course, with dry twigs, some wet ones too get burnt. It is incumbent to seek pardon and forgiveness from the Almighty for the sake of peace and order.

Recruit high-caste men for the army

It is said that Nawab Aitemaduddaulah Syed Hamid Ali Khan Bahadur also attained the distinction of appearing in the royal durbar. From his exalted grace, he has been given the responsibility of recruiting five hundred men and from his pious tongue, it was uttered that in this recruitment Syed, Mughal, Pathan—the sharif qaum—should be favoured, not the low-caste ones.

*The King is sick of the harassment of his subjects and
will retire soon to Kaba*

It is learnt that on hearing of the state of ruin and plunder being faced
by the population and the excesses of the evildoers and the chaos and
anarchy that reigns in the city, his exalted majesty has issued a note to
the effect that the soldiers often harass the population and the loyal
servants of the state and give them a lot of trouble. Formerly, the firangis
used to issue arbitrary orders as they pleased to our dear subjects and
the population was always worried and harassed. Now you people are
causing them grief and trouble and are plundering them. If this is what
you are bent upon, then in this, his last days, his majesty has no love for
the throne or for riches and that he will proceed on retirement towards
Khwaja Saheb, the shrine of Bakhtiyar Kaki at Mehrauli, and all the
subjects of his majesty too will accompany their ruler and go with him.
Or he will migrate towards Kaba and the holy places and spend the rest
of his days in prayer, repentance and remembering the Almighty. It is
said that those who heard the announcement immediately became tear-
filled. God Almighty, the provider of all causes please ensure that the city
is brought to order which may give relief to the people and also remove
the furrows of worry and apprehension from his majesty's brow.

Yesterday, a proclamation was made in the city about three things.
First, that a surcharge will be laid on the Company rupee and the
royal coin will be issued as before. Second, no resident of the city
should collect ruffians and other evildoers because of the potential for
sedition and nobody should be culpable of causing a riot or a fight. If
any untoward incident takes place, the person will be blown away from
a cannon. Third, whatever stuff or goods were stolen from the magazine
by unscrupulous people and are in possession of anyone should be
returned immediately to the city kotwali.

Most English houses have been plundered and the goods and valuables thereof taken away and they were gutted and the kothis are still being set on fire. Although it was said that a clerk had been appointed to supervise their safety, today it transpired that Thomas Saheb's kothi too has been set on fire by someone. Special and urgent efforts are needed in this direction and strong and fearless sepoys should be posted at such houses and many English houses still remain standing, which are full of goods and if no adequate protection is provided for them, then property that belongs to the government will be pilfered away. A very religious sepoy of the army says that at Kol, a treasury worth some eleven lakh rupees was wasted in plunder. It is highly regrettable that men are not going into the districts and order is not being maintained. If they can act quickly, a great deal of treasure may still be acquired and revenue too may begin to flow. It is said though that four lakh rupees have come from Bulandshahar.

Lucknow

Some people say that Munawwaruddaulah has been seated on the throne. God knows.

Treasury, etc.—the princes show the genes of Timur and Alamgir

The paper had been composed till here when it was heard that the Rohtak treasure has come in. His noble prince showed great alacrity and bravery in taking possession of the treasury immediately upon arrival there with his valiant soldiers, and swiftly returned and presented it to his majesty. The amount and the state of plunder that was committed is still unknown. It is to be hoped that the *murshidzada*s of the universe [that is, the princes] would take charge with efficiency and swiftness, in accordance with the agreement of his majesty; and would render their services with sincerity; and would take charge of whichever district they are given responsibility of and would accept whatever rank they are given and there is a strong hope that they will discharge this well.

Some of the exalted princes in their intelligence strongly resemble the Timurid gene in their valour, bravery, diligence and hard work. Some, in their seriousness and sobriety, are reminders of Shahjahan and Alamgir, and God willing, this will be elaborated at some other time. In truth, our majesty's discretion should be understood as having divine approval that he has given ranks and *mansab*s to people according to how and what they deserve.

Post

It is lamentable that no adequate arrangement has yet been made for the postal system. This is more important than everything else. Some arrangement was made, but since the troopers were not duly appointed, it was left halfway. Because of the lack of runners, some money too was lost. We can still make amends—if arrangements can be made for some troopers and some money is provided then I can get the post running.

Revenue

It is believed that if arrangements can be made right away for the revenue of the *parganas*, then the zamindars still have the money from the harvest and sharecropping—recovery will be difficult later. It would be useful for his exalted majesty to recall the earlier servants to supervise these things, especially Munshi Lala Nathmal Saheb, *sarrishtadar* collectory, and his elder son, Lala Ramji Das, deputy sarrishtadar, who are experts in their fields. Recalling them and appointing them to suitable posts would be highly profitable for the government of his exalted majesty.

Kotwali

Janab Qazi Faizullah Saheb Kotwal has come in for high praise from several quarters for his dutifulness and promptness of arrangement.

31 May 1857

Many still harbour goodwill towards the British

To date the Englishmen in hiding come out in ones and twos and are meted their just desserts. Every day and every moment and every second provides a lesson to the discerning eye and the power of the Almighty is evident. One person with his face covered [was found] buying melons at a melon seller's shop. There were three–four other shoppers there. There was some pushing around and then that man abruptly spoke up—'*tum chup rahega*'. Immediately on hearing these words, everybody there knew that this was an Englishman and the young men of the bazaar fell upon him from all sides and slew him. The eyewitnesses say that he was such a large and well-built man that he would certainly have overcome two people together, but it should be seen as a sign of divine prowess that the God Almighty deprived him even the power of moving his fingers.

We observe, however, that many with infirm beliefs are still under the spell of the Christians and harbour attachment and affection for them, but a lot of those with firm beliefs as well as the discerning and noble ones say that in truth, the English have been afflicted with divine wrath by the true avenger and their arrogance has brought them divine retribution for 'God does not love the arrogant ones'. Where now are the 'Englishmen' and the 'Friends of India' and the partisans of the wisdom and greatness of English rule who used to hurl abuses on us. They should see now what the feckless, ignorant, badly administered cities and villages of Hindustan have done to the people of good intelligence and their intentions and governance.

Near the magazine I heard an elderly gentleman giving a discourse, saying that o ye group of Muslims, compliments to you, and it is incumbent upon you to see to the progress of faith and religion and keep your faith steadfast and know that the Almighty's purpose and might is right. Follow the Quranic verse, 'The respect of God and Prophet' and do not have any faith or confidence in the greatness, arrangements or deceitful words of the Christians. God has given them such a blow that within a matter of minutes this carnage was the outcome and he imparted such courage to every humble and lowly person that his will became manifest. He has powers over everything, will he not overturn all their schemes and ploys? It is incumbent upon you to have faith in God and act on [the maxim] 'Obey God and obey the Prophet' every minute and every moment. And all courageous souls should spend all their energy in protecting and being loyal to the shadow of God on earth, his exalted majesty and should remember that they have the help and support of the Almighty himself and they have this God-given blessing. Anybody who lacks in rendering help, service or support to them will be committing impropriety before God and his Prophet and he will not come to a good end in this world or the next and he will see the result of good and bad deeds here itself.

Every day news waxes here that the troops have left for Meerut but morning gives way to night in this same way, may God quickly encourage this deed. A lot of the arrivals from Meerut reveal that the people there are expecting and awaiting help and troopers from here. While it is certain that the goras [would] have laid mines around the battery but the people of faith have a sure expectation of divine help that an assault from the victorious forces of the Muhammadi side will produce victory for them over the people in the magazine and the latter would meet their end within minutes.

Robbing soldiers find themselves robbed—a Moses for every pharaoh

Strange manifestations of divine interventions come about. Soldiers, or those dressed up as soldiers, have robbed so much money from the treasury, from banks and from the kothis of Englishmen, that many were simply unable to carry it. They have begun to convert it into asharfis and created a scenario where instead of sixteen or seventeen rupees [as was customary], asharfis were being exchanged for twenty and even twenty-five rupees. But the rascals of the city have been so smart that reason has been left a spectator. A group of Tilangas had some fifteen hundred rupees and wanted to convert them into asharfis and they ran into a seemingly decent but cunning mahajan. He showed them some asharfis, took all their money and went away. It was the gate of a lane near Dariba and the Tilangas thought that it was the mahajan's kothi. They set up a guard at the gate believing that the lala-ji would soon be bringing the asharfis while that gentleman entered the lane and made away either from the haveli at Munshi Kanwal lane or from some other side. The Tilangas, harried and worried, kept waiting for him and eventually, after a long time, entered the gate and discovered a row of houses in the lane. They started clamouring before each door and the residents stepped out and there was a big commotion. Finally, when the Tilangas realized that it was some *aiyyar* who has done his deed, they were livid and tried to extract money from the people of the mohalla to make good their loss. The people reasoned with them and said that in this lane there was not a single house belonging to a trader, moneylender or mahajan, but that it was populated entirely by *qalandar* Muslims. Someone else makes away with it and someone else should pay for it, this cannot be. Everybody was saying that there is a Moses for every pharaoh, meaning that the way the Tilangas had expropriated others' wealth, the same way theirs too was taken away.

Plunder of the magazine

The magazine is in a shambles. Thousands of maunds of gunpowder are being carried away by zamindars and Gujars. The money that the English had put together by plundering and inflicting hardships on people camouflaged in sweet talk is now being appropriated by lowly persons who have made away with property and goods worth thousands. People say that many zamindars are keeping the gunpowder for their own use while many chamars take it and sell it in the bazaars. While the opinion of some is that they take it to Karnal and Meerut, it would not be surprising if they are selling it there to the remaining Englishmen. Nevertheless, if this thing is true, then this matter should immediately be looked into. However, there is such divine retribution on the English that even if they have a lakh maunds of gunpowder and regardless of what help is rendered to them, they will still be overwhelmed. The accomplished saints and sagacious ones warn that let those who wish so lose their faith or those who want to keep it do so, but God Almighty is firmly on the side of the Muslims against the Christians and such misfortune is upon them that they will never prosper.

The kings of our country should not fall prey to British machinations

One maulvi saheb was giving a discourse saying that we are warning all the raises, rajas and jagirdars of our country that they should not fall prey to their machinations and deceitfulness and should not unnecessarily bring destruction upon themselves. Don't they see that the Englishmen had not wanted to leave even a handful of land or even an iota of government under their control and had taken over so much of the administration and had wished to destroy religion and faith? What kind of treatment did they mete out to his exalted majesty or to the kingdom of Awadh and what kind of fidelity did they show to their promises that they would now fulfil their pacts? Be warned, be careful, if you are deceived at this juncture, then all our countrymen, Hindus and Muslims, will repent greatly and will be left lamenting with their hands on their heads, and then no repentance would be of any use.

They should see the approval of the unseen and divine help and the benevolence and kindness of God Almighty on their state and how God has bestowed the miracle upon them that their own forces and army have turned against them and from all sides the Almighty has beaten and bruised them. So now any thought of helping them or supporting them or being sincere or loyal to them is akin to standing against the true God itself. And in truth there was such power and effect in the oration of the maulvi saheb that all present were deriving pleasure from it and except 'it is true and blessings upon it' nothing else was being uttered by anyone. One of those present was describing the act of the murder of Lawrence Saheb that at the time he was killed by the sepoys, he was pleading that he was a faqir, but the sepoys examined his back to ascertain the marks of the two bullets he had received at the battle of Kabul and confronted him with that. He could not say anything except to keep silent. But the differences among reporters create consternation that one is left hesitant whether to write something lest tomorrow another reporter come up with something else about the same firangi. Like yesterday somebody said he had seen Munroe Saheb lying dead with his own eyes and then it was heard that he had reached Agra. Someone reports seeing Butler Saheb dead on the road while another claims that he reached Agra and yet another that he is in Meerut. Some people say that people have gone from Peshawar to the Shah of Iran to carry news of the disturbances here and their army is reported to be in or near Qandahar. But what leaves us wondering is that there is neither a dak nor telegraph, then how did this news travel from Peshawar to here?

Précis of the royal newspaper

Mohammed Siddiq Khan, the thanadar of Guzar Faiz Bazaar, was transferred to the Lahori Gate area. It was mentioned before his majesty that one Tilanga attacked a horseman at Lal Diggi, who was of the Khatri qaum and was carrying a sword. The Tilanga forcibly tried to snatch the sword from him and when he refused to part with it, the said Tilanga shot him from force of habit. Apart from that, a vegetable seller was injured by a Tilanga at Chandni Chowk with a sword. One man presented a petition saying that fifty thousand rupees were lying in store at the Palwal tehsil and his majesty should depute a company of Tilangas to collect and deposit the money in the government treasury. Otherwise, it is likely that the zamindars of the rural areas would plunder it. Therefore an order was passed that this should be brought to Mirza Mughal's notice.

*Administration of the city–Praises for the police but
the soldiers cannot be controlled*

Everybody is full of praise at the efficiency and dutifulness of the
kotwal of the city and the vigil that he has been maintaining. But
low and high alike are helpless because of the lack of control over the
Tilangas and complaints about this are frequent. No doubt it is very
good that the soldiers are putting up at the cantonment, otherwise the
residents of the city would have been utterly destroyed. The people are
under great distress because of them. Some thanadars have also been
found to be very dedicated to the task of maintaining law and order.
But because it is the end of the month, people are very harassed and
needy. Hopefully, if the salaries are disbursed tomorrow, everybody
will get a new lease of life. Many of the poor are said to be bordering
on starvation because the *bania*s and traders have also become stingy
and the moneylenders are lying low because of the fear of Tilangas
and cannot properly conduct their business. The arrangement of two
things is highly imperative and urgent. First, the distribution of salaries
and second, the restraining of Tilangas.

14 June 1857

*Great regret that no arrangements made about
the postal system—word of guidance*

It is quite amazing that even the news of one particular place, the exalted
fort and the city itself, reported by different people varies greatly so what
can one say of accounts of places outside and farther off. That is why
we greatly regret that no proper arrangement has yet been made for the
postal system. This leads to great confusion and distress. Now some
people, quoting the arrivals from there, state that some Englishmen had
collected there but due to divine grace they are not to be found. One

elderly gentleman says that it is my conviction that since the English qaum is suffering under divine wrath, the rajas, notables and people of our country should not be apprehensive and drawing strength from the Almighty should remain steadfast in their opposition, knowing that the English no longer have the strength to stand up to our country and our people. Since God has taken away from them their government we should all stand with one body and one mind, without hesitation or scruples, to battle with them. Forgetting pleasure and leisure, they should consider it mandatory to fully submit themselves to the will and commandments of his majesty. It is binding on the troops to follow the royal instructions fully and to not demur in any way in confronting these enemies of faith and religion.

Unlike under the firangis, nobody has been persecuted for their faith in India

The followers of Hindu dharam should consider this state, and this situation, to be one of divine grace from the *nirankar jyoti* because Hindus and Muslims are after all the two leading religions in this country at this time and because mutually, nobody objects to anybody's religion or faith. It is obvious to everybody that under the rule of our exalted majesty, nobody would have ever heard any account of the persecution or harassment of Hindus, Muslims or of followers of other faiths because of their religion. In fact, since the time of Amir Timur, the heaven dweller, nobody big or small has ever faced any such trouble and people have spent their lives without any oppression or cruelty. Now they, within merely a hundred years of governing have taken matters to such a low that people began to lose their religion and Hindus and Muslims alike were traumatized. Apart from that you will find that whenever and wherever governments decline, religious controversies and conflicts abound and you can see the result of such machinations in the case of the firangis too. Especially since the army itself is composed of people of different faiths it must be remembered that if anybody errs or demurs or succumbs to deception they will repent in this life and the next and then repentance will do no good and everybody will eventually regret and cry over it. I have copied in brief the speech of that man who was speaking at one place with great eloquence and force.

But this is an object lesson that many such Hindus and Muslims exist in this realm who still are well-wishers and loyalists of those antagonists of true faith and religion, the Christians, and they are heard to be pining for their victory and rehabilitation and secretly wish well for them. It is incumbent on all Muslims and Hindus to be vigilant and dedicated to unearthing such things with the utmost exertion and effort and to ferret out such sentiments and to bring such people to task so that others can take heed from it. It is necessary to send some cavalry and infantry to Panipat via the Sonepat road to put a stop to their reinforcements. So the people of religion should consider that God Almighty is on their side and should see that it is He who has taken them to such a pass and He who has power is still around. The man was giving a discourse with such passion and force that every single listener was rapt in attention and the fervour of deen and dharam was evident in every face.

'God has power over everything and everything except God will be destroyed'—Hindu mythology and Islamic history

O countrymen, looking at the strategy and wisdom of the English, their arrangements and governance, the expanse of their dominion and their overflowing treasury and extensive revenues you perhaps feel discouraged that how can such a kingdom be overcome suddenly. But those who are Muslims may heed their precepts, and those of Hindu dharam should illuminate their hearts with the refulgence of their faith. Except the *adipurush*, the Primeval Deity, nothing is permanent. They should look at their religious stories as to how many magnificent dynasties and kingdoms came into existence in the land of Hindustan and how they all met their end. Ravana, the king of Sarandeep who had an army of demons until he was beaten by Raja Ramchandra, the Suryabanshi Rajput. Nothing can withstand divine resolution. Kans, the ruler of Mathura, what a powerful king who conquered the whole world and made to assault the Inderlok itself, when in the Yadukul family was born Sri Krishna Maharaj who so vanquished him that except his name nothing was left. Apart from that the Kshatriya clan that had become so powerful that it was vying for equality with the Brahmans, witness the workings of the Almighty that how the raja called Parsuram destroyed them and eventually after Raja Janmejaya, they were so wiped out that not even their name remained. So when you see all these mighty kingdoms and remember how God brings them to an end after a while, then why do you not comprehend that God has sent his hidden help to defeat this hundred-year-old kingdom so that this community which regarded the children of God with contempt and addressed your brothers and brethren as 'black man' and thus insulted and humiliated them, they are to be shown the prowess of the Almighty. It has been frequently observed that this fear and oppression has made a difference to the way you eat and dine, you sleep and sit. You must lose all fear and apprehension and in fact running away from the city out of fear is akin to denying divine favour and help.

O brothers of faith, the more fear you exhibit, or hesitation or apprehension or dismay you display the more will it be a sign of relinquishing faith. Don't you read in the books about the power that came into the stove of a poor old woman cooking rotis that such a storm was unleashed that the whole world was submerged? The pharaoh who out of an overflowing coffer of wealth, splendour and magnificence had begun to claim divinity for himself, his whole realm was submerged in the Nile river in an instant. Remember those Abbasid caliphs whose sleeve cuffs were sixty to seventy yards long and who never deigned to shake hands or even allow prostrations before them and whosoever could touch their sleeves in lieu of a handshake considered himself heaven-bound; after a while, the Tartars were given such manly powers and Halaku and Chengiz Khan were created and the Abbasid caliphate was destroyed and their two worlds decimated. In another age, Subuktigin and the Ghaznavid family were made prosperous and afterward the Ghurids were created who finished off the Ghaznavids and their clans and subjects. The Ghurids were pushed out of India by the Khaljis; similarly, the Safavids were replaced by the Qachars in Iran.

What then may be the hesitation in, with divine help, one man taking on and killing another? And a man who was almost equal to their arms and legs and even their swords because through him they conquered several countries and brought many realms under their subjugation. Their help and valour helped quieten the sultans of Rus, Iraq, Iran, China, Central Asia, in fact all countries of Firang and Europe who would dare not do anything opposed to them and avoided battle as much as possible. Despite this you can see that their numbers are tenfold compared to the numbers of the English and the goras. In fact if you consider yourself too a man and do not give up the beacon of bravery and keeping in mind the events described above gird up your loins then you have the same two hands as them. Each one of you, acting under divine approbation, is the king of the battlefield, like a lion in front of the enemy and in numbers a hundredfold of their figure, even a thousandfold but regretfully if one meets a fifty or hundred people then out of them maybe one or two men keep a sword as a weapon with them. Otherwise everybody blames the sepoys for showing negligence and except for agitation and commotion nothing comes forth as talk. On top of that, despite these fears and apprehensions they are not scared of God even and spread canards, panics and false stories. If only the Muslims would show greater regard for God and his Prophet.

Tilangas should emulate Arjun, Bhim and Amir Timur

O valiant Tilangas, just as in history books the bravery and courage of heroes in former kingdoms as in ancient Indian history—the achievements of the Yadubanshi clan, of Arjun and Bhim, etc.—or as in Iranian history, the feats of Rustam and Saam; and in Islamic history, the victories of Saheb Qiran Amir Timur and the brave soldiers of Chengiz Khan and Halaku Khan or the memory of the Nadirshahi contingent remains on people's lips as the epitome of bravery and valour and acts as a spur to actions, similarly this achievement of yours will go down in history books and this feat of yours will be writ large on the face of the world forever. It will forever be recounted how and with what gallantry and daring you broke the will and arrogance of this mighty kingdom and pummelled their Pharaonic pride and *shaddadi* vanity into the ground. And while many mighty rulers stood by and helplessly watched as they arrogated the kingdom of Hindustan and could not wrest it back from them, you have taken it out of their control and appropriation. And have brought relief to the people of Hindustan who had been bewitched under a cruel fate. Consider God your helper and fear only him and seek help from him for he only will help you.

Scarcity, high prices and poor hygiene—state of the city

Because of the vigilance and promptitude of the Kotwal Saheb and the other thanadars, robbery and thievery in the city are on the decline and nobody is found to complain about these things. But some people say that once this insurrection is over and if even then a similar vigil is maintained against brigandry and robbery, then it will be truly praiseworthy.

The shopkeepers of the city are being very unreasonable and the people are suffering greatly for want of essential commodities and articles of everyday use. Either the essentials cannot be found or where available, their prices are so high that they are not affordable. Either the shops are shut or where open, the situation is like there is one pomegranate and a hundred, even thousand, seekers for it. The goods available are of poor quality, but hunger is the greatest master and neediness a slave-driver, so people take what they get and consider it a boon. As is rightly said, 'If one cannot find wheat, barley will do.' Bitter and dirty ghee sells for two *ser*s for a rupee. Wheat too is expensive, but flour has become rare and in fact impossible to find. What to say of *maida* and *rava*, they are not to be found at all. Where wheat can be found, one can buy it for a rupee or half a rupee, like in the big bazaars, and then too only a little is available at one go. White wheat has become like the mythical *anqa* bird. A big problem with this is that if you give it to the grinder, they agree to grind it only after a thousand excuses and refusals and even after they accept it, they often come back saying someone seized it from them on the way.

The same thing is true for vegetables and greens. People have been found to complain that even *kaddu* and *baingan* cannot be found in the bazaars. Potatoes and yam when available are of stale and rotten variety, stored from before by far-sighted vegetable vendors. From the gardens inside the city, some produce does reach a few places, but the poor and the middle class can only lick their lips and watch as they are earmarked for the select. The dandies of the city, especially the ladies who are used to paan and tobacco, suffer greatly since paan of the size of a peepal leaf is only available at the market below Jama Masjid for as much as two paisa each! Where once upon a time the epicureans of the city would redden their mouths with paan more than the tobacco users, where every Tom or Dick would stuff their mouths with *giloris*, today, even the tobacco users are frustrated because the ingredients of paan have become so expensive. What a state has come upon us! The graceless residents of this city once found faults with the best provisions. Everybody would go only for *daudkhani* wheat, would describe flour as smelly, sometimes reject it for being sandy or would find faults with the wheat and say it gets stuck in their throats. People had so much of it to spare that a lot was left after everyday use and even the faqirs would throw it into the drain saying it was stale! Look at the Almighty's design today, may He protect us tomorrow, who knows what is in store for us because of our actions!

Apart from this there is something else which is causing a lot of hardship to the people and which needs attention and arrangement from the authorities. The water carriers have stopped filling water. Poor *shurfa* are seen carrying water in pails on their shoulders and only then the necessary household tasks such as cooking, etc., can take place. The toilet cleaners are missing, many mohallas have not been cleaned for several days and if this situation continues, then decay, deaths and disease will combine together to spoil the city's air and an epidemic will spread all over the city and even to areas adjacent and around. Undoubtedly, to those who have run away from the city and for those intending to leave the city, this kind of rot and decay provides them with a valid justification for doing so.

It is just the beginning of love, why do you cry
Let us see what is in store further ahead.

Précis of the royal akhbar—the king wants to retire

It is reported on the sixth of Shawwal, on Sunday, his majesty called all the leading notables of the realm and stated that this seeker of the highest gathering, due to the intransigence and disorderliness of the sepoys, intends to bid goodbye to the throne of the government and giving up his [Royal] dress, wishes to acquire earthy [literally, of dust] garb and go for Haj or make for the dargah of the Qudus Sarrah, Qadam Sharif and spend his last days as a servant of that shrine. All the princes unanimously obeyed his command and acquired saffron robes.

On the petition of officers of the platoon, it was stated that they are all in charge of their assignments and should keep everything in a state of readiness. On the tenth, the treasure from Hansi was entered into the royal treasury and it amounted to one lakh nineteen thousand rupees. On the eleventh, the government workshops were directed to disburse salaries and emphasis was laid on proper administration. The treasure of Mathura amounted to one lakh fifty-seven thousand rupees. On the twelfth, news came that the treasure and army are on their way from Agra. Later that news proved to be false. It was said that the goras staying at the Hindon bridge have gone towards Alipur and an order was given to the sepoys that if the claim was true, then they should prepare for battle and if this was only a ruse to kill and pillage the subjects of God, then nothing can be done for it.

The arrival of goras from Ambala via Alipur and battle, etc.—
'Faith in the King is equal to faith in the Almighty'

People in the city find out the numbers at the gora camp from the water carriers, labourers and the well-wishers of the goras and get worried. The heavy shelling day and night greatly harasses the people and some say that the English are digging a mine and that those who are helping them with provisions, etc., need to be immediately punished. It is not right for the force to stay put in the city only. They would certainly not be negligent in seeking reinforcements from Bombay and Madras and their post would be functioning—altogether the more we can hasten their suppression, the better it would be.

This was a very good thing the army did that it killed a man who was carrying provisions to them and hanged him in the kotwali. If this kind of exemplary treatment is meted out, then nobody would dare do any such thing. In fact, even in the surrounding areas, they should be hanged like this. If two or three platoons and some cavalry are deployed towards Alipur via the Sonepat–Panipat route, and every single provision supplier and helper of the British is similarly punished, then everyone will learn a lesson. The tehsildars should promptly attend to their duty in their respective areas and ensure the supply of provisions to the victorious forces; and if the zamindars are issued a warning, then all of them would tremble and take heed and everything would be taken care of. In the next raid, God willing, all the goras will be put to eternal sleep.

All people, high and low, should pray and beseech the Almighty for victory so that the prowess of our exalted majesty, the shadow of God on earth and his iqbal should increase many times. This King of ours is one of the leading saints of the era who has been approved of by the divine court. He spent years upon years, virtually in British imprisonment, never relented, and he never exhorted or incited anyone, never did he covet the throne or riches. Now of its own this divine boon has come his way. He seems bent on retiring and going to the holy places in a mendicant's garb. What has happened so far and what goes on is done entirely by the God-given army. In reality, the King, even then was helpless and was content to spend his life in a quiet corner and is now a prisoner in their [the sepoys'] hands. God Almighty helps our King in every situation. It is incumbent on the army and the people to consider the approval of the King as akin to the approval of God and his Prophet and they should not come under the awe or deception of the British—what they acquired was done either through fraud or by breaking their contract. One man came here from Lucknow and he says that in order to mislead and deceive everyone the English have put this false advertisement at all the desolate thanas en route proclaiming that at Delhi and at all other places we have regained control in, some miscreants had created a disturbance and they will be duly punished and that all the army and people remain loyal and obedient to the English. Basically, they still do not refrain from such falsehoods and deception.

21 June 1857

The kafirs are suffering for damaging our faith and ways of life

The manager saheb, a few things that I have heard and which would provide a lesson to our compatriots are being written here for the benefit of the readers of this newspaper, although these days it is very difficult to believe in any news considering how contradictory it sometimes is; but in view of their constant iteration, they are being jotted here, may its truth or falsehood fall on the reporter's head. The first exhortation of this humble writer to all the compatriots, Hindu and Muslim, is that the upturning that has taken place recently in the domain of their faith, belief and religion has been brought about only and solely because of the will of the Almighty, the true creator, and they should express great thanks to the divine power and should never be negligent in showing gratitude. They should try to earn as much grace as they can by acts of charity, by *khairat* and *punya-arth*, all their time should be spent in noble and pious deeds, and they should not allow any misgiving or fear to arise on account of fear of life or property. They should not waste their time in these worries and perturbations. It is incumbent at all times and at every moment to have complete trust and faith in the trustworthy one because the Creator without parallel has, of his own accord, removed in one stroke the fear and awe of the government of this enemy of Hindu and Muslim faith from the hearts of its dependants and servants. And no majesty of the government or regard for service or the former aura [iqbal] of the rulers remained in their hearts and all the treasures and weapons and organs of government were automatically brought to the doorstep of his exalted majesty without his asking for it. Do you then not trust the powers, ability or might of your God that you worry and panic and give vent to apprehensions? Be secure in your places and know that the kafirs had become the target of the Almighty's wrath because of their arrogance and pride and Allah detests pride and arrogance. Furthermore, these people were determined to damage faith and community and had been interfering with habits of eating, drinking and social organization and had begun even to deny the immanence of Allah in everything and had denounced the prowess of the Almighty, so why would they have not earned his wrath? Do not be misled by the daily bombardment and cannonading and noise-making of the goras, this is a very short-lived discomfort for your ears, only those will die whose death has come, nobody loses their lives before the appointed hour. Ponder as to whether death does not come to people in forms other than guns or shots or cannonballs.

The soldiers must fortify their faith and cut off supplies of the British

The victorious army must remain ever valiant and confident because God has granted them distinction in this world and the next—never let go of steadfastness. The sepoys must remember that we carry divine approval with us, when they face off with the enemies of faith in battle and even if they are seen to be advancing and gaining advantage, never fear and know that the goras are charging to their deaths. God has withdrawn the prospect of triumph and distinction from them; even if they capture one or two of our cannons in an attack, it does not matter because God Almighty who is a great avenger has deprived them of the power of prevailing upon you. Remember the battle of Badar fought by the Prophet where he succeeded in providing aid to the faithful through the angels and instilled terror in the hearts of the kafirs. Recite the prayer that the Prophet was repeatedly chanting on the day of that battle. Give strength and faith to your hearts and witness how they have deployed thousands of cannonballs against you and continue to hurl and shoot them, but you enjoy the protection of the hidden hand and therefore except for a few, nobody, old or young, was injured and rest assured that even if they deploy millions of shots, it is not going to harm anyone but would instead boomerang on them. Do not waver in your belief and confidence and have sincere faith in the Almighty and victory shall be yours. But remember never to harm the frail and the poor and be resolute in defending and providing for the subjects.

The pious and the noble and the elderly are confident that the goras are on the run and will soon vanish, but the fears and doubts that assail you are a result only of your weakness of faith and arrogance and pride. Repentance and forgiveness are the key to ridding yourself of these fears. What you must do is to cut off their supplies, it has been discovered that most of their supplies of food, etc., and of magazine come from Meerut via Baghpat, therefore it is important that cavalry, etc., should be deputed in that direction and bridges, etc., should be destroyed and some of their cavalry troops are known to be devoted specifically to this task and they should be checked. It is heard that only three hundred goras are left at Meerut, that ostensibly they rule the city, but in reality their writ does not run there. When a supplicant approaches, he is told to file an application in the office and it is the same situation in Saharanpur and Muzaffarnagar.

It is a matter of deep regret that no arrangements have yet been made here about revenue collection or about the post

A man, quoting the cavalry there, maintained that if you go towards Meerut via the Hindon bridge at Ghaziabad, you will find countless mines and tunnels on the way, therefore it would be better and wiser to attack them from the Sardanah side. Their postal system is said to be functioning at Karnal and Agra, etc. It is a matter of deep regret that no arrangements have yet been made here about revenue collection or about the post which is the foundation of everything else.

People are carrying supplies and good to the goras via very clever stratagems. It was last heard that dead bodies on cots were being used to carry bread and buns to them but showing great alertness, the Tilangas arrested them. Some steps are now being taken to stop this and it is very important to ensure that news and information from here does not reach the English. Those who are infected with the salubrious effect of their salt and those who still pine for the illicit indulgences of their time, and those who are weak of faith and hopeful of their return are the ones helping them. But know that even if one takes a lakh measures to help them, nothing is going to be of any avail because God Almighty is helping the faithful and nothing can withstand him.

Self-reform, self-strengthening and purification

> If you have a keen sight, behold the salutary lesson,
> It takes great fortune to find leisure to reform.

O compatriots, the government has changed, the zeitgeist has changed, the stewardship of administration and rule has changed—it is now incumbent upon you too to give up the habits and ways of indolence and craving for comfort which you have been reared upon since childhood and to get going in reforming yourself. Give up carelessness and adopt resolution and courage. Think of the outcome, this is a very delicate moment, the time to make amends. If you have good fortune and are capable, then promotion and high office should be as nothing to you. It was an immense impediment to your well-being and to your employment opportunities to be saddled with rulers of an alien race, an alien religion and alien language as the previous rulers were, and the differences of custom, habit, behaviour and dress were the cause of disaffection. You should be grateful and thankful that your fortunes have turned once again and right has prevailed again. Under the British rule, all the top posts which raked nothing less than hundreds of rupees every month were all given over to their countrymen. It was like the famous proverb that 'the blind man was distributing sweets, he would go around and give all to his own'.

When it came to spending that earning, as everybody knows, they were very tight fisted and stingy, they would save thousands, nay lakhs of rupees and take it all back to *vilayat* with them; therefore their money was of no benefit to our Hindustan, and we derived no advantage from their savings and profits. Of those people of the Hind who were given employment, only a handful out of hundreds would get a salary of up to a hundred rupees. Watch how, God willing, all the districts will be administered now, watch how there will be such a dispensation and so many openings that it will be difficult to find competent people to fill them up.

As opposed to this, the situation abroad, especially in the countries of Faras and Turkestan, etc., is that each of their inhabitants is skilled at least in two or three professions. At least everyone in those parts is well versed in fencing whereas when we examine our situation, in spite of this emergency, the fact is that everybody talks of using a sword with real dexterity, but most people do not even know how to tie it, let alone use it. That is why all our people are today so shell-shocked and helpless and dependent on divine intervention. The situation in Faras, etc., is radically different. The people there are well skilled in the arts of war and therefore stand shoulder to shoulder with the soldiers when needed and they have no lack of fighters and nor are they so possessed of despair and helplessness as the people here. In fact, they consider circumstances such as these to be an opportunity and a God-given gift.

Leave alone the elite and the genteel and the educated sections here, even those among the common people who are always given to quarrelling and fighting have no hesitation in doing so with ordinary planks and batons, but when it comes to more lethal weapons such as swords and daggers, they never draw upon these and the moment one or two people receive the slightest wound or begin to bleed a little, everybody runs away. Since they are not professional soldiers anyway and because of the fact that for decades governance and warfare and administration have been taken care of by others, they have rarely seen carnage and bloodshed, and therefore have no experience of looking at dead or mangled or injured bodies and cannot behold that sight. Second, experience shows that these people are better at handling batons than swords. The people of Faras and Turkestan are skilled at arts other than warfare—when they see a craft or an art flourishing they immediately pick up the art of doing it. The situation here is that since this perdition has fallen on the city, most professions are suffering. If due to good fortune somebody's trade is still plying, then it is well. Otherwise, all are faced with deprivation and if God forbid there is still some life left for the grave-destined goras, then all are headed for starvation.

Learn from foreign countries and pay attention to business and manufacturing

There is something else which needs to be condemned. I don't know what the reason for this is, but most of our people greatly look down upon business, trading and shopkeeping. Whereas the truth is that if you look at it theologically, then only those professions which are explicitly forbidden should be disdained; otherwise there is nothing wrong with business and trading. It is a different thing that out of laziness and indolence, they are loath to do any hard work. Otherwise, they can see how among the Hindus and the Muslims the groups that are wealthy are those who never sit idle, every one of them is skilled at something or the other and such is God's grace upon them that they ever prosper in their chosen field and hundreds of such people have become millionaires and billionaires and even if they don't earn so much, they are at least not dependent on anybody else and that is a big enough achievement. When one examines this closely, it turns out that each and every profession and each and every trade is only inferior until the time when it is at its lower stages and at its summit there is nothing wrong left in it. For instance, the ironsmith remains an ironsmith only until he is fixing hooves or making pipes for huqqas and when he prospers in that field and begins to manufacture guns and muskets and rifles and pistols, then he is addressed as an industrialist and a manufacturer whose ware sells for hundreds of rupees. Take the case of the swords of Faras, the maker of which, Asadullah Isfahani, is a world-famous name. Watches, English instruments of music, these are all essentially based on the principles of iron smithery.

Shawls and stoles which cost thousands of rupees are all manufactured from the same art of weaving which all of you regard with such contempt. A person is called a *dalal* as long as his turnover is small, but when his fortune turns he becomes the 'prince of traders'. A soldier may be worth a few coins when he is only a chowkidar, but hard work and progress can take him to a high position in the army. A further irony is this that all these people whom we here disdainfully address as *barhai* and *lohar*, the carpenter and the ironsmith, abroad where there is great progress and everyone is highly educated and where they themselves keep accounts and exchange lakhs of rupees with their own hands, they are well regarded and prove very equipped at that. Not at all like the progeny of nobles and notables of India where all expenses and accounts are left to the accountant diwan-ji, while nawab saheb is only capable of spending the money. Supposing suddenly that in the trades mentioned above there is some scarcity of a particular object or good or someone goes bankrupt, then the supervisor of those places would become an apprentice elsewhere or would change professions and join the learning classes or would do something else like join the army. For them, it is no big deal to leave one city and go to another. In short, people of such countries are never idle or dependent or at the mercy of friends and relatives. They do not look down upon any profession other than the forbidden ones, and in spite of following one trade, are capable of picking up another. They act on the maxim that it is better to know about a thing than to be ignorant about it and it is this that stands them in such good stead that nobody in the country goes hungry or poor. The high and low ladies of those parts do not waste their time in chewing paan or in weaving garlands, they are well versed in handicrafts and some skill or the other or are occupied in looking after their homes or engage in business and earn money. And the most praiseworthy thing is that they take out money for charity from their earnings. People of these countries prefer a trade or business to service. Remember how David used to subsist on what he made with his own hands, for him taking up a service was to be subservient to another, akin to slavery. The nobles of those lands are never idle in spite of the excess of riches at their command and are ever ready to lend a helping hand even to their junior employees.

These Englishmen who are very clever and highly skilled at many trades emulated these practices and rule us because of that. As you would have heard lately that the goras are not alone in this battle—their officers and governors, whether civilians or soldiers, are all one and united and perform all tasks equally and are not afraid to present themselves at the forefront of battle. The reason for that is they were not entirely unskilled in the arts of war, quite unlike this place where the slightest act of condescension is like a serious insult to one's high status, and the result of that is also obvious before your eyes and you are watching helplessly and are unable to do anything. The biggest regret is that we are unable to do anything in this confrontation and nor do we find anybody among our brethren and compatriots who might show valour and courage and seize the day for us. Each one of us is looking to the other or to the Almighty. The progeny of the kings of old, of stalwarts such as Abul Fazal and Khan-e-Khanan are all around, many of whom draw pensions and salaries from the jagirs and estates which their ancestors had erected for them and which the English had continued with. God Almighty has today brought us to a situation where the descendants of these stalwarts should show the glory of their lineage and aspire to the same positions and posts and achievements as displayed by their ancestors. What galls me most, however, is the knowledge that if the empire of Shahjahan, the ruler of seven worlds, was once again to return among those who are around today, he would not be able to find the servicemen and nobles and men endowed with the competence to run it! They are not a patch on their ancestors and are in fact deserving of our pity more than anything else.

Remember, however, that not all is lost, there is great space and great opportunity in the wide country of Hindustan. Until the time that the whole country is brought under one flag, they can acquire some skill or craft or the other. The persona of our Emperor, the shadow of God on earth, is very generous and we should have trust in him.

5 July 1857

The refutation of the Nazarenes' advertisement and an answer to their vain well-wishers

Previously, an advertisement had been put up at the Jama Masjid to mislead and intimidate the people of the army and the city. After hearing about its content, a reply had been prepared for the sake of the Prophet and his faith, and had become popular with all of God's creatures. Now for the sake of all the people of the watan [homeland], it has been publicized through the papers. Today, this humble writer managed to procure a copy of that proclamation courtesy a friend, who had personally acquired a copy through the darogha of the Jama Masjid. Those who have seen it and who are themselves wise, knowledgeable and worthy will know immediately that its contents are completely devoid of truth, full of fabrication and deceitful information which has been perpetrated as a stratagem to mislead the common and ignorant masses.

First, the humble one would present a verbatim copy of the said advertisement. Thereafter, each thread will be taken up one by one. Purely, as God is my witness, for the sake of the respect of deen, I will write its refutation. I am hopeful that the God Almighty, in the name of his beloved Prophet, will accept and grace this endeavour and lend force to these words so that those whose faith has weakened will become stronger and the faithful ones will become still more faithful and blessed.

But first, I find it necessary to say this in preamble and to warn all and sundry that all Hindus and Muslims should pay attention to this. The contents of the advertisement and whatever is claimed in it is completely false, fabricated and fraudulent. I have commented earlier about the debased tactics and falsehoods spread by this group who, in order to mislead the villages and the zamindars at the thanas and chowkis of the outlying regions, have put up posters and proclamations announcing that Delhi has come under their government, and that the exalted one has surrendered and the army has been subordinated. You would also learn from those arriving from Agra how they make this false proclamation every day that, God forbid, they have captured Delhi and that, God forbid, the exalted one has been sent away to Khwaja Saheb's place. Where the army has no knowledge of the events that have recently taken place everywhere, they tell them that it was nothing, merely two platoons had lost their heads and gone mad, now they have been taken care of. God save us from their shenanigans and evil machinations. For the ones far away, they take care of them, whereas for Dilliwallas they have come up with this ploy. And remember, never, never trust their word or promise. The reasons will be explained later while refuting the claims individually.

Copy of the [British] Proclamation. It goes exactly like this—

Know that the subjects are a deposit of God and the rulers are like pastors. From the day that our servants revolted in Delhi, by way of impotency and treachery, they committed excesses upon the rulers and their ladies and children, remorselessly put them to the sword and turned the fort and the city into their shelter and perpetrated cruelties on the people and looted their property and left their possessions free for the loafers of the city.

The King was also arrested and in consequence, complaints from the King about the atrocities of those wicked soldiers were regularly heard. Now, it is our duty to chasten them. Of our magnificent camps and establishments that had been set up here, it has now been learnt that some illiterate and reckless ones, who were participating in plunder along with the rebel forces, wreaked havoc in the name of jihad.

First it was necessary, in conformity with the Sharia, that the faithful Muslims should have produced witness to the violation of the Sharia, they should have presented their grievances to their King and if it was proved that there had been any excesses on our side, then they should have committed the murders and massacres.

Now we enquire from the religious leaders the conditions and justification of jihad, and taking an oath on the Bible, we say that from here to Calcutta, no ruler wished to subject Muslim soldiers to bullets laced with pig's grease or to flour mixed with pork bones and destroy their faith. If an illiterate person, out of ignorance, says that the aim was to destroy faith, then in that situation, the question arises whether eating pig's flesh is a great sin, or on partaking of it, does one instantly cease to be a Muslim. Should a tyrannical ruler impose this practice then? If you have the gumption to fight, one may refuse committing this sin. Not that one should kill their wives and children. And if they don't have the strength to fight, they should migrate.

Now, everyone should heed this carefully, it is the Hindu soldiers, real dimwits, who have prevailed upon the Muslim ones. What actually happened was that the government, with a view to the expeditions to Russia and Iran where it snows a lot, had decided to cover the bullets with the fat of cows and other kosher animals. Then the Hindu soldiers raised a hue and cry and spread this falsehood that while our bullets have been laced with cow grease, the Muslim soldiers have been given bullets laced with pig's fat. Then a group of wretched soldiers rebelled and created disorder and misled the populace. So, the people of the city know that the objects of punishment are the Hindu soldiers, and their associates and supporters will also be brought to justice. Instead of fighting against us for a baseless and unproven charge, without the approbation of any imams, you should kill all the Hindus. **This is where the proclamation ends.**

How wonderful that they say that the subjects are a special deposit of God, that is, belong to God and the rulers are like pastors or shepherds, appointed to protect them. Now pay attention to a brief reply to this. Firstly, if the subjects are a deposit and the ruler is merely a trustee and protector, then it is compulsory for the rulers to protect and safekeep their flock, that is, to return a thing in the original state without any change or appropriation in the state in which it was given to keep. They should reflect in their hearts and be ashamed that when they became the rulers of India, whether because of his exalted majesty, the manifest ruler, or from God Almighty, ruler of the seen and the unseen realms, did they find a Christian and propertyless population? Or was it the case that the Hindus and Muslims of this country, with a free run over their property and jagirs, were content and well fed and allowed to continue with their religious obligations and observances whether inside their houses or outside. Now that the trustee has returned the deposit, please tell us how many of the populace have lost their faiths, that is, [how many] have become Christians?

Had they claimed to be knowledgeable and very good Christians, then the answer too would have been along similar lines, but since their claim rests on rulership and on protection, mark all wise and just people, does it become the protector to infringe the deposit thus? Should they promote change and appropriation and alteration to what was given them in trust, and should they deprive their flock of water and food? The proof of this lies in the way thousands upon thousands of common people's currency of faith, through the enticements of priests and Evangelists, were reduced and they were encouraged to study English and the Bible in return for lucrative salaries. Thus pressure was exerted to wean away thousands from their faiths and to leave the abode of their religion and faith desolate. Although outwardly no force was exercised, behind the scenes, general tyranny raged ahead.

Thousand of subjects lost their ancestral property and jagirs, with or without excuses, within minutes of the incumbent's death, while estates were appropriated leaving thousands of people without food or water. In like manner, in many more ways, the Company government began to introduce changes and innovations in many religious duties and obligations and even banned many practices of Hindus and Muslim. For instance, Hindus could no longer perform sati nor could everyone freely perform the Id ul Zuha sacrifices. There are numerous other examples that would only prolong the argument. Briefly, the populace was subjected to greater hardship, misery and worldly and religious loss and deprivation, and it was deprived of food and water. All in all, the shepherd was thus exposed and in the words of Saadi Shirazi, 'When I saw my fate, I myself became a wolf.'

Secondly, listen to this: they call themselves pastors, does it mean that they don't consider his exalted one the ruler, or do not regard the men of the army as their subjects? Is it not incumbent upon them to protect his majesty that they protest about his lordship's patronage? (The amazing thing is that they talk about his lordship being in custody of and complaining about the soldiers and they concede that he is helpless and still they fire away night and day.) They give out that the soldiers have made him suffer although the venerable pastors had themselves rendered his majesty so dependent and without hands and feet that the helplessness of his lordship and of the populace in the present was clear and manifest to the sepoys. The reasons for which the subjects had to bear the brunt of hardships, the suffering undertaken by God's deposit, the blame for it lies squarely on the shoulders of these very same pastors, and will be written into their account on the Day of Judgement.

Status of the King under the British. His majesty was not allowed to travel outside except to a few spots like the Qutub Saheb, etc., without the Resident's mediation. No correspondence with the queen or the governor could take place, no raja or *rais* could become his majesty's disciple. Aren't they ashamed today of charging him with giving shelter that they write that first the Muslims, in accordance with the Sharia, ought to have collected evidence of transgression of contract, or the King should have enquired into the case himself and were something to be proved against us, should only then have called for a jihad to kill us?

Praise be to the Lord. Presenting the subjects now as so independent and the King as so powerful—did these kafir firangis not feel any shame when writing this? A little earlier, they had proclaimed themselves rulers and had described their 'servants' as treacherous and disloyal! In spite of the fact that the gora army has infantry and magazine aplenty, they still have not been able to reach anywhere near their servants. On top of that they blame a King and a populace that is without soldiers, funds or magazines. Verily, when iqbal or good fortune departs, your wisdom also deserts you.

When had you ever given us the power to fulfil our Sharia duties in any way that today you do not feel ashamed about using the name of the venerable Sharia? The authority to observe religious duties, celebrate Id ul Zuha, in fact, even the burial of the dead were out of the control of the venerable religious leaders. The legislation for matters of the Sharia was controlled by the great Pastor Saheb and there was no appeal. Surprising that they now say that you should have first proved it and if proven, then only you should have killed. Wonder of wonders that they say the King should have investigated the matter but do not mention the fact that his exalted majesty was not allowed to correspond except through the resident. How and why would his holiness have corresponded and had he done so, how would he have been heard there?

If they accept the King to be the ruler, then what right do they have to fight and impose hardships upon the King's city and subjects? It was incumbent upon them to file a complaint at the Shahdara or Ghaziabad thana that had returned the dispensation of his majesty's government. They should have sent a petition to his majesty and then if their case wasn't heard or the matter was left uninvestigated, then his majesty, from whom they were expecting a command, would indeed have been culpable. Instead the goras have mounted the Hindon bridge along with their cannons to fight and assault their sworn rulers and have now been incessantly firing on the fort for the last thirty-eight days.

Repenting nothing, nor showing any shame. Truly the Almighty has spoken about just such people.

From the very beginning they committed atrocities upon his majesty and upon the notables and we know to what extent that had raged. Young or old, all are well aware of how even the right and independence of communication or correspondence was denied. Remember in the case of Mirza Jahangir Bahadur what kind of promises or the terms of the contract were kept by these pastors. Ultimately, even the very throne of the kingdom was not left in our authority. This is the result of the patience shown by the real owner of the throne.

For sure, God is with those who are patient.

The greatest oppression was that at the Lal Bangla graveyard, where all the kings and princes and other members of the royal family were buried, the graves were dug up and no deference or consideration was shown for the Islamic faith or for the note sent by his majesty.

Vis-à-vis what they assert that we swear on the Bible and assert that from here to Calcutta no ruler suggested that Muslim soldiers be subjected to pig-grease bullets or to flour mixed with pork's bones with the purpose of corrupting their faith, the reply to that is that the truth of their promises and oaths, deceits and breach of contracts will be addressed point by point, a little later. For now it is enough to say that they are reaping the seeds of falsehood they sowed and, Inshallah, will continue to do so.

Alienation of Indians

And as for the statement, 'What would we have gained by perpetrating such deeds'—Answer: Aha, they have suddenly become so innocent that they do not even know its gains! We will tell you the gains, it is that eventually Muslims should lose their faith and the religion of Hindus should be corrupted and that all of them should lose place in this world and the next. Everybody's faith would be polluted and they would be expelled from their communities and they would not be allowed to eat or sit or intermingle or intermarry with their compatriots and communities. They should lose their children, wives, friends and strangers and they should not have anybody to call their own in all of Hindustan except for the English. So that ultimately, they have no choice but to accept the Christian faith. That their fate should be tied to the goras and they should spend their lives, energy and fortune in defending the English annexation—just as it has been heard that at Agra all the Christians have sided with the English and they every day acquire military training and are committed with all their might and money. In addition, many diverse subterfuges and tricks were employed so that people under them, rather all the people of the land, should eventually be so hard-pressed and oppressed that they should be forced to become Christians.

This is not the time to delve into these machinations in detail but a short speech, very interesting and apt to the point is recorded so that the great Pastor Saheb may cry and all those watching may enjoy. Witness one advantage of it that the populace is inclined to show their opposition in this way to rulers like you—who provide obvious advantages such as salaries and disbursements—despite being trained under you and being intimate with you for so long. And you were the rulers with authority and still you complain and are resentful? What about those associated with you who gained absolutely nothing except for loss of power and authority—then what would this assemblage had they been as strongly opposed, not done? In the end, it would have been like the way your sons and dependants were put to sword, or like them, would have eventually joined your religion.

The people were forced to listen to public insults against the Muhammadi faith

They themselves complain and rail about the murder of their defenceless women and children while everybody knows how the light has gone out of their kingdom . . . so much so that they hide in nooks and corners, amid the pebbles and rocks of hills, and in houses and still they do not consider the mighty soldiers who have defied the royal orders worthy of putting up a fight that they say such things. In sum, till these pastors and shepherds had power, they imprisoned many officers and suspended countless soldiers because until all the sepoys were one at heart, they did not have the ability to fight. Therefore, all the people of Delhi, etc., and several other cities, were forced to listen to public insults against the Muhammadi faith in the bazaars and madrasas and also forced to stomach stories about Lord Jesus' parentage (God forbid) and were helpless to do or say anything in return. When the sepoys all got together, when they were ready to kill and die, then what was lacking in jihad becoming a duty?

And when the gumption to fight receives such divine aid, then where is the need for Muslims to migrate? Verily, liars have no memory. They first ask what would we have gained by corrupting your religion, and then they clarify that it was only cow grease. Can someone ask them whether that does not pollute the Hindus' faith? Now how can anybody trust them when they say that there is no pig fat involved? Regardless anyhow of whether pork was used or not, the Muslims understood the way the wind was blowing and realized that the oppression being committed on the Hindus today will be visited on the Muslims tomorrow. And it would have been so.

They have flouted contracts and treaties with impunity,
their word cannot be trusted

And as for what they state that first they only wanted to punish the Hindus—Answer: What trust can one place in their word? Here it is merely a matter of talk, in absentia, without any commitment to paper or undertakings of any sort, and when the time comes, they can also resort to claiming that it was the translator's fault, like the way they did with the sections of the Bible translations which proved the truth of Mohammed's faith (they elided it, probably, certainly). They reneged on their word even where there were agreements and treaties with indigenous rulers attested with the signatures and seals of the governor-general and his council, so what of this?

Remember what happened to the agreements with Punjab and Awadh? How they took over by force the kingdoms of Jhansi and Nagpur? What happened to the loan given by Awadh? Which one of the undertakings with the throne of Hind did they fulfil? In addition, what happened to several ancestral estates such as Bahadurgarh, etc.? In fact, what signals did they send to various kings and notables under the excuse of maladministration, the condemnation of whose regimes was being penned for long by their compatriot goras?

Was this the contract that the time has come to take over the government here, is this what is called trusteeship and shepherding and keeping your word? They have taken countries and governments away from the owners on the charge of bad management and ostensibly to bring relief to the subjects. Today the same logic is reverted upon them to say that you could not administer the country or the army, therefore the exalted majesty was also bound to dismiss you from power and government because it was not your inheritance.

Jihad is an obligation for all believers, until the Day of Judgement

They write that join us and kill the Hindus and do not fight us without reason or without an imam—Answer: Praise be to God. What amazing things they say, how wonderfully they deceive in the name of the Sharia! Don't they see that the Hindus can be seen as our helpers, or the Muslims can be seen as their helpers in the fight against the people of the Book? We are well aware of the rules of the Sharia. We have given up all comfort and consider the difficulties of jihad as a sacrifice in the way of God and as agreeing with his and his Prophet's wishes. We regard it as the way of gaining permanent happiness and peace and have therefore opted for it. Oh brother Muslims, do not succumb to the deceits and treachery of those who emphasize jihad only under an imam. Listen to all and sundry and watch the deceitful sahebs—according to the Sharia books, the obligation to do jihad is clear and manifest on Islamic parties and whoever denies it is a sinner. This humble faqir, the servant of the ulemas of both sections [Sunni and Shia], will briefly note excerpts from books of both sides. The person who has both eyes, as in who can read both Farsi and Arabic, can see both kinds of texts and whoever has only one eye, that is, who can read either Arabic or Persian, can see with that, and he who lacks both can himself or through someone else at least understand it in Urdu. Therefore the précis of the texts will be written in Urdu as well.

And there is a very famous tradition of the Prophet called Hadith, meaning that offer prayers behind all who are righteous and non-righteous and launch a jihad with every Muslim or behind every sardar, as it is clearly written in Persian in *Sifar-e-Saadat* by Muhaqqiq-e-Dehlavi. The ulema of the people of the Sunnat and Jamat [Sunni sects] have held consultations and have mentioned it in devotional texts, and it is one of the signs of belonging to the Sunnat and Jamat groups. Remember what is called jihad pertains to the expenditure of strength in a fight against the disbelievers, whether with life, or goods or money or intelligence or by adding to the crowd or in any other way. Until the Day of Judgement, jihad is an obligation.

Whether there is no trumpet call for all, and when there is a public call for the reason that the disbelievers assault the city en masse, then it is compulsory for all Muslims to do jihad—whether the trumpet call is being given by a just ruler or a tyrant, it is obligatory for all people in the city, and if that is not reason enough, then a call even in the neighbouring cities makes it compulsory. Jihad and its invocation will remain till the Day of Judgement and is not conditional upon a court or a leader. This is the gist of the traditions of the Prophet's lives and books of jurisprudence according to the Sunnis.

Now listen to what the Shia texts have to say about this: Considering the state they have left Islam in and what the Nazarenes' are doing to the Muslims and Islam, it is incumbent on the community to do jihad with or without an imam or his deputy. In short, all Muslim brothers who recite the kalima should observe the calumny those base ones are visiting upon us.

All the kings are certainly helping them out, otherwise the English would have been wiped out from everywhere

Alwar and the other kings retain their governments, but the collection of revenue is much slower than before. Wherever there was English government, complete chaos rules there now. The ruler of Alwar got a Hindu killed for doing black magic while a maulvi saheb who was in voluntary confinement at the dargah of Makhdum saheb was imprisoned on the charge of conducting a spell to kill the raja saheb. And one day, a piece of the thigh bone of a swine was put into his mouth. So the Muslims of that place are in such a state that if anybody asks what your religion is, they would say we follow the raja saheb's religion. Groups from other places had tried to attack, but the presence of the large number of Rajputs deterred them. The raja has mounted the guns on the ramparts of the fort, everything now seems dependent on Delhi.

Obviously, the moment the English are defeated at Delhi, then the raja babus too would turn against them.

12 July 1857

Sunday restrictions removed

This paper is published once a week on Sundays in order to spite the Nazarenes' for whom it is an auspicious day on which no new ventures should begin. Like how the last principal forcibly declared a holiday on Sunday at the madrasa [Delhi College]. There was also a restriction on conducting business or riding a carriage on this day. Yet, by God's doing, everything went on as before even during their government. Victory ['zafar'] was achieved by Bahadur Shah and his men, and not one of them was left to raise objections ...

The point that amuses and frightens is that these angrez who fled were dressed like Hindu women and wore *lahanga*s. They were sitting in carts, and all those sahebs who never addressed men by anything other than *guddamee* [good morning] and who acknowledged the salaams of the genteel ones merely by moving an eyelid as an act of great condescension, behold, whose prowess has reduced them to this state? It was their own soldiers too. And from what we have heard, the attitude of the rest of the soldiers will soon be manifest too. Do you not see, you sceptics, the supremacy of the prowess of the Almighty over the might of the Nazarenes' that you still maintain faith in their infallibility and wonder who can stand against them? This is the reason why many of the notables, nobles and kings, especially from Rajputana, have not supported us and apart from them, there are many who are actively supporting the angrez, but such is God's doing that most of them are chastised and are punished. Remember the angrez have earned God's wrath.

Those well-wishers and supporters of the angrez who have been harassed by the riots and loss to property, or feel faithful towards them, should give up their pipe dreams about the return of the British army. No such army is going to come whether from Bombay, Madras or London; so they should not mislead the God-fearing ones. Firstly, how will the Hindustanis and the kingdoms in those parts allow the well-wishers of the angrez to come this way and if they can do so, even if they were to come from London, then can't the Irani Shah's army come from Bushahar to Bombay? Can't the Iranian army come from Kabul, Sind or Punjab?

2 August 1857

Not too many takers for the pamphlet exhorting jihad

The proclamation refuting the canards of the Nazarenes that had been mentioned in previous issues is now complete and, Inshallah, will be ready for distribution this week itself. It is a matter of deep regret however that the well-to-do, especially among Muslims, those who read this paper and have seen this advertisement have still not shown any enthusiasm. It seems as if they are still riveted on their worldly material desires and have still not overcome the fear of the return of firangi government. May God enlighten them!

Miraculous appearance of thousands of soldiers

One person, upon oath, described the state at the fronts as he had it from a grenadier who had been held captive by the kafirs and came here when he could escape. He says that when their army was about to march towards Delhi, Le Bas Saheb and the son of Thomas Metcalfe had made this disdainful and insolent remark that we shall, God forbid, have refreshments in Delhi in two or three hours. Therefore, says the man, that when the Alipur front was taken by the rebels immediately upon their arrival, they must have had a foretaste of their perdition. But we also learnt a lesson from that. When the Tirpolia was lost, we too were afraid and when they took the Bawta front, then it seemed that their conceit has come true—but such are the ways of the Omnipotent Almighty that when they made towards the city, suddenly, thousands of masked soldiers appeared on the ramparts of the city and its gates holding aloft naked swords in their hands and their mere sight was so terrifying that the English were petrified. They could not stand their ground and were madly scrambling to hide in the hills, bushes and the kothis and houses of Hindurao.

The point is this that all our brethren, Hindus and Muslims, especially those who cannot perceive the hand of the Omnipotent Almighty behind this should ponder and wonder about those uniformed soldiers who appeared in the city, whose handiwork were they? Where was this contingent when those fronts were being lost? If those masked, uniformed and scimitar-holding soldiers had not appeared, how would we have fared when we had already lost three fronts? When the aid and encouragement of the real power is inclined to your side, why then should you still be afraid and apprehensive?

Irani troops at Bombay

One person, who had it from a Haj traveller attesting its truth, described the arrival of Iranian troops at the Bombay ports. But we are surprised that the messenger who testifies to it has already arrived here while those fast riding troops have set up camp there!

The moment the ridge falls everybody will bow before the King

It is commonly held and the heart also inclines to believe it that the moment the ridge is cleared of the kafirs, all the rajas, babus and rais will assemble with folded hands before the Emperor. They say they are only waiting for that event. On the other hand, the treacherous British fraudulently proclaim their might and the strength of their government at all cities or villages where they re-establish control. They do everything they can to propagandize their power and to maintain people's fear of them. The moment they flee from the ridge, the petty zamindars of Sonepat and Baghpat would eat them alive. Inshallah then not a single gora will be able to reach even Meerut or Panipat.

23 August 1857

Still no takers for the 'Jihad' pamphlet

The pamphlet 'Jihad', which has been written as a rebuttal of the Christian proclamation, has now been printed, its price is four annas. Whoever wants to buy it can take it. But it is a matter of deep regret that our countrymen do not pay any attention to noble deeds and it is even more lamentable that at a time when there is commotion and perdition all around us and death hovers overhead on all sides, an issue of such importance and full of truth and good guidance of the Almighty and his Prophet should be so grievously ignored.

Oppression and tyranny of the evil kafirs

Outsiders report that now the kafir Christians have begun to commit grave depredations, especially upon Muslims. Wherever they gain control, they indiscriminately hang men and destroy entire villages. While they cannot cause any harm to the victorious army, they take out their anger on the subjects and in this way, burst bubbles.

The corrupting influence of Delhi's air and water

Apart from this, the thing is that the water and air of our city of Delhi is such that the troops who can act with great daring outside and can put the kafirs to sword and hand them their deaths in a flash, the moment they drink the water of the city and take a round of Chandni Chowk and stroll about in the big and small Dariba and go around Jama Masjid and enjoy the *qalaqand* of Ghantewala and its laddus, they lose all urge and determination to fight and to extirpate the enemy and become shorn of all strength and resolution. Experience as well as books of histories and biographies show us how this place [that is, Delhi] has been prone to luxury and idleness and has ever ensnared men to indulgent supineness, which is an impediment to governance, battle, warfare and the pursuit of enemies. That is the reason why wizened leaders of yore did not prefer to station their forces inside the city and the conquering rulers of the past did not favour this place of rest as an abode or place for living and the evidence of the daily goings-on is the witness to the truth of this state and this opinion.

> *The hearts of the rais remain bowed by awe, affection,*
> *loyalty and fear of the kafirs*

The turn of everyday events and the conduct and actions of people indicate that when money is demanded from people here, there are some who are genuinely without the means or ability to make any contribution to the funds and there are some who have the means and the wealth to contribute but are lacking in faith and are so possessed of love for worldly goods and possessions that they do not wish to part with it at all and for that reason are very put out at the fall of the Christians. There is no doubt that if in their hearts they did not wish for the kafir government's downfall, they regard their return as desirable. Obviously they would not spare any efforts to help and aid the kafirs and render them help and services of many kinds here and at many other places in many different ways and especially if they are harassed to part with money and are warned and threatened about that, then this would only spur them to turn into well-wishers of the English, especially since they were inclined to do so in the first place itself.

Urdu Akhbar *evokes contempt for exhorting jihad*

We have heard that since we published the pamphlet of jihad and since we constantly remind people in our articles in the newspapers about their religious duties and their obligations, the short-sighted and infirm of belief, the renegades of faith, the cravers of this world in this city, talk about us with contempt and with loathing. We are very happy and thank the Creator that they should remember us with even worse epithets and the stronger their abuse the more it gladdens our heart.

Punjab—'Till the time they receive supplies from Patiala and Meerut, we should remember, they will never be broken'

The arrivals from Lahore report the murder and destruction of the base kafirs, but some also report their control of the fort and their movement around, and it seems they have not been as completely wiped off from those parts as they have been from the eastern parts, but there is no doubt whatever that the kafirs no longer retain control over the Punjab. They survive thanks to the assistance of Patiala and other traitors to the throne. Especially the way the Patiala ruler is supporting them, nobody else is doing. We believe that if the Bombay force can be sent there via a detour, then it is better than their finding themselves unstuck, like the victorious army, in a meaningless death at the ridge. There is also no doubt that after the destruction in those parts the degenerate kafirs will lose their support from Karnal and Panipat as well, and will then find themselves isolated and hung to dry at the ridge. If that happens, the zamindars will slay them and all big and small raises will give up hope of their government. Then why would anyone help them and their awe will disappear from all sides. For as long as they continue to receive supplies from Patiala and Meerut, we should remember, they will never be broken—the longer we delay and dilate on the matter, the less disillusioned will the people be from them. We feel that a contingent of troops capable of confronting and stopping the passage of their supplies is necessary around the ridge area away from the city, and until they themselves descend, it is not necessary to climb up. But their supplies should be cut off at once.

Soldiers depart for battle from prostitutes' houses in an unclean state

Outwardly, these are the efforts we can make, but from the inside, we must repose trust in God and should be humble and repentant and should be occupied in prayer and acts of supplication towards the Almighty. A lot of people maintain that many people go for battle after spending nights at the prostitutes' quarters without bathing, and without purifying themselves, therefore all this setback and mayhem is a result of that unseemly practice. Further, a lot of atrocities are committed against the poor and goods continue to be unjustly appropriated, and we also suffer because of those things. If this is true, then may God pardon them and show them the right path and overlook our sins.

13 September 1857

The compatriots should not worry about the war's prolongation

O brothers, our compatriots, remember not to be dismayed by the prolongation of this war. Rather, you should regard this as an object lesson in divine justice and power. Between the lines, God Almighty is demonstrating the force of his power and giving you a lesson that you should not be too proud of your efforts and plans and don't turn vain about your endeavour and agency. Continue to create difficulties for the kafirs so that everyone may know his prowess and the Muslims may strengthen their faith and the kafirs may come to acquire faith in him—'Verily, he has power over everything'. It is his will that turns few into many and many into few and gives victory to the few over the many and causes the many to suffer defeat at the hands of the few; and he can instil the awe of his being into anyone's heart as he may please and may grant valour and bravery to anyone he desires.

All these developments, along with the support of the ordinary people, are proof that the goras are doomed for sure. In short, the developments at all these places, especially those places that were regarded as heavily fortified and defended and stocked with weapons and goods and armies of the goras, now that you have seen what happened to them and heard about their defeats, you should not lose heart over the impediment and the obstacle of the ridge. We should pray to God for forgiveness and enlightenment, we should make it a point to refrain from committing any excesses on fellow human beings or exploiting and injuring them in any way. We should take heed of and care for the poor and desist from sinful ways of being and earning and we should strive to be charitable and good to everyone around. Due to God's gracefulness, we indeed already enjoy his blessings and approval, and if you look around, you will find a large majority believes this.

Dilliwallas are not supporting the army

We must regret the fact that unlike other cities where the ordinary people made efforts and joined the action in killing and putting away the kafirs, the people of our city did not play their desired role and were defamed for nothing. It is also to be regretted that the victorious army, which has staked its life and is constantly facing death and is devoting itself day and night to the task of ejecting the kafirs for our sake, are not being properly taken care of by our compatriots. Their food and shelter is not being provided by those who have the means to contribute. In fact, it is often heard that they seek to defend and save themselves and wish the oppressed poor to be destroyed. It is lamentable that even at this critical juncture we people do not realize and understand. May God guide us to the right path and may it all end well.

Efforts and actions of the victorious army

Although the kafirs are well entrenched at the ridge and dig up a new front every night, the really important thing is to admire the spirit and bravery of this hardy and victorious army who attempt to storm their positions day and night. Otherwise, the situation of the ordinary residents of the city is well known, which is that let alone the infirm, unhealthy and those incapable of fighting and taking up arms, even the young and able-bodied who sport swords of silver and bronze of foreign and Isfahani make and also Indian ones, have never once shown the inclination to fight against the kafirs. In fact, many of them are actually well-wishers of the kafirs and become anxious when they hear news of their defeat and setback. It is to be greatly lamented that the majority of our compatriots have become so infected by the influence of the kafirs' salt that the influence of Islam seems to have deserted them. Many, in fact, seem to be on the side of the Christians in their hearts, though they do not have the temerity to express that partisanship openly. God willing, they will shortly be disabused of their hopes. The ones with weak faith are pitting their hopes on the prolongation of the battle for the ridge, lest, God forbid, their dreams come true on that account. But thanks to the Almighty and His omnipotence, the true believers replenish their faith and have trust that very soon the Muslims will take over the ridge and will invite all doubters there and greet them. None amongst us, of course, know the appointed time when this event shall take place, but when it comes, its signs will be manifest.

The hurly-burly of war

For four days now, a heavy gun battle has been raging. The kafirs have erected many trenches and fronts and from this side too many new fortifications have been created. Since the paper does not reach outside the city and the people of the city are witnessing first-hand all the goings-on, therefore, we have not written the details of the battle and the skirmishes. It is enough that night and day the approval of Almighty God on the side of the Muslims and his wrath against the Christians is evident and manifest every minute. The discerning and wise ones wait for his favour.

(All selections from Collection 2)

A TRIAL, AN ARCHIVE, THE MISSING MUNSHIS AND REBUILDING HINDUSTAN

The Mutiny Papers, the catalogue from which this selection is drawn, is a collection of documents mainly dealing with Delhi in 1857. Stored in the National Archives of India in New Delhi, these documents, numbering thousands, were extricated and extracted from various sources in Delhi by the occupying British army—from the kotwali, the secretariat, homes, spies—and each one diligently marked and copied, sometimes in duplicate and stored as a monument for posterity, a significant step in the formation of the colonial archive. There are thousands of these documents, all indexed in a printed catalogue. Most of them are in Shikastah (cursive) Urdu, some in Persian and a few in English translations. Collected indiscriminately at first, they were later arranged and categorized primarily as supporting evidence for the prosecution of Emperor Bahadur Shah Zafar. For all the colonial intentionality motivating this extensive, meticulous and arduous classification, they provide, as we have seen in this book, one of the densest descriptions of a city at war and at work, of administration and anarchy, and of deceit and desperation. These papers provide a street-side view, a microscopic vision of the ghadar of 1857 in Delhi.

This micro-picture compelled me to continue to use the word used by the contemporaries to describe the turmoil, namely, ghadar, alongside uprising and rebellion, to describe the events of 1857. The Urdu word ghadar (meaning outburst, mayhem, rebellion, riot and disturbance, helter-skelter, turbulence) encapsulates the multi-dimensional nature of the event far better than a more restrictive label. This does not mean that there was no conscious struggle for liberation from British rule, nor that there was no general military or civil uprising against the Company. The use of the word ghadar only emphasizes this that it was a time of immense chaos and pandemonium all around.

Commenting on these papers, Sir John Lawrence, the chief commissioner of Punjab and one of the leading architects of the recapture of Delhi, made the following observations:

> In brief terms, it may be said that the documentary evidence comprises a system in which the general government was conducted, the raising of loans, military arrangements, the communications with foreign powers and neighbouring chiefs, the passages in the native newspapers, relating to the war between the English and the Persians. The papers referring to the system of the King's government exhibit in a remarkable manner the active personal share which the King himself took in the conduct of the affairs. However wrongly he had assumed his position, it must be admitted that his orders were not unworthy of the situation. He did make some effort to preserve order in the city, to repress rapine and murder in the villages, to check malversation, to restrain the excess of the soldiery, but it is clear, from first to last, he was unable to establish an administration either within or without the city. In the tracts nominally ruled by the King, there was scarcely the semblance of authority, nor was there any protection for life or property. In but few cases did the King's agents succeed in collecting revenue from the districts. From his own records, the Mughal rule, while it lasted seems to have been a reign of terror, and a period of intolerable anarchy to the people. Then the papers show the financial straits to which the King was driven and the numerous forced loans and other contributions exacted from the moneyed classes in Delhi. The military papers do not materially elucidate the plan of the operations but they show that the mutinous army was utterly insubordinate to the government it had set up and that its discipline was entirely relaxed.[1]

I have quoted Sir John's observations at some length because they map out, with some exactitude, the terrain covered by these papers. The papers describe the administration of the city, as well as the complaints of ordinary people, showing us the strengths and limitations of the rebel establishment in the city. Except for his assessment of Bahadur Shah's role these conclusions set the palimpsest for the way the ghadar at Delhi would continue to be described. The emphasis on anarchy, shortages, the reign of terror and the ineffectiveness of royal dictates have become the standard tropes for studying 1857 in Delhi. The powerful voice of Ghalib, and his dismay at the destruction of cherished norms, as well as the soldiers' disregard for the etiquettes of courtly behaviour have added weight to this image of a world turning upside down.[2] Modern scholars too have tended to assess the situation in Delhi in these same terms of atrophy and pandemonium.[3] The princes are blamed for infighting, the soldiers are arraigned for lack of coordination and for ignoring vitals like revenue and post, and in general, the narrative of 1857 in Delhi is one long lament at yet another rebel (=Indian) failure in the event. In spite of their superior numbers and faced with a highly vulnerable enemy, the rebels, and here we can all sigh regretfully, are repeatedly unable to force the issue.

Talmiz Khaldun, writing for the collection on 1857 brought out by P.C. Joshi during the centenary of the event, first looked at these papers as a clue to the administrative order of the city. Khaldun, however, concentrated exclusively on the Court of Mutineers[4] formed by the mutineers, and even there he focused more on the legalistic norms set by the court than at actual practice. Khaldun claimed that the CoM was 'the highest judicial authority and regulated the judicial procedures for civil and criminal matters and appointed police officers and civil servants.'[5] The court was certainly a very important institutional innovation set up by the rebels in Delhi. However, it was not the summit of administrative authority but only one of the organs, or centres, along with others. It did monitor financial expenditure and propose ways of raising money, but in supervision of the overall administration, it worked closely with

Mirza Mughal, the heir apparent and the C-in-C, for long durations of the war. Accounts of the ghadar at Delhi usually portray the CoM and the princes to be working at cross purposes, even as being antagonistic towards each other. However, as shown in a lot of these documents, they worked closely together, especially with the commissariat headed by Mirza Mughal.[6] While valorizing the CoM, Khaldun's narrative of Delhi also despairs at the infighting and the chaos that marred rebel capability. William Dalrymple's comprehensive survey of Delhi, which builds on many of the documents used here, also lays great stress on the shortages and the anarchy that prevailed in the city.[7] Dissension, shortages and anarchy certainly did prevail in Delhi in 1857. However, by reiterating these themes, the extant historiography has almost completely overlooked the attempts at order, discipline and organization that also marked the uprising at Delhi. My endeavour in this book has been to highlight structures of authority, point out attempts at imposing order and discipline and to indicate that in spite of the unruliness of the soldiers, some bureaucratic and administrative norms can be delineated. It is time to pay attention to these aspects of rebel actions.

The very existence of such a large cache of documents in the National Archives of India points to a system of governance that allowed for their production. Government papers cannot be produced without a government even if its foundations or authority may be shaky. It bears repeating that the reason why the British could collect and sort these papers is because they existed in the first place. Only sporadic records survive from other theatres of 1857, which prompts the question as to whether they didn't produce enough paperwork, or not enough was preserved. However, the recent unearthing of over a hundred documents, letters and petitions, between Tatya Tope's office (for want of a better word) and some of his lieutenants,[8] leads to the conjecture that records of rebel administration and correspondence must have been voluminous and with some diligence at the local archives, may still be recovered.

Moreover, the existence of this immense archive presupposes also the existence of the entire paraphernalia of writerly, clerical establishments that was characteristic of Indian governments. Apart from professional writers, mohurrirs or munshis, attached to the police thanas and to the regiments, this would have also necessitated a large number of harkaras or carriers and, obviously, a sufficient supply of paper. The petitions submitted by ordinary people and soldiers, many of whom were illiterate, exhibit a uniformity of style and presentation, adherence to protocols of correct form of addressing superiors and a terminology that would only be available to the initiated. In other words, there would have been scribes for hire who would transmit grievances into a standardized format and commit them to paper before they could be admitted to a court or a thana. We have no records, or testimonials, for the existence of this class, nor do we have any modes of celebrating their services to the cause of the uprising. Their presence, however, is inscribed in the documents. The existence of this class points, once again, to the complexity of the administrative effort that informed the uprising at Delhi and presumably at other places. The information order of north India rested on a dense network of literate and literacy-aware subcultures and these did not vanish overnight because of the uprising.[9]

This aspect can be highlighted from the other side of the fence as well. The British returned to Delhi in the first week of June and after defeating the rebel forces in two battles, occupied the ridge on 8 June and began the siege of Delhi. For the first two months there was immense confidence in the British camp that they only needed to march back and the city would be theirs. The protracted and intricate negotiations about storming the city, which eventually came to naught, were dragged on and on because the rebels showed not only greater will power than expected, but also seemed better organized.[10] Their gunners were more accurate, they seemed to have an endless supply of soldiers and they could make sorties deep inside the English camp. The rebels' achievement, to hold out so well for so long and to repeatedly threaten the precarious British position, should itself offer a corrective to the unshakeable stereotype of anarchy and chaos. The city held out for as long as it did because there was some order, organization and method to the outward chaos. In this, Delhi was not unique. Other centres of rebel power seemed to have quickly developed administrative norms and organization in order to prepare for and manage a war effort which entailed a lot more than military discipline and revenue collections.[11]

These papers should offer some corrective to the picture of anarchy and chaos that dominates narratives of 1857 in Delhi. The administration put together by the rebels and the royal government was a combination of pre-existing institutions, such as the police establishment, and some improvizations, like the CoM, but it was surprisingly effective. By the end of May, a skeletal administrative structure was in place. When fighting resumed with the British forces in the first week of June, it was able to provide for and manage that war to a surprising degree of efficiency. Administrative norms were bureaucratized, everything was committed to paper and rules of hierarchy and accountability were insisted upon, and enforced. Soldiers and rebel leaders were well aware of the need to secure the hinterland, to collect revenues and to form new strategies for encircling the British. Indeed the *Dehli Urdu Akhbar*[12] ceaselessly iterated the necessity of destroying the hegemonic awe enjoyed by the East India Company. The rebels' undoing, which begs the question as to what their success may have comprised, lay not in their lack of awareness or efforts, but in their inability to effectively implement what they devised over areas beyond their control.[13]

Dehli Urdu Akhbar

Although the *Dehli Urdu Akhbar* does not form a part of the Mutiny Papers, I have included selections from it here for two reasons. One, it is listed in the Mutiny Papers catalogue and is stored under its head in the archives, making it technically a part of the collection. Second, it is an eyewitness account of the city of Delhi during the uprising and can serve as a very useful source, especially for those who are looking for ideological material on the Mutiny. Where the rest of the Mutiny Papers largely eschew sentiments, or ideology, with its apocalyptic rhetoric, its constant exhortations and morale building and its lamentations about the ineptitude of soldiers and citizens, the *Dehli Urdu Akhbar* is a patriot's delight. It was edited by Maulvi Mohammed Baqar, an eminent Shia scholar of the city and a friend of the poet Zauq, as well as of some of the leading Britishers of the city. The paper is an important and independent source for studying the material and emotional state of the city during the uprising. It has been seen as a transitional publication, poised mid-way between medieval Persian *akhbarat*s and the modern newspaper,[14] but it really came into its own during the four months of the uprising when its reportage and editorializing took on a very modern colour. A recent study of the issues of 1857 by Shireen Moosvi correctly points out that the paper modified its tone as time went on. Beginning with a shrill religious rhetoric it evolved into appealing in the name of all countrymen or compatriots.[15]

One way of looking at the *Dehli Urdu Akhbar* is as a source of propaganda, which consistently refuted news that could upset the morale of the rebels. It fought, consciously and creatively, what it declared was the disinformation campaign launched by the British and instead sought to present the 'true' picture to its readers so that they would not lose heart and assume a British victory. At the same time it was not a text that was commissioned or printed by a rebel leader as such, therefore it can be treated as an independent source, possibly also as a neutral voice between soldiers, civilians and the court. We don't know enough about the number of copies circulated, its readership and its place in the city's imagination to know how decisively it influenced the city's make-up or the soldiers' morale.[16] But it did create an ideological space from which a coherent, secular critique of the British could be mounted. Plus, the very fact that it was a newspaper meant for a general readership forced the editor to appeal to his readers to act as judge and arbiter. He was therefore not only addressing, in incipient form of course, but also creating an 'imagined community', long before we can date the rise of nationalism proper.[17]

The issues of 14 and 21 June are of particular importance because they anticipate two very important ways of conceiving and addressing the watan or homeland. In the first, Maulvi Baqar yokes Hindu mythology, Puranic lore, Quranic fables and medieval Turkish history into a seamless whole in order to convince his readers of the transitory and ephemeral nature of political rule. Adducing the stories of Krishna, Rama, Parshuram is the counterpart, an exceptional one, of the constant appeals to Tulsi–Gangajal–Saligram which we encounter elsewhere in the official proclamations of the uprising. It is exceptional because otherwise in the rebel proclamations we find relatively fewer appeals to history, other than the history of British perfidies and malicious, false conquests. The invocation of religion and faith seems to make history redundant. But Maulvi Baqar, perhaps because of his exposure to the discipline of history at the Delhi College, situates this struggle on the grounds of history and the inevitability of historical change, in addition to divine approval and intervention.

In the issue of 21 June, Maulvi Baqar produced a set of arguments that seem to presage, word for word, the later nationalism of the nineteenth century, including what was once called economic nationalism. He first brought up the cultural differences between the former rulers and Hindustanis and how that was an impediment to good governance as well as to opportunities of employment, etc., for the subjects. He mentioned the drain of wealth from India and the unwillingness of the colonial rulers to spend (to invest?) their savings within India and lamented the Indian disdain for business and industry and the fact that they did not pay enough attention to the crafts. Presaging the militant strands of the Indian national movement, he talked about the declining martial ability of Indians and the fact that they did not know the use of arms or weapons. He compared the scenario in India disadvantageously with that in the firang lands or in Faras, which can qualify as exhortative or competitive nationalism (nationalism as 'catching up'), and was, in general, full of 'secular' notions about progress, self-strengthening and reform. This presents a contrast, outwardly, with his usual religious rhetoric, but only if we expect the notion of progress to be neatly compartmentalized between the religious and the worldly spheres. For Baqar there was no clash between the two because both were manifestations of divine power and progressing in one while lagging in the other did not make sense. If this is religious anti-colonialism then it is one that partakes very strongly of country, homeland and people which is, explicitly, the land and people of Hind or Hindustan.

Other than repeatedly, and consciously, attempting to demolish the British hegemony, the awe, the iqbal that had come to mark

British reputation in India, the *Akhbar* also acted as an organ of self-criticism. It castigated the soldiers for displaying idleness, attacked rebel leaders for not paying enough attention to the organization of posts and collection of revenues from the hinterlands and lashed out at the citizens of Delhi for not showing the required spirit and support. It expressed concern at the state of hygiene in the city, at the scarcity and dearth that characterized the vegetable and food markets and harped incessantly about the need to show consideration and charity to the poor. In the issue of 23 August, for instance, these are the appropriate steps recommended by the editor—control over nearby areas, collection of revenues and the importance of disabusing the 'awe' of the English.[18]

Baqar's attitude towards the soldiers certainly changed over time, as pointed out by Moosvi. He began by calling them Tilangas, the somewhat disdainful term employed by Dilliwallas towards the Company soldiers, and was greatly distressed at their atrocities against the city's population. He described the comeuppance of some soldiers, who had amassed great wealth from looting and were cheated while trying to convert the money into gold coins, as a case for having a Moses for every Pharaoh. This resentment at their insolence gradually turned into admiration and he begins to address the army as *Afwaj-e zafar mauj*, a play on Bahadur Shah's poetic title Zafar, which means victory. Thus the army became the victorious forces, those who had won the empire for the Company and who would now lick their former employers. The country, and particularly the city, was reminded of their enviable deeds, their great bravery and urged to support them, to valorize them. While his attitude towards the soldiers and the citizens changed inversely to each other—from being concerned about the people's welfare he turned to berating them for their lack of spirit—he remained consistent in his visceral dislike, even hatred, for the British. His tone towards them was of immense glee when describing their rout or massacre or plight, but one of shrill refutation when dealing with their claims and propaganda. Each British death is a matter of joy, each setback a tribute to their vileness, the extreme racism displayed by him comes as a surprise because he had been friends with many Britishers before the uprising and had served in their administration. In some measure, Baqar's attitude was symptomatic of the groundswell of popular resentment against the British. The intensity of violence which marks the uprising everywhere cannot be made sense of except through the racism, violence and wanton humiliation that Indians felt subjected to in the decades leading up to the uprising.

However, the *Dehli Urdu Akhbar* is suffused with religious terminology and exhortations. It based its appeal, in the last analysis, on the manifest working of divine approval which is clearly on the Islamic-Indian side. Forever, Baqar fell back on this ultimate proof of right and victory being assured to the victorious armies, the fact that the mighty English were annihilated by their own armies and so swiftly too, cannot be but the Almighty's doing. Divine approval and intervention became a validating authority, exactly like the invocation of the good name and deeds of Bahadur Shah Zafar, who was an object of the greatest veneration for Baqar. Fight on for the good King Bahadur Shah, fight against the perfidies of the faithless British, fight for the good of your country and fight above all because God is on your side. Not everybody in the city was as enthusiastic, however. The pamphlet that Baqar prepared to propagate jihad found few takers. Repeated advertisements in the papers and repeated pleas to buy and distribute it as a national service evidently fell on deaf ears because issue after issue carried the same appeal. Few shared Baqar's enthusiastic and rousing religious defence of the uprising.

There is a letter addressed to William Hodson, the chief of the English intelligence at Delhi, preserved in the Delhi State Archives, unsigned and in an English translation, which purports to be a note from Mohammed Baqar the editor of the *Delhi Urdu Akhbar*.[19] In the letter Baqar describes the dissension between Hindus and Muslims in the city over the killing of five butchers by some soldiers. The tone of the letter implies some regularity of correspondence. Baqar could therefore have been a spy. However, whether or not he was one does not affect the substance of what he articulated in his newspaper. The British did not see him as a sympathizer either, he was arrested and hanged soon after they reoccupied the city.

The *Dehli Urdu Akhbar* certainly presents irrefutable evidence for the uprising being informed by religion. Being informed by religion does not equal a religious uprising, however. Moreover, Baqar was not as obsessed with jihad and this shows that appeals to religion did not ipso facto imply invocations to jihad.[20] Yet it also shows that the domain of religion extended to areas that denote attachments to ways of life rather than to specific doctrines. Attempts to denigrate Christianity are far fewer compared to the indignities perpetrated by the Christians. The Hindustan that Baqar conjures up shows an ecumenical doctrinal expanse but one which concurrently needed to be enriched by material advancement. For Hindustan to prosper, attachment to religion and best practices of religion needed to go hand in hand with self-reform and self-improvement. Spiritual progress, material advancement, anti-colonialism and communal fraternity are conjoint, under the necessary leadership of Bahadur Shah Zafar, into a whole which would become wholly elusive after the liberal-ization of India post-1857.

Notes

1. See 'Introduction' in *Press List of Mutiny Papers* (Calcutta: Imperial Records Department, 1921).
2. 'Every worthless fellow, puffed up with pride, perpetrates what he will ... The jewels of the city's fair-faced women ... fill the sacks of the vile, dishonoured thieves and pilferers', From Mirza Asadullah Khan Ghalib, *Dastanbui*, translated by Ralph Russell and Khurshid ul Islam, in Ralph Russell (ed.), *The Oxford India Ghalib: Life, Letters and Ghazals* (New Delhi: Oxford University Press, 2003), p. 119.
3. Iqbal Hussain, 'The Rebel Administration in Delhi', *Social Scientist*, 26 (296–99), January–April 1998, pp. 25–39.
4. Also known as Court of Administration, the constitutional body set up by soldiers to administer the city. See chapter 'The Court of Mutnieers' in this text.
5. See 'The Great Rebellion' by Talmiz Khaldun in P.C. Joshi (ed.), *Rebellion 1857* (New Delhi: National Book Trust of India, 2007), p. 1–72. Khaldun is the pen name of Surinder Singh (information courtesy Professor Amar Faruqi). However, Shahid Amin correctly reminded me that

Mahdi Hasan had first used the CoM papers for his English biography of Bahadur Shah, published in 1957/58.

6. Collection 57, No. 483, Mutiny Papers, the National Archives of India (NAI), and several other documents included in this book in the chapter on the CoM.

7. William Dalrymple, 'Introduction' in *The Last Mughal: The Fall of a Dynasty, Delhi, 1857* (London: Bloomsbury, 2006), p. 3.

8. Rajesh Tope, '1857 from the perspective of Tatya Tope', paper presented at the 1857 Commemoration Seminar at Delhi University in 2007.

9. This phrase is from C.A. Bayly's *Empire and Information: Intelligence Gathering and Social Communication in India, 1780–1870* (Cambridge: Cambridge University Press, 1996).

10. For the intense discussions and for the British disappointment, see John Kaye, *History of the Sepoy War in India*, Vol. 1 (London, 1877), Preface, pp. 525–54, 576–79.

11. For more on Awadh and the administration of the rebels, see Rudrangshu Mukherjee, *Awadh in Revolt, 1857–58: A Study of Popular Resistance* (New Delhi: Oxford University Press, 1984), p. 146.

12. A detailed discussion on its role can be found in the next section of this piece.

13. In a similar vein, Cobb writes of the French revolution, 'The approach has been throughout to replace the question commonly asked: "Why did the popular movement fail in the course of the French revolution?", a question largely irrelevant since the "movement" never had any chance at all of success, at least under its own momentum and without outside help, by the question: "How did a popular movement in its own right ever emerge at all?": for this is perhaps the most astonishing fact about the history of the French Revolution' (Richard Cobb, *The Police and the People: French Popular Protests, 1789–1820* [London: Oxford University Press, 1970], p. xiv).

14. Margrit Pernau, 'The Dehli Urdu Akhbar: Between Persian Akhbarat and English Newspapers', *Annual of Urdu Studies*, 18, 1993, pp. 105–131.

15. Shireen Moosvi, 'Rebel Journalism, *Dehli Urdu Akhbar*, May–September 1857', *People's Democracy*, xxx1 (17), April 2007.

16. I received the following communication from Professor C.M. Naim about this: 'In 1848, its circulation was 79 copies. See J. Natarajan, *History of Indian Journalism*, p. 50. Quoted in Nadir Ali Khan's *Urdu Sahaft Ki Tarikh*. Of course, each copy had at least four or five readers, and perhaps

one or two listeners.' One can therefore speculate that at least five to six hundred people from the educated and presumably the better-off classes were familiar with the paper's contents.

17. For this I rely on the many different kinds of arguments by Christopher Bayly in order to push back the period of the emergence of nationalism, and more particularly, of patriotism in nineteenth-century Indian history. See his *Origins of Nationality in South Asia: Patriotism and Ethical Government in the Making of Modern India* (New Delhi: Oxford University Press, 1998) and *Empire and Information: Intellignece Gathering and Social Communication in India, 1780–1870* (New York: Cambridge University Press, 1996).

18. Baqar also launched into a long passage about how Dehli's luxurious air makes idlers of us all, which is why the rulers of yore forever avoided staying too long in this city, and how the laddus and the *pedas* of Ghantewala, the famous sweets shop at Chandni Chowk, turn valiant soldiers into cowards. See *Dehli Urdu Akhbar*, 23 August 1857, Collection 2, NAI.

19. *Translation of a letter from Moonshee Mahomed Bakarr, Editor of Delhi Oordoo Akhbar*, Newsletter during the Mutiny, File No. 50, 28 July 1857, Delhi Archives.

20. See the introduction in this book to the section 'The Ideologue'.

IN THE NAME OF SARKAR

The terms rebel government and rebel administration have been used interchangeably in this book. Neither term is meant to convey a coherent, organized and regimented structure of authority. As has been noted, there were multiple power centres in the city, which sometimes clashed with each other. The main constituents of these centres of power included leading members of Bahadur Shah's court, the CoM set up by the soldiers, the commissariat headed by Mirza Mughal and the staff of the commander of the Bareilly forces, Bakht Khan, who had been appointed lord governor. The administrative structure included also the police force of the city, the darogha or the superintendent of the magazine, the regiment officers including such prominent ones as Mir Rajab Ali, the head of the sappers and miners regiment, the officers in charge of hospitals and royal functionaries such as the darogha of supplies. Together these formed a skeletal administration sometimes at odds with each other, sometimes working in unison. By using the term administration, or government, my intention is to delineate structures of authority from the outward picture of anarchy. The orders issued by the head of any of these power centres could translate into action at the ground level, as for example, in the movement of goods or people. The response to these orders in the form of acknowledgements or refusal or issuing of receipts, mostly in writing, also indicates some degree of bureaucratic functioning and the pursuit of established norms. Moreover, the fact that ordinary crimes such as gambling and stealing continued to be prosecuted, that missing persons were searched and other kinds of complaints were registered and dealt with also points to the continuation of some kind of settled administration. It is in this limited sense that the word government has been used here.

An additional reason for persisting with these terms is the wide prevalence of the Urdu word sarkar, meaning government, in these documents. The term is used alike by the petitioners authorities and soldiers. All of them regarded the government to have changed hands and the King to have assumed the reins of the new government. Constant appeals and exhortations to 'reasons of government', 'needs of government' and 'responsibilities of government' imply a rationality of governance. Conscripted workers are deemed to be working for the sarkar. Exhortations to officers and soldiers are also made in the name of the sarkar. Families of workers killed in the magazine conflagration are assured compensation by and in the name of the sarkar. Whether or not there was a unified structure in Delhi, many of the participants assumed it to be there and expected it to perform as such. The word sarkar here needs to be correlated to another word that recurs frequently in the *Dehli Urdu Akhbar, amaldari*. The latter uses the term to denote a change of government. 'The English have lost the amaldari at Panipat', is the phrase used by the paper to describe the fall of the British government there. It denotes the taking over of actual governance by Indians and sometimes acted as a synonym for *hukumat*, governance. This needs to be placed in the context of the exact phrase used for government proclamations, even by the East India Company. The phrase used by the town crier went, 'The creation/people belong to god, the country to the Emperor and the government [that is, amaldari] to the Company.' The use of the word amaldari implies a change of control or governing authority and has nothing to do with sovereignty, which remains where it always was, with the King. According to the implied understanding of the newspaper, the rebels were merely (re)taking over actual control of administration, not instituting a new regime.

However, even as the structure of authority is designated as a rebel government, it needs to be underlined that it is not exclusively a government formed of rebel soldiers or civilians. It should more properly be described as the rebel-royal government. While formal rebel structures such as the CoM played a crucial role in running the administration, court functionaries and institutions fashioned or controlled by the British—police and lawcourts—too were a part of it. Daroghas of different royal departments such as the ice factory, the officer in charge of supplies, the superintendent of the royal mint and others participated in the city's governance. The royal secretariat which issued parwanas, *shuqqas* and firmans from the King remained active through out.[1] Informally, the members of Bahadur Shah's court, notably his sons and grandsons, also enjoyed substantial authority.

The emphasis on ghadar as well as on *order and organization*, which are the twin leitmotifs of this book, may seem immediately contradictory, but in a larger protean event, the presence of smaller circles of authority and structure are not altogether anomalous and this book attempts to highlight them.

The initial turmoil created by the arrival of soldiers at Delhi and the widespread plunder had a dimension of class war.[2] The soldiers' mistreatment of the city's elites, even of the person of Bahadur Shah, has been well documented.[3] Jiwan Lal, a former judicial functionary who turned into a British spy and whose diary was compiled by Metcalfe as part of his *Two Native Narratives*, reported that,

> . . . several respectable men were seized and made to carry burdens to intimidate them and extort money, all valuable property had by this time been buried, and a private police force had been raised by the better class of citizens to protect themselves and their property.[4]

Private guards continued to remain in place for the well-to-do, almost right till the end. The house of Mufti Sadruddin Azurda, an important judicial authority under the British and a leading city intellectual, had to be guarded by the volunteers.[5] People's houses could be raided on the charge, or pretext, of protecting the British or containing stolen goods and arms from the magazine. This, of course, created room for ambiguity and high and low were affected alike. There are numerous complaints of this kind in the section titled 'The Personal Becomes Public: Dilliwallas and the Uprising'. The *Dehli Urdu Akhbar* reported a case where some ruffians, in this case, low-caste ones, were roaming the city dressed as soldiers.[6] For the Delhi elites the uprising, particularly its initial days, was a rough period. However, this picture of turmoil needs to be offset by other features which were simultaneous to it. By the 21st of May, barely ten days after the soldiers arrived, it had become customary to hold an evening parade, and in his entry for the day, Jiwan Lal reported that some two hundred soldiers were found missing on that date from the parade. Clearly, supervision and organization were required to discover and to report this fact.

The administrative order extended to many areas, military and civilian. The exact sequence and specifications of platoons which went to the battle front, and a schedule of sorties and assaults were made almost every day, in consultation with the CoM. The decision was communicated in a written form to the regiments, which were duly acknowledged by their adjutants. The regiments deployed on guard or sentry duty at each of the gates were specifically appointed to those positions. As suggested by *Sadiq-ul Akhbar*, one of the two weekly newspapers of Delhi, soldiers from specified units were stationed at each police station in order to buttress the authority of the police, possibly also to protect it from other soldiers, and these came to be known as police platoons.[7] The arrival of every fresh batch of soldiers, or armies, from different parts of the country was usually known in advance and arrangements were made to receive them and put them up in previously specified localities.[8]

Military necessities required an inexhaustible supply of labour of many different kinds, both skilled and unskilled. Tailors, masons, thatchers, watercarriers, construction workers and many others were required daily at the battle front and beyond, for military as well as semi-military duties. These had to be sourced and kept in readiness, every day. This task was usually carried out by the police who often resorted to coercion. Monetary contributions were levied repeatedly, often targeting the same people but there was some record of who had paid how much and when, and people could sometimes be exempted if they had already paid their dues. Money collections could sometimes assume arbitrary dimensions; anybody and everybody could set himself up as a royal collector but equally, the poor could lodge a complaint if harassed and hope to get some relief.[9]

Soldiers were deputed to tend to sick and wounded comrades. All who absented themselves because of medical reasons required a medical certificate to sanctify their leave, the lack of which could lead to prosecution. Absconding soldiers who came and hid in the city, and there were many of them, could also be arrested on occasion. According to Jiwan Lal, soldiers were tried, and shot, for showing cowardice.[10]

Apart from the management of soldiers, and supplies and money, the city's administration had also to deal with other necessities such as fixing prices of goods, announcing and maintaining a daily schedule of rates and fixing the exchange rate for gold coins and for the older company coins and new royal coins. It had to ensure that shops remained open and well stocked and that official proclamations, resolutions and decisions were conveyed to all in the city. This everyday matrix of tasks was further sharpened by the new kinds of regulations that were in put place in the troubled months of 1857. These included restrictions on favourite pastimes such as flying kites or consuming opium, gambling and blowing the bugles during Muharram. Military requirements necessitated a ban on private possession of lead or any other commodity that could be used for manufacturing gunpowder and the implementation of the ban involved the police and soldiers deployed as guards. The administration also had to arrange the funeral of soldiers and of unclaimed corpses. Periodically, the police also had to round up particular sections of the population: Punjabis, Bengalis and bankers.

Studying rebel governmentality[11] in Delhi in 1857 sometimes leads to very startling revelations. The prison, which was 'freed' and emptied of all prisoners early in the uprising, after 'the spirit of insubordination became rife in every class', as testified by Jiwan Lal, seemed to have been quickly filled up again. Even more significantly, in spite of the heavy money shortages the prisoners were paid an allowance of half an anna every day. They found the amount inadequate and clamoured for more![12] A recent study of the coins minted by the rebel government of Delhi establishes the self-consciousness of the regime as well as its aspirations to be new and novel.[13] The lunatic asylum remained functional right through. Clearly, the administration not only felt responsible for conducting the war but also attempted to fulfil the normal functions of government. In doing so, it was forced to form a relationship with its subjects which was in many ways unprecedented in pre-modern South Asia. At moments, it had to act as the guardian for the subjects, to take care of their well-being and to ensure that their losses were compensated at the same time as it had to exploit them for labour and resources. This will become clearer after a brief look at the aftermath of the explosion of the government-run armaments manufactory which was called the magazine.

The explosion of the magazine on the 7th of August brought into salience the relationship of the government to its servants as well as to the subjects whom it was supposed to be serving. A terrible explosion convulsed the magazine, over five hundred labourers working there lost their lives while shrapnel and debris were strewn all over the city.[14] For two days the fire kept raging, the administration made several efforts to douse it, demanding annihilators, pyrotechnists and any other specialists it could manage. The police did yeoman service during that accident and came in for much praise from the newspapers. In response, the government immediately moved to take insurance for those who had lost their lives in the explosion, promising compensation, jobs and pensions to the family members of all who had lost their lives. Welfare of the subjects, it appears, was an important consideration. One offshoot of this incident was that furious soldiers grew more obsessed with the possible treachery and connivance of Hakim Ahsanullah Khan, the King's physician and confidant, in bringing this about. They surrounded his house, humiliated his family and did not let go until the King offered his own variant of the later satyagraha by refusing to appear in public and by announcing his decision to go and become a sweeper at the shrine of Bakhtiyar Kaki, popularly known as Khwaja Saheb, regarded as the patron saint of Delhi, at Mehrauli.[15]

Other than the well-known components such as the police there were other administrative units and positions that remained in place throughout. The judicial courts continued to function, albeit under new functionaries. Cases presented at the court were processed in the same manner as before; recording of statements, presentation of witnesses, the mode of cross-examination, these norms and practices remained in force. The functioning of these courts should have been the first casualty of widespread anarchy. However, even the police could not simply lock up people at will. Older functionaries of the royal court who had earlier exclusively served the royal household now came to work for the wider rebel government. The darogha of the *barfkhana* or the royal ice factory continued to supply ice to the royal and presumably other elite households and strongly complained to the King about the intervention of the soldiers in its management. The *darogha-i-saman*, officer of the royal household became the officer in charge of supplying tents and marquees to the army. Officials who could not be yoked directly to the cause of the government found themselves eased out of authority. The Jama Masjid was wholly taken over by the soldiers, especially by the jihadis who turned it into a kind of base camp for themselves. As a result, the darogha of the Jama Masjid found himself redundant and urged the King to direct the jihadis to recognize his overlordship of the mosque, to no avail.[16] This fusing of the royal household with the wider structures of government may at first sight seem a throwback to the previous ways of government. That would, however, be misleading because this was not government for the King or even by the King. This will become clearer through a close examination of the police establishment which came to form the most important executive wing of the government.

Police[17]

Prior to the uprising the police in Delhi was under the control of the British magistracy. How and why it moulded itself to service the rebel cause is something that still needs investigation. Most of the officers in charge of police stations came from upper-caste Muslim families with ties to the local gentility. Perhaps it was the prestige of the Mughal court which drew the higher police officials to it so easily. Moreover, in the older Mughal dispensation, the kotwal, the city police chief, was one of the most important officials of the city and normally reported directly to the King.[18] In medieval kingdoms, the kotwal combined the functions of the executive chief as well as a police official. Thus, when the King exerted his authority, it did not prove very difficult for the officers of the police force to switch their loyalties to him. The King encouraged this by corresponding directly with the leading police officers. At his express bidding, on the occasion of the festival of Baqrid, all the thanadars appeared before him and paid him a ritual tribute called nazar. In this way the rebel administration successfully managed to reintegrate the police into the older symbolic, ritualistic world of obedience and service.[19]

The organization of war as well as the maintenance of a general administrative order in Delhi was in the main the work of the pre-existing police force. Working mainly on the orders of the commissariat headed by Mirza Mughal, the C-in-C, as well as on the instructions of the CoM, the police formed the bulwark of the administrative order of the city. In an early attempt to stake claim over it, the King wrote to the officers, or thanadars, of all the thanas or police stations in the city, in the second week of the uprising, urging them to remain in position and to follow commands issued to them. The ease with which the old administrative machinery began to service the rebels' cause was truly remarkable. The daily reports of the thanas show that almost all thanadars and their subordinates remained in place; in fact, there were new recruitments. By the end of May, some degree of order had clearly been fully established. The *Dehli Urdu Akhbar* remarked on this when it praised the new kotwal for his effectiveness.[20]

The soldiers evidently saw the police as a representative of the royal establishment or of the government that had been established because from the first few days they demanded rations, provisions and shelter from the police. The civilian population of Delhi too recognized the police as the representative of the new government that had come into being because they complained to the police about the soldiers' excesses and expected to be redressed. In the symbiotic relationship between the government, the soldiers and the ordinary people, it was the police which acted as the major interface and the intermediary. Naturally, the police was called upon to perform tasks that were earlier wholly outside its purview.

The police were petitioned when people's houses were plundered by soldiers, when women ran away or children went missing, when shops and grains were required for soldiers' camps, when affrays occurred between citizens, and when the administration had to implement orders and commandeer resources. Police duties could range from arranging for a charpoy and fuel for cremating the dead body of a subedar,[21] to ascertaining whether those standing bail had the property they claimed,[22] to getting the refuse cleared from the city,[23] to making sure that dead bodies were allowed through by the guards at the city gates,[24] to issuing general proclamations and informing the citizenry of the orders of the commissariat and the CoM[25] and issuing notice of a general levy,[26] to awarding and maintaining contracts to different contractors for shops.[27] Its indispensability to the administrative set-up of the rebels' makes a study of the police establishment an exploration not just into the management of the uprising but also of the very nature of the rebellion. It emerges that the administration kept itself going by the force it could exert on the subalterns—the subalterns who serviced this rebellion through skilled and unskilled labour, as well as the subalterns within the police force, the barqandazes, the ordinary constables, who actually implemented the orders on the ground.

Before exploring in greater detail the functioning of the police, it may help to get an idea of their distribution and arrangement in the city, particularly since these terms and positions recur many times in the documents. The kotwali was the main police station of the city and was headed by the kotwal, the chief of police. The kotwal had twelve police stations or thanas under his charge, each of which was headed by a thanadar (also called a darogha). In addition to these, jamadars and mohurrirs, or clerks, were the other officer ranks. Finally, there were the barqandaz, the semi-armed ordinary policemen or constables who did most of the running around. We do not have the exact figures for the number of policemen employed in Delhi. But the daily diary of the kotwali shows that on 27 July there were in all forty-two people employed there. There was a kotwal and two deputy kotwals, eight mohurrirs or clerks, one jamadar and twenty-five barqandazes. Of the people employed at the kotwali, ten were Hindus and thirty were Muslims, while the religion of two cannot be determined. We don't know exactly how many of these had been employed from before the mutiny but the numbers had certainly increased since the uprising.[28] During the uprising, the thanadar was paid four rupees a month, the old barqandazes were getting two rupees and the new ones fifty paise each.[29] Extrapolating from these figures, taking twenty men for each thana, and considering that there were twelve thanas in the city, one can arrive at a rough figure of four hundred for the total police strength in the city. In addition to the regular policemen, every thanadar also had some sweepers, drum-beaters and chowkidars, the last paid by local dues, which functioned under him.[30]

As should be evident by now, the police was at the forefront of collecting supplies, provisions and labour that were essential to waging a war, in addition to performing normal policing duties. Money contributions were raised through the police it was the force which arrested, detained, browbeat and escorted bankers and merchants. The supply of provisions to different regiments was also the responsibility of the police. Thus the police had to make sure that enough shops were billeted and open for business wherever the regiments were stationed. In addition to supplying the regiments with food (and with delicacies like puri-kachauri and sheerini as the occasion demanded[31]), the police also had to provide resources for the war effort. This included not just the materials of war but also the manpower required to fight it. Coolies, labourers, bakers, water carriers, farriers, masons, anything and anyone that was required was supplied by the police. A very large section of the Mutiny Papers consist of documents to and from different thanadars. At a frantic pace, handling nearly a hundred documents a day, the thanas provided for or managed this complex gamut of tasks. A list of objects and persons they were providing makes for staggering reading: oxen, cobblers, coolies, water carriers, cattle, rations, doolie-bearers, conveyances, grocers, gunny bags, daggers, spades, axes, ghee, baskets, pulses, sulphur, saddle makers, molasses, wood, husk sellers, carpenters, shoesmiths, *ekka*s, mares, carts, sweepers, butchers, blacksmiths, corn, curds, flour, milk, sugar and doctors, and this is only a selection.

Even as the police conscripted and requisitioned labour it could also speak up for their grievances. In one of many such missives, the kotwal raised the question of wages of forty doolie-bearers who had been sent to the platoon of the forty-eight regiment.[32] As did the thanadar of Turkman Gate.[33] Whatever it supplied, however, the police expected the price to be paid.[34] Instead of the demand being routed through the commissariat or the CoM, soldiers could directly go to the concerned thana and ask for supplies.[35] Soldiers could also write directly to the police in case of other requirements.[36]

Apart from trying, often ineffectually, to protect the residents from the excesses of the soldiers the police faced fundamental problems even in making arrangements for their supplies. Grain merchants posted to serve the encampments at Delhi Gate protested to the kotwali that the men of the platoon rarely paid up for the wares they bought and they showed cruelty to the shopkeepers. In this case, the King inscribed on the margins of the application an instruction for the secretary of the commissariat to deduct the dues from their salaries.[37] Similar was the case of the shopkeepers billeted at the lunatic asylum who complained that soldiers forcibly took their goods and beat them up in the bargain, and if things continue in the same way they would go on a strike.[38] The relations between the soldiers and the citizens were always fraught with tension and the police had to constantly negotiate its way through this logjam of dire necessity, lack of money and the refusal of the soldiers to abide by the compulsions of the administration.

The kotwali records are replete with efforts to summon the leading bankers and traders of each area. Dealing with bankers and raising money presented a double bind for the police. On the one hand they were constantly commanded to arrest, detain and put under house arrest recalcitrant bankers and merchants who refused to make contributions. On the other hand they were constantly restrained by orders urging them to avoid offending the public. The thanadar of Chandni Chowk wrote to the kotwal reporting on the bankers of the famous and rich

Katra Neel where, 'Some people disappear inside their houses and do not give any response while most of them make one excuse or another to keep this servant at bay and are forever on the lookout for creating trouble or making complaints'. Accordingly he was sending some bankers hoping that 'A strong rebuke will be administered to them for unless that happens the money will not come forth'.[39] Sometimes it could work in reverse, the police could forward petitions from the people requesting to be exempted from making money contributions as the deputy kotwal indicated to the C-in-C in the case of the poor people of the Faiz Bazaar area.[40] But excessive zeal could earn censure. The same file contains an admonition from the kotwal to the thanadar of Kashmiri Gate, reprimanding him for raiding the shop of Bahauddin without permission. He is instructed specifically that no house is to be raided without permission from the kotwali [41]

Sometimes the tasks assigned to the police required an impossible degree of resourcefulness, while simultaneously putting enormous powers into its hands. The kotwal was asked, in one communiqué from the C-in-C, to make sure that no one bought or sold plundered or looted articles, and anyone caught doing so was to be strongly punished.[42] A similar occasion was when Bakht Khan went to the kotwali and asked the officers to issue a general proclamation that anybody found flying kites, discharging fireworks, idly firing a weapon or flying pigeons was liable for punishment.[43] Sometimes the police, already overburdened, could display zeal for taking on more work. On 24th July, one and a half months into the uprising, it struck the kotwal that 'Clandestine gambling continues again in the areas commanded by thanadars posted in the city'. He therefore wrote directly to the King to ask whether the gamblers should be peremptorily arrested.[44] Then, as now, gambling came accompanied by other vices. On 3rd August Mir Akbar Ali, a resident of Faiz Bazaar lodged a complaint stating that there was a gambling house near his home and that the gamblers used abusive language and stared at the females of his home.[45]

The dilemmas and problems faced by the police in acting at once as the preventive arm as well as the chief executive wing of the government were exemplified on the occasion of the Muslim festival of Baqrid, when a general order banning cow slaughter was passed in the city at the behest of the King and of the C-in-C. The police was not only urged to make sure that the ban was implemented; it was also persuaded to take preventive steps to ensure that cows weren't slaughtered.[46] Apart from circulating the order to all the thanadars and issuing a general proclamation everywhere, the kotwal wrote to all the thanadars asking them to send him a list of all the cow-owning Muslims in their respective areas.[47] The problem arose when the King issued an order instructing the kotwal to collect all the cows owned by the Muslims and to keep them in the kotwali.[48] In order to further ensure that no slaughter happened surreptitiously, the C-in-C wrote to the kotwal to count all the skins of dead animals and the amount of grease available with the butchers, an order that was sent to all the leading butchers as well.[49] One can only wonder what this would have meant for the citizenry at large for the police could arrest any Muslim on any one of the following charges: sacrificing cows, owning cows and not giving an undertaking, possessing skins or showing an intention of killing cows. The section of documents on cow slaughter gives important glimpses into the mentality of the government and the techniques it adopted as it tried to prevent cow slaughter.

The biggest stumbling block for the police was the presence of an enormous body of armed soldiers who would demand things off them but not allow them to function without hindrance. Not only would soldiers interfere in police work but they would also lean on the police to, significantly, legalize actions which they had undertaken directly. They would arrest people and bring them to the kotwali or to a particular thana, or assault the thana and free a particular accused as they saw fit.[50] The soldiers guarding the Farrashkhana gate routinely asked for bribes to allow the movement of goods and documents.[51] Sometimes soldiers would interfere with the police when they were busy raising supplies or commandeering labour.[52] Then there was interference in its investigative agency, well illustrated by the case of the prostitute Vaziran. After she was arrested on the charge of theft, a large group of soldiers descended on the kotwali and forcibly freed her. An exasperated kotwal reported to the C-in-C, 'The situation is this *that the soldiers interfere in everything* . . . and this prostitute has been brought to the *thana* in several cases earlier'.[53] In a directive on 1st July, the C-in-C wrote to the kotwal asking him to stop soldiers from forcibly searching houses with the instruction that 'without the order of the government and the presence of the informer no [forced] searches will be conducted at any respectable person's house'.[54] These cases may at first sight confirm the picture of anarchy. However, we should not completely dismiss the constant attempts of the administration to impose order and to make the soldiers amenable to discipline.

The police force itself was regularly monitored for discipline, attendance and punctuality. All thanadars were urged to maintain a regular daily diary, a practice of the past, and send it punctually to the kotwali.[55] Every circular, whether from the kotwal and thanadars, or parwanas, orders from higher-ups, was supposed to be copied in hand and a receipt signed on the document itself. When circulars returned unsigned, it indicated absenteeism, a misdemeanour which did not go unnoticed even in spite of the turbulence.[56] The vigilantism over police discipline and responsiveness seems to have been an area of concern from the very beginning. This is evident from the case of Faiz Mohammed Khan, a merchant artisan and resident of Turkman Gate, who made a complaint that on the night of Id his house was broken into but when he went into the thana to lodge a complaint, he couldn't find anyone there.[57] What is remarkable here is the eagerness shown by the thanadar to deny the charge of dereliction of duty, whether he was doing this out of fear of censure or out of a lure for reward remains unclear.[58]

Not only was the performance and attendance of the thanadars well monitored, their jurisdiction too was closely watched. Although they were being asked to perform all sorts of extra-policing duties, they were not allowed to step beyond their exact imprimatur during their execution. On 19 August, when the kotwal, replying to an order of the C-in-C, wrote that the particular case being enquired into had already been compromised, he earned a sharp rebuke from General Taleyaar Khan, member secretary of the CoM.[59] If the jurisdiction of the kotwals was closely guarded, on occasion, the police too could refuse a chore by saying it was not a part of their duties. When asked to remove carcasses of dead camels strewn around Daryaganj, the kotwal refused to comply and clarified, to the King, no less, that it was the duty of Mir Amir Ali, the superintendent of roads, and he should be made to do it.[60]

There could sometimes be graver problems. In one of the rare documents which allows the barqandaz to speak, a barqandaz refused to obey an order in the middle of the night. He is reported to have said that 'Such urgent orders come every day, we are not going out just now, we will only go in the morning,' whereupon, a panicked kotwal wrote to the C-in-C saying that 'If this happens and the barqandazes refuse to obey the officer's orders then how will government work be done.' Even earlier the concerned thanadar had sent in a note complaining about his barqandazes: 'If every barqandaz gets the courage to do ghadar[61] then they would do ghadar whenever an urgent task comes up. Therefore I submit that Ghazi Khan etc., the four barqandazes, should be dismissed which would prove salutary to the others otherwise they would not obey anyone's orders.'[62]

We don't know whether the barqandazes were actually dismissed but it is noteworthy that neither the thanadar nor the kotwal had the power to dismiss or appoint anyone under their command. Requests from the kotwal or thanadars seeking dismissal of blind or infirm or old barqandazes or their transfer had to be routed through the C-in-C.[63] Even as small a matter as the room rent that a barqandaz could pay had to be cleared by the C-in-C.[64] The thanadar of Guzar Itiqad Khan, Faiz Talab Khan, wrote on 27 May stating that the older employees of the thana have not been paid their salaries of two months, let alone the newer ones.[65] The police was functioning as the strongest arm of the ghadar but it was not an arm which was free to move on its own. While its material conditions of work—cramped spaces, delayed salaries, insufficiency of staff—may paint a picture of chaos, the restrictions on its field of operations can be read to substantiate the notion of ghadar, as well as detract from it. In a scenario where the police was the chief executive wing of an emergency government, it would not have been surprising for it to arrogate all sorts of powers to itself. That the administration attempted to keep a constant check on its powers and performance can then be read as indicative of the authority and discipline that could still be maintained, against the odds.

If the police was troubled by soldiers it could also, sometimes, harass the residents. On 24th June, barely a month into the uprising, the residents of Chandni Chowk sent in a petition to the C-in-C complaining about the oppression of Hafiz Aminuddin Khan, the thanadar of Chandni Chowk.[66] We don't know if the thanadar was reprimanded but he was replaced sometime in July. The police mainly procured goods and services through conscription, expropriation and confiscation. In the process it often faced stiff resistance, from civilians as well as soldiers. The same Chandni Chowk thanadar, mentioned above, wrote to the kotwal on 3rd July complaining about a certain Punjabi tailor who had refused to obey orders from the thana. The Punjabi tailor, the thanadar claimed, was a rogue who has abused the barqandazes and 'has made many tailors run away and unless he is properly punished he will not obey the orders given out'.[67] Similarly, a thanadar wrote in to complain about a badmash called Afzal who assaulted some barqandazes while they were trying to conscript labor. Afzal's remarkable little speech went thus: 'I too rule this place, if you take people away by force we will confront you ... if you have arms, we too are armed, you cannot take them away like this.'[68] In many cases the soldiers stepped in to release arrested workers.[69] However, we need to remember that considering the degree and intensity of expropriation committed by the police, the number of cases of active resistance seem remarkably low. What comes as a surprise is the relative ease with which the police got away. The order maintained by the police, therefore, appears to be effective and substantial.

Along with all this, the police had to deal with an inordinate number of cases of missing women. Women were eloping with soldiers, soldiers' wives were deserting them, courtesans and prostitutes were colluding with soldiers. This was happening at a rate that ensured that at any given time during the uprising at least one thana in the city was dealing with a disappeared woman. There were, to give only a few instances, communiqués from the thanadar of Bhojla Pahari on 16 August reporting the missing wife and property of Hyder Ali, a horseman of the sixth cavalry, fourteenth regiment, arrived from Datiya in Jhansi;[70] from the thanadar of Faiz Bazaar regarding the case of the groom of a risaldar, Ghulam Mohiuddin of eighteenth cavalry running away with Dilpasand Kaur;[71] from the kotwal to all thanadars regarding the wife of Pir Bakhsh who had run away with his goods and valuables, and scores of others. In the case of these missing women, often a physical description of the woman accompanies the report. Pir Bakhsh's wife was described as being twenty-five years old, of wheatish complexion, average height, slim body wearing a pajama choli, with close-knit eyebrows. In the circumstances then prevailing in the city, when the population had nearly doubled, it was no mean task to try and locate a particular missing woman. Not surprisingly, there were few instances of reported recovery for any of these women. And even the policemen were not spared. The missing wife of Gopal, barqandaz of thana Paharganj, was spotted with Jiwan Khan and Nawab Khan, havaldars of third company, sappers and miners, and they were said to be looking after her. In case of arrest, wrote the kotwal, it was highly likely that there would be a riot and 'His lordship is well aware of the situation of the soldiers of war'.[72]

Amidst all the chaos, the ghadar and given the enormity of burdens it was operating under, it is remarkable that the police could actually recover some of these missing women. However, recovery itself wasn't a solution because in some cases missing or eloped wives contested the versions given out by their spouses. Pir Bakhsh complained that the wife of his deceased brother, whom he treated with great consideration, had recently run away with a soldier, Jabar, of the volunteer platoon and when he located her and urged her to return the hundred rupees she had made away with, she declined and in fact threatened him by saying that 'I will get you beaten up by soldiers'.[73] In cases like these it was impossible to detect who was lying and who was giving out the truth. Eventually, it was decided that no charge could be proven against the woman; therefore she was allowed to go free but the case was finally decided on 11 September, three days before Delhi fell. That a case was being discussed, reported and processed as part of a normal procedure, merely three days before the city was stormed, tells us something important about the disciplinary order of the city. The administrative norms remained in place almost to the day that the city was assaulted; there are a large number of documents dating from 14th September, the day of the British assault.

Then there were disturbances created by prostitutes of different hues. The establishments of courtesans and prostitutes were points of congregations for soldiers and civilians and clashes often ensued there. We have already encountered the case of Vaziran, the prostitute with military clout, but there were several others. Kunwar Lal, the thanadar of Dariba, wrote to the kotwal at the end of June reporting the case of the dispute between a prostitute, Sundar, and her tenant Abdurrazzaq. Over a dispute about payment of rent, three soldiers then present in her quarters came and fired upon Abdurrazzaq. After the thanadar had brought both of them to the thana a further set of soldiers dropped in, this time claiming to speak for Abdurrazzaq: 'He is our brother, we will take him and this prostitute to the court of the Commander in chief'. The thanadar managed to stay his ground and send the disputed parties to the kotwali for the case to be decided as the kotwal saw fit.[74] Sundar Kasbi managed to make a name for herself. In an undated communication the clerk of the Dariba thana wrote to the kotwal requesting him to reprimand a bad character called Gopal who frequented her place. His visits, he wrote, could cause an 'untoward incident and that if he continues he will be punished'.[75]

The reason the police became so indispensable to the administration and to the war effort in Delhi was because it was the only organized body available to the rebel government. The magnitude of tasks the government was compelled to perform in 1857 were without precedent in the pre-modern era. Governing a city, fighting a war and commandeering resources from within the city—these called for an exceptional bureaucratic and disciplinary effort. In order to successfully wage the war effort the administrative order in Delhi perforce needed a mechanism to implement and act on its orders, which were, often, coercive in nature. At the same time the administration was relying quite intensively on public morale and support. At all times, therefore, the police had to walk a tightrope between executing decrees and not stepping on too many toes. Apart from the soldiers who constantly thwarted it, the authorities were not in favour of granting the police too many summary powers. The police, therefore, had to tax the public without offending it. An impossible task at all times, but made even more difficult by the lack of money. Further, given the way the police was acting, and given the presence of such a mass of soldiery, one would expect the citizens to be coerced into silence. But the evidence of a vast number of complaints by the people shows that rather than abandoning faith in the administration the people were rather looking to it to for succour. This was true for complaints against the police itself. The people could speak out against injustices and expect the government to respond to them.[76] The police could not always bend everyone to its will; intransigence was encountered not merely among the subalterns it was pressing into service but also by other citizens: the Punjabi tailor who quarreled with barqandazes or Afzal the ruffian who freed conscripted labourers or the citizens of Chandni Chowk who complained against their bullying thanadar.

By and large, the police force held its discipline. There are plenty of documents where thanadars express helplessness in executing commands because of lack of money or unavailability of goods. But there is not a single document where a thandar could be said to have displayed insubordination of any kind. Instances of outright refusals are equally conspicuous by their absence. There may have been other instances of a barqandaz refusing work which I have not stumbled upon, but instances of outright insubordination are rare for the subordinates and officers alike. Considering that the thanadar could neither appoint nor dismiss a barqandaz of his free will, the lack of documented instances of insubordination is immediately noticeable. The remarkable achievement therefore was the degree of order that could still be, and was, maintained. The bureaucratic norms that had been established for the mode of receiving grievances as well as for the way in which they were addressed remained in force. As the inordinate amount of paperwork indicates, orders and commands issued by the commissariat could reach a particular thana on the same day. The thanadars, with the help of their clerical staff, could produce or reply to dozens of missives daily. As mentioned above, this implies that carriers or runners were in place to carry this correspondence from one place to another. Every order sent by the C-in-C to the kotwal or to the thanadars was copied in hand and recorded in the register of the thana or the kotwali. Not only were documents zealously produced, they were also supposed to be sealed and covered properly.[77] It is telling that thanadars who had conscripted coolies, to take only one instance, to send them to the C-in-C, insisted on getting a receipt for it and insisted that the workers be paid. Receipts for all goods and persons were sent at all times—this imperative complicates the coercion through which many of those things were procured. The receipts do not necessarily add up to any particular reward for any of them; in fact, some of them remain unpaid themselves, but they are an indication of the relatively healthy nature of the administrative order that had taken charge of the city.

While affrays and fracas between civilians and soldiers were quite common, as was the violence involved in plundering and looting, there were distinct limits to this violence. It is remarkable that in spite of all the violence, terror and tyranny, very few murders or assassinations seemed to have taken place in the city. The police records don't mention any single incident of murder, very few merchants or bankers are actually killed. House arrest is another matter, but extortion of bankers does not seem to extend to abduction or murder for gain. In fact the *Dehli Urdu Akhbar* expressly praised the efficiency of the police and quoted others who echoed this sentiment.[78] There was pandemonium in the city but it did not endanger the safety of life.

While the police served as the main executive wing of the rebel government in Delhi, it is difficult to discern the motivations which informed its actions. The documents do not show any particular partisanship of the police towards the rebels. If they had sympathy or feeling for the rebel side, it is not reflected in the documentary evidence. The official nature of the correspondence, conducted and composed by professional scribes in all cases, never betrays any emotional attachments. In exhorting the subordinates, or in directives or commands issued to officers, there is a near universal absence of exhortation on religious or patriotic grounds. At no point does any police functionary mention religion or the cause of religion and country. This ideological gap is intriguing, given the surfeit of emotional appeals in official proclamations to soldiers. Was the police simply doing its duty, like it had always done? Was it serving the King, not the wider uprising? Where did the loyalty of the police force lie? The bureaucratic nature of the corps seems to provide the strongest impelling force for its actions.

Delhi was peculiar compared to other centres of the uprising in so far as that it did not have a hinterland to feed off. There was no body of *talukdars* sending in supplies and men to service the cause.[79] Soldiers were more or less left to fend for themselves, therefore they constantly impressed the authorities with their needs. The constant importunation of the soldiers may seem to detract from their spirit and devotion, but it needs to be underscored that they had nowhere else to turn to. The lukewarm attitude, even downright hostility, of the residents of the city towards the army was criticized not just by the soldiers but also by the editor of the *Dehli Urdu Akhbar* who found their lack of fervour quite alarming.[80] As Gautam Bhadra has pointed out in the case of Lucknow, the soldiers' fear and suspicion of courtly circles originated from the awareness that the interests of the elite and those of the common insurgents were not identical.[81] Further, the soldiers' insolent behaviour and the display of wanton luxury has been described by the same author as a 'festival of the oppressed' denoting festivity as well as defiance against the higher orders.[82] The picture that emerges of the soldiers in these documents has to be offset against other accounts which describe their bravery and desperation in battle. Being in nature administrative documents, the Mutiny Papers do not throw any light on the emotions involved in fighting the war but as shown by other accounts, for instance the *Dehli Urdu Akhbar* which is included here, there was no dearth of these. The soldiers were after all fighting a voluntary war, without resources.

However, formal structures of authority such as the C-in-C, the CoM, the police and the functionaries of the royal establishment were only as important to the city's running as the countless smaller power centres which were spread throughout the city. These could take the form of groups of soldiers, platoons billeted at the police station, groups of armed strong men in the locality or even the establishments of the leading courtesans, singers and prostitutes. Poring over these documents creates an impression of a miasma of panic and suspicion descending on the city, a scenario where beggars, mendicants, lunatics, funeral processions, nothing was beyond the pale of suspicion. The events of the uprising and the rebel takeover of the city turn everything into a political act. Opening or closing shops, stocking goods or not, underselling, aimless wandering, carrying flour, carrying lead, visits to prostitutes, consumption of opium, nothing remains simple or apolitical as in the past. One can call this the personalization of the public and the politicization of the personal.[83] Everything could be an act of enmity or subversion; vigilantism could sometimes turn inward too, as when the soldiers clash with the menial police officers checking their bags. When this is placed against the intense physical mobility in the city, the movement of troops, police, labour, guards for private and public establishments, the picture of flux gets further accentuated, further justifying the nomenclature of ghadar. Yet this ghadar was not without its own structures of order. The despotism of the soldiers was subject to checks, accountability and prosecution, in many cases. As the section on in this book on soldiers shows, there was also some deterrence at work.

The uprising provided a huge boost to the prestige and influence of the soldiers and the officers among them consciously harnessed this by promoting themselves to the highest ranks. Generals Sidhara Singh, Hira Singh, Taleyaar Khan, Shyam Singh, formerly junior officers in the colonial army, promoted themselves to ranks and positions which could match the princes and nobles in their grandeur. Posts such as colonels, generals, brigade majors, even governor generals, were awarded, or arrogated to themselves, by these former subaltern officers. At one point the kotwal was seriously confused about the protocols of addressing these newly elevated officers.[84] The soldiers were trying to match the pomp of the traditional feudal nobility, as well as the formality of the superior ranks of the British army. In some ways this inversion was extended to other areas, for instance the use of British army marching songs when assaulting their positions.[85]

The CoM at Delhi was a formalization of this newly-acquired power. Similar councils of war, with soldiers leading them, were formed at other places as well. Lucknow saw the formation of a 'military cell' as well as a 'parliament'.[86] These institutions asserted the soldiers' power and differentiated their bid for power from earlier dispensations. The governments they sought to form can be described as forms of constitutional monarchies. Scholars have usually seen the uprising as a war of restoration, which attempted nothing more than a conservative throwback to the earlier practices. However, the soldiers' councils were an emphatic assertion of the refusal to simply follow the old. We should distinguish between the prestige of the traditional courts and the actual power enjoyed by them in rebel administrations.[87] In asserting their difference from the nobility as well as the common people, the soldiers tried to combine the new committee or council with older forms of consultative assemblies such as panchayats.[88] As I have shown in the section earmarked for the CoM, the word 'court' came to stand as a verb for a widespread practice, so *kot karna* became an acceptable mode of reaching a consensus. Soldiers 'did court' to devise a suitable punishment for a negligent soldier, or to scrutinize the conduct of their superior officers and could even seek to dismiss them.[89] It is possible that in these instances the word court represents the persistence of the military court martial—a practice which soldiers would have been familiar with because of the service in the Company army.

The ghadar of 1857 was a radical moment in several ways. The attacks on British people and property, the destruction of official records, the burning of moneylenders' ledgers—and the humiliation they were subject to—is mirrored at Delhi in the constant attacks on the merchants, bankers and the well-off. There was turbulence; there was rumour; there was a threat to and dissolution of established authority; there were over 70,000 professional soldiers, the best in the world; there were about 30,000 volunteers, joined by thousands of ordinary people, maulvis, pandits, zamindars, servicemen, poets, scholars, gamblers, sellers of bhang, all of these were involved in the war for Delhi. Mobs were looting houses on the charge, or pretext, that the inhabitants were sheltering or supporting the British. Crowds were resisting rampaging soldiers. Princes were rediscovering power; paupers were aggrandizing themselves; the price of gold was touching the sky; the British were dressing like Indians; the armies fighting against them were playing English bands and their songs; the sharif were being forced to eat kaddu and baingan; women were eloping with lovers; courtesans and prostitutes were thriving; Indians were appointing themselves commissioners and collectors and colonels and generals; grain was being hoarded; a cacophonous contest for information was continuing apace in the midst of the felling of telegraph wires; ideologues were thundering the language of apocalypse and doomsday and of the hundredth anniversary of the battle of Plassey, and reminding their 'Hindu brothers of the Mahabharata and of Krishna'—a world did turn upside down in Delhi. The soldiers' initial violation of courtly etiquette shows impatience with traditional protocol. The rebellious soldiers, who were radical enough to threaten traditional rulers, to modify monarchical systems of government and on occasion, as shown later, challenge their own officers, did not attempt to refashion the world, in spite of being steeped in devotional cults[90] which condemned power and material wealth. Why was this so? What we need to uncover is the nodes along which this radicalization proceeded and the processes that accelerated or decelerated it. What did the soldiers think about legitimate and illegitimate power, did they wish to reorganize society along any new lines, did caste and gender play any role in their calculations, what were the limits of this radicalization? An overwhelming concentration on victory and defeat has prevented us from unravelling the threads—of protest, resistance and racism—that constituted the ghadar in Delhi, and at other places.[91]

We also need to know more about the motivations and mechanisms through which people volunteered to fight against the British. This pertains especially to people who travelled from distant regions to participate in the war. It was not enough, at least at Delhi, to simply turn up and start fighting. Volunteers found it necessary to formally present themselves to the King, get his approval and register themselves on the official rolls before joining the battle. It may have been the peoples' war but the people needed, or desired, an official endorsement before participation.[92] Stray deserters from the British army routinely demanded compensation for the loss of pay and for the plunder on which they had perchance missed out. It was important for people to achieve an official rank. Former soldiers needed acknowledgement of their ranks, civilians applied for specific positions. It was possible to collect a band of men, form a unit, earn an official position and then flaunt one's authority in the city. This is shown by the complaint against one Banda Husain by a woman who reported that, 'When the *disturbances broke out* he collected a group of people and petitioned before his lordship and was awarded the rank of a subedar and now he is committing excesses upon people.'[93] The prospect of a good opportunity may have been as important in attracting people to military service, in some cases, as anti-British feeling. This places some limits on the degree of voluntarism exhibited in the uprising.

By the end of August and the beginning of September, the participants at Delhi were well aware of the impending doom. Exhortations from the officers as well as the leaders, in this phase, impress upon the people the salience of this being a fight about deen and dharam and that they ought to fight to the bitter end. In this endgame, the government looked to the wider population as a support base which ratified its existence, as well as sought to serve them by enlisting their support. From exhorting soldiers and men of religion with phrases like, 'If we don't attack now we will be doomed, know that this is the moment to show valour and bravery,' to widening the ambit of the war to everybody in the city, the attempt was to turn this explicitly and consciously into a 'people's war'.[94] Spies reported that the guards seemed to be more alert than ever before and that the guns were mounted on all sides.[95] As the endgame drew near there were repeated assurances of rewards for everyone who achieved martyrdom while fighting. In addition to monetary rewards, the families were also promised pensions and jobs. What is remarkable is that in spite of this awareness of defeat, the administrative order remained more or less intact. There are letters and documents dating even from

14 September, the day the British launched their final assault on Delhi, which indicate that the officials remained in position, that commands sent to various regiments were still being officially received in writing, that people were still making complaints to the police, almost as usual. It emerges, therefore, that while the realization of the end being near was clear, there was no exact knowledge, as the *Dehli Urdu Akhbar* never ceased to lament, of British plans, nor any anticipation of how completely, eventually, the city would be routed.

Finally, I must insert a word of caution. As I have explained in the preface to this book, is the selections from the Mutiny Papers included here are as much a record of rebel governmentality as of medieval and pre-modern modes of governance. Practices of administration that had continued from an earlier era are reflected better here than novelties brought in specifically by the rebels. For instance, the functioning of the police, the attitudes to gambling and prostitution, the existence of distillers and sellers of bhang, these exhibited continuities over a longer period. The fact that skilled workers are usually summoned through their chaudhris or clan heads gives us a glimpse into the social organization of labour which pre-dated the uprising. The cross examination of 'disputed' women indicates the agency they enjoyed in stating their preference for a spouse or in determining the paternity of a child. These documents can therefore be read for the uprising as well as for the social study of a pre-colonial city. Further, these are mostly government papers, so to say. Withal, this is a fragmentary record. In order to recover the sentiments, feelings and thoughts of the rebels we will need to recover other sources and hear other voices.

Notes

1. A firman is a formal royal edict, a shuqqa is a less formal royal order, and a parwana is both summons and a permission letter which could be royal as well as non-royal.
2. By this I mean the attack on the property of the well-to-do by the soldiers, aided by what are called the badmashes, the lowly ruffians.
3. William Dalrymple, 'Introduction' in *The Last Mughal: The Fall of a Dynasty, Delhi, 1857* (London: Bloomsbury, 2006), pp 20–23.

4. Jiwan Lal's narrative, *Two Native Narratives*, on http://www.kapadia. com/TheMutinyinDelhi.html, p. 8.

5. Collection 151, No. 87, Mutiny Papers, National Archives of India (NAI).

6. 24 May 1857, *Dehli Urdu Akhbar*, NAI.

7. 27 July 1857, *Sadiq ul Akhbar*, Vol. 4, No. 4, NAI.

8. The *Dehli Urdu Akhbar* reported on 10 August on the impending arrival of the large Nimach contingent: 'On the 4th the petition of the thanadar of Badarpur regarding the arrival of the Nimach camp at Barah Pula was received and a response issued that Husain Bakhsh Khan should go to receive them and provisions and supplies should be arranged. Notes were issued to the General Bahadur, etc., that they should be brought to the Durbar.' (See section on the *Dehli Urdu Akhbar*, 'The Ideologue' in this volume, the issue dated 10 August). That this was duly done was reported later by the *Sadiq ul Akhbar*, 'Yesterday, the Nimcha contingent that had defeated the angrez at Agra entered Delhi with great pomp and celebration in a contingent of 15,000 men.' Similarly, the Jhansi troops were received by officials. When the impressive Bareilly army arrived, it was received by a high ranking noble, Ahmed Quli Khan, outside the Delhi Gate.

9. See the chapter 'Merchants, Bankers and Wages: Raising Money for the War' in this volume for details.

10. Jiwan Lal's narrative, p. 30.

11. I am aware of the dangers of using this Foucauldian concept in the special and short-lived conditions of the ghadar, but there is a definite mould in which the administration was trying to cast and apprehend subjects. The rationalities, mentalities and techniques of governance can be fruitfully analyzed using this theoretical grid.

12. 4 July 1857, Collection 132, No. 20, Mutiny Papers, NAI. Also see Jiwan Lal's narrative, p. 6

13. Paper presented by Shailendra Bhandari of the Ashmolean Museum, Oxford, at *Mutiny on the Margins*, a conference on 1857, organised at Edinburgh Univeristy in July 2007.

14. Reporting on the details of that incident, the *Dehli Urdu Akhbar* wrote that 'On Friday, at 4 p.m., the building housing the magazine, located at Mohalla Choonriwala, suddenly erupted with fire and some twenty-five to thirty maunds of gunpowder exploded. Six hundred and nine labourers, fifty of whom were residents of the same mohalla, were burnt to cinders

and in the heavy, smoked air of powder, were cast away like crows and ravens in the sky. It was such a terrible and heart-rending site, a sample of doomsday perhaps, that on one side the residents of the mohalla, fearing lest their houses too be blown up and on the other side were the poor workers who had died and the lamentations and grief of their family members' (10 August 1857, *Dehli Urdu Akhbar*, Vol. 4, No. 6, Mutiny Papers, NAI.

15. For details, see Jiwan Lal's narrative, p. 68.

16. Collection 102, No. 47, Mutiny Papers, NAI. For more on jihadis, see Dalrymple, *Last Mughal*.

17. Richard Cobb provides interesting parallels. The mentalities and functioning of the police during the French upheavals reflected a long medieval ethos, as did the police functioning in Delhi during 1857. See Richard Cobb, *The Police and the People: French Popular Protests, 1789–1820* (London: Oxford University Press, 1970).

18. For a very brief discussion on the importance of the kotwal in the ancien regime, see Narayani Gupta, Delhi Between Two Empires, 1803–1931: Society, Government and Urban Growth (New Delhi: Oxford University Press, 1981), p. 3.

19. I am thankful to Rashmi Pant for drawing my attention to the abiding importance of older loyalties for explaining the relative ease with which the police force switched its loyalty.

20. See the *Dehli Urdu Akhbar* dated 31 May 1857, NAI.

21. 7 August 1857, Collection 111c, No. 127, Mutiny Papers, NAI.

22. 10 August 1857, Collection 111c, No. 159, Mutiny Papers, NAI. See also Collection 111c, No. 160, Mutiny Papers, NAI.

23. 16 June 1857, Collection 128, No. 64, Mutiny Papers, NAI.

24. 10 June 1857, Collection 128, No. 34, Mutiny Papers, NAI.

25. Undated, Collection 57, No. 543, Mutiny Papers, NAI.

26. Undated, Collection 120, No. 129, Mutiny Papers, NAI.

27. 26 July–3 September 1857, Collection 45, Mutiny Papers, NAI.

28. 25 July 1857, Collection 103, No. 213, Mutiny Papers, NAI.

29. 27 May 1857, Collection 123, No. 6, Mutiny Papers, NAI.

30. In 1841, the colonial Delhi government attempted to transfer the charge of the chowkidari tax to the Bakhshis, in lieu of the citizens' panchayats, but had to back down in the face of popular protest. See Gupta, *Delhi Between Two Empires*, p. 11.

31. 1 August 1857, Collection 103, No. 220, Mutiny Papers, NAI.

32. 26 July–3 September 1857, Collection 45, Mutiny Papers, NAI.

33. In the second week of the rebellion, he wrote to say that twenty-three cobblers were being sent in, but that the diggers who used to reside in that area had all left town and these cobblers too 'have emerged from their houses after great difficulty and if they are not paid their wages, they will also leave the city in a day or two' (23 May 1857, Collection 61, No. 1, Mutiny Papers, NAI). On 29 August, the deputy kotwal wrote in to say that coolies had been sent to the Teliwara trenches from the kotwali and they have not been paid their daily wages for two days. He requested that their wages be paid 'because if wages are not paid to coolies how will they do the work of the government . . . as it is scores of coolies have run away from the city' (29 August 1857, Collection 129, No. 80, Mutiny Papers, NAI).

34. The kotwal said while supplying fifty sacks and three maunds of rope, 'bought from the market and sent to his lordship. We hope their price would be repaid as quickly as possible by the government' (28 July 1857, Collection 111c, No. 34, Mutiny Papers, NAI).

35. See the case of rider Imam Bakhsh. In response, the kotwal sent in a requisition to the different thanas to supply him with various kinds of grains and the order was complied with. See 27 July 1857, Collection 103, No. 215.

36. The subedar of the thirtieth regiment wrote to the kotwal demanding six thatchers for making fences at the hospital, and, as the bureaucratic norm demanded, the kotwal responded by inscribing on the margins that a note had been sent to the thanadar of Turkman gate demanding thatchers (29 July 1857, Collection 111c, No. 49).

37. 11 June 1857, Collection 125, No. 12, Mutiny Papers, NAI.

38. 23 August 1857, Collection 124, No. 306, Mutiny Papers, NAI.

39. Undated, Collection 61, No. 547, Mutiny Papers, NAI.

40. 16 August 1857, Collection 63, No. 46, Mutiny Papers, NAI.

41. 'When and if you intend to raid somebody's house, you should immediately inform the kotwali. Until permission is granted by the kotwali, no raids should be conducted' (19 May–10 August 1857, Collection 53, Mutiny Papers, NAI).

42. 13 August 1857, Collection 101, No. 26, Mutiny Papers, NAI.

43. 31 August 1857, Collection 120, No. 190, Mutiny Papers, NAI.

44. Fortunately, the King showed some restraint and asked the kotwal to first issue a general proclamation banning gambling before arresting people. See 24 July 1857, Collection 111c, No. 11, Mutiny Papers, NAI.

45. 3 August 1857, Collection 62, No. 80, Mutiny Papers, NAI.

46. On 30 July, the C-in-C wrote to the kotwal asking him to issue a general proclamation to make sure that no one commits cow slaughter and to 'arrest anyone who so much as even thinks of doing so. It has been heard that some mujahideen intend to perform this act, so go to the Maulvi saheb and ask him to talk to them ... This year no one should think of doing so otherwise there will be an unnecessary riot and the enemy's hands will be strengthened' (30 July 1857, Collection 111c, No. 64, Mutiny Papers, NAI).

47. 26 July–3 September 1857, Collection 45, Mutiny Papers, NAI.

48. The kotwal explained to the King that there was not enough room in the kotwali to hold all the cows owned by the Muslims in the city. In turn, he suggested that thanadars should be directed to get bonds executed by the Muslims to the effect that they would not sacrifice cows. See 29 July 1857, Collection 111c, No. 44, Mutiny Papers, NAI.

49. 29 July 1857, Collection 111c, No. 45, Mutiny Papers, NAI.

50. On 22nd June, some barqandazes of thana Bhojla Pahari were doing their customary rounds near the Lahori Gate when they noticed two sacks. Suspicious, they inquired into it, whereupon the soldiers posted there proceeded to give a solid thrashing to the hapless barqandazes. See 22 June 1857, Collection 103, No. 24, Mutiny Papers, NAI.

51. The thanadar of Guzar Qasimjan wrote to the kotwal saying that when challenged by the barqandazes of the thana, the soldiers threatened to beat them up and explicitly told the thanadar to mind his own business, who would have let it pass but for the fact that they were now demanding money to allow documents to pass. See Undated, Collection 110, No. 293, Mutiny Papers, NAI.

52. 26 July–3 September 1857, Collection 45, Mutiny Papers, NAI.

53. Emphasis added. 26 July–3 September 1857, Collection 45, Mutiny Papers, NAI

54. 1 July 1857, Collection 60, No. 253, Mutiny Papers, NAI. Accordingly, when the soldiers were insistent on searching the house of a rich magnate, Ajudhia Parshad, the kotwal instructed the thanadar to 'Tell the soldiers that they should first go to the General Bahadur with the informant and submit an application there. When an order is passed from there only then

can a search be conducted. Without the application of the spy/informant no searches will be conducted at respectable people's houses' (1 July 1857, Collection 60, No. 253, Mutiny Papers, NAI.)

55. On 24 July, the C-in-C wrote to all the thanadars and the kotwal to make sure that all thanadars sent in their diaries by 8 a.m.—an instruction which was repeated several times. See 24 July 1857, Collection 120, No. 134, Mutiny Papers, NAI.

56. See the response by the thanadar to the deputy kotwal on the complaint that there was no officer in the Dariba thana to receive petitions except for two illiterate barqandazes. Kotwali records, 26 July–3 September 1857, Collection 45, Mutiny Papers, NAI.

57. 25 May 1857, Collection 61, No. 4, Mutiny Papers, NAI.

58. Upon this, the thanadar sent in an indignant reply, refuting the report that he was not on duty and impugning the complaint's motive. He said he had gone to offer Id prayers while the clerk was in the toilet and when asked to wait, the complainant had chosen to go back home. The thanadar added that Faiz Mohammed Khan had concocted the report of the break-in in order to take over the goods by stealth as in these situations, the complainant generally never desired a search or registered claims against anyone.'As far as being absent or present is concerned, the situation is this that this devoted one never absents himself from duty even for a moment and the clerk of this thana is an outsider and he never goes anywhere' (25 May 1857, Collection 61, No. 3, Mutiny Papers, NAI).

59. Acting as the secretary of the CoM, General Taleyaar Khan wrote, 'That the plaintiff had first made a claim and then you write they have compromised with each other, it is not clear whether the complainant's case was true or false. Therefore you are directed that you should not, for any case, make a decision and send it to our court. Send both parties to our court now' (19 August 1857, Collection 103, No. 303, Mutiny Papers, NAI).

60. 3 July 1857, Collection 111b, No. 14, Mutiny Papers, NAI.

61. This is one of the few contemporary references I have found to this word which has come to stand for the uprising itself. Here it definitely means disobedience and rebellion.

62. The matter involved the requisitioning of four water carriers, an order for which arrived at the Turkman Gate thana at midnight. When the barqandazes were called out, Ghazi Khan, leading four others, refused to comply. Only in the morning, after the jamadar had given them a

written order, did they go. Kotwali records, 26 July–3 September 1857, Collection 45, Mutiny Papers, NAI.

63. On 22nd June, the kotwal wrote to all the thanadars asking them to report if any posts of barqandaz or jamadar or mohurrir were vacant in their respective thanas or 'if any barqandaz was inefficient or negligent in carrying out the orders of the government' (22 June 1857, Collection 120, No. 16, Mutiny Papers, NAI).

64. The thanadar of Bhojla Pahari, Mirza Amani Beg, wrote to the C-in-C on 30th July saying that, 'Since the time the royal government took over, the number of barqandazes has increased and there is not enough room for charpoys for all to fit in'. So he requested the sanction of two rupees a month for renting a room for them. See 30 July 1857, Collection 122, No. 22, Mutiny Papers, NAI.

65. 27 May 1857, Collection 123, No. 6, Mutiny Papers, NAI.

66. They said that he was a badmash who spent all his time loitering around with bad characters and that he had proved so cruel that if he continued, 'the subjects are sure to be ruined' (24 June 1857, Collection 61, No. 95, Mutiny Papers, NAI.

67. 3 July 1857, Collection 61, No. 117, Mutiny Papers, NAI.

68. 29 July 1857, Collection 61, No. 256, Mutiny Papers, NAI.

69. See section 'Pillage, Extortion and Dereliction' on soldiers in this volume.

70. 16 August 1857, Collection 121, Number 105, Mutiny Papers, NAI.

71. 25 July 1857, Collection 120, No. 137, Mutiny Papers, NAI.

72. Emphasis added. 26 July–3 September 1857, Collection 45, Mutiny Papers, NAI.

73. 7 September 1857, Collection 60, No. 686, Mutiny Papers, NAI. An order was then sent to Kalwant Singh, commander of the fourth platoon, thirty-eighth regiment, asking him to produce the woman along with the soldier Jabar (see 7 September 1857, Collection 75, No. 22, Mutiny Papers, NAI). The soldier was duly arrested and the woman was produced in the court. Her version of the events was that Pir Bakhsh assaulted her and threw her out of the house, after which she had gone away. See 11 September 1857, Collection 60, No. 688, Mutiny Papers, NAI.

74. 30 June 1857, Collection 106, No. 31, Mutiny Papers, NAI.

75. Undated, Collection 104, No. 67, Mutiny Papers, NAI.

76. In a remarkably similar vein, Cobb writes of the people during the French revolution: 'Even at the height of the Terror and of the Thermidorian

Reaction, people talked loud and clear. One is constantly amazed at their impudence and their imprudence' (Cobb, *The Police and the People*, p. 51).

77. 14 August 1857, Collection 61, No. 367, Mutiny Papers, NAI. Syed Nazar Ali, the thanadar of Chandni Chowk, wrote an apologetic note to the C-in-C on 14 August stating that all documents were to be sealed properly and that the incorrect sealing was done not by him, but by the mohurrir of the thana Durga Prashad.

78. *Dehli Urdu Akhbar*, 31 May 1857, Collection 2, Mutiny Papers, NAI.

79. The earlier channels of revenue and grain collection had broken down in Delhi and the British control of Punjab and other surrounding areas had cut it off from its traditional agrarian and other commodities markets. Compare the situation in Awadh in Rudrangshu Mukherjee, *Awadh in Revolt*, 1857–58: A Study of Popular Resistance (Delhi, New York: Oxford University Press, 1984). However, Bahadur Shah did receive money from former and nominal vassals such as the raja of Ballabgarh, the raja of Kishangarh, the nawabs of Jhajjhar and Bahadurgarh, and occasionally, from the contingents that poured in from other cities. See Eric Stokes, *The Peasant Armed: The Indian Rebellion of 1857*, edited by C.A. Bayly (New York: Oxford University Press, 1986), and also the text of this volume.

80. *Dehli Urdu Akhbar*, 14 June 1857, Collection 2, Mutiny Papers, NAI.

81. Gautam Bhadra, 'Four Rebels of Eighteen-Fifty-Seven', in Ranajit Guha (ed.), *Subaltern Studies IV* (New Delhi: Oxford University Press, 1985, p. 268.

82. Ibid., p. 266. One example of this kind of merry-making came on 23 June, the centenary of the battle of Plassey when a 'gun constructed in the reign of Shahjahan was mounted on the walls, a he-goat was tied to the mouth, twenty five seers of sweetmeats were placed inside the barrel, and a necklace of flowers was hung around the muzzle. Then several Brahmins and astrologers were summoned and directed to consult their almanacks as to whether the mutineers would be victorious' (Christopher Hibbert, *The Great Mutiny*, *India 1857* [New Delhi: Penguin, 1980], p. 275). A similar sentiment was displayed when the common people, regular bystanders at the batteries, would behead each slain Englishman and carry their impaled heads in a procession to the city, and earn five rupees from the King as a reward. See Hibbert, *Great Mutiny*, p. 277.

83. Once again, there are interesting parallels with the situation in revolutionary France. See Cobb, *The Police*, p. 23.

84. 14 August 1857, Collection 61, No. 369, Mutiny Papers, NAI.

85. Ranajit Guha has developed some insightful hypotheses about the use of inversion in moments of resistance. See his *Elementary Aspects of Peasant Insurgency* (New Delhi: Oxford University Press, 1983), Chapter 2.

86. These English terms appear in the Urdu documents. See Mukherjee, *Awadh in Revolt*, pp. 138–50.

87. For both, see Mukherjee, *Awadh in Revolt*, p. 154.

88. Sabyasachi Dasgupta has developed some useful insights about the soldiers' councils. See his 'The Rebel Army of 1857: At the Vanguard of the War of Independence or a Tyranny of Arms', *Economic and Political Weekly*, Vol. 42 (19), 2007, pp. 1729–33.

89. See section 'The Court of Mutineers' in this volume.

90. I mean particularly the Rajputs, Bhumihars and Brahmans of Baiswara and eastern India, in general, where *Ramcharitmanas*, a long devotional poem composed in the Persian form of *masnavi* (a 'communiqué' as translated by Professor Mujib Rizvi), which closely followed Persian and Hindavi sufi creations, was a highly popular and culturally significant poem. See also Ram Vilas Sharma, *Nirala-Jivan va Vyaktitva* (Delhi: Rajkamal, date of publication unknown). These hypotheses, however, need more detailed investigation.

91. One has to reiterate here, this is with the exception of Ranajit Guha.

92. See section 'Give us money, rank and compensation' on volunteers in this volume.

93. 13 August 1857, Collection 70, No. 210, Mutiny Papers, NAI.

94. For a brief discussion of the concept and how it may apply to 1857, see Kaushik Basu, 'The Beginning of 'People's War' in India', *Economic and Political Weekly*, Vol. 42 (19), 2007, pp. 1720–28.

95. Hibbert, *Great Mutiny*, p. 279.

GLOSSARY

Anqa	A mythical bird
Asharfi	A gold coin, also a Mughal coin
Badmash	Ruffian, goonda, criminal, lower classes
Baqrid	Id ul Zuha, the Muslim festival of thanksgiving
Barqandaz	A semi-armed Police constable
Challan	Charge sheet
Chana	Chick pea, staple army food
Chaudhri	Headman, of a clan or caste etc.
Chowkidar	Watchman
C-in-C	Commander in Chief, Mirza Mughal
CoM	Court of Mutineers
Dak	Post, also a carriage for hire
Dalal	A broker or a middleman
Diwan-e Khas	Hall of special audience in the Red Fort
Faras	Iran
Ghazi	Religious warrior
Havaldar	Officer in the British Indian army
Halwai	Confectioner
Hartal	Strike
Hirkara	A runner for post and messages
Kalima	Muslim declaration of faith
Kebab	Roasted meat
Khwaja Sara	A eunuch, the keeper of the interior palace
Jamadar	Subaltern rank in the army

441

Jagirdar	Holder of a jagir
Jharoka	A window, also a Mughal practice of giving darshan to their subjects
Jihad	Holy war
Jihadi	Holy warrior/volunteer
Kafir	Heathen, unbeliever
Kahar	A doolie or carriage bearer
Kalima	Islamic profession of faith
Khairat	Obligatory charity that is enjoined upon all Muslims
Kotwal	Head of the police force of a city.
Khalifa	Caliph, also a leading disciple of a master
Kuchehri	Courts, also the court compound or a secretariat
Laddu	Sweetmeat
Lambardar	A revenue official in a village
Lohar	Ironsmith
Maafidaar	Holder of a rent and revenue free grant of land
Mahajan	Trader, moneylender
Mahurat	Auspicious moment
Maida	A kind of flour
Malin	Female gardener
Mann	Same as maund, measure of weight, roughly equal to forty kilograms
Maulvi	A devout or learned Muslim
Mohalla	Neighborhood, locality
Muharram	Shia holy month, month of mourning
Muharrir	Clerk
Mujahideen	Plural of jihadis, also stands for other volunteers
Naik	A subordinate officer
Nazar	An offering or tribute presented to the King
Parwana	Summons, an order from a higher authority
Patwari	Keeper of revenue and land records
Pensiondar	Holder of grant of land as a pension
Punya-arth	Acts of charity.
Purabiya	Easterners, refers to the Company soldiers as they mostly came from Eastern parts of UP and Bihar

Qiladar	Commander or Captain of the Palace guards, a British position
Qanungo	Revenue official
Rais	Notable
Rava	Granualted wheat flour
Risala	Cavalry unit
Risaldar	Officer in the Army, non-commissioned
Saheb	Honorific, master, employer, ruler, lord
Sati	Hindu practice of the burning of a widow in her husband's pyre
Ser	A measure of weight, slightly less than a kilo
Sharia	Islamic law
Shastras	Hindu traditions
Sheerini	Sugary syrup, a sweet
Subedar	Officer of the infantry in the English Army
Tehsil	Sub-district revenue unit
Tehsildar	Revenue and executive officer of a tehsil
Teli	Oil-presser
Telin	Female oil-presser
Thana	Police station
Tilanga	Company soldiers, deriving from the Telengana region where they were first recruited from and given uniforms
Turkestan	Turkey
Vakil	Representative, also a lawyer
Vilayat	Foreign lands. Referred formerly to Iran and Central Asian lands but later came to denote Europe
Zafar	Victory, name given to the armies by Bahadur Shah
Zamindar	Landholder
Zenana	Segregated female section of the household

ACKNOWLEDGEMENTS

This book would have been materially impossible without William Dalrymple. It was while researching at his behest, and with his support, that I first encountered the Mutiny Papers and it was he who first exhorted me, and the publisher, to bring out a separate collection of these translations. Our collaboration during the making of *The Last Mughal: The Fall of a Dynasty, Delhi 1857* was made delightful by his generosity and gifts as a writer. To him, therefore, I owe my first and most important thanks.

First books can sometimes be unbalanced in that the passions exhibited in their acknowledgement pages can sometimes be greater than the labour put in the book itself. Nevertheless, there is a long list of people who have wanted me to write a book, and I must thank them for keeping faith as well as seek grace for the fact that they may have to wait longer for the kind of book they want, and expect, me to write. Over the years I have disappointed as many people as I have pleased. That list has included family, friends, teachers and employers. All, but I, have been sure that my calling lay in being a historian and to them I present this meagre result as proof that perhaps they weren't so right.

My mother has taught me all I know of eloquence; I literally owe my languages, of speech and being, to her. The *lazzat-e taqreer* that she imparted to us is now beginning to even prove lucrative for me! My father, one of the most dedicated readers I have known, first built a library for me, then has shown me, through my life, the importance of books, and has passionately wished me away from my present indulgences to a more austere life. My uncle, S.R. Faruqi, scholar extraordinaire, astute theorist and the great excavator of hidden visions of Urdu and Indian literature, showed great indulgence in teaching me by precept and example. In disappointing him continuously, my only plea is the necessary modesty of what I could hope to achieve after him. My father-in-law, Professor Mujeeb Rizvi, Gandhian-Bhakt-Sufi, disputant of all orthodoxies, Hindu-Muslim-Urdu-Hindi, has taught me ways of scholarship where praxis always comes before pedantry, and has been an inspiring resister of falsehoods of all kinds. Shahidbhai and Shahidchi, the other two Shahids in my life, have always been objects of my admiration for the sincerity, diligence and honesty of their scholarship. I thank them all for showing me the possibilities of what I could become.

I was immensely fortunate to earn a Government of India scholarship to study at the Doon School, Dehradun. It provided me a wonderful life and a platform to explore myself that is otherwise entirely denied to *mofussil* childen. To teachers, seniors and staff who shaped me there, particularly to Shomie Das, I remain deeply grateful. My teachers at St Stephen's where I first learnt the rudiments of history—P.S. Dwivedi, David Baker, Shiv Shankar Menon, Rohit Wanchoo and others—instilled such joy in the discipline that I wasn't able to replicate it thereafter; I deeply and humbly thank them all. David Washbrook, Lawrence Goldman, Peter Carey, my tutors at Oxford and Chris Bayly, my supervisor at Cambridge, showed me how passion can infuse profession and how brilliance can be married with diligence. To them too I owe profound thanks.

Over the last few years of my wayward peregrinations, Sarai, that extraordinary intellectual oasis at Delhi, became a glorious abode for me and has sustained and nourished me with supreme kindness. Without its exhortation and support, I would have neither become a dastango, nor would this book have been possible. To friends, teachers and guides there who have enriched me, and to Ravikant, Vivek, Shuddha, Jeebesh, Dipu and others I offer my gratitude and thanks. It was also through Sarai that I first encountered, for it is a sight and an experience, that extraordinary performer among scholars and scholar among performers, Professor Shahid Amin. His encouragement, support and inputs at various stages have had a determining influence on the shape of the book. One day, I hope, he will 'come out' and become a dastango. Professor Amar Farooqui of the University of Delhi, Professor C.M. Naim of the University of Chicago, Professor Narayani Gupta and Rudrangshu Mukherjee, the reluctant prince of 1857 historiography, have all encouraged me at various stages and I am thankful to them all.

My stints at the National Archives were made highly pleasant by the superb staff at the research room. Thanks to Jaya Ravindran who facilitated with great warmth all the research that has gone into this book. To Roy saheb, Pradip, Naresh, Abrar and to all others there, I express my deepest regards and thank that institution for allowing me access to this wonderful material.

A few papers and articles, based on these papers, were published or presented at conferences at Edinburgh University, Jamia Millia Islamia, Delhi University and at Jaihind College, Mumbai. I thank the organizers for providing me this opportunity to think through the material.

My publishers and editors at Penguin, Ravi Singh, Ranjana Sengupta and Anupama Ramakrishnan, showed such strong belief in the book that even my repeated phases of truancy did not shake it. I thank them for their indulgence and support.

Rajit K. Mazumder closely read the first draft of the collection and saved me innumerable blushes. I cannot thank him enough for his inestimable suggestions about the language, tone and content of this book. Two of my closest friends also happen to be my brothers, Masood and Rumi, and this is an insufficient recompense for the way they have doted on me. The love and material support of several friends has been indispensable during the impecunious and often pointless struggles which I have led over the past decade and a half. Aamir, Mazum, Ashish, Bhanu, Fazal, Yug, PC, Osama, Sourabh, Chris, Tish, Radhika, Danish and countless others, spread over three continents, have allowed me to stay afloat. It would be an affront to thank them.

My biggest intellectual collaborator and closest friend, the one who first taught me to argue and think independently, my rival, beloved, intellectual, savant, actor, Shardul Chaturvedi, is not around to see this book. This will be my deepest regret in this and in all other endeavours to come, I only hope that some day I can measure up to the pride he had in me.

Many have desired this book but none has been so indispensable to its making, and none have actually created the conditions in which I could have worked on it as my wife, Anusha Rizvi. For being the first reader and listener of everything I do, for putting up with the extremes of discomfort and deprivation, for always putting my interest and well-being before hers, for passionately sharing my slightest achievement and for putting up often with excruciating pettiness on my part, I gratefully offer this book to her, *tum ho to jahan bhi hai*.

ABOUT THE TRANSLATOR

Mahmood Farooqui studied history at St Stephen's College, Delhi, and at the Universities of Oxford and Cambridge. He has been a journalist and a newspaper columnist and, over the last few years, has effected a major revival of Dastangoi, the art of Urdu storytelling. Farooqui co-directed the highly acclaimed Hindi feature film *Peepli Live* with his wife, Anusha Rizvi. He lives in Delhi.

INDEX